China's Rise and Its Global Implications

Shaoguang Wang

# China's Rise and Its Global Implications

Shaoguang Wang
Institute of State Governance
Huazhong University of Science and Technology
Wuhan, China

Translated by Lei Xiong

B&R Book Program

ISBN 978-981-16-4340-8     ISBN 978-981-16-4341-5 (eBook)
https://doi.org/10.1007/978-981-16-4341-5

Jointly published with CITIC Press Corporation
The print edition is not for sale in China (Mainland). Customers from China (Mainland) please order the print book from: CITIC Press Corporation.

Translation from the Chinese language edition: 《中国崛起的世界意义》 by Shaoguang Wang, © CITIC Press Corporation 2020. Published by CITIC Press Corporation. All Rights Reserved.
© CITIC Press Corporation 2021
This work is subject to copyright. All rights are solely and exclusively licensed by the Publisher, whether the whole or part of the material is concerned, specifically the rights of reprinting, reuse of illustrations, recitation, broadcasting, reproduction on microfilms or in any other physical way, and transmission or information storage and retrieval, electronic adaptation, computer software, or by similar or dissimilar methodology now known or hereafter developed.
The use of general descriptive names, registered names, trademarks, service marks, etc. in this publication does not imply, even in the absence of a specific statement, that such names are exempt from the relevant protective laws and regulations and therefore free for general use.
The publishers, the authors, and the editors are safe to assume that the advice and information in this book are believed to be true and accurate at the date of publication. Neither the publishers nor the authors or the editors give a warranty, express or implied, with respect to the material contained herein or for any errors or omissions that may have been made. The publishers remain neutral with regard to jurisdictional claims in published maps and institutional affiliations.

Cover illustration: Shaoguang Wang

This Palgrave Macmillan imprint is published by the registered company Springer Nature Singapore Pte Ltd.
The registered company address is: 152 Beach Road, #21-01/04 Gateway East, Singapore 189721, Singapore

# Preface

Ever since 1949, there have been recurring predictions about PRC's imminent collapse. Many are convinced that China's system would not work, and its development would sooner or later hit a wall. Why do so many people have repeatedly made wrong predictions? It has to do with their tacit theoretical basis and dogmas in the heads of those who make such predictions. The Preface briefly discusses some of prevailing "theories" and reveals their unspoken premises: Only systems possessing certain talismans of power would prevail, and all others are doomed to fail unless they follow the path suggested by the "theories." China's rise overturns these theories. The book attempts to explain why China, once an extremely poor country in the East with no history of colonialism, could take off after it embarked on the road of socialism. The story of China tells the world that if China can, so can all others.

Wuhan, China  Shaoguang Wang

# Contents

| | | |
|---|---|---|
| 1 | **Introduction** | 1 |
| | *Ridiculous Prediction* | 2 |
| | *Ridiculous Theory* | 5 |
| | *What Does China's Rise Mean to the World?* | 11 |
| 2 | **Revelation: State Capacity and Economic Development** | 15 |
| | *Many Countries (Regions) Carried Out Reform and Opening-Up* | 15 |
| | *Conditions Required for Successful Reform and Opening-Up* | 19 |
| | *State Capacity and East–West Divergence* | 20 |
| | *State Capacity and China–Japan Divergence* | 48 |
| | *Summary* | 58 |
| 3 | **Groundwork: From Old China to New China** | 65 |
| | *National Reality Before the Founding of New China* | 69 |
| | *From the Founding of New China up to 1978, Before the Reform and Opening-Up* | 87 |
| | *Summary* | 110 |
| 4 | **Exploration: From New China's First 30 Years to Next 40 Years** | 115 |
| | *Explorations in the 30 Years Pre-reform* | 117 |
| | *Explorations in the 40 Years Post-reform* | 131 |
| | *Summary* | 152 |

vii

| | | |
|---|---|---|
| 5 | **Steering: From Planning to Programming** | 155 |
| | *Planning Well for Decision Made, Action Taken with Success Secured* | 157 |
| | *Preparedness Ensures Success, Unpreparedness Spells Failure* | 173 |
| | *Summary* | 181 |
| 6 | **Pillar: State-Owned Enterprises and Industrialization** | 185 |
| | *New China's Starting Point* | 188 |
| | *From an Agricultural to an Industrial Country, 1949–1984* | 209 |
| | *From Industrial Country to Industrial Power, 1985–2019* | 229 |
| | *Summary* | 252 |
| 7 | **Direction: From Economic to Social Policies** | 253 |
| | *Take Economic Construction as the Central Task* | 253 |
| | *Reduce Inequality* | 258 |
| | *Reduce the Sense of Insecurity* | 264 |
| | *Summary* | 281 |
| 8 | **Leapfrogging: Striding from Middle Income to High Income** | 287 |
| **Appendix: A Look at the "Great Famine" from a Historical and Comparative Perspective** | | 301 |

# List of Figures

| | | |
|---|---|---|
| Fig. 2.1 | Economic development in China and Soviet-Eastern European countries (1985 = 1) (*Source* The Conference Board, Total Economy Database: Output, Labor and Labor Productivity, 1950–2018, March 2019) | 17 |
| Fig. 2.2 | Economic development in China and the nine countries (1985 = 1) (*Source* The Conference Board, Total Economy Database: Output, Labor and Labor Productivity, 1950–2018, March 2019) | 18 |
| Fig. 2.3 | Number of conflicts in Europe and China, 1450–1839 (The dotted line represents Europe, the solid line China) t (*Source* Adopted from Tonio Andrade, *The Gunpowder Age: China, Military Innovation, and the Rise of the West in World History*, p. 6) | 30 |
| Fig. 2.4 | GDP per capita in China and Japan, 1661–1900 (*Source* Maddison Project Database (Version 2018) by Jutta Bolt, Robert Inklaar, Herman de Jong and Jan Luiten van Zanden, https://www.rug.nl/ggdc/historicaldevelopment/maddison/data/mpd2018.xlsx) | 50 |
| Fig. 2.5 | Tax revenues per capita (koku of Rice) in China and Japan, 1650–1850 (*Source* Adopted from Sng Tuan-Hwee and Chiaki Moriguchi, *Asia's Little Divergence: State Capacity in China and Japan before 1850, Journal of Economic Growth*, Vol. 19, No. 4 [December 2014], p. 441) | 51 |

## LIST OF FIGURES

Fig. 2.6 Railway operational mileage in China and Japan 1871–1907 (*Source* B. R. Mitchell, *International Historical Statistics: Africa, Asia & Oceania, 1750–1993*, 3rd Edition [London: Macmillan Reference Ltd. 1998], pp. 683–684)   53

Fig. 2.7 Rebellions during the Tokugawa shogunate and early years of Meiji Restoration (*Sources* Roger W. Bowen, *Rebellion and Democracy in Meiji Japan: A Study of Commoners in the Popular Rights Movement* [Berkeley, CA: University of California Press, 1984], p. 73)   56

Fig. 2.8 Pattern of per capita GDP growth: Korea, Brazil, India, and Nigeria, 1960–2000 (*Source* Atul Kohli, *State-Directed Development: Political Power and Industrialization in the Global Periphery* [Cambridge: Cambridge University Press, 2004], p. 24)   61

Fig. 2.9 State capacity and economic growth (*Source* Atul Kohli, *States and Economic Development*, 2010, http://www.princeton.edu/kohli/docs/SED.pdf)   61

Fig. 2.10 State capacity and level of economic development (*Source* Susan E. Rice and Stewart Patrick, *Index of State Weakness in Developing World* [Washington, DC: The Brookings Institution, 2008])   62

Fig. 3.1 The past and present of the state Farm 850 in Heilongjiang Province (Wang Zhen and demobilized soldiers carry earth to build the dam of the Farm 850 today Yunshan Reservoir on the Farm 850 in 1958)   68

Fig. 3.2 The situation in the far east (*Source* The cartoon was created by Xie Zuantai [Tse Tsan-tai, 1872–1937], and it was first published by the Journal of Furen Literary Society, in Hong Kong in July 1898)   70

Fig. 3.3 The economic growth rate, 1913–1936 (*Source* Liu Wei, Calculation of China's GDP, 1913–1936, *The Journal of Chinese Social and Economic History*, No. 3 [2008], pp. 90–98)   80

Fig. 3.4 GDP per capita in China, India and African countries, 1950 (International U.S. dollar in 2017) (*Source* The Conference Board, Total Economy Database, April 2019, http://www.conference-board.org/data/economydatabase/TED1)   81

LIST OF FIGURES    xi

Fig. 3.5   GDP per capita in China, India and African countries, 2019 (International U.S. dollar value in 2017) (*Source* The Conference Board, Total Economy Database, April 2019, http://www.conference-board.org/data/economydatabase/TED1)   82

Fig. 3.6   Crime rates in the first three decades (*Source* Cited from Xiaogang Deng and Ann Cordilla, To Get Rich is Glorious: Rising Expectations, Declining Control, and Escalating Crime in Contemporary China, *International Journal of Offender Therapy and Comparative Criminology*, Vol. 43, No. 2 [June 1999], p. 212)   92

Fig. 3.7   Initial land distribution and economic growth (Average GDP growth, 1960–2000 [%]) (*Source* Klaus Deininger, *Land Policies for Growth and Poverty Reduction: A World Bank Policy Research Report* [Washington, DC: World Bank, 2003], p. 18)   95

Fig. 3.8   Average life expectancy of New China, 1949–1980 (*Source* Data of 1953–1959 are from Judith Banister, *China: Changing Population* [Stanford: Stanford University Press, 1987], p. 116, Table 4.18; data after 1960 are from World Bank: World Development Indicators 1960–2018, http://databank.worldbank.org/data.download/WDI_excel.zip)   98

Fig. 3.9   Window period of China's demographic transition (*Source* Misbah T. Choudhry and J. Paul Elhorst, Demographic Transition and Economic Growth in China, *India and Pakistan, Economic Systems*, Vol. 34, No. 2 [2010], pp. 218–236)   99

Fig. 3.10  Window period of India's demographic transition (Source: Misbah T. Choudhry and J. Paul Elhorst, Demographic Transition and Economic Growth in China, India and Pakistan, *Economic Systems*, Vol. 34, No. 2 [2010], pp. 218–236)   100

Fig. 3.11  Student enrollments at various types of schools (10,000) (*Source* Department of Comprehensive Statistics of National Bureau of Statistics, *China Compendium of Statistics 1949–2008*, Statistical Database of Chinese Economic Social Development)   101

xii   LIST OF FIGURES

Fig. 3.12   Number of reservoirs in China (*Source* Ministry of Water Resources of the People's Republic of China, *China's Water Conservancy Statistics Yearbook*, Statistical Database of Chinese Economic and Social Development)   103

Fig. 3.13   Construction of large reservoirs 1949–2007 (*Source* Ministry of Water Resources of the People's Republic of China, *China's Water Conservancy Statistics Yearbook*, Statistical Database of Chinese Economic and Social Development)   104

Fig. 3.14   Area of effective irrigation (unit: 1,000 hectares) (*Source* Ministry of Water Resources of the People's Republic of China, *China's Water Conservancy Statistics Yearbook*, Statistical Database of Chinese Economic and Social Development)   105

Fig. 3.15   Total grain output and per capita grain output (*Source* Department of Comprehensive Statistics of National Bureau of Statistics, *China Compendium of Statistics 1949–2008*,*China Statistics Yearbook*, Statistical Database of Chinese Economic Social Development)   106

Fig. 3.16   Shares of industry, agriculture and tertiary industry in national economy (*Source* Department of Comprehensive Statistics of National Bureau of Statistics, *China Compendium of Statistics 1949–2008*,*China Statistics Yearbook*, Statistical Database of Chinese Economic Social Development)   107

Fig. 3.17   Economic growth rate of China, 1950–1978 (%) (*Note* The figures for 1949–1952 refer to the growth rate of national income, and those since 1953 refer to the growth rate of GDP. *Source* Department of Comprehensive Statistics of National Bureau of Statistics, *China Compendium of Statistics 1949–2008*,*China Statistics Yearbook*, Statistical Database of Chinese Economic Social Development)   111

Fig. 3.18   Comparison of HDI in five countries (*Note* The figure after each country is related to the added value of its HDI from 1950 to 2014. *Source* Data of 1950 are from Nicolas Crafts, *Globalization and Growth in the Twentieth Century*, IMF Working Paper No. 00/44 (March 1, 2000); data of 1980–2014 are from the UNDP webpage http://hdrstats.undp.org/indicators/14.html)   113

LIST OF FIGURES    xiii

Fig. 4.1   Varieties of goods under unified allocation
           and department-managed goods (*Source* Li Jingwen,
           *Direction of Reform on China's Goods Management
           System,Research on Economics and Management*, No.
           1 (1980), pp. 56–62; Zhang Jianqin, *A Comparative
           Study of Traditional Planning Economic System in China
           and the Soviet Union* [Wuhan: Hubei People's Publishing
           House, 2004], p. 217)                                              126
Fig. 4.2   China's GDP growth rate, 1949–2018 (%) (Table 3]
           *Source* Data for 1953–2004 are from National Accounts
           Department of National Bureau of Statistics, *Data
           of Gross Domestic Product of China 1952–2004* [Beijing:
           China Statistics Press, 2007: Growth rate of GDP; data
           for 2005–2008 are from National Bureau of Statistics,
           *China Statistical Abstract 2009* [Beijing: China Statistics
           Press, 2009], p. 22)                                                130
Fig. 4.3   Employment in urban units of public ownership (*Source*
           National Bureau of Statistics, *China Statistical Abstract
           2009* [Beijing: China Statistics Press, 2009], p. 45)              136
Fig. 4.4   Historical stages in China's development (2018 value
           of U.S. dollar) (*Source* The Conference Board, Total
           Economy Database, April 2019, http://www.conference-
           board.org/data/economydatabase/TED1)                               140
Fig. 4.5   Poverty of rural dwellers (*Source* Comprehensive Statistics
           Department of National Bureau of Statistics, *China
           Statistical Yearbook; China Statistical Abstract*; Statistical
           Database of Chinese Economic Social Development)                   149
Fig. 5.1   Frequency with which English phrase "five-year plan"
           appears in Google Book Ngrams 1900–2000                            163
Fig. 5.2   GDP per capita and HID rankings in each economy,
           1980 (*Source* UNDP, 2010 Report Hybrid-HDI data
           of trends analysis, http://hdrundp.org/en/media/
           2010_Hybrid-HDI-data.xls)                                          164
Fig. 5.3   Variation of GDP per capita of countries in transition,
           1989–2019 (calculated at 2018 international US dollar)
           (*Source* The Conference Board, Total Economy Database,
           April 2019, http://www.conference-board.org/data/eco
           nomydatabase/TED1)                                                 166

| | | |
|---|---|---|
| Fig. 5.4 | Quantity of planned metrics and their fulfillment rate (*Note* The fulfillment rate of planned metrics refer to the ratio of the number of metrics fulfilled (at and above 100%) and the overall number of planned metrics. *Source* Yan Yilong, *Metrics Governance: Visible Hand of Five-Year Planning*, Beijing: China Renmin University Press, 2013: 293–295; 326–340) | 175 |
| Fig. 6.1 | Shares of traditional and new economy in the gross industrial and agricultural output value (*Source* Xu Dixin and Wu Chenming, *History of the Development of Chinese Capitalism*, Vol. III [Beijing: People's Publishing House, 2003], p. 756) | 189 |
| Fig. 6.2 | GDP composition in 1952 (*Source* National Bureau of Statistics, *China Compendium of Statistics 1949–2008*; *China Statistical Yearbook*; Statistical Database of Chinese Economic and Social Development) | 190 |
| Fig. 6.3 | Number and employment of state-owned industrial enterprises (*Note* Unless otherwise noted, all the data of figures and tables in this and the next section are sourced in the *Statistical Database of China's Economic and Social Development* on the China National Knowledge Infrastructure [CNKI]) | 214 |
| Fig. 6.4 | SOEs' contribution to industrial growth, 1949–1984 | 215 |
| Fig. 6.5 | Profits and taxes made by state-owned industrial enterprises, 1952–1984 | 216 |
| Fig. 6.6 | Rapid growth of state-owned fixed capital investment, 1952–1984 | 218 |
| Fig. 6.7 | Funding sources shares in state-owned economy's fixed asset investment, 1953–2000 | 219 |
| Fig. 6.8 | Share of state-owned institutions' fixed asset investment in state financial resources, 1953–1984 | 220 |
| Fig. 6.9 | Shares of various sources in state financial revenue, 1950–1984 | 221 |
| Fig. 6.10 | Original value of state-owned industrial fixed assets and their shares, 1952–1984 | 222 |
| Fig. 6.11 | Per capita national income, 1949–1984 (*Source* Department of National Economy Statistics of National Bureau of Statistics: *Compendium of National Income Statistics 1949–1984*, Beijing, China Statistics Press, 1987, p. 10) | 229 |
| Fig. 6.12 | Breakdown shares in state financial revenue, 1950–2010 | 233 |

| | | |
|---|---|---|
| Fig. 6.13 | Geographical distribution of total investment in fixed assets | 235 |
| Fig. 6.14 | Number of state-owned industrial enterprises and their employment | 236 |
| Fig. 6.15 | Profit volume and profit-making percentage of SOEs, 1980–2018 | 239 |
| Fig. 6.16 | Total assets of state-owned and state-holding industrial enterprises, 1999–2017 (Unit: 100 million yuan) | 239 |
| Fig. 6.17 | Number of Chinese, United States, and Japanese enterprise in the Fortune 500 list | 240 |
| Fig. 6.18 | State-owned fixed asset investment and share, 1980–2017 | 241 |
| Fig. 6.19 | Original value of state-owned industrial fixed assets and share, 1980–2016 | 242 |
| Fig. 6.20 | Comparison of power generation between China and the United States, 1949–2018 (*Source* US data are from US Energy Information Administration, Annual Energy Review, http://www.eia.gov/totalenergy/data/annual/index.php) | 246 |
| Fig. 6.21 | Countries' GDP share in global total, 1950–2019 (*Source* The Conference Board, Total Economy Database, April 2019, https://www.conference-board.org/data/economydatabase/TEDI) | 250 |
| Fig. 6.22 | China: Toward high-income economy | 251 |
| Fig. 7.1 | Shares of consolidated fiscal revenue and expenditure in GDP (*Source* Unless noted by specific sources, all the data used in this chapter are based on a databank the author compiles from various sources) | 257 |
| Fig. 7.2 | Central authorities' transfer payments to localities (100 million yuan) | 260 |
| Fig. 7.3 | Coefficient of variation of interprovincial GDP per capita | 261 |
| Fig. 7.4 | Urban–rural income and consumption gaps (rural areas as 1), 1978–2017 | 263 |
| Fig. 7.5 | National Gini index in China, 1995–2017 | 264 |
| Fig. 7.6 | Urban and rural minimum living security coverage, 2001–2018 (10,000 people) | 266 |
| Fig. 7.7 | Composition of China's total health cost, 1965–2018 | 271 |
| Fig. 7.8 | Participation in China's endowment insurance (10,000 people) | 273 |
| Fig. 7.9 | Units of indemnificatory housing completed, 2006–2018 | 278 |
| Fig. 7.10 | Participation of unemployment insurance, work injury insurance and maternity insurance, 1994–2018 (Million) | 279 |
| Fig. 7.11 | Public spending on social security (100 million yuan) | 283 |

xvi  LIST OF FIGURES

| | | |
|---|---|---|
| Fig. 7.12 | Share of public spending on social security in GDP (*Source* Chinese data are from a databank the author compiles from various sources; data for other countries are from International Labor Organization, *World Social Protection Report Data 2017–2019*, http://www.social-protection.org/gimi/gess/AggregateIndicator.action#expenditure) | 284 |
| Fig. 8.1 | Evidence for "middle-income trap" (*Source* The World Bank, Development Research Center of the State Council, the People's Republic of China, *China 2030: Building a Modern, Harmonious, and Creative Society*, 2013:12) | 292 |
| Fig. 8.2 | Year an economy turned lower-middle income and number of years it spent as lower-middle income (*Note* The line shown is obtained from the regression of the number of years in LM on the year the economy turned LM. The regression result is shown in the figure. Both the constant and the coefficient on "year turned LM" are statistically significant at the 1% level of significance. See Appendix Table 1 for the codes of each economy. LM = lower-middle income, N = Sample size, R-sq = R-squared. *Source* Jesus Felipe, Utsav Kumar, and Reynold Galope, Middle-Income Transitions: Trap or Myth? *Journal of the Asian Pacific Economy*, Vol. 22, No. 3 [2017], pp. 429–453) | 295 |
| Fig. 8.3 | Year an economy turned upper-middle income and number of years it spent as upper-middle income. (*Note* The line shown is obtained from the regression of the number of years in UM on the year the economy turned UM. The regression result is shown in the figure. The constant and the coefficient on "year turned UM" are statistically significant at the 5% and 10% level of significance, respectively. See Appendix Table 1 for the codes of each economy. N = Sample size, R-sq = R-squared, UM = Upper-middle income. *Source* Jesus Felipe, Utsav Kumar, and Reynold Galope, Middle-Income Transitions: Trap or Myth? *Journal of the Asian Pacific Economy*, Vol. 22, No. 3 [2017]) | 296 |
| Fig. A.1 | Variation of average crude death rate: Finland (unit: ‰) (*Source*: Palgrave Macmillan Ltd., *International Historical Statistics* [Basingstoke: Palgrave Macmillan; April 2013]) | 305 |

|  |  |  |
|---|---|---|
| Fig. A.2 | Variation of average crude death rate: Germany (unit: ‰) (*Source* Palgrave Macmillan Ltd., *International Historical Statistics* [Basingstoke: Palgrave Macmillan; April 2013]) | 306 |
| Fig. A.3 | Variation of average crude death rate: Greece (unit: ‰) (*Source* Palgrave Macmillan Ltd., *International Historical Statistics* [Basingstoke: Palgrave Macmillan; April 2013]) | 306 |
| Fig. A.4 | Variation of average crude death rate: United States (unit: ‰) (*Source* Palgrave Macmillan Ltd., *International Historical Statistics* [Basingstoke: Palgrave Macmillan; April 2013]) | 307 |
| Fig. A.5 | Variation of average crude death rate: South Africa (unit: ‰) (*Source* Palgrave Macmillan Ltd., *International Historical Statistics* [Basingstoke: Palgrave Macmillan; April 2013]) | 308 |
| Fig. A.6 | Variation of average crude death rate: China (unit:‰) (*Source* National Bureau of Statistics, *China Statistics Yearbook* [every year]) | 308 |
| Fig. A.7 | Comparison of before and after Great Leap Forward: different estimates (unit: ‰) | 312 |
| Fig. A.8 | Compare with India: UN data (unit: ‰) (*Source* United Nations Department of Economic and Social Affairs Population Division, *World Population Prospects: The 2012 Revision*, http://esa.un.org/unpd/wpp/index.htm) | 313 |
| Fig. A.9 | Compare with India: World Bank data (unit: ‰) (*Source* World Bank, http://data.worldbank.org/indicator/SP.DYN.CDRT.IN) | 314 |
| Fig. A.10 | **a** GDP per capita and crude mortality rate: 1960. **b** GDP per capita and crude mortality rate: 1962 (*Source* World Bank, http://data.worldbank.org/indicator/) | 316 |
| Fig. A.11 | **a** Height and year born (Chinese men) (Year born). **b** Height and year born: 1935–1975 (Chinese women) (*Source* Stephen Lloyd Morgan, *Stature and Famine in China: The Welfare of the Survivors of the Great Leap Forward Famine, 1959-61* [February 2007], Available at SSRN: http://dx.doi.org/10.2139/ssrn.1083059) | 318 |

# LIST OF TABLES

| | | |
|---|---|---|
| Table 2.1 | Growth rate of GDP per capita around the formation of modern countries Unit: % | 23 |
| Table 2.2 | GDP per capita of the world around the formation of modern countries Unit: 1990 international value of US dollars | 24 |
| Table 2.3 | War-making capacity since 500 CE | 28 |
| Table 2.4 | Men under arms, Europe 1500–1980 | 29 |
| Table 2.5 | Annual tax revenue per capita, 1500–1909 unit: gram silver | 45 |
| Table 2.6 | Comparison of infrastructures between late Qing China and Japan in the Tokugawa shogunate | 52 |
| Table 2.7 | Duration of samurai rebellions | 57 |
| Table 3.1 | Distribution of wars in China, 1912–1930 | 72 |
| Table 3.2 | National education level in 1949 | 83 |
| Table 3.3 | Estimates of mortality rates before the founding of New China | 85 |
| Table 3.4 | Growth rate of major industrial products | 109 |
| Table 4.1 | Shares of different economic sectors (Unit: %) | 119 |
| Table 6.1 | Comparison of China and India's economy | 190 |
| Table 6.2 | Private industry in 1949 | 192 |
| Table 6.3 | Output of major industrial products at early stage of New China | 194 |
| Table 6.4 | Comparison of major industrial products between China and India in 1949 | 195 |

| | | |
|---|---|---|
| Table 6.5 | Composition of Capital Volume, 1947–1948 (Unit: Fiat money100 million yuan in 1936 value) | 197 |
| Table 6.6 | Variation of total volume of industrial capital II in 35 years up to the founding of New China (Unit: fiat money, 100 million yuan, 1936 value) | 199 |
| Table 6.7 | Shares of items of industrial capital II in its total volume in 35 years up to the founding of New China (Unit: %) | 200 |
| Table 6.8 | SOE share in major industrial products in 1949 | 206 |
| Table 6.9 | Labor productivity of workers in Industrial Enterprises Nationwide (Unit: Yuan/Per Capita/Year) | 208 |
| Table 6.10 | Structural changes in ownerships 1952–1957 (Unit: %) | 209 |
| Table 6.11 | Improvement of overall labor productivity of state-owned industrial enterprises (Counted at the constant price of 1970) | 216 |
| Table 6.12 | Changes in internal composition of gross output by industry (Unit: %) | 224 |
| Table 6.13 | Variations in output ranking of major industrial products in the world | 225 |
| Table 6.14 | Geographical distribution of industrial production, 1952–1984 (Unit: %) | 226 |
| Table 6.15 | State capital dominated sectors, 2016 | 244 |
| Table 6.16 | Top 10 economies' CIP index and sub-indexes, 2016 | 248 |
| Table A.1 | Number of years taken for mortality rate to drop from 20 to 10 per thousand in countries, regions, or races | 310 |
| Table A.2 | Age distribution of mortality in rural Guizhou, 1958 and 1960 (Unit: %) | 319 |

# CHAPTER 1

# Introduction

On September 21, 1949, ten days before the founding of the People's Republic of China, the First Plenary Session of the Chinese People's Political Consultative Conference (CPPCC) opened in the Hall of Huairen, or Cherished Compassion, inside Zhongnanhai, the seat of China's central leadership in Beijing. The historical mission of this conference was to prepare for the founding of New China. The assembly unanimously adopted the following resolutions: (1) The capital of the People's Republic of China would be settled in Beiping (which would be renamed Beijing beginning from September 27, 1949). (2) The People's Republic of China would use the Anno Domini dating system. (3) The *March of the Volunteers* would act as the national anthem until a formal national anthem was created. (4) The five-star red flag would be the national flag of the People's Republic of China. The Conference also adopted the *Common Program of the Chinese People's Political Consultative Conference*, which was of the nature of an interim constitution, and formulated the *Organization Law of the Central People's Government of the People's Republic of China*, and the *Organization Law of the Chinese People's Political Consultative Conference*. The session elected Mao Zedong chairman of the Central People's Government, and also elected vice chairmen and members of the Central People's Government. At the opening ceremony of the congress, Mao Zedong, chairman of the Central Committee of the Communist Party of China, delivered an opening speech, warmly celebrating the victory of the People's Liberation War and the People's

© CITIC Press Corporation 2021
S. Wang, *China's Rise and Its Global Implications*,
https://doi.org/10.1007/978-981-16-4341-5_1

Revolution, and celebrating the founding of the People's Republic of China. He solemnly declared: "The Chinese people, comprising one quarter of humanity, have now stood up."

Toward the end of this great speech to the founding of the republic, Mao Zedong made some remarks that sounded very majestic: "Let the domestic and foreign reactionaries tremble before us! Let them say that we are no good at this and no good at that. By our own indomitable efforts we the Chinese people will unswervingly reach our goal."[1] Mao Zedong was in anguish to say these words, because until 1948, not only the United States, but also the Soviet Union, believed that China would be unified under a Kuomintang government, rather than under the Communist Party. Among those who were saying that China was no good at the time was not only the United States who was hostile to the Socialist Camp, but even the Soviet Union, the "Big Brother" of the Socialist Camp, also had the doubts. Hence the saying that China was "no good at this and no good at that."

## Ridiculous Prediction

In fact, ever since the founding of the People's Republic of China in 1949, there have constantly been remarks that China is "no good at this and no good at that," and there have constantly been people predicting when the New China will collapse, fall, break down or even disintegrate. At that time, many people in the world did not believe that China had embarked on a broad road of modernization, and even we ourselves estimated that the road ahead would be very tortuous and long. What those outside were arguing about at the time was not the question of whether China was going to collapse, but when and how it would collapse, and what impact the collapse would have on the interests of the neighboring powers. In 1991, the Soviet Union, the world's first socialist country, disintegrated. Since then, predictions about China's collapse have been even more deafening. In the summer of 1995, for example, *Foreign Policy* published a long article by political scientist Jack Goldstone, entitled *The Coming Chinese Collapse*, predicting that "the most likely future scenario

---

[1] Mao Zedong, *The Chinese People Have Stood Up!* (September 21, 1949) *Selected Works of Mao Tse-tung*, Vol. V (Foreign Languages Press, Peking, 1977), p. 18.

is for a replay of 1911."[2] Of course, in retrospect today these sayings are obviously not scientific, which only reflect the dark mindset of some people and a vicious expectation on their part.

It's needless to mention those endless predictions throughout the 1950s to the 1970s. After we entered the twenty-first century, the crow-mouthed prophets still tirelessly repeated such "prophecies" that had been proven false time and again. In August 2001, a book was published in the United States with the title quite sensational—*The Coming Collapse of China*, authored by Gordon G. Chang (Zhang Jiadun), a Chinese-American. No sooner than it came off the press did the book make into the *New York Times* bestseller list, and Gordon Chang became a celebrity invited by various institutions across the United State, and the U.S. Congress specially invited him to a hearing. In English, the expression of "coming" implies that something would happen soon. But how soon would this "coming" he emphasized could be? A few days? A few weeks? A few months? A year or two? Chang didn't say.

There should be quite some people who believe in such an unreliable prediction. In March 2002, the non-simplified Chinese edition of the book was published in Taiwan, and Lee Teng-hui personally wrote a recommendation for it, saying "this book gives a specific description of the reality of the mainland, which is worth recommending." This Taiwan secessionist knew nothing about the reality of the mainland, how could he know that this book by Gordon Chang "gives a specific description of the reality of the mainland"?

Even more ridiculously, another version of the book in Taiwan put my name on the cover, saying, "Even scholars from Chinese official institutions, Wang Shaoguang, Hu Angang and Ding Yuanzhu, have to give the 'most serious warning' to the Chinese government." Yes, in the summer of 2002, the three of us did publish an article in *Strategy and Management* entitled *The Sternest Warning: Social Instability Behind the Economic Boom*, but what we discussed were some of the challenges facing China at the time, we never predicted that China's political system would collapse.

Gordon Chang's original prediction was that the collapse was "impending," which should mean soon. Yet 10 years passed and China did not collapse. So a lot of people challenged, "How come things you predicted haven't come true?" At the end of 2011, Gordon Chang wrote

---

[2] Jack A Goldstone, *The Coming Chinese Collapse*, Foreign Policy, No. 99 (Summer 1995), pp. 35–53.

another article titled *The Coming Collapse of China: 2012 Edition*. He admitted that his previous prediction was a bit wrong, but this time it would be a nail in the coffin. To appear prudent, he affectedly said: "I admit it: My prediction that the Communist Party would fall by 2011 was wrong. Still, I'm only off by a year. Instead of 2011, the mighty Communist Party of China will fall in 2012. Bet on it."

The year 2012 passed, again China did not collapse. Still Gordon Chang would not give up. In September 2015, he made a new version of the forecast: *2015: The Year China Goes Broke?* Such a person is really birch-headed, stubborn, and diehard as the beak of dead duck. He has not made any more predictions since, but who knows if he will come up with a new one in the future.

In fact, Gordon Chang is not alone. Also in 2015, David Shambaugh, an American expert on China, published an article in the *Wall Street Journal* entitled *The Coming Chinese Crackup*, which drew extensive attention. The article claimed that "the endgame of communist rule in China has begun." He later argued that he did not mean that. But the title was so eye-catching, the article so certain, which could not be excused in a few words of explanation.

In 2017, a couple walking out from the Chinese mainland wrote a book called *China's Collapse without Break*. The man is named Cheng Xiaonong, who used to work in the department for institutional restructuring while in China; and the woman is named He Qinglian, who was a reporter at home. I could never comprehend the title of the book, how can things collapse but not break? They seemed to have the intention of arguing that China is going to collapse, but they were not sure, so to make themselves not so absurd, they fabricated such a tune of a collapse without break.

In 2018, a famous U.S. magazine, *The National Interest*, published an article, which made a fuss to ask, *Are We Ready If China Suddenly Collapsed?* Later in 2018, the *New York Times* published a lengthy article under the headline, *The Land Failed to Fail*, which meant that China should be bound to fail, but it did not. The headline revealed a tremendous disappointment. It indicated the West's perception of China, their disagreement with China's social system, which led them to the assumption that China's system and road of development will certainly not succeed, and will fail sooner or later. But they have waited for 70 years, and their expected collapse is still not in sight, yet still they are not reconciled.

## Ridiculous Theory

Ever since 1949, we have constantly heard people saying that China's system is no good, China's road leads to nowhere, and the Chinese are bound to run head against a wall. Seven decades have passed, in retrospect, all the predictions about China's collapse have been proven wrong. This book will indicate with a large amount of data that China has crossed the mountains and embarked on an increasingly broader road. The question is, why have so many people been making false forecasts about China's future for so long, and insisting in going all the way to the dark in spite of irrefutable facts? This involves the theoretical basis of such predictions. Although some people who have made false predictions may not be clear about what their theoretical basis is, they might have some dogmas in their minds, and they assume that as long as there is a system that operates following the dogmas, the state will succeed, or it will surely fail. More specifically, the Western countries have followed these dogmas, so they could be and have already been successful. And these people think that only the road taken by the West is the correct one, which is bound to be the only way every state must take to succeed, and has become a paradigm, with no other option. No other road is likely to work, China's road included. However, the predictions made on the basis of these dogmas have failed time and again, for 70 years in a row, evidencing that these dogmas or theoretical basis for such predictions are completely wrong.

The "dogmas" and "theoretical basis" mentioned here are actually written in a large number of textbooks in the West, which circulate day after day in various media. Such theories have cropped up layer upon layer and in all kinds. And books about them are so many. Here, I'd briefly cite a few to show what they are saying, and with their experience and what they have done in contrast, we'd examine where China's road to rise is different at all.

In 1963, William McNeil, a prominent historian at the University of Chicago, published a book entitled *The Rise of the West: A History of the Human Community*,[3] which was intended to sing a different tune with Oswald Spengler's *The Decline of the West*. The book was well received as soon as it came out, and won several book awards. The key

---

[3] William Hardy McNeil, *The Rise of the West: A History of the Human Community* (Chicago: University of Chicago Press, 1963).

of the book is *Part III, The Era of Western Dominance, 1500 A.D. to the Present*. The author suggested that "Europeans of the Atlantic seaboard possessed three talismans of power by 1500 which conferred upon them the command of all the oceans of the world within half a century and permitted the subjugation of the most highly developed regions of the Americas within a single generation. These were: (1) a deep-rooted pugnacity and recklessness operating by means of (2) a complex military technology, most notably in naval matters; and (3) a population inured to a variety of diseases which had long been endemic throughout the Old World ecumene."[4] More than 20 years later, the author himself confessed that the book was in fact "an expression of the postwar imperial mood in the United States" and "a form of intellectual imperialism."[5]

Similar to this book is Eric Jones's *The European Miracle: Environments, Economies and Geopolitics in the History of Europe and Asia* published in 1981.[6] Since the 1980s, we've often heard about the "Japanese miracle," "East Asian miracle" and "Chinese miracle," but before that, there had long been talks of the "European miracle" in Europe and the United States. The book title itself is obvious enough about its main point of view and there is no need to give a detailed introduction. Other scholars later commented on the book, saying that it is full of European centrism and even tinged with "cultural racism."[7]

Over the past 20 years and more, such books have also become fashionable. In 1997, American scholar Jared Diamond published *Guns, Germs and Steel: The Fates of Human Societies*,[8] with a Chinese version available. The author recognized the fact that Europeans massacred or conquered other nations, but he tried to focus on answering the question: Why was it the European societies (the societies that colonized the Americas and

---

[4] William Hardy McNeil, *The Rise of the West: A History of the Human Community* (Chicago: University of Chicago Press, 1963).

[5] William Hardy McNeil, *The Rise of the West After Twenty-Five Years*, Journal of World History, Vol. 1, No. 1 (Spring 19901), pp. 1–21.

[6] Eric Jones, *The European Miracle: Environments, Economies and Geopolitics in the History of Europe and Asia* (Cambridge: Cambridge University Press, 1981).

[7] James Morris Blaut, *The Theory of Cultural Racism*, Antipode: A Radical Journal of Geography, Vol. 23, No. 4 (1992), pp. 289–299; James Morris Blaut, *The Colonizer's Model of the World: Geographical Diffusionism and Europcentric History* (New York, NY: The Guilford Press, 1993), p. 64.

[8] Jared Mason Diamond, *Guns, Germs, and Steel: The Fates of Human Societies* (New York: W. W. Norton, 1997).

Australia), rather than the Chinese, Indian or other societies that were technologically advanced and politically and economically dominant in the modern world? The answer he gave was that the geographical factor was crucial, because geographically Europe was divided into dozens or hundreds of independent and competing small states and centers of invention and creation. If one state failed to pursue some kind of reform and innovation, another state would do so, compelling its neighbors to do the same, or it would be conquered or economically lag behind. In other words, European countries are more competitive by nature, and the need to survive has driven them to constantly compete, innovate and develop. Whereas China was just too gigantic, too unified, and was too short of competition, so it had been hard for it to develop.[9]

There is hardly anything new in Diamond's talks. As early as in 1898, Zhang Zhidong[10] made this passage in his *Exhortation to Study*:

> There are many states in Europe, each confronting the other like groups of tigers eagerly awaiting an opportunity to devour, no one could survive unless it evenly matched others. Therefore new methods of governance that cultivates wealth and strength, and new skills that measure heaven and earth, study the nature and benefit the people have been put up every day, which have been imitated mutually and vied to dominate and stay long. With their territories interconnected, their interflows have become ever more convenient and they have become ever more well-informed since railway and ship transport went into smooth operation, which has led to great refreshing changes over the past 100 years, and the progress has been especially rapid in the past 30 years. For those who live around transport hubs, they are well-informed without much effort to learn. For those students with esteemed friends, they gain a lot without much labor. The periods of Spring-Autumn (770-476 B.C.), Warring States (476-221 B.C.) and Three Kingdoms (220-280 A.D.) in China's history witnessed more talents than other eras. But once the states were amalgamated into one country in the bygone dynasties, as a unified country towering alone in the East, its neighbors were all remote barbarians or desert tribes, and none of them had a ruling art or academic studies better than China's.

---

[9] Jared Diamond, *How to Get Rich*, http://www.edge.org/conversation/how-to-get-rich.

[10] Zhang Zhidong, or Chang Chi-tung (1837–1909), one of the prominent officials of the late Qing Dynasty (1644–1911) and a leading Chinese reformist in the nineteenth century for the country's industrialization and modernization—*Translator*.

So it was enough for China to rule without troubles just by following the old ways with some modifications when necessary, and adhering to the old learning without going beyond the range. As it gets farther away from the ancient times, old defects have piled up increasingly and quintessence of the old ways and old learning gradually paled, then we find ourselves to appear deficient in comparison with others as all the five continents are interconnected today.[11]

As a theoretical hypothesis, Diamond and Zhang Zhidong's notions are quite interesting. The question is, geographical features won't change much for tens of thousands of years, but the development momentums in various countries could be reversed in decades or hundreds of years. It doesn't seem to make sense to interpret variables with constants. China is still very gigantic and unified today, isn't it true that it has nonetheless developed? How could Diamond and Zhang Zhidong's theoretical assumptions explain it?

In 1998, an influential book was published in the United States, which is *The Wealth and Poverty of Nations: Why Some Are So Rich and Some So Poor*[12] authored by David Landers, a retired professor at Harvard University, with Chinese version available. The book cites several key variables to explain the wealth and poverty of nations. The first is geographical position, or more accurately, climate, as "the rich countries lie in the temperate zones, particularly in the northern hemisphere; the poor countries, in the tropics and semitropics." Climate has always been an important factor in Western theories that explain social and political changes, one example is Montesquieu's *The Spirit of Laws*. In addition to climate, other variables include competitive politics, economic freedom, and approaches toward science and religion. In other words, the West succeeds because they are Western countries and they have done things in compliance with Western values. Some have criticized Landers as a Western centrist, and he does not deny it. According to the theory in *The Wealth and Poverty of Nations*, it should be impossible for socialist China under the leadership of the Communist Party to succeed, because its geographical location and climatic conditions are all wrong, and it

---

[11] Zhang Zhidong, *Exhortation to Study* (Zhengzhou: Zhongzhou Ancient Books Press, 1998).

[12] David Landers, *The Wealth and Poverty of Nations: Why Some Are So Rich and Some So Poor* (New York: W. W. Norton, 1998).

lacks the political, economic and cultural factors for success that he has emphasized.

Ten years later in 2008, American political scientist Jack Goldstone published *Why Europe? The Rise of the West in World History 1500–1850*.[13] According to the author, it was not colonialism and conquest that made the rise of the West possible; on the contrary, it was the rise of the West (technically) and the decline of other regions that allowed European power to extend completely throughout the entire planet. Having whitewashed colonialism, the author claimed that there was not a single but multiple factors for Europe's success. He cited six factors: (1) new findings leading to the emancipation of mind; (2) mathematical and scientific way of thinking; (3) research methods of experimental science; (4) tool-driven experiments and observations; (5) tolerance and pluralism; and (6) interaction between entrepreneurs, scientists, engineers, and artisans. He believed that these are the most important explanatory variables developed in Europe and the United States. If we use the six factors to explain China, arguably the six of them seem to be there but are not real. Suppose China has always had these factors, why did modern China fall so low? But if China has always missed them, then how do we explain the rapid economic development in the 70 years after the founding of New China?

In 2010, Ian Morris, an archeologist and historian at Stanford University, published *Why the West Rules: For Now—The Patterns of History, and What They Reveal About the Future*.[14] The book's main explanatory variables are also geographical conditions. According to the author, biology and sociology can explain global similarities, while geography can explain regional differences. In this sense, geography can be used to explain why the West dominates the world: Europe has the Mediterranean Sea, while China does not have its own Mediterranean. Along the Mediterranean Sea, European countries were able to get involved in maritime trade through the development of navigation technology, with a relatively large trading. Moreover, the navigational technology also enabled European countries to discover new continents at an early stage, and expand markets and sources of raw materials. These were what China missed without

---

[13] Jack A Goldstone, *Why Europe? The Rise of the West in World History 1500–1850* (New York: McGraw-Hill Education, 2008). He is the very scholar who predicted in 1995 that China's collapse was bound to happen.

[14] Ian Morris, *Why the West Rules—For Now: The Patterns of History, and What They Reveal about the Future* (New York: Farrar, Straus and Giroux, 2010).

its own Mediterranean. The question again is that although geographical factors are constant, the level of economic development could be up and down. China's geographical conditions have not changed much as compared with what it was like hundreds or thousands of years ago, which was even more so at the time around the founding of New China. Then why the New China has succeeded but the Old China failed? How to explain this?

In 2011, British historian Niall Ferguson published *Civilization: The West and the Rest*.[15] The author is very interested in China and often comes to China for exchanges with various universities. He concluded that the West could rise after 1500 and led the rest of the world (including China) just because their political institutions had six "killer apps" which were not existent in other countries: the first was the competition, the second was science, the third was the rule of law, the fourth was medical science, the fifth was consumerism, and the sixth was work ethics. The inherent logic of this saying is not clear, but much like a jumble. It just intends to imply that they lead the world just because they have their family heirloom unique to them, which is not available to others. According to this logic, there is no chance for other countries to turn over, unless they holistically copy the six killer apps from the West. The question is, even if you want to copy, could you really do it? Will they give up their killer apps they have treasured so much?[16]

Finally, I'd mention a book published in 2012, entitled *Why Nations Fail: The Origins of Power, Prosperity and Poverty*, authored by Daron Acemoglu, an economist at the Massachusetts Institute of Technology, and James Robinson, a political scientist at Harvard University.[17] Their argument is simple but powerful, holding that some countries fail because their political institutions are extractive and other countries succeed because they are within a system that is inclusive. Western countries have inclusive systems, so they succeed. The Communist-led countries are of course within the system that is extractive, so it is impossible for such

---

[15] Niall Ferguson, *Civilization: The West and the Rest* (New York: Penguin, 2011).

[16] Ferguson even believes that China's rise after 1978 (rather than after 1949) has benefited from its opening up, whereby it has learned the West experiences. His *Civilization* was translated by Zeng Xianming and Tang Yinghua into Chinese and published by the CITIC Press Group, Beijing in 2012.

[17] Daron Acemoglu and James A. Robinson, *Why Nations Fail: The Origins of Power, Prosperity and Poverty* (New York, Crown Publishers, 2012).

countries to succeed; even if they look like successful in a short period, it is not a real success, it must be short-lived, a flash in the pan, and is bound to doom. Let's say nothing about whether this theory could explain the rise of the West (in what sense were Europe and the United States "inclusive" throughout the eighteenth and early twentieth centuries?), will it be able to explain China's performance in the recent decades? The authors put on an air of prophets and said unquestionably: "China under the rule of the Communist Party is another example of society experiencing growth under extractive institutions and is similarly unlikely to generate sustained growth unless it undergoes a fundamental political transformation toward inclusive political institutions." Perhaps ignorance could magically give people the guts to look down upon everything.

## What Does China's Rise Mean to the World?

The arguments of the books cited above vary, so do their approaches to the accomplishments China has made, but their unspoken basic assumptions are the same, that is, the Western experience is the key to understand the success or failure of all nations. The experience of other countries does not seem to be worth mentioning; and if one insists in mentioning it, it's nothing more than some painful lessons.

The reason why I've taken pains to present these prominent Western scholars' theories on economic rise above is nothing more than to illustrate that some Western scholars have a common problem, that is, they are often conceited about the achievements their own countries made in the past few centuries, always seeking to find some secrets to their success that can be universally applied, and measure the realities of other countries (China included) with the framework of these theories about Western success. In fact, it seems to me that the so-called theories offered by those voluminous works not only could explain China, but also they could hardly explain the West itself. Some of them admit that imperialism, colonialism, slavery and slave trade played a considerable role in the success of the West. But what marvels is that with a neat twist, they suddenly halt the discussions about how much of a role these brutal, bloody and ugly pasts have played, but rather move to shift people's attention to the so-called bright spots of the West, such as "democracy," "market," "private ownership," "competition," "rule of law," and "science," things that mainstream Western ideology has always advocated. These rhetoric expressions of theirs are the mainstream in the West, which some people in the Third World (China included) have accepted and believed blindly. Once such theories are internalized, the prediction about China will only point to one direction, that is, it is impossible for China's system to function sustainably and effectively, and even if some achievements are made in a short period, it will eventually go bankrupt. Unfortunately for them, none of their predictions has come true. Now the New China has gone through 70 years, the country is going ever higher up step by step, getting ever richer and stronger, and it will soon become a member of the high-income club. Seventy years are not a short period. For human beings, it was rare to see people living to 70 years old in ancient times. So the predictions made by some people in the West are completely unscientific, with their theoretical foundation totally wrong, and they have become a laughing stock of history.

To sum up, over the past 200 years, many Western scholars have tried to put forward theories to explain the following questions: Why could the West dominate the world? Why are some countries prosperous but other countries decaying? Why have China and other developing countries lagged behind? They all try to point out that this is because the West has something unique (institutional, cultural, racial, geographical, and climatic) that is not available to other countries. Now their predictions about China have proven mistaken, and China has walked out a road of its own, suggesting that their theories cannot answer their own questions and that China's rise is significant to the world.

In realistic sense, the practice of China's rise tells the world:

1. A poorest country in the world (in 1950, China was one of the poorest countries in the world) can turn over.
2. A country that has never invaded other countries or imposed colonialism can develop. (The early stages of development or primitive accumulation in Europe and the United States, including some Nordic countries, were all accompanied by aggression into other countries and colonialism.)
3. An ancient civilization in the East (not Anglo-Saxon, Protestant, South European or East European culture) can develop. (The TV documentary series *River Elegy* once asserted that our cultural genes impeded our own development.)
4. A socialist country can develop, which resembles neither those early capitalist countries like Britain and the United States (with the mortality rate rising rather than declining in the early days of

industrialization) nor Japan and South Korea—they are vassals of imperialism and have the support and preferential treatment from the United States.
5. A country with a population of more than one billion can develop. There are precedents of rapid development realized in small economies over a period of time, like former Yugoslavia. But it is much more difficult for big countries, and China's population is about the size of the 36 member countries of the Organization for Economic Co-operation and Development plus Russia's population put together.
6. A country's economy on the right road of development can grow sustainably over a long term and it could constantly make self-adjustments on its way.

The six points above tell the world that if China can succeed, so can other countries.

In theoretical sense, the Western model emphasizes that some preconditions (in culture, politics, etc.) are necessary for modernization; but China's road indicates that the rise of a country does not have to copy the Western model. China's road is equivalent to a more profound Protestant Revolution: the West tells the world that people could only follow its way if they want to develop; while China tells the world that so long as people persevere in walking on their own way, every country could get developed. The word "road" in the expression of China's road can be understood as "way," and as China's sixth-century BC sage Laozi noted in the famous philosophical work *Tao Te Ching*, "The way that can be explained is not the Unchanging Way." China's road does not refer to any single policy, mechanism, and institution, its essence is "independence, seeking truth from facts, getting adapted according to local conditions."

This book attempts to explain why the New China as a poor country, a country of peace, an Eastern country, a socialist country, and a country with a big population could rise. As a Chinese scholar, I am not like some Western scholars who are so explosive with their self-confidence that whenever they speak they would utter some "killer apps," and whenever they write they would burst into lengthy works with theoretical frameworks that could explain all countries and regions throughout thousands of years of history. This book focuses on the explanation of China's rise, but it will examine the case of China in the context of comparison and historical perspective, in an attempt to tell clearly a Chinese story, while straightening out lines of other countries' rise. Chapter 2 explores an important prerequisite for economic rise from a comparative perspective—"state capacity." Chapter 3 examines from a historical perspective why things the Old China failed to accomplish could be done by the New China, with the standing point still on the "state capacity." Chapter 4 summarizes the continuous explorations the New China has made over the past 70 years. Chapter 5 introduces a secret weapon in China's development, which is the "medium- and long-term planning." Chapter 6 discusses the unique contributions of state-owned enterprises and state capital to China's industrialization and economic modernization. Chapter 7 shifts the focus from economic development to social progress, demonstrating China's unprecedented great leap forward in social security over the past 20 years. Chapter 8 argues from the perspective of theory and comparison that there is no such a thing as "Middle Income Trap," and even if such a trap does exist, China will certainly be able to stride over it and enter the high-income stage. This book "does not listen to false talks and does not follow impractical methods," but uses a large number of charts and tables while making theoretical reasoning, in the hope to speak with data. After all, "one real thing overwhelms a thousand false ones.'

CHAPTER 2

# Revelation: State Capacity and Economic Development

Since its founding, the New China has made great achievements recognized all over the world. No matter compared with whatever economies or measured in whatever dimensions, these achievements are superb and one for the books. However, could China's experience prove that a country is bound to succeed so long as it is engaged in reform and opening-up? I'm afraid not. Whether in the last 400 years, or in the past 40 years, many countries and regions carried out reform or opened up, but in most cases they failed, the successful were only a minority.

## MANY COUNTRIES (REGIONS) CARRIED OUT REFORM AND OPENING-UP

At the end of the nineteenth century and the beginning of the twentieth century, in the face of the formidable military and economic pressures from Western powers, many countries embarked on the road of reform and opening-up, with the aspirations to realize modernization. In the mid-nineteenth century, Governor of Egypt Mohamed Said Pasha began to carry out land, tax, and legal reforms, founding the Bank of Egypt and building the country's first standard-gauge railway. The Ottoman Empire underwent reforms for nearly a century up to its collapse (1923). In Iran, Reza Shah (1878–1944), the founder of the Pahlavi dynasty, modeled after the West in carrying out a series of reforms, including the construction of the Trans-Iranian Railway, founding the University of

Tehran, parliamentary reforms, and so on. At the end of the nineteenth century and the beginning of the twentieth century, after the Westernization Movement and the Reform Movement of 1898, China's Qing rulers introduced the New Policies of the late Qing Dynasty (1644–1911), which covered political, economic, military, judicial, cultural, and educational fields. None of the above reforms and opening-up was successful. Only Japan, after the Meiji Restoration in 1868, enhanced its national strength and embarked on the road of modernization.

Similar examples are numerous in the past 40 years. In 1980, Turkey announced to begin economic reforms. In the same year, Eastern European countries also successively carried out economic restructuring. Throughout the 1980s, sub-Saharan African countries (Cameroon, Gambia, Ghana, Guinea, Malawi, Madagascar, Mozambique, Niger, Tanzania, and Zaire) all began to reform, so did India. In 1983, Indonesia carried out reforms of economic liberalization. In 1986, Vietnam initiated the Renovation reforms. In the same year, Gorbachev began his "New Thinking"-oriented all-round reforms. In the late 1980s, a group of Latin American and Caribbean countries underwent structural reforms. By 1989 and 1990, the 15 republics of the former Soviet Union and the socialist countries of Eastern Europe all abandoned socialism and thoroughly transformed following the Western capitalist system. Some of the above-mentioned reforms are relatively successful (like those in Vietnam); others have slowly embarked on the right track after many trials (as what happened in India); but most of them failed, and some were even catastrophic, such as the cases in some Eastern European countries.

Figure 2.1 compares the economic growth trend of China with those of the former Soviet Union republics and Eastern European countries. With the year 1985 as the base line, China's GDP per capita (gross domestic products per capita) grew nearly sevenfold by 2018, leaving other countries far behind. Among the former Soviet Union republics and Eastern European countries, Turkmenistan performed the best, which ranked fourth in oil and gas resources in the world with a population size similar to that of Bao'an District in Shenzhen. Of the rest 25 countries, only six had their GDP per capita more than tripled in the 33 years.

In Fig. 2.1, the growth curves of 26 countries, excluding China, huddle together, covering up some of the countries with the poorest performance. Pick out the nine such countries and compare them with China, as shown in Fig. 2.2, their GDP per capita barely improved from 33 years ago, with four of them even seeing it going down instead of up.

2 REVELATION: STATE CAPACITY AND ECONOMIC DEVELOPMENT 17

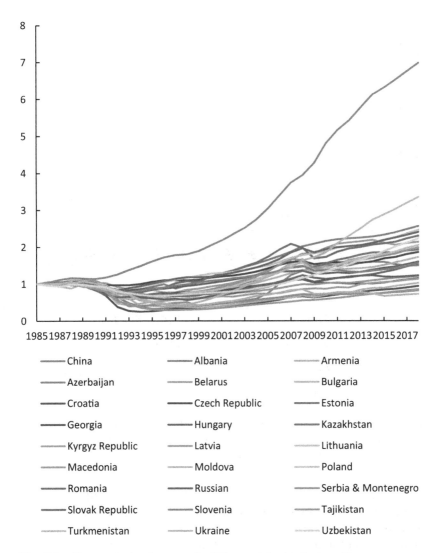

**Fig. 2.1** Economic development in China and Soviet-Eastern European countries (1985 = 1) (*Source* The Conference Board, Total Economy Database: Output, Labor and Labor Productivity, 1950–2018, March 2019)

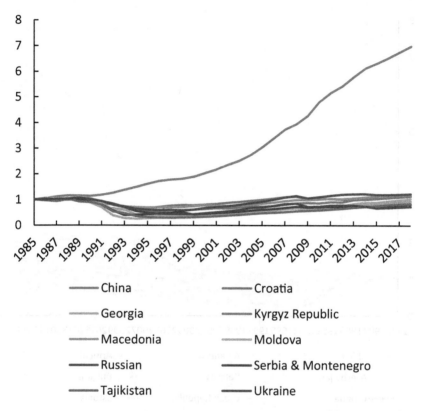

**Fig. 2.2** Economic development in China and the nine countries (1985 = 1) (*Source* The Conference Board, Total Economy Database: Output, Labor and Labor Productivity, 1950–2018, March 2019)

The worst case is Ukraine, where the GDP per capita in 2018 was 27% lower than in 1985. By Western standards, Ukraine's reform and opening-up is perhaps the most radical, carrying out both market economy and democracy, but it ended in tragedy. Slow economic growth is a common scenario throughout human history, but it is rare to see an economy go backward so severely over such a long period of time. The mainstream media in the West never tell people that reform and opening-up following their scheme could have such catastrophic consequences.

The above comparison reveals a simple fact that there are many cases of reform and opening-up, but not many successful. Many people assume without much thinking that as long as the reform and opening-up is carried out, it will inevitably lead to prosperity. This view is unfounded both in theory and in practice. The so-called reform and opening-up alone may not realize the goal of getting both the country and people rich.

Therefore, it is worth asking what conditions are necessary for rapid economic development aside from the policy of reform and opening-up.

## Conditions Required for Successful Reform and Opening-Up

In my opinion, the success of reform and opening-up requires two types of preconditions.

The first type is to have a solid foundation, including political basis (independence, national unity, social stability, eradication of "distributional coalitions"), and social basis (social equity, public health, universal education), and material basis (water conservancy facilities, farmland capital construction, initial scale of a large and complete industrial system). The success of China's reform and opening-up over the past 40 years is just due to a very solid foundation laid in the first three decades since the founding of New China. The importance of laying the foundation can never be overemphasized too much.

The second type is to have an effective government, that is, a government with the infrastructural state capacity. The reason is actually very simple: each reform will inevitably lead to regrouping of the existing pattern of vested interests; the more drastic the reform, the greater the breadth, depth and intensity of the regrouping of interests, and the more likely the capsizing of the ship. To cope with this situation, an effective government is a must, which should be able to control the overall situation, adopt various ways to ease and mitigate the corresponding impact, and overcome all kinds of resistance and obstacles, so that reform and opening-up could be successful. In other words, the arguments in this chapter can be summed up in one sentence: To realize the economic growth, one factor is necessary aside from reform and opening-up, that is, there must be an effective government with infrastructural state capacity.

What is state capacity? It is the ability of the state to turn its will into action and reality. Every country has its own will, or things it wants to be done, but it is never easy to turn the will into action and reality, or there won't be so many troubles in the world.

What is infrastructural state capacity? After years of research, I think that seven types of state capacity are essential, including (1) coercive capacity: the state should be able to monopolize the legitimate use of violence so as to encounter external threat to the sovereignty and internal threat to social order; (2) extractive capacity: the state should be able to extract from the population a share of the yearly product of its economic activities, such as fiscal taxation; (3) assimilative capacity: the state should be able to shape national identity and cultivate a set of core values among the people so as to retain a high degree of moral unity in the country. In addition, there are capacities to identify, to regulate, to steer, and to redistribute. As for such infrastructural state capacity, I have discussed it in detail in several books and papers, and I will not repeat them here.[1]

What is the relationship between reform and opening-up, state capacity and economic growth? It would become clear once we analyze the three major divergences in history: the Great Divergence between the East and the West, the Great Divergence between China and Japan, and the Great Divergence that occurred among the developing countries after World War II.

## STATE CAPACITY AND EAST–WEST DIVERGENCE

The Great Divergence of the East and the West means that there had been not much difference between the two over a long period of time, but then the West gradually rose, and finally dominated the world (some people call it the "European miracle"), while the East remained in a slump and lagged far behind. Historians do not seem to dispute over the Great Divergence between the East and the West, they only disagreed on its timing and causes. Some scholars hold that the Great Divergence took place in the eighteenth century, others argue that it occurred earlier, between 1500 and 1600. The dispute over the timing of the divergence is in fact a one over its causes. Either way, however, most might agree

---

[1] Wang Shaoguang and Hu Angang, *Report on China's State Capacity* (Shenyang: Liaoning People's Publishing House, 1993); Hu Anguang and Wang Shaoguang, *The Second Transformation: State Institutional Building*, Revised Edition (Beijing: Qinghua University Press, 2009).

that the Industrial Revolution in the mid-eighteenth century was the real watershed between the East and the West.

To explain why the Industrial Revolution took place in Europe rather than elsewhere, it is necessary to take a look at whether some events had happened in Europe before the Industrial Revolution, but yet to happen in the East. These events may be related to the Industrial Revolution, because the time sequence foreshadows the logical cause and effect.

In retrospect, six major events had already taken place in Europe before the Industrial Revolution (the latter half of the eighteenth century to the nineteenth century): the Scientific Revolution (sixteenth–eighteenth centuries), the Military Revolution (sixteenth–seventeenth centuries), the emergence of fiscal-military states (seventeenth–eighteenth centuries), large-scale colonialism (sixteenth–nineteenth centuries), large-scale slave trade (sixteenth–nineteenth centuries), and tax revenue growth (seventeenth–twentieth centuries).

Many people believe that the Scientific Revolution played a great role in promoting the Industrial Revolution. Especially with the rise of "New Economics" or the theory of endogenous growth in the 1980s and 1990s, many people believe that the economy could achieve sustained growth just relying on endogenous technological progress instead of relying on external force. An American economic historian even wrote a book to prove this, which is entitled *The First Knowledge Economy: Human Capital and the European Economy, 1750–1850*.[2] The book uses some fashionable new concepts such as "knowledge economy" and "human capital," but its arguments are not new, much the same as another book published 45 years before titled *Science and Technology in the Industrial Revolution*.[3] However, the relationship between the Scientific Revolution and the Industrial Revolution has been debated in academia for nearly 100 years, and there are not many people who ascertain that the Scientific Revolution promoted the Industrial Revolution. A consensus reached in this domain is that the Second Industrial Revolution (around 1870–1914) did benefit from scientific research, but it is still controversial as to how

---

[2] Margaret C. Jacob, *The First Knowledge Economy: Human Capital and the European Economy, 1750–1850* (Cambridge: Cambridge University Press, 2014).

[3] Albert Edward Musson and Eric Robinson, *Science and Technology in the Industrial Revolution* (New York: Gordon and Breach, [1989], c1969). The first edition of the book was published in 1969, and the introduction to the second edition was written by Margaret C. Jacob, which indicates the inner context of the two books.

much the Scientific Revolution had to do with the First Industrial Revolution (around 1760–1840). The prevailing view in academia is that up to the seventeenth century, the scientific evolution was non-cumulative and had little to do with technological progress. It was not until the late nineteenth century when the scientific evolution became cumulative and closely related to technological progress. Throughout the seventeenth and mid-nineteenth centuries, science did not contribute significantly to technological progress and therefore had little to do with the Industrial Revolution. During the period, artisans with little formal schooling and no scientific research literacy were the main force in technological innovation.[4] For example, the textile and smelting industries that dominated the First Industrial Revolution had little to do with the scientific research of the time.[5]

The other five events reflect changes in state capacity from different aspects, and the strengthened state capacity is likely to be associated with the emergence of the Industrial Revolution.

Let's look at a simple fact first. Before modern states (states with certain capacity to coerce and extract) emerged in Europe, different regions in the world were in similar situation: the long stagnated economy with little growth. But things changed when modern states emerged in Europe (after 1500), as their economic growth began to pick up. At first the growth rate was not significant, with the average annual growth rate of GDP per capita in Western Europe rising from 0.12% in the years of 1000–1500 to 0.14% in 1500–1820, a mere difference of 0.02%. However, as the infrastructural capacity of those Western European states improved, their economic growth rate gradually increased, rising from 0.98 in 1820–1870 to 1.33% in 1870–1913. In the first half of the twentieth century, Western Europe experienced two World Wars, when the growth rate dropped to 0.76%. After World War II, European capitalism entered a golden age for its development, when the growth rate climbed up to 4.05%. China throughout the nineteenth to the first half of the twentieth centuries recorded a very low growth rate of GDP per capita, which was even negative (see Table 2.1). In contrast, it was a very apparent trend of Great Divergence.

---

[4] Abbot Payson Usher, *A History of Mechanical Inventions* (New York: McGraw-Hill, 1929).

[5] Herbert Kisch, *From Domestic Manufacture to Industrial Revolution: The Case of the Rhineland Textile Districts* (Oxford: Oxford University Press, 1989).

**Table 2.1** Growth rate of GDP per capita around the formation of modern countries Unit: %

|  | 1–1000 | 000–1500 | 1500–1820 | 1820–1870 | 1870–1913 | 1913–1950 | 1950–1973 |
|---|---|---|---|---|---|---|---|
| Western Europe | −0.03 | 0.12 | 0.14 | 0.98 | 1.33 | 0.76 | 4.05 |
| Eastern Europe | 0.00 | 0.04 | 0.10 | 0.63 | 1.39 | 0.60 | 3.81 |
| United States | 0.00 | 0.00 | 0.36 | 1.34 | 1.82 | 1.61 | 2.45 |
| Latin America | 0.00 | 0.01 | 0.16 | −0.04 | 1.86 | 1.41 | 2.60 |
| Japan | 0.01 | 0.03 | 0.09 | 0.19 | 1.48 | 0.88 | 8.06 |
| China | 0.00 | 0.06 | 0.00 | −0.25 | 0.10 | −0.56 | 2.76 |
| India | 0.00 | 0.04 | −0.01 | 0.00 | 0.54 | −0.22 | 1.40 |
| Africa | −0.01 | −0.01 | 0.00 | 0.35 | 0.57 | 0.91 | 2.02 |
| World | 0.00 | 0.05 | 0.05 | 0.54 | 1.31 | 0.88 | 2.91 |

*Source* Angus Maddison—*Contours of World Economy, 1–2030 AD*– Essay in Macro-Economic History (2007)

The Great Divergence also manifested in the change of GDP per capita. Calculated in the 1990 international value of U.S. dollar, in the first year of Common Era, the GDP per capita of Western Europe was 576, and in China it was 450. By 1000 AD, it was still 450 in China, but in Western Europe it fell to 427. In other words, in 1000 AD, China was slightly more developed than Western Europe as a whole, because after the collapse of the Roman Empire, Europe was divided and there was no country there decent enough to speak of. By the beginning of the sixteenth century, GDP per capita in Western Europe reached 771, while in China it went up to 600. In the following 100 years, the gap between China and Europe widened further, with China's GDP per capita remaining at 600 while in Western Europe it climbed up to 889. In the next 300 years, the GDP per capita gap between the East and the West became a huge divide (see Table 2.2). The point here is that before modern states emerged, Europe like the rest of the world witnessed little economic growth. As the prototype of modern states began to take shape in the sixteenth and seventeenth centuries, the economic growth there began to pick up and lead the rest of the world. This is no accident.

Thomas Hobbes (1588–1679), an English philosopher who lived in that era saw this very well. In the absence of a common power to keep

**Table 2.2** GDP per capita of the world around the formation of modern countries Unit: 1990 international value of US dollars

|  | 1 | 1000 | 1500 | 1600 | 1700 | 1820 | 1870 | 1913 |
|---|---|---|---|---|---|---|---|---|
| Western Europe | 576 | 427 | 711 | 889 | 997 | 1202 | 1960 | 3457 |
| Eastern Europe | 412 | 400 | 496 | 548 | 606 | 683 | 937 | 1695 |
| United States | 400 | 400 | 400 | 400 | 527 | 1257 | 2445 | 5301 |
| Latin America | 400 | 400 | 416 | 438 | 527 | 691 | 676 | 1493 |
| Japan | 400 | 425 | 500 | 520 | 570 | 669 | 737 | 1387 |
| China | 450 | 450 | 600 | 600 | 600 | 600 | 530 | 552 |
| India | 450 | 450 | 550 | 550 | 550 | 533 | 533 | 673 |
| Africa | 472 | 425 | 414 | 422 | 421 | 420 | 500 | 637 |
| World | 467 | 450 | 566 | 596 | 616 | 667 | 873 | 1526 |

*Source* Angus Maddison—*Contours of World Economy, 1–2030 AD*—Essay in Macro-Economic History (2007)

all people in awe, they are in that condition which is called war, in which every man is against every man.[6] "In such condition, there is no place for Industry; because the fruit thereof is uncertain: and consequently no Culture of the Earth; no Navigation, nor use of the commodities that may be imported by Sea; no commodious Building; no instruments of moving, and removing such things as require much force; nor Knowledge of the face of the Earth; no account of Time; no Arts; no Letters; no Society; and which is worst of all, continual fear, and danger of violent death; And the life of man, solitary, poor, nasty, brutish, and short."[7] This means that an effective state is a necessary prerequisite for economic growth and social progress.

Adam Smith (1723–1790) lived in an era more than a century later than Hobbes. As the popular theory goes, Adam Smith only emphasized the "invisible hand" of the market and strongly opposed state intervention, but this greatly misreads him. A careful reading of Smith's writings (such as Book III of *The Wealth of Nations* and *Lectures on Justice, Police, Revenue and Arms*) will find that violence was always a focus of his attention. In his view, Europe's economic stagnation following the collapse of the Roman Empire was due to the rampant violence. On the one

---

[6] Thomas Hobbes, *Leviathan* (Oxford at the Clarendon Press, Oxford University Press reprinted from the edition of 1651 in 1965), p. 96.

[7] Ibid., pp. 96–97.

hand, "in the infancy of society, as has been often observed, government must be weak and feeble, and it is long before its authority can protect the industry of individuals from the rapacity of their neighbors. When people find themselves every moment in danger of being robbed of all they possess, they have no motive to be industrious. There could be little accumulation of stock, because the indolent, which would be the greatest number, would live upon the industrious, and spend whatever they produced." On the other hand, "among neighboring nations in a barbarous state there are perpetual wars, one continually invading and plundering the other, and though private property be secured from the violence of neighbors, it is in danger from hostile invasions. In this manner it is next to impossible that any accumulation of stock can be made."

To Smith violence was so crucial that he made this summary: "Nothing can be more an obstacle to the progress of opulence."[8] Accordingly, Smith concluded, "Commerce and manufactures can seldom flourish long in any state which does not enjoy a regular administration of justice; in which the people do not feel themselves secure in the possession of their property; in which the faith of contracts is not supported by law; and in which the authority of the state is not supposed to be regularly employed in enforcing the payment of debts from all those who are able to pay."[9] In other words, an effective state is the basic premise of Smith's political economy; without the guarantee of an effective state, market entities are simply unable to function properly.

Up to the years of Adam Smith, royal absolutism had prevailed in many parts of Europe after centuries of game playing with feudal princes. A well-known scholar on Adam Smith, Istvan Hont (1947–2013), summed up what had happened since then this way: "The suppression of the power of the feudal nobility led to strong central governments or, in other words, to royal absolutism. This change coincided with the military revolution and had two effects. The first was the emerging dominance of Europe over the rest of the world." This was also the Age of Discovery and the age of expansion, the beginning of European colonial adventures. "But because of the discoveries and the superiority of European shipping

---

[8] Adam Smith, *Lectures on Justice, Police, Revenue and Arms* (Oxford at the Clarendon Press, 1896), pp. 223–224.

[9] Adam Smith, *The Wealth of Nations: An Inquiry Into the Nature and Causes of the Wealth of Nations* (Chicago: University of Chicago Press, 1977), p. 1227.

and military technology, Europe also acquired a huge external market [and used its weaponry to force especially favorable terms of trade]. The result was spectacular acceleration of economic growth."[10]

The concept of "royal absolutism" was mentioned in the above paragraph. The concept prevailed for a long time, but John Brewer challenged it in 1989 in his book *The Sinews of Power: War, Money and English State 1688–1783*, suggesting that it should be replaced with fiscal-military state.[11] Harvard historian Nicholas Henshall also pointed out in his 1992 book *The Myth of Absolutism: The Change & Continuity in Early Modern European Monarchy* that the term "absolutism" is rather misleading and he also proposed replacing it with fiscal-military state.[12] Therefore, in the last 20 years, more and more historians have begun to use the term "fiscal-military state" to refer to the new type of states that emerged in Europe from the seventeenth to the nineteenth century.

Since it is called a "fiscal-military state," it should have at least two infrastructural state capacities: coercive capacity (military state) and extractive capacity (fiscal state). As historian Li Bozhong put it, "fire gun plus accounting book" was a feature of the early-day economic globalization.[13] It is exactly the political innovation of "fiscal-military state" that has led the technological innovation and economic development in the West.

In fact, "fiscal-military state" should be called "military-fiscal state," because in the perspective of historical development, the military revolution preceded the financial innovation, and the financial innovation initially served the military and war. The concept of Military Revolution was first proposed by British historian Michael Roberts in 1956.[14] After decades of debate, most relevant scholars now agree with Roberts that in the sixteenth and seventeenth centuries, a military revolution took place

---

[10] Istvan Hont, *Politics in Commercial Society: Jean-Jacques Rousseau and Adam Smith* (Cambridge, MA: Harvard University Press, 2015), p. 113.

[11] John Brewer, *The Sinews of Power: War, Mondy and the English State, 1688–1783* (Cambridge, MA: Harvard University Press, 1989).

[12] Nicholas Henshall, *The Myth of Absolutism: Change & Continuity in Early Modern European Monarchy* (London: Longman, 1992).

[13] Li Bozhong, *Fire Gun & Accounting Book: China & the East Asian World In the Early-Day Economic Globalization* (Beijing: SDX Joint Publishing, 2017), p. 392.

[14] Michael Roberts, *The Military Revolution, 1560–1660: An Inaugural Lecture Delivered Before Queen's University of Belfast* (Belfast: M. Boyd, 1956).

in the West, that is, revolutionary changes were witnessed in weapons, military organization, and scale.

This certainly was not the first military revolution in human history. Geoffrey Parker, a famous British military historian, pointed out that the previous military revolution was created by China's Qin Shi Huang, or the First Emperor of the Qin Dynasty (221–210 B.C.), which laid the foundation for a long-standing imperial system that lasted more than 2,000 years without much change. What happened in the West was the second military revolution. In Parker's view, "The superior military organization of the Ch'in(Qin) enabled them to conquer all of China; that of the west eventually allowed them to dominate the whole world. For in large measure, 'the rise of the West' depended on the exercise of force."[15] Many other Western scholars have also been outspoken about the role of violence in the "rise of the West." For example, Charles Tilly, a famous American scholar on state formation, put forward the following equation in his book:

Militarization=Civilization.[16]

Ian Morris, a famous American scholar on history, wrote a book titled *The Measure of Civilization: How Social Development Decides the Fate of Nations*. In his view, an important dimension of civilization is the war-making capacity. In the chapter he discussed this war-making capacity, the first sentence is: "Nothing made Western domination of the world quite so clear as the First Opium War of 1840-42 CE, when a small British fleet shot its way into China, threatened to close the Grand Canal that brought food to Beijing, and extracted humiliating concessions from the Qing government."[17]

Morris calculated the war-making capacity of the East and the West over the past 6,000 years. Table 2.3 indicates that from 500 to 1400 AD, the East was more capable of war-making than the West. But after the sixteenth century, the West went through the Military Revolution,

---

[15] Geoffrey Parker, *The Military Revolution: Military Innovation and the Rise of the West, 1500–1800* (Cambridge: Cambridge University Press, 1996), pp. 3–4.

[16] Charles Tilly, *Coercion, Capital and European States, AD990–1990* (Cambridge, MA: Wiley-Blackwell, 1992), p. 122.

[17] Ian Morris, *The Measure of Civilization: How Social Development Decides the Fate of Nations* (Princeton, NJ: Princeton University Press, 2013), p. 173.

**Table 2.3** War-making capacity since 500 CE

*Source* Data from Ian Morris, *The Measure of Civilization: How Social Development Decides the Fate of Nations*, pp. 180–181

and its war-making capacity began to surpass that of the East. By the eighteenth century, the gap in the war-making capacity between the East and the West was already huge. Up to the twentieth century, the West was five times more capable of war-making than the East, with an overwhelming superiority, and at that time, there was little doubt that the East was beaten by the West.

Morris' calculation did not come from nothing. In European countries where data are available, one sign of the Military Revolution was the rapid expansion of the size of the army. Table 2.4 cites changes in the troops and their percentage in the national population in five European countries, which shows that from the beginning of the sixteenth century to the beginning of the eighteenth century, both the absolute size of the army and the troops' percentage in national population were rising rapidly. Throughout the sixteenth and seventeenth centuries, Spain was the dominant power in Europe; in the eighteenth century, the leading roles went to France and England. In other words, European countries became greatly more capable to coerce in these few centuries.

**Table 2.4** Men under arms, Europe 1500–1980

| | Thousands of troops under arms | | | | | | Troops as percent of national population | | | | | |
|---|---|---|---|---|---|---|---|---|---|---|---|---|
| | 1500 | 1600 | 1700 | 1850 | 1980 | | 1500 | 1600 | 1700 | 1850 | 1980 |
| Spain | 20 | 200 | 50 | 154 | 342 | | 0.3 | 2.5 | 0.7 | 1.0 | 0.9 |
| France | 18 | 80 | 400 | 439 | 495 | | 0.1 | 0.4 | 2.1 | 1.2 | 0.9 |
| England/Wales | 25 | 30 | 292 | 201 | 329 | | 1.0 | 0.7 | 5.4 | 1.1 | 0.6 |
| Netherlands | 0 | 20 | 100 | 30 | 115 | | | 1.3 | 5.3 | 1.0 | 0.8 |
| Sweden | 0 | 15 | 100 | 63 | 66 | | | 1.5 | 7.1 | 1.8 | 0.8 |
| Russia | 0 | 35 | 170 | 850 | 3663 | | | 0.3 | 1.2 | 1.5 | 1.4 |

*Source* Charles Tilly, *Coercion, Capital and European States, AD990–1990*, p. 79

Gunpowder was invented in China, where also appeared the earliest bombs, guns and artillery, several hundred years ahead of Europe, but why did the Military Revolution take place first in Europe, not in China? There could be many factors that played in it, yet a very crucial one might be the frequency of wars. Every country's history is a history of wars, but the history of Europe is particularly bloody, with almost one war after another. Frequent military conflicts often prompt the warring countries to make great efforts to innovate weapons, innovate military organizations, and expand the size of armed forces, thus bringing about a military revolution.

Someone drew the Fig. 2.3 based on historical data, where dark lines represent China and light lines represent Europe. Analysis shows that from 1450 to 1550, there were not many armed conflicts in China, where the military innovation stagnated; but in the same period, military conflicts took place frequently in the West, with one war after another, which accelerated military innovation. By the end of the fifteenth century, Europe was already superior to China in artillery. As one stagnated and the other advanced, the first small military divergence came up consequently. In the 200 years after 1550, the East Asian region was beset with

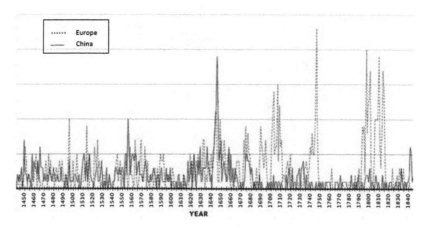

**Fig. 2.3** Number of conflicts in Europe and China, 1450–1839 (The dotted line represents Europe, the solid line China) t (*Source* Adopted from Tonio Andrade, *The Gunpowder Age: China, Military Innovation, and the Rise of the West in World History*, p. 6)

uprisings of war everywhere, forcing China in turn to learn from Europe the technology to make advanced guns, which led to a military parity with European countries. In the meantime, Zheng Chenggong (Koxinga) defeated the inalienable Dutch colonists and regained Taiwan.[18] But from 1740 to 1839, China was free from warfare, where military innovation halted, yet wars in Europe never stopped, leading to leaps and bounds of military innovation. This rendered the second military divergence on a larger scale.[19] The outcome of this military divergence was the First Opium War mentioned by Morris, which has become a permanent disgrace to China.

What is noticeable here is that the timing of the Great Economic Divergence, or more specifically, the timing of the British Industrial Revolution happened to take place in the years from 1760 to 1820–1840, almost completely coinciding with the timing of the Great Military Divergence between China and the West. This is no coincidence, but because the Military Revolution had created modern states with greater coercive capacity, and the modern states with greater coercive capacity in turn laid the foundation for economic growth.

Then how does the coercive capacity influence the economic growth? From the history of Europe we could see that its role manifested in both internal and external aspects.

Internally, the coercive capacity could help keep the "reform and opening-up" of the time on course and create a peaceful internal environment that Hobbes and Smith had aspired for. The first standing army in the world came into being in the sixteenth century in Spain, which then dominated the world. A careful reading of Adam Smith's *The Wealth of Nations* will reveal that although Chapter I of Book V is entitled *On the Expenses of the Sovereign or Commonwealth*, it actually argues that the standing army is a symbol of modern society, because "it is only by means of a well-regulated standing army that a civilized country can be defended."[20] Throughout Adam Smith's lifetime, the professional police force was yet to come into being in the world. The first dedicated police

---

[18] Tonio Andrade, *Lost Colony: The Untold Story of China's First Great Victory over the West* (Princeton, NJ: Princeton University Press, 2013).

[19] Tonio Andrade, *The Gunpowder Age: China, Military Innovation, and the Rise of the West in World History* (Princeton, NJ: Princeton University Press, 2016), pp. 5–7.

[20] Adam Smith, *The Wealth of Nations: An Inquiry Into the Nature and Causes of the Wealth of Nations* (Chicago: University of Chicago Press, 1977), Book V, Chapter I.

force was founded in London in 1829 and it was soon introduced to other parts of Britain and the United States and many other European countries, with a fundamental mission to protect private property rights from infringement.[21]

Externally, the coercive capacity could facilitate three actions: the first is to plunder overseas resources, including labor resources; the second is to open up overseas markets; and the third is to bring up management talents.

The way to plunder overseas resources was through colonialism and the slave trade. European colonialism lasted about 500 years, from the beginning of the fifteenth century to the end of the nineteenth century. Portugal and Spain were the first two to promote colonialism, who extended their claws to Africa, Asia and the newly "discovered" Americas in the fifteenth and sixteenth centuries. In the first year or two of the seventeenth century, Britain and the Netherlands separately established their own "East India Company," thereafter for more than 100 years they and France successively established overseas colonies, with their contention focusing on the Americas. Starting from the mid-nineteenth century, more European countries got involved in the contention for Africa and Asia, with Africa almost thoroughly carved up and many Asian countries falling to be colonies.

In the rise of Europe, nearly all the European countries, large and small, were involved in colonial plunder, including the Nordic countries (Sweden, Denmark, Finland and Norway). Belgium, for example, had colonies in Africa 80 times the size of its own; its colonization left a death toll of 10–13 million people in the Congo, about half of its population, and even if they had survived, many would have their hands chopped by the colonists as punishment, when people with hands chopped were seen everywhere in the Congo, the cruelty even exceeding the rule of Nazi Germany, which is hardly mentioned today. In 1897, Belgium began to invest in China with the money it had seized in the Congo, planning to send Congolese soldiers to China and ship Chinese laborers to the Congo, and it purchased several small islands in China and named them the "Congo Free State" (Etat Independent du Congo). Someone found in surprise among the unequal treaties signed by China that one of them was a "Special Tianjin Chapter" in the treaty signed between China and the

---

[21] Sam Mitrani, *The Rise of the Chicago Police Department: Class and Conflict, 1850–1894* (Campaign: University of Illinois Press, 2013).

"Congo Free State" in 1898, which provided that the Congo also enjoyed extraterritorial rights in China.[22] Of course, The Congo at that time was nothing more than a "black glove" for Belgium. Li Hongzhang[23] allegedly remarked in surprise when meeting with the Congolese negotiating delegation, "I thought Africans were all dark-skinned," because the members were all Belgians. As a member of the Eight Nation Alliance that suppressed China's Yihetuan Movement or Boxer Uprising in 1901, Belgium established a concession in Tianjin covering an area of nearly 50 hectares, which it withheld until 1929.[24]

In Part 7 of Volume I of *Capital, The Accumulation of Capital*, Marx quoted William Howitt as saying, "The barbarities and desperate outrages of the so-called Christian race, throughout every region of the world, and upon every people they have been able to subdue, are not to be paralleled by those of any other race, however fierce, however untaught, and however reckless of mercy and of shame, in any age of the earth."[25] Having cited the plagues of colonialism based on a large number of materials in the nineteenth century, Marx hit the nail at the head on the relationship between colonialism and the primitive accumulation of capital: "The colonial system ripened, like a hot-house, trade and navigation. The 'societies Monopolia' of Luther were powerful levers for concentration of capital. The colonies secured a market for the budding manufactures, and, through the monopoly of the market, an increased accumulation. The treasures captured outside Europe by undisguised looting, enslavement, and murder, floated back to the mother-country and were turned into capital."[26]

Colonialism was accompanied by a large-scale transatlantic slave trade. The slave trade began in the first countries pushing colonialism: Spain and Portugal began the long-distance slave trade in the early sixteenth

---

[22] Gao Fang, *Unequal Treaties in Recent Modern China, Nanjing Journal of Social Sciences*, 1999 (2).

[23] Li Hongzhang (1823–1901) was a politician and diplomat of the late Qing Dynasty, holding a position equivalent to that of prime minister and foreign minister—*Translator.*

[24] Adam Hochschild, *King Leopold's Ghost: A Story of Greed, Terror, and Heroism in Colonial Africa* (New York: Houghton Mifflin, 1999).

[25] William Howitt, *Colonization and Christianity: A Popular History of the Treatment of the Natives by the Europeans in All Their Colonies* (London: Longman, 1838), p. 9.

[26] Karl Marx, *Capital*, Vol. I (Moscow, USSR: Progress Publishers, online edition, 2015), p. 535.

century; the Netherlands, England, and France followed closely behind, and ever expanded the slave trade; which later involved other European countries, including Denmark, Norway and others. At that time, the word "factory" in Western languages usually referred to slave-trading depots on West African coast before it invoked site of industrial production.[27]

Over a long period of more than 300 years, an estimated 12 million people were shipped from Africa to the Americas as slaves, and some scholars estimate that the figure is even bigger: With the slaves who died in the shipment and trading (about 10 million), Africa could have lost a population of as much as 30 million. Some scholars estimate that at the beginning of the seventeenth century, sub-Saharan Africa accounted for 18% of the global population, but 300 years later, this share fell to 6%; while during this period, the population of Europe and the United States grew by several folds.[28]

In Part 7 of *Capital* Vol. I, *The Accumulation of Capital*, Marx also talked about the relationship between the slave trade and primitive accumulation: "The discovery of gold and silver in America, the extirpation, enslavement and entombment in mines of the aboriginal population, the beginning of the conquest and looting of the East Indies, the turning of Africa into a warren for the commercial hunting of black-skins, signalized the rosy dawn of the era of capitalist production. These idyllic proceedings are the chief momenta of primitive accumulation." He particularly cited Liverpool, a leading business port in England, as an example, pointing out that: "Liverpool waxed fat on the slave trade. This was its method of primitive accumulation."[29]

Not only the slave trade, but also the slavery was an important cause for the Industrial Revolution to break out first in Europe and America. As early as 1944, Eric Williams, a Caribbean historian, made a famous argument in *Capitalism and Slavery*: Profits obtained from the sugar produced out of sugarcanes slaves grew in the British Caribbean colonies and the transatlantic slave trade provided one of the main streams of the

---

[27] Sven Beckert and Seth Rockman, eds., *Slavery's Capitalism: A New History of American Economic Development* (Philadelphia: University of Pennsylvania Press, 2016), p. 11.

[28] Paul Adams, Erick Langer, Lily Hwa, Peter Stearns, and Merry Wiesner-Hanks, *Experiencing World History* (New York: NYU Press, 2000), p. 334.

[29] Karl Marx, *Capital*, Vol. I (Moscow, USSR: Progress Publishers, online edition, 2015), pp. 533, 538.

primitive accumulation of capital in Britain which financed the Industrial Revolution, making it the world's first modern economy. It was not until after manufactures gained a foothold and the profits obtained from slavery were no longer secured as compared with them when Britain began to advocate for slavery abolition.[30] Williams' arguments sparked decades of debate. Although his methodological framework may seem dated today, no historic or economic analyst has been able to undermine his basic theses.[31]

Robin Blackburn, a British historian, published *The Making of New World Slavery: From the Baroque to the Modern, 1492–1800* in 1997, in which he discussed in detail how slavery was related to British economic growth. He pointed out that in the late eighteenth and early nineteenth centuries (a critical period of the British Industrial Revolution), exchanges with the slave Caribbean plantations had far outstripped any other factor, domestic or international, to promote the British economic growth at home. In this sense, this factor "helped British capitalism to make a breakthrough to industrialism and global hegemony ahead of its rivals."[32]

On the other side of the Atlantic, the development of American capitalism was more directly related with slavery. There has been a long-lingering myth in the American studies—slavery and its impact were confined to the south of the United States only. Yet in fact, the industrial takeoff of the entire United States was inextricably associated with slavery. Studies in the last decade or two have revealed some previously untold facts: slave-grown cotton was the most valuable export made in America (since textile was an emerging pillar industry in Europe and the United States at the time, cotton was as important to the United States then as oil is to Saudi Arabia today); the capital stored in slaves exceeded the combined value of all the railways and factories in the United States; the highest concentration of steam power in the United States was to be found along the Mississippi dotted with slave plantations rather than along the Merrimack River in New England (it is usually assumed that

---

[30] Eric Eustace Williams, *Capitalism and Slavery* (Chapel Hill: The University of North Carolina Press, 1994).

[31] Selwyn H. H. Carrington, *Capitalism & Slavery and Caribbean Historiography: An Evaluation, Journal of African American History*, Vol. 88, No. 3 (Summer, 2003), pp. 304–312.

[32] Robin Blackburn, *The Making of New World Slavery: From the Baroque to the Modern, 1492–1800* (London: Verso, 1997), p. 572.

the textile mills along the Merrimack River had played an important role in the American Industrial Revolution); the management of slaves in the southern plantations was similar to grouping in a factory, and their scale was generally larger than that of the northern enterprises; America's early management innovations largely originated in plantations that combined grouping and violence, rather than in railroads, as Alfred Chandler claimed; the maritime insurance and slave life insurance related to slave trade played a tremendous role in promoting the early development of American insurance industry; and loaning and re-loaning, with slaves and their children as mortgage, greatly promoted the early development of American banking. All this means that the spatial distance did not restrain the beneficiaries of slavery to owners of the southern plantations; on the contrary, slavery had provided cotton for textile mills in Rhode Island, delivered enormous wealth to banks in New York City, created markets for manufacturers in Massachusetts, financed the construction of cities in Connecticut, such as Bridgeport, and rendered a steady stream of business opportunities to merchants shipping and selling southern farm produces and northern industrial goods.

All in all, the contribution of slavery to the economic development of the United States at that time could not be overestimated. This is understandable as to why a few years before the start of the American Civil War, an article carried by the southern magazine *DeBow's Review* entitled *North and South* declared slavery the "nursing mother of the prosperity of the North;"[33] why Sven Beckert, author of *Empire of Cotton: A Global History* and a scholar on the history of American capitalism, would name a new book he co-edited about the history of American economic development *Slavery's Capitalism*, and conclude that "American slavery is necessarily imprinted on the DNA of American capitalism."[34]

With the horizons of time and space further extended, we would see that the slave trade and slavery connected Africa, the Caribbean areas, Latin America, North America, Britain, and Europe together, thereby got further related with China. "Slave-mined silver in the Americas first provided European empires the opportunity to gain access to Chinese

---

[33] Sven Beckert and Seth Rockman, eds., *Slavery's Capitalism: A New History of American Economic Development* (Philadelphia: University of Pennsylvania Press, 2016), p. 2.

[34] Ibid., p. 3.

markets and consumer goods, and slave- grown agricultural commodities gave England specifically the possibility of supplanting China by escaping the environmental constraints on its population growth. As Kenneth Pomeranz has argued, one factor in England's ability to break the 'Malthusian trap' was that nation's access to calories and fibers in the form of sugar and cotton harvested on American plantations."[35] This also explains why the Industrial Revolution that changed human history took place in Britain first, and why the Military Revolution, colonialism, slave trade and slavery in Europe led to the so-called Great Divergence between the East and the West.

Why were Europe and the United States so nasty to develop economy by hook or by crook? A remark made by Mr. Stapleton, a British Parliament member to his constituents in 1873 fully expressed the European people's sense of urgency: "If China should become a great manufacturing country, I do not see how the manufacturing population of Europe could sustain the contest without descending to the level of their competitors."[36] It sounds almost identical with what former U.S. President Donald Trump has said. It is in this context that the Great Divergence occurred, just to the desire of Westerners.

Aside from plundering resources, Western colonizers also relied on their superior ships and guns to shoot their way around the world and seize the market. Sir Walter Raleigh (1554–1618), a British adventurer who had been involved in colonial expansion in North and South America, admonished Elizabeth I out of his own experience: "Whosoever commands the sea commands the trade; whosoever commands the trade of the world commands the riches of the world, and consequently the world itself."[37] It is said that these words deeply impressed the Queen, which ballooned her ambitions for overseas colonization, and she began to attach importance to building the naval fleet, and granted more and

---

[35] Sven Beckert and Seth Rockman, eds., *Slavery's Capitalism: A New History of American Economic Development* (Philadelphia: University of Pennsylvania Press, 2016), p. 8.

[36] Karl Marx, *Capital*, Vol. I (Moscow, USSR: Progress Publishers, online edition, 2015), p. 430.

[37] George Modelski and William R. Thompson, *Seapower in Global Politics, 1494–1993* (London: Palgrave MacMillan UK, 1988), p. 7. In the mid-seventeenth century, Raleigh's sayings were copied and modified by John Evelyn (1620–1706), and became more widely known.

larger private companies the permit to colonize and plunder overseas. To this end, Britain established the East India Company at the end of 1600 as a tool for its predatory colonial policies in India, China, and other Asian countries. Beginning from the mid-eighteenth century, the company owned an army and fleet and became a huge military force, with which it occupied India completely and acquired the power to colonize it, manipulating the country's most important governance functions, not to mention the monopoly on India's trade.

The East India Company established by the Dutch government came into being two years later than its British counterpart, but it was also a violent group with its own army and fleet that could issue currency, sign formal treaties with relevant countries, and execute colonial ruling in occupied areas (like Indonesia, Malacca, and China's Taiwan). Jan Pieterszoon Coen, holding two terms as governor of Indonesia at the start of the Dutch East India Company, was known for his ruthlessness, and his basic belief was that the use of violence was the only path to prosperity. In a 1614 letter to the Council of Seventeen (the decision-making hub of the Dutch East India Company), he wrote bluntly: "Your Honors should know by experience that trade in Asia must be driven and maintained under the protection and favor of Your Honors' own weapons, and that the weapons must be paid for by the profits from trade; so that we cannot carry on trade without war, nor war without trade."[38]

With the force backing them, wherever these two companies stretched their tentacles, their markets were extended there; in case the locals were unwilling to deal with them, they would open the market with guns and imposed unfair trade "rules" on the opponent. The Opium War was an example of the way they opened up their markets. Forcing others to buy or sell made huge business benefits for the two companies, as well as for the United Kingdom and the Netherlands, raking in enormous profits for them. Thomas Papillon, an English merchant and politician who was an influential figure in the City of London in the second half of the seventeenth century and a director of the British East India Company, published a famous booklet in 1696 entitled *The East-India-Trade A Most Profitable Trade to the Kingdom*: the very title itself speaks volumes about the importance of the British East India Company to the United

---

[38] Stephen R. Bown, *Merchant Kings: When Companies Ruled the World, 1600–1900* (New York: Thomas Dunne Books, 2010), pp. 7–56.

Kingdom.[39] At its peak, the Dutch East India Company had 70,000 employees (one fifth of whom were mercenaries), and its value soared to the equivalent of 7.4 trillion US dollars today, nearly eight times the value of Apple, and is described as a most valuable company of all-time.[40]

In *Capital*, Marx called Holland a nation "of the colonial administration" and "the head capitalistic nation of the seventeenth century." For quite a long time, it was "in almost exclusive possession of the East Indian trade and the commerce between the south-east and north-west of Europe. Its fisheries, marine, manufactures, surpassed those of any other country. The total capital of the Republic was probably more important than that of all the rest of Europe put together."[41] His description of the British East India Company is equally stunning: "The English East India Company, as is well known, obtained, besides the political rule in India, the exclusive monopoly of the tea-trade, as well as of the Chinese trade in general, and of the transport of goods to and from Europe. But the coasting trade of India and between the islands, as well as the internal trade of India, were the monopoly of the higher employees of the company. The monopolies of salt, opium, betel and other commodities were inexhaustible mines of wealth. The employees themselves fixed the price and plundered at will the unhappy Hindus. The Governor-General took part in this private traffic. His favorites received contracts under conditions whereby they, cleverer than the alchemists, made gold out of nothing. Great fortunes sprang up like mushrooms in a day; primitive accumulation went on without the advance of a shilling."[42]

Besides Britain and the Netherlands, the East India Company was also set up in Denmark (1616–1772), Portugal (1628–1633), France (1664–1794), Sweden (1731–1813), and Austria (1775–1785). In addition to these East India companies, in various countries, the European powers established many kinds of other chartered companies with exclusive rights

---

[39] Thomas Papillon, *The East-India-Trade A Most Profitable Trade to the Kingdom* (London, 1696).

[40] Jeff Desjardins, *The Most Valuable Companies of All-Time*, http://www.visualcapitalist.com/most-valuable-companies-all-time/, December 8, 2017.

[41] Karl Marx, Karl Marx, *Capital*, Vol. I (Moscow, USSR: Progress Publishers, online edition, 2015), pp. 534–535.

[42] Ibid., p. 534.

in different regions, all of which were tools to colonize and expand overseas markets for their mother countries, rather than purely commercial entities.

In short, following the Military Revolution in Europe, various powers sought to expand overseas markets by various means while plundering overseas resources. "Due to the huge costs and security risks of the ocean-going trade, both the ocean exploration and global trade of the European merchant groups were 'armed trade.'"[43] This period is known in Europe as the "Age of Heroic Commerce." By the end of the eighteenth century, the European powers had opened up large tracts of overseas markets, "thereby laying a decisive foundation for the burst of the Industrial Revolution. Without a world market, there could be no Industrial Revolution."[44]

In addition to capital, other resources and markets, to develop the economy requires relevant human resources, such as entrepreneurs and engineers. In this aspect, military organizations (the standing army of a country and private mercenaries) and defense projects also played a considerable role. Both military organizations and economic organizations are large organizations of people, and they share many similarities in their operation. In fact, the word "company" was originally used to refer to "a group of soldiers" before it was used to refer to commercial entities. Similarly, an earlier form of the word "entrepreneur" appeared in the fourteenth century, throughout the sixteenth and seventeenth centuries the most frequent usage of the term connoted a government contractor, usually of military fortifications or public works.[45] Throughout the sixteenth and eighteenth centuries, there were constant wars between political bodies in Europe, when large social organizations were not economic entities but military ones. Those who organize a battle often have a sense of adventure and the courage to bear risks, and know how to operate from a distance, which are all aligned with the so-called entrepreneurship. To this day, there are people in different countries who believe that the military is the best school to cultivate entrepreneurs.

---

[43] Wen Yi, *The Great Industrial Revolution in China: Political Economics of Development, Outline of Critique on General Principles* (Beijing: Qinghua University Press, 2016), First Section, Chapter 7.

[44] Ibid.

[45] Robert F. Hebert and Albert A. Link, *A History of Entrepreneurship* (Routelege, 2009), p. 5.

What's more, many organizations by nature at that time were mixed, as the commercial and military functions were often merged in the same one, such as various militarized overseas monopoly trading companies. Then the wars themselves created various business opportunities, such as large and small-scale production of military goods, supplies to the army and navy, contractors and subcontractors for building warships and fortifications, cross-border banking services, and vendors trailing the military to provide services. The operators of these businesses were often inextricably tied with the army, while many active or demobilized soldiers and officers could use their organizational capabilities acquired in the army to go between the military and companies and become entrepreneurs influential in the business circles. In this sense, the Military Revolution created an environment in which groups after groups of entrepreneurs and company operators and managers walked out of the military. Historical studies have also found that "the entrepreneur was typically found among the ranks of merchants or the military at that time. Military leaders especially qualified, because wars were often fought for economic reasons. The general who designed and executed a successful strategy in battle took considerable risks and stood to gain substantial economic benefits."[46]

Capital, resources, markets, human resources, and technology all played an essential role in the rise of Britain and other countries in Europe. With regard to their transition from an agricultural society to an industrial society, textbooks in general talk abstractly about the role of these so-called production factors, but completely evade the intrinsic relationship between these factors and violence. However, the above analysis tells us that these colorless abstract nouns are in fact based on violence or the state coercive capacity. Priya Satia, an Indian professor of British history at Stanford University, published a book in 2018, and its very title clearly points to the relationship between violence and the Industrial Revolution—*Empire of Guns: The Violent Making of the Industrial Revolution*.[47] This is certainly not a new point of view, as Blackburn already concluded in the final paragraph of *The Making of New World Slavery*:

---

[46] Ibid., p. 2.

[47] Priya Satia, *Empire of Guns: The Violent Making of the Industrial Revolution* (New York: Penguin Press, 2018).

"The British path to industrialization had been smoothed by the aggressive and relentless application of force."[48] With this, we could not but appreciate what Karl Marx incisively pointed out more than 150 years ago: The methods Britain and other European countries used to develop economy depended "in part on brute force... But, they all employ the power of the State, that is, the concentrated and organized force of society, to hasten, hot-house fashion, the process of transformation of the feudal mode of production into capitalist mode, and to shorten the transition. Force is the midwife of every old society pregnant with a new one. It is itself an economic power."[49] Whether or not a moral judgment is to be made, Marx's remarks made a simple fact clear: A state with a strong coercive capacity could take one step ahead at the critical moment of its economic takeoff.

However, the coercive capacity or the monopoly on violence has to be backed with financial resources, and the improvement of this capacity also requires a corresponding enhancement of the state extractive capacity. With the Military Revolution throughout the sixteenth to the seventeenth centuries, the armies of various countries grew ever more sizable, with the way they were organized becoming more and more complex, while the spatial scope involved in the battlefield expanded globe wide, and all this led to a dramatic increase in the expenses of war. To sustain a war (which was profitable), the state had to enhance its extractive capacity, or more bluntly, the government must use financial and banking instruments to raise money for military operation. Of course, in turn, the military race could also force the fiscal and financial means to advance, so that the government could learn how to raise money. As for the importance of the extractive capacity, Jean Bodin (1530–1596), a French thinker known as the father of modern political science, had realized it as early as the sixteenth century, when the modern state was in its infancy, and he talked about the issue of taxing and war in several of his books,[50] and in his masterwork *The Six Books of the Commonwealth*, there is a famous

---

[48] Robin Blackburn, *The Making of New World Slavery: From the Baroque to the Modern, 1492–1800* (London: Verso, 1997), p. 573.

[49] Karl Marx, Karl Marx, *Capital*, Vol. I (Moscow, USSR: Progress Publishers, online edition, 2015), p. 534.

[50] Martin Wolfe, *Jean Bodin on Taxes: The Sovereignty-Taxes Paradox*, Political Science Quarterly, Vol. 83, No. 2 (June 1968), pp. 268–284.

saying: "Financial means are the nerves of the state."[51] This phrase has been quoted over and over again, especially in the seventeenth and eighteenth centuries, when the Military Revolution was in rapid progress and colonialism began to sweep the globe.

Hobbes also paid much attention to war and taxation, and several books he published around the time of the English Civil War talked about taxation,[52] and whenever it came to the necessity of taxation, he would mention war without exception: "Those levies therefore which are made upon men's estates, by the sovereign authority, are no more but the price of that peace and defense which the sovereignty maintains for them."[53] And "customs and tributes are nothing else but their reward who watch in arms for us, …the labors and endeavors of single men may not be molested by the incursion of enemies."[54] "For the impositions, that are laid on the people by the sovereign power, are nothing else but the wages, due to them that hold the public sword, to defend private men in the exercise of their several trades, and the callings."[55]

Reviewing the history throughout the seventeenth and nineteenth centuries, it is clear that the military demand gave a strong impetus to the gradual establishment of more developed fiscal institutions in various countries of Europe. Tilly made some to-the-point comments on this issue: Over the millennium from 990–1990 as a whole, "war has been the dominant activity of European states. State budgets, taxes, and debts reflect that reality. …War wove the European network of national states, and preparation for war created the internal structures of the states within it. …With a nation in arms, a state's extractive power rose enormously."[56]

---

[51] Rudolf Braun, *Taxation, Sociopolitical Structure, and State-building: Great Britain and Brandenburg-Prussia*, in Charles Tilly, ed., *The Formation of National States in Western Europe* (Princeton, NJ: Princeton University Press, 1975), p. 243.

[52] Dudley Jackson, *Thomas Hobbes Theory of Taxation*, Political Studies, Vol. 21 (June 1973), pp. 175–182.

[53] Sir William Molesworth, ed., *The English Works of Thomas Hobbes of Malmesbury* (London: John Bohn, 1839–45), Vol. IV, p. 164.

[54] Sir William Molesworth, ed., *The English Works of Thomas Hobbes of Malmesbury* (London: John Bohn, 1839–45), Vol. II, p. 159.

[55] Sir William Molesworth, ed., *The English Works of Thomas Hobbes of Malmesbury* (London: John Bohn, 1839–45), Vol. III, pp. 333–334.

[56] Charles Tilly, *Coercion, Capital and European States, AD990–1990* (Cambridge, MA: Wiley-Blackwell, 1992), pp. 74, 76, 82–83.

When a state works on both coercive and extractive capacity, the evolution will result in the so-called fiscal-military state, that is, the state that can guarantee the operation of large-scale wars through taxation and other innovative fiscal means. Fiscal-military states conquered large tracts of land around the world between the seventeenth and nineteenth centuries and became global overlords, showing how important the extractive capacity could be.

When it comes to the extractive capacity, some people often believe that it is a by-product of economic growth, and that it can get strengthened only after the economic growth, which is an essential condition for the strengthening of the extractive capacity. It is true that a strong economy is likely to enhance the extractive capacity. For instance, up to the nineteenth century, the Netherlands was the locomotive of economy, dubbed as the "first modern economy."[57] Its per capita tax revenue was higher than in any other country throughout the seventeenth century, twice or several times higher than in Britain; and the situation sustained until the eighteenth century, when its per capita tax revenue was still 30–70% higher than in Britain.[58] This does not mean, however, that the economic growth could always go ahead of the growing extractive capacity, as the former is not necessarily a precondition for the latter. In fact, it is completely possible for the extractive capacity to precede and then drive the economic growth. In Britain, for example, its fiscal revenues (in terms of average per capita revenue in silver grams) rose significantly after the Glorious Revolution, from 38.5 grams in 1650–1659 to 91.94 grams in1700–1709, and soared to 315.05 grams at the peak of the First Industrial Revolution (1820–1829). During the same period, however, the economy did not grow as fast, while the growth rate of tax revenue was much higher than the rate of economic growth. It is estimated that from 1688 to 1815, Britain's GDP grew threefold, but its real tax revenues increased 15 times. It was similar in France, where the GDP per capita doubled from 1650 to 1899, but the per capita tax revenue grew 33 times.[59] The situation in other European countries

[57] Jande Veris and Advander Woude, *The First Modern Economy Success, Failure and Perseverance of the Dutch Economy, 1500–1815* (Cambridge: Cambridge University, 1997).

[58] Revenues in Europe in History, http://ata.boun.edu.tr/ata.boun.edu.tr/files/faculty/sevket.pamuk/database/a-web_sitei.xls.

[59] Mark Dincecco, *The Rise of Effective States in Europe*, *The Journal of Economic History*, Vol. 75, No. 3 (September 2015), pp. 907–908.

Table 2.5  Annual tax revenue per capita, 1500–1909 unit: gram silver

| Year | England | Dutch R | France | Spain | Austria | Russia | Prussia | Ottoman |
|---|---|---|---|---|---|---|---|---|
| 1500–09 | 5.50 |  | 7.16 | 12.86 |  |  |  |  |
| 1550–59 | 8.93 |  | 10.88 | 19.11 |  |  |  | 5.58 |
| 1600–09 | 15.22 | 76.19 | 18.13 | 62.56 |  |  | 2.40 | 5.76 |
| 1650–59 | 38.70 | 113.96 | 56.55 | 57.26 | 10.55 |  | 8.96 | 7.43 |
| 1700–09 | 91.94 | 210.58 | 43.52 | 28.61 | 15.57 | 6.25 | 24.63 | 7.99 |
| 1750–59 | 109.14 | 189.41 | 48.75 | 46.21 | 23.04 | 14.92 | 53.19 | 9.06 |
| 1780–89 | 172.35 | 228.16 | 77.61 | 59.00 | 42.95 | 26.75 | 35.00 | 7.10 |
| 1820–29 | 315.05 | 151.71 | 137.12 | 49.70 | 49.48 | 39.61 | 72.81 | 18.56 |
| 1850–59 | 257.59 | 173.84 | 185.00 | 120.61 | 70.78 | 55.67 | 96.47 | 39.06 |
| 1880–89 | 361.52 | 303.91 | 464.75 | 271.06 | 287.81 | 128.07 | 247.57 | 98.16 |
| 1900–09 | 927.28 | 525.21 | 1026.13 | 436.36 | 731.38 | 266.26 | 807.60 | 199.82 |

Source The European State Finance Database, Nine-year moving averages of total revenue per capita in England, 1490–1815 (inconstant prices of 1451–75), http://www.esfd.org/Table.aspx?resourceid= 11287

was about the same, with per capita tax revenues increasing many folds, although some countries (Britain, France, Prussia, and Austria) displayed a faster growth of the extractive capacity than others (Ottoman Empire, Russia, Spain, and the Netherlands) (see Table 2.5). This indicates that the state extractive capacity is not a simple by-product of economic growth. With the increase of per capita tax revenue, the overall tax revenue in these countries certainly went up by big margins accordingly.

China was an entirely different case at that time. Compared with Britain and the rest of Europe, the Qing Dynasty was very incapable of extracting and showed no improvement in this regard. It is estimated that the annual fiscal revenue of the central government was about 35 million taels (of silver) in the Reign of Kangxi (1662–1722), about 40 million taels in the Reign of Yongzheng (1723–1735), and 43 million to 48 million taels in the Reign of Qianlong (1736–1795), with the situation sustaining up to the Opium War. The fiscal revenues at all government levels swung in between 60 and 80 million taels. Considering that this was a period of rapid population growth, the per capita fiscal income of the Qing Dynasty not only did not grow, but it continuously declined.[60] Peer Vries estimated that the Qing government's tax revenue before the

---

[60] Peer Vries, *Public Finance in China and Britain in the Long 18th Century*, LSE Working Paper No.167/12, 2012, pp. 18–19.

Opium War would not exceed 300 million tales of silver, which is a very high estimate, far higher than those made by other scholars, such as Zhang Zhongli, James Lee, Roy Bin Wong, Pierre-Etienne Will, and Mark Elliot. Compared with Britain at that time, this figure was far too low: 300 million taels were about 11 billion grams of silver, while China's population then reached 350–360 million, that was a tax revenue of about 30 grams of silver per capita, only a small fraction of Britain's, and also much lower than other European powers'.[61]

A number of studies have evidenced the close relationship between state capacity and the early economic performance.[62] A 2011 study by Patrick O'Brien, an economic historian at the London School of Economics and Political Science, found that up to 1815, Britain's state capacity to provide external security, maintain internal order and protect the property had enabled it to increase investment and international trade and become a precocious industrial state.[63] As a negative example, Mauricio Drelichman and Hans-Joachim Voth noted in their 2014 work that Spain's failure to make efforts to improve its extractive capacity with its unexpected gains (silver revenues from the Americas) reduced the once overlord to its gradual decline in the seventeenth century.[64] A study by two Dutch scholars also found that the Netherlands' unbalanced extraction (over-reliance on one province's fiscal revenues) compromised its extractive capacity and then the national defense capacity of the Dutch Republic, which eventually led to its eradication by France in 1795.[65] Another study illustrates that in the era of Great Divergence between the

---

[61] Peer Vries, *State, Economy and the Great Divergence: Great Britain and China, 1680s–1850s* (London: Bloomsbury Academic, 2015), pp 84–98; S. A. M. Adshead, *China in World History* (London: Palgrave Macmillan UK, 2000), pp. 245–247.

[62] Mark Dincecco, *The Rise of Effective States in Europe*, The Journal of Economic History, Vol. 75, No. 3 (September 2015), pp. 901–918.

[63] Patrick O'Brien, *The Nature and Historical Evolution of an Exceptional Fiscal State and Its Possible Significance for the Precocious Commercialization and Industrialization of the British Economy from Cromwell to Nelson*, The Economic History Review, Vol. 64, No. 2 (2011), pp. 408–446.

[64] Mauricio Drelichman and Hans-Joachim Voth, *Lending to the Borrower from Hell: Debt, Taxes and Default in the Age of Phillip II* (Princeton, NJ: Princeton University Press, 2014).

[65] Jan Luiten van Zanden and Arthur van Riel, *The Strictures of Inheritance: The Dutch Economy in the Nineteenth Century* (Princeton, NJ: Princeton University Press, 2004).

East and the West, there was a clear correlation between the country's extractive capacity and its economic performance.[66]

Such observations have led more and more scholars to the belief that an important cause for the Great Divergence was the strong or weak state capacity. Dutch scholar Peer Vries maintained that the root cause of "what the 'East' lacked in contrast to the 'West'" in the early modern era would be the "major difference" in "the importance, role and function of the state."[67] Warren Sun, a scholar of Chinese origin, also held that "China failed to become a leading sheep in the world economy in modern history because it did not become a country based on war finance (fiscal-military state)."[68]

Ha-Joon Chang, a Korean professor of political economy at Cambridge University, published a book entitled *Kicking Away the Ladder: Development Strategy in Historical Perspective*, which talks about developed countries trying to "kick away the ladder" by which they have climbed up to the top they have reached today, and sell "good institutions" and "good policies" to developing countries.[69] In the early stage of economic development in Europe and the United States, wars gave them the impetus to strengthen their state capacity, which in turn helped them grab the "first barrel of gold." The state capacity was the ladder the developed countries had used, which they are trying to hide away now and ask the developing countries to do as they say, not as they did. This is simply the act of "Bad Samaritans."[70] The developing countries (including China) today must not fall in their trap.

---

[66] Mark Dincecco, *The Rise of Effective States in Europe*, p. 910.

[67] Peer Vries, *State, Economy and the Great Divergence: Great Britain and China, 1680s–1850s* (London: Bloomsbury Academic, 2015), p. 2.

[68] Warren Sun, *China's Role in Modern Global Economy* [EB/OL], (December 21, 2015), http://www2.scul.edu.cn/economy/2015/1221/c1805a31351/page.htm.

[69] Ha-Joon Chang, *Kicking Away the Ladder: Development Strategy in Historical Perspective* (Anthem Press, 2002).

[70] Ha-Joon Chang, *Bad Samaritans: The Myth of Free Trade and the Secret History of Capitalism* (Bloomsbury Press, 2001).

## State Capacity and China–Japan Divergence

In the latter half of the nineteenth century, Japan's development outpaced that of China by far, defeating China in the 1895 Sino-Japanese War, then encroaching on northeastern China and finally trying to occupy the whole of the country. To this day, Japan remains much more advanced than China in terms of technology and economic development indicators. How should we interpret the China–Japan Divergence?

There are two prevalent views on this question. One holds that up to the Meiji Restoration, China and Japan were similar, both were backward countries with economic stagnation, and the rulers had no intention to make any progress. The other perceives that the gap between China and Japan widened after Japan's Meiji Restoration in 1868, since Japan went through a thorough reform, while China's reform was not thorough enough.[71] A Chinese book published in 2018 still holds this perception, which has been highly recommended by a number of renowned scholars. The author of the book argued that "Since it entered the era of Meiji Restoration, Japan had opened up to the outside world externally and carried out reforms internally, embarking on a road of modernization for a prosperous country and powerful army, Japan was more thoroughgoing in guiding the Meiji Restoration to success," and "in case Japan failed to pursue reforms and struggle hard, it would have declined and decayed like China!"[72] In fact, quite a few studies have challenged the above-mentioned prevailing views.

With regard to the first prevailing view, studies over the last decade or two have evidenced that China and Japan experienced extensive commercialization and early industrialization (non-mechanical industrialization) as Western Europe did. To borrow a notion from American scholar Kenneth Pomeranz, "the core regions in China and Japan circa 1750 seem to resemble the most advanced parts of western Europe, combining sophisticated agriculture, commerce and non-mechanized industry in similar, arguably even more fully realized, ways."[73] According

---

[71] John Fairbank, Edwin Reischauer and Albert Craig, *East Asia: Tradition and Transformation*, Revised Edition (Boston: Houghton Mifflin, 1989).

[72] Ma Guochuan, *Enlightenment of a Nation: Origin of the Rise of the Japanese Empire* (Beijing: CITIC Press Group, 2018).

[73] Kenneth Pomeranz, *The Great Divergence: Europe, China and the Making of the Modern World* (Princeton, NJ: Princeton University Press, 2000), p. 17.

to economist Angus Madison's estimate, China's share of world GDP rose from 22.3 to 32.9% from 1700 to 1820, against Europe's growth from 24.9 to 26.6%; China's annual average growth rate was 0.85% during the period, against Europe's 0.58%, both higher than the world average (0.52%), but China's even higher than Europe's.[74] Accordingly, Chinese scholar Li Bozhong also held that "in the several centuries leading up to the Industrial Revolution in Europe, China was not inferior to Europe in many aspects of its economic development."[75] However, in criticizing the first prevailing view, Pomeranz overemphasized the commonality between China and Japan while ignoring the differences between them.

The second prevalent view noticed the differences between China and Japan, but emphasized that these differences only emerged after the Meiji Restoration, as if the differences cropped up just because the efforts put in the reform and opening-up varied between the two countries. Recent studies have found that the divergence between China and Japan did not occur after the Meiji Restoration, but was already in existence before it, only their gap further widened after the Restoration. Before the Meiji Restoration, the gap between China and Japan manifested in two aspects: in GDP per capita, and in state capacity, the latter was likely to be closely related to the former.

Based on the latest edition of Madison database, Fig. 2.4 shows that in the year when Emperor Kangxi took the throne (1661), China's GDP per capita was higher than Japan's; but by the 31st year of Qianlong (1766), Japan had surpassed China in GDP per capita. A study published in 2017 found that in the 130 years following 1720, the average annual growth rate of GDP per capita in Japan significantly increased to 0.25%, while China's GDP per capita barely grew. This continuously widened the gap between the two countries, and by the last decade or so of the nineteenth century, the two countries had become vastly different. It is clear that the divergence between China and Japan in terms of GDP per capita appeared before, not after, the Meiji Restoration: "These earlier growth

---

[74] Angus Maddison, *Chinese Economic Performance in the Long Run, 960–2030 AD*, Second Edition (OECD Publication, 2007), p. 44.

[75] Li Bozhong, *Early Industrialization South of the Yangtze River (1550–1850)*, Revised Edition (Beijing: China Renmin University Press, 2010).

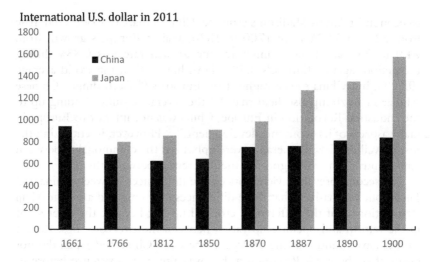

**Fig. 2.4** GDP per capita in China and Japan, 1661–1900 (*Source* Maddison Project Database (Version 2018) by Jutta Bolt, Robert Inklaar, Herman de Jong and Jan Luiten van Zanden, https://www.rug.nl/ggdc/historicaldevelopment/maddison/data/mpd2018.xlsx)

spurts thus helped to lay the foundations for the transition to modern economic growth after the Meiji Restoration in 1868."[76]

On par with the divergence in GDP per capita, there also came a divergence in the state extractive capacity between China and Japan. Figure 2.5 is taken from a comparative study on the Tokugawa shogunate (1603–1867) in Japan and China's Qing Dynasty. As its authors made it clear that the data in this chart much underestimate Japan's extractive capacity, the actual gap between China and Japan in terms of extractive capacity was much greater than what is illustrated. Nevertheless, Fig. 2.5 indicates that from 1650 to 1850, Japan's level of extraction remained largely stable, while China's extractive capacity drastically declined, resulting in an ever widening gap between the two countries in terms of state extractive capacity. The authors of the study estimated that up to the First Opium War, China's tax revenues were only about 2% of national income,

---

[76] Jean-Pascal Bassino, Stephen Broadberry, Kyoji Fukao, Bishnupriya Gupta and Masanori Takashima, *Japan and the Great Divergence, 730–1874*, Discussion Papers in Economic and Social History, University of Oxford, Number 156, April 2017, p. 3.

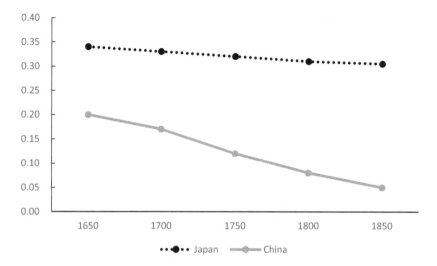

**Fig. 2.5** Tax revenues per capita (koku of Rice) in China and Japan, 1650–1850 (*Source* Adopted from Sng Tuan-Hwee and Chiaki Moriguchi, *Asia's Little Divergence: State Capacity in China and Japan before 1850, Journal of Economic Growth*, Vol. 19, No. 4 [December 2014], p. 441)

against 15% in Japan. This study is important because it evidenced with substantial data that the huge gap between China and Japan in terms of state extractive capacity occurred before, not after, the Meiji Restoration.

The relatively greater state extractive capacity may explain why Japan embarked on the path to modernization ahead of China with the pace smoother and faster. With a relatively stronger state capacity, Japan during the Tokugawa shogunate period and the Meiji Restoration was able to provide more and better infrastructures and public goods, such as roads, bridges, harbors, lighthouses, firefighting facilities, and disaster reliefs. Table 2.6 displays comparative data only in four aspects. Before the Meiji Restoration, China's urbanization rate was only about one-third of that in Japan, and thereafter it would take nearly 100 years for China to reach Japan's then level in urbanization rate. Japan had also done far better than China in terms of ecological conservation, with the damage to forest taken as an indicator.

Yes, the total length of China's highways was much longer than that in Japan, but China was much larger in land area, and when it is converted

Table 2.6 Comparison of infrastructures between late Qing China and Japan in the Tokugawa shogunate

| | China | Japan |
|---|---|---|
| Urban population (urbanization rate) | 20.50 million (5.8%) | 5.1 million (%) |
| Length of trunk roads (km) | 11,370 (imperial routes) | 1440 (Gokaido) |
| Density of highways (square kilometer) | 0.26 | 0.51 or 3.37 |
| Forest coverage (million hectares) | 18.5 (in 1700) down to 9.6 (in 1850) | 27 (in 1600) down to 25.5 (in 1850) |

Source Sng Tuan-Hwee and Chiaki Moriguchi, *Asia's Little Divergence: State Capacity in China and Japan before 1850*, Journal of Economic Growth, Vol. 19, No. 4 (December 2014), p. 461

into road density per square kilometer, China lagged far behind Japan. China's first railway was built in 1876 and was demolished the next year because of resistance, while the Tokugawa shogunate had planned to build railways before the Meiji Restoration.[77] This engaged Japan in the rapid construction of national railway network guided by the government investment shortly after the Meiji Restoration, with ever increasing operational mileage, leaving China far behind (see Fig. 2.6).

Moreover, Japan is a long and narrow island nation, and China is 25 times the size of Japan. Prior to 1887, the core areas of Japan had accessed to railways, and by 1907, railway lines had extended to almost all the Japanese islands. In contrast, the total length of railways in China before the 1895 Sino-Chinese War was slightly more than 400 kilometers, which, placed on the map of China, was just a short line. Even up to the 1907, few provinces in China accessed to a railway, and many of the railway lines were controlled by foreign powers (see Fig. 2.6).

The provision of public goods requires the support from fiscal revenues, and it is possible to do more things only when the government is more capable of extracting, while public goods like transport networks are the infrastructures for further economic development. There is no doubt that the foundation laid before the Meiji Restoration in Japan paved the way for the development thereafter. According to William

---

[77] Dan Free, *Early Japanese Railways 1853–1914: Engineering Triumphs That Transformed Meiji-era Japan* (Tokyo: Tuttle Publishing, 2012).

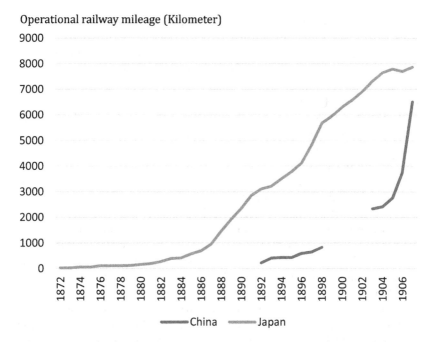

Fig. 2.6 Railway operational mileage in China and Japan 1871–1907 (*Source* B. R. Mitchell, *International Historical Statistics: Africa, Asia & Oceania, 1750–1993*, 3rd Edition [London: Macmillan Reference Ltd. 1998], pp. 683–684)

Beasley, a famous historian on Japanese history, even the relevant reform plans rolled out before the Meiji Restoration can be counted as a kind of public goods, which "was a blueprint for 'wealth and strength' on the lines which the Meiji government was later to follow."[78]

In the initial stage of modern economic growth, the coercive capacity is as important as the extractive capacity that is the central authority's monopoly on the legitimate use of violence.

During the shogunate or bakufu period that spanned 682 years from 1185 to 1867, Japan did not have a unified central government in its true

---

[78] William Beasley, *The Rise of Modern Japan* (New York: St. Martins Press, 1990), p. 50.

sense, but various parts of the country were ruled by warriors.[79] In the latter half of the sixteenth century, Japan experienced a military revolution: the almost universal adoption of firearms, the development of tactics for the effective deployment of those firearms, a change in the composition and organization of armies, which led to the professionalization of warfare. This was very similar to the military revolution in Europe, but it happened without central authority. Nevertheless, by revolutionizing the way armies were organized and the wars were fought, there emerged new notions of centralized authority that were critical to the creation of a unified modern state.[80]

Circa 1850, both China and Japan faced internal and external problems, to which the two countries responded in very different ways, with profound impact on their respective ability to enforce.

In order to suppress the Taiping Heavenly Kingdom Uprising, the Qing government at first mobilized the standing armies of the Eight Banners and the Green Standard to fight the Taiping Army, but their fighting qualities deteriorated so that they were frustrated successively. Reluctantly, Emperor Xianfeng had to encourage local gentries around the country to set up their own militias, with the most prominent being the Hunan Army organized by Zeng Guofan in 1852 and the Huai Army organized by Li Hongzhang in 1862, both composed of village farmers. Not only the armies were under the command of local forces, but even the military expenditure depended on money raised by local forces in various pretexts. Hence China with a long-standing tradition of centralized power began to move towards decentralization, despite the several attempts the Qing court made later to recover the power, the spilled water could hardly be recollected, and what was lost could not come back.

Also dealing with its internal and external crises, Japan, where the military power was rather decentralized, moved toward centralization of the military power. As an island nation with limited land area, the Japanese came to realize through the Western threats from the sea that the decentralized feudal political structure before the Meiji Restoration was outdated. The shogun bakufus and daimyos who had dealt with the powers or even had brief combat experience with them, had taken

---

[79] Marius Jansen, *Warrior Rule in Japan* (Cambridge: Cambridge University Press, 1995).

[80] Matthew Stavros, *Military Revolution in Early Modern Japan, Japanese Studies*, Vol. 33, No. 3 (2013), pp. 243–251.

measures to enhance their military strength, but restrained with decentralized financial resources, they were obviously unable to resist Western invasions by fighting separately. In fact, even before the brief civil war (the 1868–1869 Boshin War), both the Tokugawa supporters and the opponents had realized that only a unified centralist system could save Japan, and they sought to change the bakufu-daimyo system. What they fought over was who and how should dominate the centralization. The civil war put an end to the samurai feudal system spanning more than 600 years and led to the establishment of the imperial system and a new type of administrative institutional framework.

The most critical reform of the Meiji Restoration was the abolition of feudal lords' domains which were transformed into prefectures in 1871, a reform that was no less significant than the abolition of the feudal dukedoms and setup of counties by Qin Shihuang, the First Emperor of the Qin Dynasty in China. Often overlooked, on par with the abolition of feudal lords' domains was the reform that ordered the daimyos to disband the private armies and hand over their weapons to the government. Despite the resistance from some samurai, a national army and navy were formally created by early 1872. In early 1873, Japan officially introduced universal conscription, which replaced the samurai class with soldiers from ordinary civilian families.[81] By then, Japan had established a centralized and unified standing army. While creating a unified national military system, Japan set up a local and national police system. Based on its monopoly on violence, the Japanese government was able to launch a series of bold reforms in a short period of time, including the introduction of the new currency system (1871) and the land tax system (1873) to centralize financial power. By 1877, Japan had established a unified fiscal system, further strengthening its extractive capacity.

The Qing government in China, in contrast, did not begin to model after Germany and Japan to form a standing army until after the outbreak of the 1895 Sino-Japanese War, which was the New Army under the command of Yuan Shikai (1859–1916), that was nearly a quarter of a century later than Japan. Even more embarrassing for the Qing Empire, this New Army of northern China "knew only Marshal Yuan but was ignorant of the Qing Dynasty" and eventually became the main force of the 1911 Revolution that dethroned the Qing emperor. Regretfully for

---

[81] Edward J. Drea, *Japan's Imperial Army: Its Rise and Fall, 1853–1945* (Lawrence, KS: University Press of Kansas, 2009).

China, it was not until after the Communist Party of China took power when a unified military system was formed throughout the country that monopolized the legitimate use of violence, nearly 80 years later than in Japan.

Similar to China, Japan also witnessed strong resistance from various parties to its reforms. It is rarely known that there were more frequent uprisings in the early period of the Meiji Restoration than in the Tokugawa shogunate (see Fig. 2.7). For instance, from 1873 to 1874, peasant rebellions against the new tax system, the new education system, and the conscription broke out wave upon wave. And there were frequent samurai unrests from 1874 to 1878.

Unlike China, Japan with the backing of a centralized and unified army and police was largely able to quench the unrest resolutely in a short period of time. Yamagata Aritomo (1838–1922), "the father of

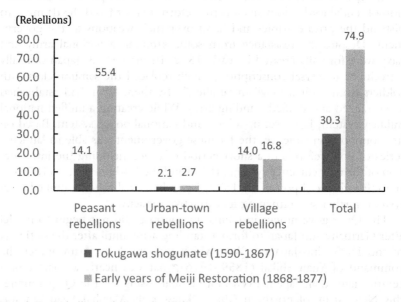

Fig. 2.7 Rebellions during the Tokugawa shogunate and early years of Meiji Restoration (*Sources* Roger W. Bowen, *Rebellion and Democracy in Meiji Japan: A Study of Commoners in the Popular Rights Movement* [Berkeley, CA: University of California Press, 1984], p. 73)

Table 2.7 Duration of samurai rebellions

| Rebellion | Duration |
| --- | --- |
| Saga Rebellion | February 26–April 9, 1874 |
| Shipuren Rebellion | October 24–25, 1876 |
| Akizuki Rebellion | October 27–November 14, 1876 |
| Hagi Rebellion | October 28–December 8, 1876 |
| Satsuma Rebellion | January 29–September 24, 1877 |
| Takebashi Incident | August 23–24, 1878 |

militarism" in modern Japan who founded the Japanese army, had foreseen while setting up the first standing army that the first task of the national army was to suppress internal chaos.[82] The following events verified this view. The Japanese police were actually a branch of the army at the time, while the army itself was nothing more than a militarized police force whose main task was not to resist external enemies but to eliminate internal insurrections.[83] There were frequent peasant rebellions during the Meiji Restoration, with 185 in the 10 years from 1868 to 1878, some involving tens of thousands of peasants. But all these rebellions were quickly quelled by the army and police.[84] Perhaps the greater challenge to the authorities was the samurai rebellions, with more than 30 such rebellions erupting in defense of samurai privileges between 1874 and 1877.[85] However, the local samurai rebellions were no match to the newly organized regular army.[86] Table 2.7 lists several samurai rebellions with considerable scale and impact between 1874 and 1878: the shortest of them lasted just one day or two, and the longest sustained no more than eight months. The Satsuma Rebellion or Southwest War was the last civil war in Japan's history to date, in which the newly formed

[82] Stephen Vlastos, *Opposition Movements in Early Meiji Japan*, in *Cambridge History of Japan: Vol. V, The Nineteenth Century* (Cambridge: Cambridge University Press, 1989), p. 386.

[83] Hyman Kublin, *The "Modern" Army of Early Meiji Japan*, The Far Eastern Quarterly, Vol. 9, No. 1 (November 1949), p. 39, note 53.

[84] Zhou Yiliang, *Peasant Movements around the Meiji Restoration in Japan*, Journal of Beijing University (Philosophy & Social Sciences), 1956, 1 (3), pp. 52–78.

[85] Patricia Ebrey and Anne Walthall, *Modern East Asia from 1600: A Cultural, Social, and Political History*, Third Edition (Boston, MA: Wadsworth, 2014), p. 351.

[86] D. Colin Jaundrill, *Samurai to Soldier: Remaking Military Service in Nineteenth-Century Japan* (Ithaca, NY: Cornell University Press, 2016).

standing army won the complete victory, marking the end of the samurai era thoroughly.

After the domestic political situation stabilized, Japan improved its national strength rapidly. Between 1870 and 1900, Japan's GDP per capita rose from 985 to 1,575 U.S. dollars (calculated at 2011 international value), an increase of nearly 60%. During the same period, China's GDP per capita rose from 751 to 840 U.S. dollars, an increase of merely about 12%.[87] Based on its ever growing national strength, Japan abolished the unequal treaties signed with Western powers step by step over the 20 years after 1877; by 1899, it had completely abolished extraterritorial rights. Some scholars thus believe that Japan "rapidly rose to sovereignty" while China was still "struggling for it."[88] One thing the Japanese learned from their opponents in the game with the Western powers was Might Is Right. Once it grew strong, it began to emulate the Western powers for external colonial expansion, embarking on a road to "expand by force and develop with war." When summing up Japan's development experience later, Yamagata Aritomo said quite proudly, "It has been more than 40 years since the great Meiji Restoration was accomplished, and to ponder on the course, the nation's development has mainly depended on the strength of the armed forces."[89] Almost at the same time when he made these remarks, he put forward the strategic objective that Japan should pursue: to occupy China's northeast, before seeking to take a "dominant position" over the whole of China.[90]

## SUMMARY

The discussion above shows that the Great Divergence that occurred between the East and the West, and between China and Japan was closely related to the state capacity. There were some other similar divergences in history, in which again, the strong or weak state capacity was an important explanatory variable. For instance, there was another Great Divergence

---

[87] Maddison Project Database (Version 2018).

[88] Kayaoglu Turan, *Legal Imperialism, Sovereignty and Extraterritoriality in Japan, the Ottoman Empire, and China* (Cambridge: Cambridge University Press, 2010).

[89] Wu Yin, *A Look into Japan from Historical Depth: An Analysis of the Social Basis and Historical Roots of Japanese Militarism*, Yanhuang Chunqiu, 2001 (10), pp. 42–45.

[90] Sun Yaozhu, *Yamagata Aritomo and Japan's Aggression to China*, Japan Study Papers, 2002 (Tianjin: Tianjin People's Publishing House, 2002), pp. 248–259.

after the Second World War, in which the East Asian economies stood out in the Third World for a long period of time, with the emergence of several "little dragons," constituting the so-called East Asian miracle.

When this miracle first drew people's attention in the 1970s, economists explained that the success of Japan, South Korea, Singapore, and China's Taiwan and Hong Kong should be attributed to the undisturbed free market. Several of these economists are Chinese. As Edward Chen Kwan-yiu, a professor at the University of Hong Kong, asserted, "State intervention is largely absent" in these economies[91]; Professor John C. H. Fei of the Yale University and Professor Shirley W. Y. Kuo of the Taiwan University did not completely negate the presence of government intervention, but believed that there was much less government intervention in these economies than elsewhere.[92] Without an understanding of East Asia at all, Milton Friedman nevertheless asserted full of confidence that "Malaysia, Singapore, South Korea, Taiwan and Japan– all relying extensively on private markets – are thriving."[93]

However, a large number of empirical studies in the 1980s have evidenced that in the development of Japan,[94] China's Taiwan,[95] and South Korea,[96] the government played a crucial and essential role.[97] By the 1990s, even the World Bank had corrected its previous conclusions[98] and acknowledged that in these economies, "in one form or another, the

---

[91] Edward Chen Kwan-yiu, *Hypergrowth in Asian Economies: A Comparative Study of Hong Kong, Japan, Korea, Singapore and Taiwan* (London: Macmillan, 1979), p. 41.

[92] John C. H. Fei, Gustav Ranis and Shirley W. Y. Kuo, *Growth with Equity: The Taiwan Case* (Washington, DC: The World Bank, 1979), p. 34.

[93] Milton Friedman and Rose Friedman, *Free to Choose: A Personal Statement* (New York: Harcourt Brace Jovanovich, 1980), p. 57.

[94] Calmers Johnson, *MITI and the Japanese Miracle: The Growth of Industrial Policy, 1925–1975* (Stanford: Sanford University Press, 1982).

[95] Alice H. Amsden, *The State and Taiwan's Economic Development*, in Peter B. Evans, Dietrich Rueschemeyer, Theda Skocpol, eds., *Bringing the State Back In* (Cambridge: Cambridge University Press, 1985), pp. 78–106.

[96] Alice H. Amsden, *Asia's Next Giant: South Korea and Late Industrialization* (New York: Oxford University Press, 1989).

[97] Robert Wade, *Governing the Market: Economic Theory and the Role of Government in East Asian Industrialization* (Princeton, NJ: Princeton University Press, 1990).

[98] The World Bank, *World Development Report 1991: The Challenge of Development* (New York: Oxford University Press, 1991), pp. 31, 70, 145.

government intervened – systematically and through multiple channels – to foster development."[99] Obviously, a government able to play such a great role is impossible to be the one that lacks the infrastructural state capacity. As Alice Amsden, a professor at the Massachusetts Institute of Technology, put it, South Korea's success "rests heavily on a strong state, one that is capable of implementing its own policies." This is true to not only South Korea, Amsden reasoned, "Without a strong central authority, a necessary although not sufficient condition, little industrialization may be expected in 'backward' countries." Throughout the economic transition, even if the government does not intervene in the market, it must have a strong capacity to cope with the pressure from the groups with impaired interests in the transition, so as not to interrupt the process of economic growth. Such strong state management is precisely what "backward" countries lack.[100]

When comparing East Asian economies with others, the importance of state capacity becomes even more prominent. In his 2004 book *State-Directed Development: Political Power and Industrialization in the Global Periphery*, Atul Kohli, an Indian professor of Princeton University, compared the trajectory of four countries in the latter half of the twentieth century (see Fig. 2.8): "These cases provide a wide range of variation in state capacities to pursue economic transformation: from a fairly effective, growth-promoting state in South Korea, to a rather ineffective and corrupt Nigerian state, with Brazil and India providing mixed cases." Professor Kohli concluded that "the creation of effective states in the developing world has generally preceded the emergence of industrializing economies."[101] A few years later, he expanded his research to 31 economies, including many countries in Africa and Latin America, and the key role of the state capacity was once again evidenced: the quality of government institutions and staff was a measure of the state capacity, the greater the state capacity, the higher the long-term economic growth rate (see Fig. 2.9).

---

[99] The World Bank, *The East Asian Miracle: Economic Growth and Public Policy* (New York: Oxford University Press, 1993), p. 5.

[100] Alice H. Amsden, *Asia's Next Giant: South Korea and Late Industrialization* (New York: Oxford University Press, 1989), pp. 18, 147–148.

[101] Atul Kohli, *State-Directed Development: Political Power and Industrialization in the Global Periphery* (Cambridge: Cambridge University Press, 2004), p. 2.

2 REVELATION: STATE CAPACITY AND ECONOMIC DEVELOPMENT    61

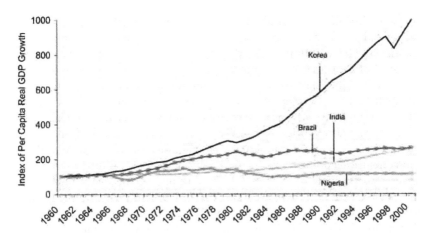

**Fig. 2.8** Pattern of per capita GDP growth: Korea, Brazil, India, and Nigeria, 1960–2000 (*Source* Atul Kohli, *State-Directed Development: Political Power and Industrialization in the Global Periphery* [Cambridge: Cambridge University Press, 2004], p. 24)

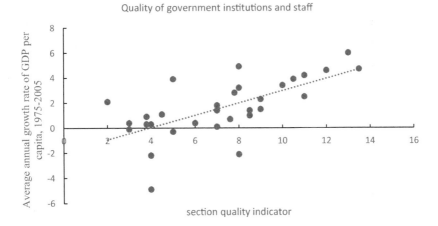

**Fig. 2.9** State capacity and economic growth (*Source* Atul Kohli, *States and Economic Development*, 2010, http://www.prince-ton.edu/~kohli/docs/SED.pdf)

Two scholars at the Brookings Institute used an even larger database to measure the state capacities of 141 developing countries or economies in transition. They also found that the stronger the state capacity, the higher the level of economic development (see Fig. 2.10).

I've taken the pains to cite so many studies and data here just to prove that, whatever indicators are used to measure the state capacity, whether they have involved historical or present cases, whether the comparison is made on similar or different cases, whether the study is based on limited or sizable samples, and no matter it is qualitative or quantitative analysis, the conclusions point to the same direction: in most countries, there are fewer cases in which reforms and opening-up are successful but mostly they have failed, and there are fewer cases in which the economic growth has sustained but mostly it's short-lived. Many people take it for granted that as long as there is the determination to carry out market-oriented reform and opening-up, it is bound to succeed, and as long as a nation perseveres in reform and opening-up, the economy is bound to grow sustained and result in economic prosperity. Of course, without reform and opening-up, there may not be economic prosperity. But we have

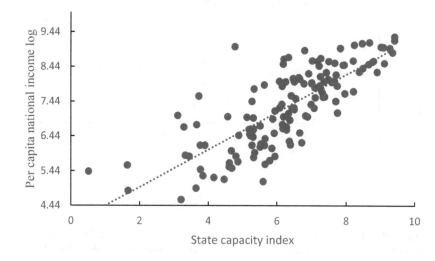

**Fig. 2.10** State capacity and level of economic development (*Source* Susan E. Rice and Stewart Patrick, *Index of State Weakness in Developing World* [Washington, DC: The Brookings Institution, 2008])

proved with the above transnational comparisons that not all reforms and opening-up can be successful.

The success of reform and opening-up depends on an effective government. Historical, comparative and contemporary studies have shown that in some countries where the transformation of political and economic institutions (reform and opening-up) was relatively smooth and modern economic growth emerged rather early are the ones whose state capacities were enhanced before the development of economy. This time sequence has revealed a logical correlation, that is, economic development is likely to be more than just the outcome of reform and opening-up. In addition to the correct direction and measures of reform and opening-up, an effective government is also required as a prerequisite. In other words, it won't work just with the reform and opening-up but with no state capacity to pave the way.

Of course, we cannot put it the other way around to say that as long as the state capacity is strong enough, economic prosperity will be possible without reform and opening-up. The effective state is only a necessary condition for economic prosperity, while reform and opening-up is another, and reform and opening-up and the construction and maintenance of state capacity are complementary and indispensable to each other. Neither is a sufficient condition. As we mark the 40th anniversary of reform and opening-up, we should have a clear mind about why China is successful.

Finally, why is it necessary and crucial to have an effective government with infrastructural state capacity for reform and opening-up and economic growth? First, a strong state capacity could lay a more solid foundation for reform and opening-up, including institutional guarantee, human capital, and infrastructures. Second, a strong state capacity could create a more favorable internal and external environment for reform and opening-up. For example, only with a certain national strength can we independently formulate our own economic policies. Third, a strong state capacity could allow a better control of the direction and pace of reform and opening-up. Reform and opening-up is not a linear movement, not to go straight toward one direction at one speed without turns, it sometimes has to take a detour, or adjust the pace. Fourth, a strong state capacity could enable the government to adjust the distribution of losses and gains brought about by reform and opening-up, making necessary and appropriate compensations on the groups whose interests are impaired, so as to avoid intensifying social contradictions and prevent political disturbances.

The state capacity is so important that in our future journey on the road of reform and opening-up, we must go along cherishing it.

CHAPTER 3

# Groundwork: From Old China to New China

Today's China is like a skyscraper towering into the clouds. Looking at such a building, people usually focus their attention on its parts above the ground, that is, the building's brilliant and magnificent outlook. However, the most arduous work in building such a structure is not the construction of those parts above the ground, the most time- and energy-consuming work is probably to carry out those cumbersome and complicated preliminary preparations, including the relocation of the original occupants of the site, the demolition of the original buildings, the "seven-accesses" and "one leveling" (namely, accessing it to road, water supply, electricity, drainage, heating supply, telecommunications, and gas supply, and land leveling), earth excavation, foundation piling, cement pouring, and basement or underground garage building.

To lay the foundation for a country's undertakings is similar to that of the construction industry. There are three characteristics in laying the foundation at the early stage of building a mansion. First, the time it involves probably accounts for a large proportion of the entire process of construction, as if it will never finish, and once the foundation is laid, the above-ground parts are built quickly, as if the building grows taller every day, with the result easy to see. Second, the ground-breaking process seems to be messy, very dirty, very troublesome, with dust and noise all around, which is very disturbing, and it requires strenuous efforts to have the work done, while the construction of above-ground parts impresses the people as orderly and methodical. Third, during the foundation-laying

© CITIC Press Corporation 2021
S. Wang, *China's Rise and Its Global Implications*,
https://doi.org/10.1007/978-981-16-4341-5_3

period, none of the benefits that the building could render in the future is visible or could be enjoyed; yet without laying the foundation or if the foundation is not solid, the gains could never come by. Therefore, whether for a real estate project or for a great cause of nation-building, the foundation laying is extremely critical.

In 1954, at the opening ceremony of the First Session of the First National People's Congress of the People's Republic of China, Chairman Mao Zedong declared majestically, "We are fully confident that we can overcome all difficulties and hardships and make our country a great socialist republic. We are advancing. We are now engaged in a great and most glorious cause, never undertaken by our forefathers. Our goal must be attained. Our goal can unquestionably be attained."[1] At the time he delivered the speech, the New China was in a difficult period of foundation laying. The focus of this chapter is the three decades of foundation laying from 1949 to 1979.

With regard to the relationship between the first three decades and the following 40 years since the founding of New China, no matter within China or internationally, there are two views, one believes that the first 30 years and the next 40 years evolved in the opposite direction, and the other holds that the first 30 years laid a solid foundation for the longer-term development of the next 40 years and beyond.

Let's first take a look at two English books published in recent years. One is quite an influential book published in 2015, *The Great Surge: The Ascent of the Developing World* authored by Stephen C. Radelet, an economist once holding senior positions in several U.S. government departments, and the book was highly recommended by George Soros, Francis Fukuyama, and Larry Diamond (known as "Mr. Democracy"). There is a strange sentence in the book, "In 1976, Mao (Zedong) single-handedly and dramatically changed the direction of global poverty with one simple act: he died."[2] This sounds as if Mao Zedong was the biggest obstacle to solving the problem of poverty for humankind. The other is *Enlightenment Now: The Case of Reason, Science, Humanism, and Progress* published in 2018, which has been well reported by Chinese media and I'm told that someone has planned to translate it into Chinese because its

---

[1] Mao Zedong, *Strive to Build a Socialist Country* (September 15, 1954) *Selected Works of Mao Tse-tung*, Vol. V (Peking: Foreign Languages Press, 1977), p. 149.

[2] Steven Radelet, *The Great Surge: The Ascent of the Developing World* (New York: Simon & Schuster, 2015), p. 35.

author is Steven Pinker, a well-known experimental psychologist, cognitive scientist and Harvard professor. In the book, Pinker wrote: "Though China's rise is exclusively responsible for the Great Convergence (which refers to the trend of slow fusion of developing and developed countries), and the country's sheer bulk is bound to move the total around, and the explanations for its progress apply elsewhere. The death of Mao Zedong is emblematic of three of the major causes of the Great Convergence."[3] Exactly the same as the previous author, Pinker also believed that when Mao Zedong was alive, China was poor, weak, and unable to do anything; but once he passed away, China and the world began to open up and develop. Neither of the authors of the two books is an ignorant nobody or a China-hand, but how comes they embraced such an absurd perception of the Mao Zedong era? Obviously, it's because it reflects the mainstream perception of the West. I'm afraid there are quite a few people in China who hold the same perception.

Another view is withheld by the CPC Central Committee with Comrade Xi Jinping at its core. In his report to the CPC 19th National Congress, Xi Jinping assessed the first three decades this way: "Our Party… united the people and led them in completing socialist revolution, establishing socialism as China's basic system, and advancing socialist construction. This completed the broadest and most profound social transformation in the history of the Chinese nation. It created the fundamental political conditions and institutional foundation for achieving all development and progress in China today. Thus was made a great transition: The Chinese nation reversed its fate from the continuous decline of modern times to steady progress toward prosperity and strength." The central leadership's perception of the first 30 years and the following 40 years of the New China is entirely different from that of the previous two foreign scholars, holding that the first 30 years laid the foundation for the development in the next 40 years.

As for these two views, the former can be called "breach theory," and the latter can be called "continuity theory." The breach theory assumes that no foundation is necessary, and reform and opening-up alone could be enough to produce great achievements. No matter it was in 1978, or in 1949, as long as there was no Mao Zedong, things would have worked out easily. The continuity theory looks at things just the other

---

[3] Steven Pinker, *Enlightenment Now: The Case of Reason, Science, Humanism, and Progress* (New York: Viking, 2018), p. 90.

**Fig. 3.1** The past and present of the state Farm 850 in Heilongjiang Province (Wang Zhen and demobilized soldiers carry earth to build the dam of the Farm 850 today Yunshan Reservoir on the Farm 850 in 1958)

way around, believing that only with a solid political, social and material infrastructure could the reform and opening-up yield brilliant results.

Let me cite a simple example first. Not long ago, there was a post on WeChat about the Farm 850 in Heilongjiang Province in northeast China. The Farm 850 today is already a very modern one (see picture on the right in Fig. 3.1). Following the breach theory, what the Farm 850 has achieved today is the outcome of reform and opening-up, while the pioneering endeavors for development in the pre-reform period were all unnecessary z-turns. However, even with a little understanding of a bit of history and a bit of historical materialism, one could see that this is nonsense. Look at the picture on the left of Fig. 3.1, which captures Wang Zhen, minister of farm and land reclamation, working together with demobilized officers and soldiers at a reservoir on the Farm 850 in 1958. As those who took part in the reclamation of the wild land recalled, life was really hard at that time, and the pioneers had to live in make-shift shelters and huts. Without the efforts to lay the foundation in those years, how could the Farm 850 become so beautiful today?

Su Zhe[4] wrote in his essay *On Things New*: "Those who plan to build a house will deal with the foundation first, and only when the foundation is completely leveled, then the stone and wood will be added up, thus the house built up will stand firm." The truth in these words is clear to us all, which is to build a solid house, the first thing to do is to lay its

---

[4] Su Zhe (1039-1112), was a famous Chinese politician and essayist in the Northern Song Dynasty (960-1127).—*Translator*.

foundation, and once the foundation is laid solid and stable, bricks and tiles can be added to build the house up, which can be strong.

Similarly, a prosperous and powerful country requires a foundation of three types of infrastructures, namely, political infrastructure, social infrastructure, and material infrastructure.

There are four points for the political infrastructure: independence, national unification, social stability, and eradication of "distributional coalitions." The social infrastructure emphasizes social equity, people's health, and universal education. The material infrastructure consists of three aspects: agriculture-based, industry-led, and the establishment of an integrated industrial system. These words are all but of common sense that sounds simple and plain, yet it was tremendously difficult to lay the three types of infrastructures in the first three decades of the New China, let alone on the basis of self-reliance, which was utterly impossible in the Old China, in the more than 100 years before the founding of New China.

## NATIONAL REALITY BEFORE THE FOUNDING OF NEW CHINA

Before the founding of New China, China repeatedly suffered external aggressions, and internally it was divided up, with powerful "distributional coalitions" politically, disunity of people like a sheet of loose sand socially, the economy backward and poor, no people's livelihood to speak of, illiteracy universal, and the health level so low that the country was dubbed as "sick man of East Asia" by Westerners.

### *Repeated External Aggressions*

Many people are familiar with the cartoon of *The Situation in the Far East* in Fig. 3.2, which is described as "self-evident and clear at one glance." It exposed the Western powers' ambition to partition China at the end of the nineteenth century.

From 1840 to 1949, a series of wars took place on the Chinese land, some were foreign powers' direct invasions into China, others were fought by rivaling foreign powers in the Chinese territory, and then there was the War of Resistance against Japanese Aggression which lasted more than a decade, when China faced Japan's all-round invasion and occupation. China lost almost all of these wars, with serious losses in every

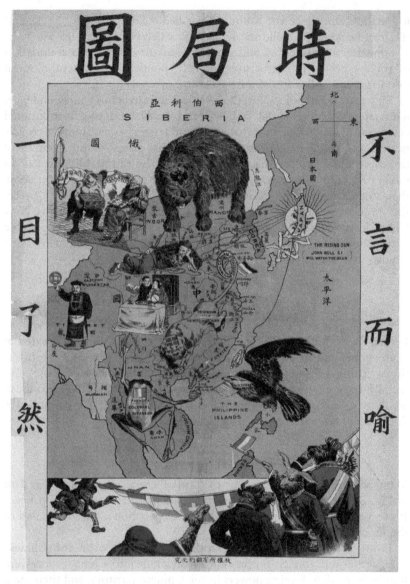

**Fig. 3.2** The situation in the far east (*Source* The cartoon was created by Xie Zuantai [Tse Tsan-tai, 1872–1937], and it was first published by the Journal of Furen Literary Society, in Hong Kong in July 1898)

battle. It only won the last one, the War of Resistance against Japanese Aggression, but it was a bitter victory—a victory which cost dearly to China.

*The Dictionary of China's Foreign Relations Treaties (1689–1949)* contains 1,356 treaties signed between China and foreign countries from 1689 to 1949, and the majority of them were signed after 1840.[5] As Professor Gao Fang of the Renmin University of China interpreted, all these treaties are not necessarily unequal, some are treaties signed between sovereign states, but among them are 745 unequal treaties signed with 22 countries, almost all of them the powers of the time. But one of them was signed with the Congo of Africa, and the treaty China signed with the Congo of Africa back then was also an unequal one, and one can imagine how poor and weak China had become.

Of the 745 unequal treaties, 411 were signed by the Qing government from 1841 to 1912, and 243 were signed by the Beiyang Government in its 15 years in power (1913–1927). In terms of annual average, the Beiyang Government signed more unequal treaties than the Qing government. Even under the Kuomintang's National Government, in the 22 years since it took power in 1928, 91 of the treaties it signed could be considered unequal. This was the case before 1949, in which China was subject to others' predation. So it has to rely on the Communist Party of China to get out of this plight thoroughly.

### *Internal Division*

Table 3.1 lists how many provinces were affected by wars in China each year throughout 1912–1930, and how many soldiers were involved in them, which were all civil wars. Whether from high school history class or from college Party history class, we would learn that internally China had always remained in a certain state of war since 1912, with serious internal division. First there was the Second Revolution in 1913 (also known as the War against Yuan Shikai, the 1913 War and the Battles of Jiangxi and Nanjing), followed by the National Protection War in 1915–1916. After Yuan Shikai's death in 1916, there were constant wars among warlords. After the Northern Expedition, the National Government in Nanjing once declared national unification, but the only places it could

---

[5] Zhu Huan and Wang Hengwei, *The Dictionary of China's Foreign Relations Treaties (1689–1949)* (Changchun: Jilin Education Press, 1994).

Table 3.1 Distribution of wars in China, 1912–1930

| Year | Provinces affected | Soldiers involved (10,000) | Year | Provinces affected | Soldiers involved (10,000) |
|---|---|---|---|---|---|
| 1912 | 1 | 64.9 | 1921 | 7 | 105.0 |
| 1913 | 6 | 57.2 | 1922 | 10 | 106.0 |
| 1914 | – | 45.7 | 1923 | 6 | 119.0 |
| 1915 | – | 52.0 | 1924 | 8 | 133.0 |
| 1916 | 9 | 70.0 | 1925 | 13 | 147.0 |
| 1917 | 5 | 69.0 | 1926 | 15 | 158.0 |
| 1918 | 9 | 85.0 | 1927 | 14 | 170.0 |
| 1919 | 2 | 91.4 | 1928 | 16 | 183.0 |
| 1920 | 7 | 90.0 | 1929 | 14 | – |
|  |  |  | 1930 | 10 | – |

Source Phil Billingsley, *Bandits in Republican China* (Stanford University Press, 1988), Table 3..1

really control were provinces surrounding Shanghai, and the rest of the country was still held by local warlords. In fact, China had never been truly unified before 1949. It has to rely on the Communist Party of China to realize national unification.

### Powerful Distributional Coalitions Politically

The "distributional coalition" is a concept put forward by Mancur Olson, a famous American economist, in his 1982 book *The Rise and Decline of Nations*. In his view, an over-stable polity tends to breed powerful "distributional coalitions," whose main goal is not to expand the overall social incomes and make the cake bigger, but to do everything possible to go for "rent seeking" and find ways to get a few more pieces from the overall social incomes available and cut a bigger portion from the existing cake for themselves, even at the cost of hindering the social progress. The existence and expansion of "distributional coalitions" could impede the social progress and reduce the country into recession step by step.[6]

Before the founding of New China, the biggest and most stubborn "distributional coalition" in China was the landlord class that oppressed the mass of poor peasants. How powerful was this political "distributional coalition"? Zhang Jingjiang (1876–1950), one of the Four Elders

[6] Mancur Olson, *The Rise and Decline of Nations* (Yale University Press, 1982).

of the Kuomintang who served as chairman of the Standing Committee of the Central Executive Committee of the Kuomintang and governor of Zhejiang Province among other senior titles, was honored by Chiang Kai-shek as his "revolutionary mentor." Zhang was a mastermind of the April 12 Coup in 1927, which led to the purge of Communists and leftists in the KMT and a massacre of them, known as the White Terror. From 1928 to 1929, the rural Zhejiang under Zhang's rule carried out a moderate land reform (with 25% of rent cut). It was just about one year after the KMT established the National Government in Nanjing in the wake of the Northern Expedition. Sun Yat-sen, the founding father of the Kuomintang, had advocated the equalization of land rights and land reform, which the KMT should be well aware of. The man who presided over the 25% rent cut in Zhejiang at the time was Xiao Zheng, a member of the Standing Committee of the KMT Zhejiang Provincial Headquarters, who also led the 1927 KMT purge in Zhejiang. The land reform was essential, but even the one as mild as that in Zhejiang met with fierce opposition, obstruction and destruction from the rural gentry group within the KMT. "They falsely accused the peasants who had obtained the rent-cut of being Communists and called the police to arrest them, or threatened to withdraw the rented land under the pretext of taking it back to farm on their own, or hired local hooligans and mobs with handsome pay to resist the rent reduction by force. In Tiantai, Sui'an, Wuyi and several other counties, county KMT instructors were beaten or even killed as they promoted the rent cut."[7] Under the pressure from the landlord class, Zhang Jingjiang soon gave up the 25% rent reduction, and labeled Xiao Zheng a "Communist" and ordered his arrest, with an attempt to put him to death. Xiao was spared the death only after Chen Lifu, a senior KMT official, pardoned him.[8]

Struck by what happened, a KMT member with vision wrote an article entitled *My Defeat, My Party's Defeat* in 1929, in which he wrote: "My defeat is not a frustration to the time, but to my Party colleagues. The land reform is not a policy position unique to the radicals, but should also be policy position shared by all us revolutionaries." The essayist was well aware that the land reform was very important, and he wrote, "Unless the

---

[7] Gao Lu, *On the Root Cause of the Failure of Land Reform When the KMT Ruled the Mainland, Historical Research in Anhui*, No. 3 (1998), pp. 81–82.

[8] Xiao Zheng, *The History of Land Administration in China* (Taipei, Taiwan: The Commercial Press Ltd., 1979), pp. 271–273.

ownership of the land is reformed, it is impossible to inspire the peasants' militant might to support the revolution, gather the labor force for the development of big industries, break the domination of clan power and patriarchy in villages, and shatter the local rural gentry groups within the Party. Unless the ownership of the land is reformed, we will be doomed on it sooner or later!"

It never occurred to this essayist that such a gentle and mild land reform policy should have died like that because of the internal subversion among the KMT colleagues, for which he was really heartbroken. He wrote, "I was beaten today, beaten by the agents of the local gentry within my Party. I feel bitter, as I'm afraid that years later my Party would fail due to the same reason, beaten by the radicals' land revolution!"[9] The radicals here refer not only to those within the KMT, but also to the radical land reform to be carried out by the Communist Party. He worried about "years later" in 1929, and 20 years later, his worries came true.

In 1948, the last year the National Government ruled the Chinese mainland, Chiang Kai-shek issued an order that wherever the Communist Party distributed land to the peasants, the Kuomintang should acknowledge the CPC's land reform achievements once it recovered the place, and four counties in northern parts of Jiangsu Province were designated as pilot areas for that. He understood that land reform was very important and wished to carry it on, but no sooner than the pilot areas were designated did the landlords protest it, and once they protested it, the pilot areas could not get run.[10]

It is clear that Chiang Kai-shek, like some people within the Kuomintang, was well aware that in China, it would be a must to carry out land reform in order to promote the social progress. Yet they just couldn't get the reform going, even if they made the determination and came up with methods. Once it came down to the stage of practice, the "distributional coalitions" dashed out and resisted desperately. The very "distributional coalitions" were within the KMT, involving its members in making troubles up and down, and once a real move was to be taken, problems would pop up.

---

[9] It has been circulated online, with the author unknown. It is said that the article was authored by Zhang Jingjiang, which should not be true.

[10] Zhu Zongzhen, *The KMT Response to CPC's Land Reform Policy After World War II*, Proceedings of International Symposium on Epoch-Making Historical Turn—China in 1949 (Chengdu: Sichuan People's Publishing House, 1999), pp. 208–234.

In February 1949, Chiang Kai-shek resigned from the presidency and claimed he would hold no more official titles at all. When he retreated to his hometown of Fenghua in Zhejiang Province, he found that the area had not changed much since he left decades before. In his diary, he reflected: "I bitterly feel that nothing in the countryside has been reformed from more than 40 years ago, and I bitterly feel how conservative, corrupt and selfish the Party and government have been in my 20 years of ruling, who have done nothing for the social and popular welfare. This is because the Party and government, the military and educational departments have focused only on holding official positions but did not pay attention to the implementation of the Three Principles of the People. From now on, all education should be based on the Principle of People's Livelihood Rights. It is not too late to mend the fence even after some of the sheep have been lost."[11] It sounds as if he understood better than anyone that inequality in rural land distribution was a persistent disease in China which must be addressed, but during the 40 years when he was away from his hometown, nothing had changed there. For this he had no other one to blame, because for at least 22 years out of the 40 years the country was ruled by the Nationalist Government of the Republic of China under his leadership. He mentioned in his diary that the Three Principles of the People were not implemented. We know that one of the Three Principles is the people's livelihood rights, which means socialism once put into English. Even if he had the mind for it, he did not have the force to do it, because the "distributional coalitions" within the KMT were too powerful. It has to rely on the Communist Party of China to smash the decadent "distributional coalitions."

### A Sheet of Loose Sand Socially

Before the founding of New China, the Chinese society was a sheet of loose sand. The phrase of "a sheet of loose sand" originated in Sun Yat-sen, which means that China is such a large country allegedly with a big population and a vast land area, but in many places the people were confined to the narrow family and geographical identification, loyal only to family or hometown, while ignoring China, or not knowing how important this recognition would be.

---

[11] Yang Tianshi, The Land Reform Initiated by Chiang Kai-shek and Chen Cheng in Taiwan, *Journal of Literature, History and Philosophy*, No. 6 (2018), p. 80.

Sun Yat-sen deplored this fact. According to some people's statistics, throughout his lifetime he publicly mentioned "a sheet of loose sand" at least 25 times, "a dish of loose sand" twice, and "loose sand" eight times. The first time he put it up was on April 10, 1912, and the last time was April 13, 1924, shortly before his death.

In January 1924, Sun Yat-sen began his series lectures on the Three Principles of the People, and the first one was on nationalism. He described the situation at the time this way: "Compared with other nations in the world, China has the largest population, being the largest as a nation in size, with a civilization of more than 4,000 years, and we should have run parallel with the countries in Europe and America. But people in China have only family and clan groups and do not worship the national spirit, so although there is a China combining 400 million people, it is really a sheet of loose sand, which has become the poorest and weakest country in the world today, ranking lowest internationally. 'We have become the fish and the meat while the rest of mankind is the carving knife and chopping board.' We are in the most dangerous state at this moment. If we do not care to advocate nationalism and integrate the 400 million people into an unified nation, I'm afraid China will go toward national doom and extinction."[12]

In less than 10 years, his worries became a nightmare that turned into reality. In 1931, the Japanese occupied the entire territory of northeast China and waged the all-round aggression into China in 1937. Japan's aggression seemed irresistible because the disunited Chinese society at that time was a sheet of loose sand. That's why the first of Sun Yat-sen's Three Principles of the People is nationalism, and he wished to integrate the disunited Chinese into such a union as the Chinese nation. However, the society then was a sheet of loose sand, and it also has to rely on the Communist Party of China to mobilize and organize the tens of millions of Chinese people.

In a society like a sheet of loose sand, bandits ran wild in China at the time. How rampant were the bandits? Following citations may offer some suggestions.

The first citation is from the February 10, 1924 issue of *Oriental Magazine*, when the KMT was yet to take power, and the Northern

---

[12] Sun Yat-sen, *The Three Principles of the People—Nationalism (January 1924), Complete Works of Sun Yat-sen*, Vol. 9 (Beijing: Chung Hwa Book Company, 1986), pp. 188–189.

Warlords were still dominant: "In China where warlord troops and bandits are dominant, the most eye-catching incidents to the nationals are of course within the range of warring disasters and banditry; and the most eye-catching figures are of course the leading warlords and chief bandits. But in the last three years, if ignoring everything but only taking sensationalism as the standard, then among all the happenings, the Zhili-Fengtian Warfare[13] was much overshadowed by the rampant bandits in Henan and the train hijacking in Lincheng of Shandong, in which the influential figures ... we'd better directly pick the bandit chief nicknamed Lao Yangren or Old Foreigner, and Sun Meiyao who was responsible for the Lincheng train hijacking, rather than randomly naming some warlord leaders like a certain general or marshal."[14]

The Old Foreigner mentioned here refers to Zhang Qing, a bandit ringleader in western Henan back then.[15] It is recorded that in November 1923, the Old Foreigner captured the town of Liguanqiao in Xichuan County of Henan, killing 4,326 local people and burning 26,000 houses.[16] And Zhang Qing was just one of bandit chiefs in the three volumes of *Records of Bandits in Modern China*, and the book itself just cited the most noteworthy of them, as minor rings of bandits were as many as cattle hair, who cannot be cited completely.

The second citation is from a booklet published in 1931, titled *China's Rural Economic Relations and Their Features*, authored by Zhu Qihua under the penname of Zhu Xinfan, who was a former member of the Communist Party of China in its early stage but had quit the Party when the booklet was published. Using statistics of the time, the book gave a detailed account of disasters in various provinces. What is noticeable is that apart from natural disasters such as droughts, floods, and locust plagues, there were manmade disasters of wars and banditry in nearly every province: "The conservative estimate of the bandit population was about 20 million in 1930. By and large, the turbulent Republic of China is

---

[13] Military conflicts between the Anglo-American backed warlords who controlled Hebei and Beijing and the Japanese backed warlords in Liaoning.—*Translator*.

[14] Nan Yan, *Old Foreigner Is Also Dead, Oriental Magazine* (February 10, 1924).

[15] Phil Billingsley, *Bandits in Republican China* (Stanford University Press, 1988), Chapter 3.

[16] Su Liao, *"Old Foreigner" Zhang Qing*, Editorial Board of Hebei Literary and Historical Materials, *Records of Bandits in Modern China*, Vol. 3 (Beijing: Qunzhong Publishing House, 1992), p. 262.

bandit-ridden everywhere and all the time."[17] China's population at the time was about 450 million or 500 million, with the adult male population absolutely no more than 200 million. If some 20 million adult men were bandits, that means one-tenth of them were bandits, which was indeed bandit-ridden everywhere. Even Shanghai, the largest metropolis in the Far East at the time, was no exception. It is commonly known that Shanghai is just the name of the city Shanghai, but in the past the word Shanghai in English also implied the meanings of kidnapping, coercion, abduction, and trafficking. Someone who got hurt could say "I got Shanghaied." People today perhaps have no idea that "Shanghai" could mean this, and "Shanghai" at that time had this implication just because of the mega environment it lived in.

The third citation is from *Bandits in Republican China* authored by Phil Billingsley, an American. In this book, the author made a very interesting observation: "By the end of the Resistance War the contrast between Communist-controlled areas and the rest of the country had become startling. In the government areas, predatory banditry actually increased during the war. Harsh military conscription quotas left farms without labor, heavy taxation and merciless grain requisitions caused widespread impoverishment and frequent famine, and half-starved soldiers deserted in huge numbers. Military suppression merely heightened the problem, and the most of the old 'white areas' the Communists inherited after 1945 were rife with predatory activity. In the Communist areas, on the other hand, reports both from the Communists and from travelers passing through had by 1944 ceased to mention banditry at all, even in the 'nest of plunderers' of northern Shaanxi."[18] Bandits were wiped out in the Communist-led areas, but they were on the rise in the KMT-controlled places, what a striking contrast! The eradication of banditry was a Chinese dream for decades and centuries. It still has to rely on the Communist Party of China to realize this dream. A few years after the founding of New China, the country was completely free from the plague of banditry.

---

[17] Zhu Xinfan, *China's Rural Economic Relations and Their Features* (Shanghai: Shanghai Publishing Company, 1931).

[18] Phil Billingsley, *Bandits in Republican China* (Stanford University Press, 1988), Chapter 9, p. 265.

## Backward and Poor Economy

The ten years throughout 1928–1937 was dubbed by some people as the "Golden Decade" under the Nationalist Government. Was there any economic growth during this period? Yes, of course. But it was really far from qualified to be called the "Golden Decade."

The economic structure at the time was very backward. In 1933, for example, the modern sectors consisting of manufacturing, mining and utilities accounted for only about 3.4% of the net GDP volume, and the overwhelming majority of the population was engaged in agriculture. Of the 500 million people, only about 2 million were engaged in industry. Russia before the October Revolution in 1917 was often regarded as a model of backwardness, but China in the period of the KMT Republic was even more backward. In the pre-October Revolution Russia, 53% of workers were employed in big factories with 500 workers and more; while in China, even in 1953, only 167 of the 150,000 private firms hired 500 workers or more.[19] Up to the founding of New China, big factories were few, while most of the surviving factories were merely small workshops.

According to the descriptions by those who always put "the model of the Republic of China" on their lips today, cities in the Republican period were simply wonderful, with many people living in extravagant mansions and driving luxury limos. How many people know that until 1956, the total volume of private capital investment across China amounted to just 2.2 billion yuan (about 900 million U.S. dollars),[20] of which 1.2 billion yuan was concentrated in Shanghai, with very little elsewhere? The 2.2 billion yuan investment was owned by 1.14 million people, with only 69 capitalists whose investment exceeded 1 million yuan nationwide, and only 1,439 capitalists whose investment exceeded 100,000 yuan. Compared with investors today, theirs was only tiny in terms of scope. China's utmost industry at that time was agriculture, the overwhelming majority of people lived in rural areas, and the industrial structure as a whole was very backward.

The economic growth was slow at the time. Figure 3.3 depicts the

---

[19] Unless otherwise illustrated, please consult Chapter 6 for sources of the data cited in this section.

[20] Premier Zhou Enlai's *Talk with William Hinton and His Family* (November 14, 1971), www.crt.com.cn/news2007/News/jryw/2008/930/08930151816782AJ7B ECEG96DFCI55I.html.

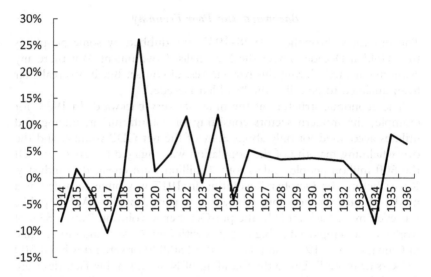

**Fig. 3.3** The economic growth rate, 1913–1936 (*Source* Liu Wei, Calculation of China's GDP, 1913–1936, *The Journal of Chinese Social and Economic History*, No. 3 [2008], pp. 90–98)

annual growth of China's GDP from 1913 to 1936. Throughout these years, the GDP growth was sometimes high, and sometimes low, at an average annual rate of 2.7%. If these 24 years are divided into the Beiyang Government period (1913–1927) and the Nanjing Nationalist Government period (1928–1936), this chart shows that the average annual GDP growth rate in the first period was 2.78%, and that in the latter period was 2.57%. In other words, in terms of the economic growth rate, the Nanjing Nationalist Government period could not even match the Beiyang Government period. In this case, the "Golden Decade" of the National Government was really unworthy of the name.

The outcome of economic backwardness was universal poverty. To the question of whether African countries or China was richer in 1950, I'm afraid that most people today would probably reply that African countries have always been poorer than China. But in fact, when the New China was just founded, China was even poorer than most of the African countries (see Fig. 3.4). China's GDP per capita at that time was only slightly higher than that of four African countries, and many other African countries led

3 GROUNDWORK: FROM OLD CHINA TO NEW CHINA  81

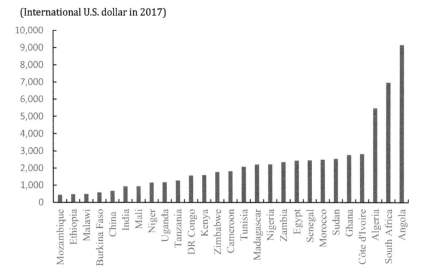

**Fig. 3.4** GDP per capita in China, India and African countries, 1950 (International U.S. dollar in 2017) (*Source* The Conference Board, Total Economy Database, April 2019, http://www.conference-board.org/data/economydatabase/TED1)

China by one fold, three folds, five folds, eight times or even more than a dozen times in GDP per capita. India's GDP per capita then was also higher than China's, by 40% more. We now often believe that sub-Saharan Africa represents poverty, but at that time we were even inferior to most sub-Saharan African countries. So Sun Yat-sen had good reason to say that China was the poorest and weakest country in the world. Very few people today know about this fact, we ourselves do not know, Africans do not know, neither do people in other parts of the world.

Seventy years have passed, China is no longer what it used to be. Figure 3.5 illustrates the GDP per capita in China and African countries in 2019. China's GDP per capita today has exceeded that of all the African countries and is twice that of India.

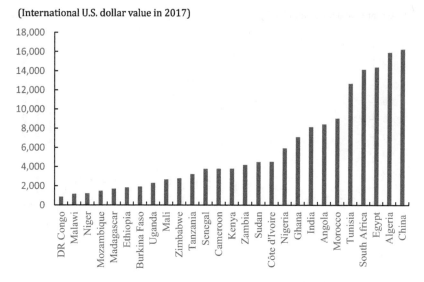

**Fig. 3.5** GDP per capita in China, India and African countries, 2019 (International U.S. dollar value in 2017) (*Source* The Conference Board, Total Economy Database, April 2019, http://www.conference-board.org/data/economydatabase/TED1)

## Universal Illiteracy

Some people seem exhilarated when talking about the education in the Republican period today, claiming how excellent the Republican education was, with academic masters here and there, as if the academic level of the higher learning institutions was exceptionally high. In fact, the overall academic level of the universities then could not match what we have today, whoever has read Qian Zhongshu's *Fortress Besieged* should know about it. More important, with or without academic masters, whether the universities were well or poorly run, it simply didn't matter much to the overwhelming majority of people.

In 1936, there were barely 100 universities nationwide. Prior to the founding of New China, there were only 89 universities and 52 colleges in China, with slightly more than 80,000 students. Today in Zhengzhou University alone there are 72,000 students, while the college students nationwide total 26.958 million. In the 38 years throughout 1912–1949, only a total of 218,000 people acquired college diplomas, barely 6,000 a year on average. How many people receive a college diploma every year now? More than 5 million students are graduated from universities each year over the past ten years, and in 2018 the figure topped 8.2 million. Therefore, putting the quality aside, the institutions of higher learning then and now are not in the same order of magnitude in terms of quantity and scale, and before the founding of New China, universities had nothing to do with the vast majority of people.

James Lee, Dean of the School of Humanities and Social Sciences of the Hong Kong University of Science and Technology, co-authored with mainland scholars *A Silent Revolution*, which analyzed the social origins of students enrolled by Peking University and Soochow University from 1949 to 2002. The book mentioned a survey conducted by the Nationalist Government in 1931, which indicated that most students able to attend colleges at that time were from families of landlords, rich farmers, merchants, academic scholars, politicians, doctors, military and police, and very few of them were from the working class and peasantry background.

In fact, in the Republican China, even secondary and primary education was a luxury, not to say college education. Primary education was divided into elementary (grades 1–4) and sub-secondary (grades 5–6) level, and those who had finished a six-year schooling were considered "minor intellectuals." The overwhelming majority of people were illiterate, who never had an elementary schooling, and many people could not even recognize or write their own names. For the national education level in 1949 please see Table 3.2.

Table 3.2 National education level in 1949

|  | *Graduates (10,000)* | *Percentage in population (%)* |
| --- | --- | --- |
| College graduates | 18.5 | 0 |
| High school graduates | 400 | 0.7 |
| Primary school graduates | 7 000 | 13 |
| Illiterate population | 43 200 | 80 |
| Total population | 54 000 | 100 |
| Average education level (years) |  | 1 |

Source *China's Three Major Strategies and Programs: Education, Talents and Sci-Tech* (2011), http://www.50forum.org.cn/home/article/detail/id/450.html

## Low Health Level

There are many indicators today that can be used to measure the health level. But when the health level is low, one indicator could be enough, and that is mortality. Table 3.3 lists the estimates of mortality rates during the Republic of China period since 1918. The first column in the table is a list of people who made the estimates, among them are Chinese, foreigners, officials, and academic scholars. Other columns list the targets of estimates, their corresponding timing, crude mortality rates, corresponding data from India, and comparisons with countries with data available at the time.

As Table 3.3 indicates, different estimates vary greatly, and China's annual mortality rate at the time ranged from 25 to 45 per thousand, or 25–45 deaths out of every 1,000 people, which was higher than the mortality rate in India at the time and the highest among all countries with data available. The high mortality rate before the founding of New China was mainly due to the high infant mortality rate, which was as high as 200 per thousand. Infant mortality is the death of young children under the age of one, and the infant mortality rate is the probability of deaths of children under one year of age per 1,000 live births. The infant mortality rate of 200 per thousand means among every 1,000 live births, 200 or one fifth would die short of one year of age. The infant mortality is one of the direct factors affecting the average life expectancy. Because of such a high infant mortality rate before the founding of New China, the average life expectancy of the country was then only about 35 years. This was the case before 1949.

It should be noted that from 1959 to 1961, China was hit by severe natural disasters coupled with mistakes of the Great Leap Forward, when the peak mortality rate in 1960 was around 25 per thousand. In other words, after the founding of the People's Republic of China, the peak mortality rate was just about the average level during the Republic of China period. After the three years of natural disasters, great famines that perplexed Chinese for thousands of years have never recurred. For details of the 1959–1961 "Great Famine" please consult the appendix to this book.

All in all, with analyses of all external, internal, political, social, economic, people's livelihood, education, and health affairs, a general conclusion can be made, that is, up to 1949, no matter it was under the

Table 3.3  Estimates of mortality rates before the founding of New China

| Targets | Corresponding timing | Crude mortality per thousand | India | Countries with data available | Sources |
|---|---|---|---|---|---|
| National population | 1916 | 30–40 | | | Chen Changheng, *On China's Population* (Shanghai: The Commercial Press, 1918), pp. 72–73 |
| National population | 1925 | About 30 | 31 | Almost the highest | Yan Xinzhe, *Outline of Rural Sociology* (Shanghai: Chung Hwa Book Company, 1934), pp. 95–96 |
| Rural population | 1929–1931 | >30 | 24.9 | The highest | Frank W. Notestein, A Demographic Study of 38,256 Rural Families in China, *The Milbank Memorial Fund Quarterly*, Vol. 16, No. 1 (January, 1938), pp. 57–79 |
| Rural population | 1929–1931 | 41.9 | | | George W. Barclay, Ansley J. Coale, Michael A. Stoto and T. James Trussell, A Reassessment of the Demography of Traditional Rural China, *Population Index*, Vol. 42, No. 4 (October, 1976), pp. 606–635 |
| National population | 1931 | 40–45 | 26 | The highest | Iida Shigesaburo, *A Study of China's Population* (Tokyo: Tachibana Publishing, 1934), pp. 108–109 |
| National population | 1934 | 33 | 23.6 | The highest | Ta Chen, Births, Deaths, and Marriages, *American Journal of Sociology*, Vol. 52, Supplement (1947), pp. 25–42 |

(continued)

**Table 3.3** (continued)

| Targets | Corresponding timing | Crude mortality per thousand | India | Countries with data available | Sources |
|---|---|---|---|---|---|
| Rural population | 1936 | 30 | 23.6 | The highest | Qiao Qiming, *China's Rural Socioeconomics* (Shanghai: The Commercial Press, 1945), pp 101–106 |
| National population | 1936 | 27.6 | | | Editorial Board of the China Economy Yearbook under the Industrial Department of the National Government, China Economy Yearbook, 1936, Part III (Shanghai, The Commercial Press, 1936), p. 33 |
| National population | 1938 | 28.2 | | | Interior Department of the National Government, Applied Statistics for Wartime Administration, Type 5, Statistics of Health, 1938, pp. 114–118 |
| National population | 1945–1949 | 36 | | | Mi Hong and Jiang Zhenghua, A Study and Assessment of Demographic Surveys and Materials in the Republic of China Period, *Population Research*, Vol. 20, No. 3 (1996), p. 49 |
| National population | 1910–1943 | 33.4 | | | United Nations, Future Population Estimates by Sex and Age, Report IV: The Population of Asia and the Far East, 1950–1980, *Population Studies, No. 31* (New York: United Nations, Dept. of Economic and Social Affairs, 1959), pp. 81–86 |

(continued)

Table 3.3 (continued)

| Targets | Corresponding timing | Crude mortality per thousand | India | Countries with data available | Sources |
|---|---|---|---|---|---|
| National population | 1912–1949 | 25–35 | | | Hou Yangfang, *The History of Chinese Population, Vol. 6, 1910–1953* (Shanghai: The Fudan University Press, 2001, pp. 384–390) |

Qing government, the Beiyang Government or the Nationalist Government, the least state capacity was absent in China, so it was impossible to become prosperous and strong on the basis of the Old China. It has to rely on the Communist Party of China to lay the foundation for the national reconstruction.

# From the Founding of New China up to 1978, Before the Reform and Opening-Up

Now let's have a look at the first three decades of the New China, we'd use the same analytical framework: the political, social and material infrastructure.

## *Political Infrastructure*

*Independence*
The most crucial in the political infrastructure is that China became completely independent, with which it already obtained the most basic state coercive capacity.

We can say that beginning from the late Qing Dynasty, it had been hard for China to be independent, and it was still hard for China to stand on its own by the Beiyang Government period, even during the "Golden Decade" of the Republic of China, it was also hard to be independent, and there was no independence to speak of when the country was faced with great crises like the Japanese invasion and civil war. China was a loser in every war with foreign forces.

The War to Resist U.S. Aggression and Aid Korea after the founding of New China was not a war we chose to fight, but the one imposed on us by imperialism, and we had to fight this war, and the outcome of that war was we won.

For a very, very long time in the United States, there were very few books on the Korean War although there were very many books on other wars, so the Korean War was known in the United States as "The Forgotten War," or "The Unknown War," or "The War Before Vietnam." They were unwilling to talk about it simply because this war was a disgrace to Americans. They would insist that they tied with China in the war, but how should they cover it up if they broke even with China? This was the first war that China won after the founding of New China, and it was also a landmark war, as thereafter China has lost no other war or suffered from any aggressions by foreign enemies.

As recorded in *Chronicles of Mao Zedong*, on October 25, 1950, the Chinese People's Volunteer fired the first shot of the War to Resist U.S. Aggression and Aid Korea. Two days later, Mao Zedong invited Wang Jifan, his teacher at the Hunan First Normal School, and Zhou Shizhao, his close friend and classmate at that school, to Zhongnanhai for a discussion on relations between politics and religion. Zhou Shizhao asked, How comes you the chairman has this leisure to talk about issues of religion and philosophy today? Isn't the situation in Korea very tense? Mao Zedong said, The tension in Korea has been escalating, and over the discussion on this issue we have been unable to sleep for many days. But today we can rest at ease, because our volunteer army has marched out of the border. Zhou Shizhao expressed his concerns that now the reactionary KMT rule was overthrown and the whole country was liberated, it was a golden opportunity to build a new country. The people of the whole country looked forward to peaceful construction, but the volunteer army went out to aid Korea, would this affect the peaceful construction? Mao Zedong replied, In case the U.S. imperialists did bring down the Democratic People's Republic of Korea, even though they would not cross the Yalu River, our northeast would live under its menace, then it is difficult to carry out peaceful construction. So we can only "strike with one punch to avoid a hundred ones."[21] Indeed, suppose we failed to respond to the fierce acts of aggression of the "No. 1 power in the world" but worried about the invasion of foreign enemies all day long, how could we concentrate on our construction?

*National Unification*
As populous as it used to be, why was China before 1949 unable to beat Japan but dared to challenge "the No.1 power in the world" when the New China was just established? This was because the Chinese strength was concentrated. This relates to another major accomplishment made in China after 1949—after a century of warring turmoil and upheavals since 1840, China finally achieved lasting unification.

It seems that current studies have not quite hit the nail on the head about this issue. People often take it for granted that when the Communist Party of China defeated the KMT in 1949, the unification came by naturally, as if it were an easy thing to do. In the historical perspective, it really did not come by so naturally.

We won't mention events too far away. Just have a look at what happened in 1927 when the Kuomintang completed the Northern Expedition and felt it could declare the reunification of China. Chiang Kai-shek's advisor Yang Yongtai worked out a policy to eliminate local warlords for him: the first step was to destroy their nests after transferring them away, by moving Yan Xishan from Shanxi, Feng Yuxiang from Henan, Li Zongren from Guangxi, Liu Xiang and Liu Wenhui, uncle and nephew of the Lius, from Sichuan, Li Jishen from Guangdong, and Zhang Xueliang from the northeast all to the central government with an official post conferred to them, so as to root them out from their old nests and strengthen the centralization; and the second step was to unify the armies throughout the country and dissolve the capital on which all kinds of forces depended for their survival and activities. But it wasn't long before these new warlords started fighting each other.

In the 1948 China, the Chinese People's Liberation Army under the command of the Communist Party had four major field army groups. Each of them had hundreds of thousands or even millions of soldiers from different regions whose commanders were more powerful than the KMT-era warlords. Why could all of them become a unified force after the

---

[21] Literature Research Office of the CPC Central Committee, *Chronicles of Mao Zedong, 1949–1976*, Vol. 1 (Beijing: Central Party Literature Press, 2013), pp. 226–231.

founding of New China in 1949? Further in-depth studies are required on this issue.

A combing of historical records will reveal that at the end of 1947 and early in 1948, when the prospect that the civil war might be coming to an end was slowly becoming clear, leaders of the Communist Party like Mao Zedong began to lay out their lines to create a sustained unification. In the beginning of 1948, Mao Zedong drafted a document for the CPC Central Committee on January 7, *On Setting Up a System of Reports*. As the first step to unification, a strict system of reports was required to set up. This step seemed irrelevant but actually it was significant. As the Northeast Bureau did not report to the Party Central Committee as required, Mao Zedong drafted three consecutive telegrams criticizing Lin Biao and the bureau.

In April 1948, a circular was issued on *Unifying All the Powers Possible and Necessary to Be Unified to the Central Committee*, requiring that "all the powers that are possible and necessary to be unified should be concentrated to the Central Committee." With a careful reading of Mao Zedong's works in sequence, we can see how Mao Zedong and the CPC Central Committee arranged step by step to unify all the field armies under the leadership of one central government after the founding of New China. China did not realize a complete and solid unification until about 1956. It was by then when Mao Zedong had the confidence to say in February 1957, "Never before has our country been as united as it is today. . . The days of national disunity and chaos which the people detested are gone, never to return."[22] It required tremendous efforts to make the layout from 1948 to 1956, including a series of careful military, economic, financial, and administrative arrangements, before a solid state of national unification could be created.

Therefore, the national unification was hard-won. Without the guarantee of the political infrastructure of national unification, it would be totally impossible to achieve the ensuing rapid economic growth and prosperity. In Mao Zedong's words: "The unification of the country, the unity of the people and the unity of our various nationalities – these are the basic guarantees for the sure triumph of our cause."[23]

---

[22] Mao Zedong: *On the Correct Handling of Contradictions Among the People* (February 27, 1957), *Selected Works of Mao Tse-tung*, Vol. V (Peking: Foreign Languages Press, 1965), p. 384.

[23] Ibid.

*Social Stability*
The previous section mentioned the rampant banditry in the Republican China period. In fact, the New China was still not free of the banditry trouble in its early years. Bandits caused great damage to the rural areas, especially in mountainous areas of Guangxi, Yunnan and Guizhou, and in many places of western Hubei and Hunan, bandits were also rampant. I am afraid many of our young people may have no idea that at its early stage and even years after the founding of New China, civil servants in many places had to carry guns with them for self-defense while on business trips because of banditry problems. From 1950 to 1953, the People's Liberation Army mobilized 1.5 million troops from more than 140 divisions of 39 armies to annihilate bandit forces and special KMT agents of more than 2.6 million, including those who surrendered. The move ended the history of bandits plaguing in China for long and wild, effectively secured the people's peaceful living and work, and stabilized the social order.

Perhaps some people feel that it was only easy to eliminate bandits. But just think about the fact that the banditry that plagued the Old China in the previous decades, centuries or even millenniums was wiped out in a matter of a few years after the New China was founded, one should realize how remarkable the accomplishment was. It laid a solid social infrastructure for the New China to grow prosperous and strong.

The New China's social stability was also manifested in the very low crime rate. Figure 3.6 depicts the trajectory of crime rates over the first three decades of the New China. The chart shows that in the early years of the New China, the crime rate remained relatively high, at 90 per 100,000 people. At that time, the hostile political forces were not reconciled to their failure and carried out all kinds of sabotage. "In the six months from spring to autumn 1950, nearly 40,000 cadres and activists were killed by counter-revolutionary elements." Meanwhile, "rogues, robbers, ruffians and prostitutes were active around, disturbing the social order." Afterward, crime rates declined rapidly. From the early 1950s to the late 1970s, crime rates fluctuated largely within the range from 30 to 60 per 100,000 people. The statistics during the 1966–1972 period were absent, because the institutions of public security, prosecution and court were smashed at the height of the Cultural Revolution and systematic data were not collected.

Is the ratio 30–60 per 100,000 high or low? A comparison with other countries makes it clear: the crime rate in the United States during the

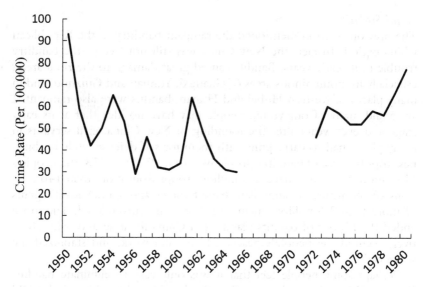

**Fig. 3.6** Crime rates in the first three decades (*Source* Cited from Xiaogang Deng and Ann Cordilla, To Get Rich is Glorious: Rising Expectations, Declining Control, and Escalating Crime in Contemporary China, *International Journal of Offender Therapy and Comparative Criminology*, Vol. 43, No. 2 [June 1999], p. 212)

same time span was 2,000–6,000 per 100,000 people, and in Britain it was 1,000–2,000 per 100,000 people. The crime rate in the New China was not a bit lower, but much lower.

*Eradication of "Distributional Coalitions"*
Another important part of the political infrastructure is the eradication of "distributional coalitions."

Olson was mentioned earlier, and his book about "distributional coalitions" *The Rise and Decline of Nations* was published in 1982. He died in 1998, and in his book posthumously published in 2000, *Power and Prosperity*, Olson compared China more directly with the Soviet Union, arguing that one of the reasons for China's success in reform and opening-up was that the various movements in the previous three decades had destructed the rigid system, decimated nearly all those "well-entrenched coteries of administrators" in the country, thus cleared the way for the later reform and opening-up.[24]

Olsen's subtext was that a "movement" every once in a while should be a good thing, which could smash any elite interest groups and be conducive to subsequent economic growth. It was in this sense that Susan Rose-Ackerman, a professor at Yale Law School, asked an interesting question: "Was Mancur a Maoist?"[25]

## Social Infrastructure

The social infrastructure of prosperity and strength is also very important, which covers three respects: social equity, people's health, and universal education.

### Social Equity

One of the most important reasons for the Communist Party of China to be able to triumph and rule the country was the land reform. The land reform benefitted the overwhelming majority of peasants in China, which ensured the utmost equality in land distribution. In recent years, some people have tried every means to negate the land reform in some media. Indeed, the land reform does not conform to the theory of property rights and the principle of market economy, but who has stipulated that a revolution must follow the theory of property rights and the principle of market economy under the capitalist system? When a society is extremely unequal, the principle of revolution precedes these two things.

For thousands of years, the unequal distribution of land has been an important cause of social instability and economic stagnation. The previous citation of *My Defeat, My Party's Defeat* indicates that even

---

[24] Mancur Olson, *Power and Prosperity* (New York: Basic Books, 2000), pp. 166–168.

[25] Susan Rose-Ackerman, *Was Mancur a Maoist? An Essay on Kleptocracy and Political Stability*, Economics and Politics, Vol. 15 (2003), pp 135–162. What Susan Rose-Ackerman did not know is that early in the 1990s, Chinese scholar Zhang Yuyan had several talks with Olson. Olson was keenly interested in what Mao Zendong said about "capitalist-roaders within the Communist Party," "bombard the headquarters," "mix sand and cut the ground from under one's feet," and "from great chaos to great order." When he learned that Mao Zedong held the Cultural Revolution should be staged "once in seven or eight years," he was so excited that he stood up from his sofa. Please consult Zhang Yuyan, *Learn Political Economics from Professor Olson, ABC of Economics* (Fuzhou: Fujian People's Publishing House, 2005), p. 145.

people with vision in the Kuomintang were clear that nothing could be done without land reform. How important is the land reform? Through comparisons among countries, one could see that countries with or without (or without thorough-going) land reform vary in the later economic performance—Those with the land reform register a rapid economic growth later, while those without it show a slow growth. The contrast between China and India is a case in point.[26]

In 1997, two World Bank researchers published a report examining the relationship between inequality and economic growth. They found that in countries where the unequal distribution of land was serious in 1960, the economic growth in the next 30 years thereafter was often slow; while in countries where the average annual GDP growth rate was higher than 4.5% from 1960 to 1992, the land was fairly equally distributed without exception. A chart in the report clearly depicts the negative correlation between unequal distribution of land and subsequent economic growth.[27] More than 10 years later, one of the authors of the above-mentioned report drew Fig. 3.7 with bigger database. Readers with a little understanding of statistics are able to decipher the meaning of this diagram.

We can even say that the achievements of the New China's land reform continued to function until the reform and opening up. As we all know, the rural reform began with the family contract responsibility system. Imagine, if the land before its division to the household was not collectively owned, if there were still landlords and rich peasants who owned large amounts of land while others had little or no land, if the land allocation was seriously unequal, then I'm afraid the production contract to the household could only lead to the intensification of class conflicts, it would be impossible to achieve any results. If the rural reform could not start, how could there be the follow-up urban reform? It is known to many that the land distribution was quite fair when the production contracting to households was carried out at the end of the 1970s and in the beginning of the 1980s, and some even criticized that it was too equal, because the distribution was equal not only in terms of the area of land plots, but also in terms of the land quality, resulting in the fragmentation of land in

---

[26] Lin Chun, *A Discussion on the Land Reform Once More: Revelations from China and India*, Open Times, 2016 (2).

[27] Klaus Deininger and Lyn Squire, *Economic Growth and Income Inequality: Reexamining the Links*, Finance & Development, Vol. 34, No. 1 (March 1997), pp. 38–41.

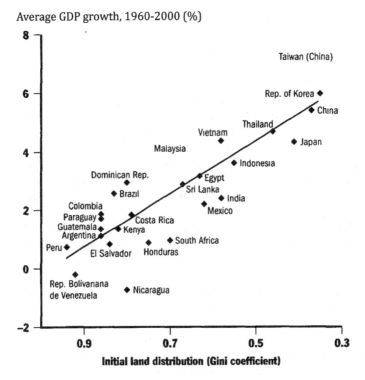

**Fig. 3.7** Initial land distribution and economic growth (Average GDP growth, 1960–2000 [%]) (*Source* Klaus Deininger, *Land Policies for Growth and Poverty Reduction: A World Bank Policy Research Report* [Washington, DC: World Bank, 2003], p. 18)

several pieces to each household, rather than a stretch of land as a whole. Without such equity, the rural reform could not be advanced. Therefore, the land reform in the early years of New China is a great cause for the Chinese society to achieve equality to a great extent.

Another point in China's social equity before the reform and opening-up was the fairly equal distribution of income.

One indicator for equality or inequality is the Gini coefficient. The coefficient can take any values between 0 and 1. A coefficient of 0 indicates a perfectly equal distribution of income within a population, and a coefficient of 1 represents a perfect inequality in income distribution. Of course the two extremes won't occur in the real world. In general, a Gini coefficient at and below 0.2 indicates absolute equality, a one between 0.2 and 0.3 means the distribution is fairly equal, a figure between 0.3 and 0.4 means relatively reasonable, while a coefficient between 0.4 and 0.5 indicates that the income gap is wide, and a value higher than that indicates a very unequal distribution. Up to the early 1980s, China's Gini coefficient was less than 0.3, and its inequality was well below the world average.[28] In the first few years of reform and opening-up, a very important thing the Chinese economic theoretical circles did was criticize the "big pot of rice," saying that it was too equal at that time, and that it was necessary to create a little inequality artificially in order to produce material incentives. This evidenced from a negative side that the society was very equal at the time.

And the equal distribution of income plays a very important role in the subsequent economic development. Similar to the role of equitable distribution of land, the equal distribution of income also plays a positive role in promoting the subsequent economic growth, while inequality often leads to economic stagnation.[29] A large number of comparative empirical studies have evidenced a negative correlation between income inequality and subsequent economic growth: The greater the inequality in a country, the slower the subsequent economic growth; but in places where the income distribution is more equal, a rapid economic growth is often witnessed subsequently. Francois Bourguignon, former chief economist of the World Bank, sighed: If one interprets literally the potentially negative relationship between inequality and growth, then the redistribution policy to guarantee that growth is pro-poor would lead progressively to faster growth.[30] These studies show that equity and efficiency are not necessarily contradictory; on the contrary, the more equitable a society is, the faster, rather than slower, its subsequent economic growth is likely to be; efficiency and equity can be synchronic, and equity is conducive

---

[28] World Bank, *China 2020: Development Challenges in the New Century* (Washington, DC: World Bank, 1997), p. 8.

[29] Alberto Alesina and Dani Rodrik, *Distribution, Political Conflict and Economic Growth*, in Alex Cukierman, Zvi Hercowitz, and Leonardo Leiderman, eds. *Political Economy, Growth and Business Cycles* (Cambridge: MIT Press, 1992), pp. 23–50.

[30] Francois Bourguignon, The Poverty-Growth-Inequality Triangle, Indian Council for Research on International Economic Relations Working Paper, No. 125 (2004), http://www.icrierorg/pdf/wp125.pdf, p. 17.

to accelerating the economic growth. Therefore, an equal social structure is one of the institutional guarantees for China's rapid economic growth after the reform and opening up.

*People's Health*
The second respect of social infrastructure is people's health. In the Mao Zedong era, what was emphasized was the public consumption, not individual consumption, especially in the fields of health care and education.[31] At that time, China was still very poor, but nearly all the urban and rural populations enjoyed some form of basic health care, which greatly improved the health indicators of the Chinese people. Then the equity and accessibility of China's health services were highly recommended by the United Nations Children's Fund, the World Health Organization and the World Bank.[32] China's low-cost but extensive-coverage mode of health care was also promoted at the Almaty Conference in 1978 as a model of primary health services by the World Health Organization.[33]

One indicator to measure a country's health level is the average life expectancy of its population.

---

[31] Mao Zedong said, "If a socialist society does not undertake collective efforts, what kind of socialism is there in the end?" He criticized the *Textbook on Political Economy* of the Soviet Union, saying in too many places this book speaks only of individual consumption and not of social consumption, such as public welfare, culture, health, etc. This is one-sided. Please consult *Mao Zedong's Notes and Talks on Socialist Political Economy* (Abridged), pp. 282–284.

[32] For instance, the World Bank in its *World Development Report 1993: Investing in Health* called the New China's health care guarantee was "a unique achievement for a low-income developing country." (Washington, DC: World Bank, 1993), p. 111; Kenneth W. Newell, *Health by the People* (Geneva: World Health Organization, 1975); World Health Organization, United Nations Children's Fund, *Meeting Basic Health Needs in Developing Countries: Alternative Approaches* (Geneva: World Health Organization, 1975); Matthias Stielfel and W. F. Wertheim, *Production, Equality and Participation in Rural China* (London: Zed Press for the United Nations Research Institute for Social Development, 1983).

[33] World Health Organization, *Primary Health Care: Report of the International Conference on Primary Health Care* (Geneva: WHO, 1978); Dean T. Jamison, et al., *China, the Health Sector* (Washington, DC: World Bank, 1984); BMJ Editorial Board, *Primary Health Care Led NHS: Learning from Developing Countries*, BMJ, October 7, 1995 (April 19, 2009), http://bmj.bmjjournals.com/cgi/content/full/311/7010/891; Therese Hesketh and Wei Xing Zhu, *Health in China: From Mao to Market Reform*, BMJ, May 24, 1997 (April 19, 2009), http://bmj.bmjjourns.com/cgi/content/full/314/7093/1543.

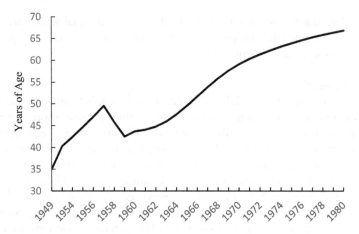

**Fig. 3.8** Average life expectancy of New China, 1949–1980 (*Source* Data of 1953–1959 are from Judith Banister, *China: Changing Population* [Stanford: Stanford University Press, 1987], p. 116, Table 4.18; data after 1960 are from World Bank: World Development Indicators 1960–2018, http://databank.worldbank.org/data.download/WDI_excel.zip)

China's average life expectancy in 1949 was around 35 years.[34] Of course, not everyone lived for 35 years only. But the infant mortality rate was so high at the time that many people died young, driving the average down. Young people today may not know but those in their 60s and 70s perhaps remember that when they were young, some families could only have the third, fifth, and seventh of the children alive, while the rest had unfortunately died at an early age. So the average life expectancy was very low then.

After the founding of New China, the average life expectancy of the people increased rapidly except in a few years (see Fig. 3.8). By the beginning of reform and opening up, China's average life expectancy had reached 68 years, nearly double that of 1949.

The people's health level was improved and the mortality rate declined, which in itself is an important demand in people's livelihood. Equally important, the rapid improvement of the people's health also brought a

---

[34] National Health and Family Planning Commission, *China Health and Family Planning Statistics Yearbook 2015* (Beijing: Peking Union Medical College Press, 2015), p. 233.

demographic dividend to China in advance. A comparison of the demographic transition data from China and India shows that the crude birth rate of both countries in 1950 was about 45 per thousand, with the crude death rate at about 25 per thousand. But the demographic transition curves from 1950 to 1980 varied between the two countries: In China, both the birth rate and mortality rate declined rapidly, to 20 per thousand and 5 per thousand, respectively; while in India the birth rate and mortality rate went down slowly, to 35 per thousand and 12 per thousand, respectively. This resulted in a time difference in the occurrence of the so-called demographic dividend between the two countries.

Figure 3.9 reveals that China's demographic dividend occurred in the late 1970s. In nearly 40 years thereafter the percentage of people aged 0–14 in the population shrank, while the percentage of people aged 15–59 increased, and the percentage of people aged 60 and over remained at a low level. In other words, during this period, the working-age population accounted for a big ratio of the total population with a relatively low dependency rate, creating favorable demographic conditions for the economic development. China's reform and opening-up coincided with this window period of demographic dividend which has sustained to this day.

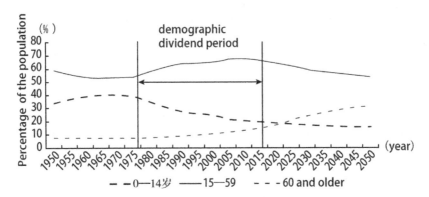

Fig. 3.9 Window period of China's demographic transition (*Source* Misbah T. Choudhry and J. Paul Elhorst, Demographic Transition and Economic Growth in China,*India and Pakistan, Economic Systems*, Vol. 34, No. 2 [2010], pp. 218–236)

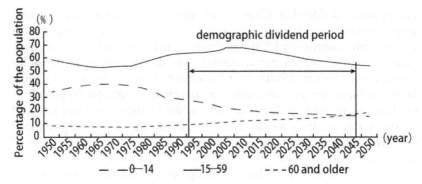

**Fig. 3.10** Window period of India's demographic transition (Source: Misbah T. Choudhry and J. Paul Elhorst, Demographic Transition and Economic Growth in China, India and Pakistan, *Economic Systems*, Vol. 34, No. 2 [2010], pp. 218–236)

The window period of demographic dividend in India came about 25 years late, and it did not occur until the mid-1990s (see Fig. 3.10). Its starting point was at about the same time with China, but India lagged behind China by one generation in terms of the occurrence of window period of demographic dividend. This is exactly because China's mortality rate began to plunge by big margins rapidly in the early years of the New China.

The window period of demographic dividend is conducive to economic growth. China and India have varied in their economic performance over the past 70 years, with the former outpacing the latter by far. There are many reasons for this difference, but one point that is undeniable is that the rapid improvement of the health level and the rapid decline in mortality rate enabled us to enjoy the benefits of the demographic dividend in advance.

*Universal Education*

The improvement of health level is very important, so is the improvement and popularization of education. For a country's economic growth, especially in the early stages, what weighs more is not the higher learning or a focus on elite education, but the basic education, namely, the primary and secondary including junior and senior high school education, because

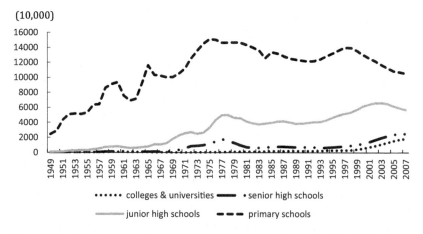

**Fig. 3.11** Student enrollments at various types of schools (10,000) (*Source* Department of Comprehensive Statistics of National Bureau of Statistics, *China Compendium of Statistics 1949–2008*, Statistical Database of Chinese Economic Social Development)

if most people in a country are illiterate or have little schooling, it is hard for the country to register a sustained economic development.

In the Mao Zedong era, education at all levels, especially the basic education, developed at high speed. The enrolment rate of school-age children grew rapidly from about 20% in 1949 to 97.1% in 1976, while the adult illiteracy rate fell drastically from 80% in 1949 to 22.8% in 1982.[35] Figure 3.11 depicts the student enrollments in various types of schools at all levels from 1949 to 2006. The chart shows that the basic education developed rapidly in the first 30 years. The primary school student enrollment increased six folds, that of the junior high schools increased 55 folds, and of the senior high schools grew 62 folds. Even the student enrollment of institutions of higher learning, which were once suspended during the Cultural Revolution, increased many times over that in 1949.[36] What is noticeable is, Fig. 3.11 also indicates that in the

---

[35] Lai Li, Zhang Zhupeng and Xie Guodong, *China's Adult Illiteracy Reduced by Nearly 100 Million in Ten Years, with Big Cut in Female Illiteracy*, China Education Newspaper (August 1, 2007).

[36] Department of Comprehensive Statistics of National Bureau of Statistics, ed., *China Compendium of Statistics 1949–1999* (Beijing: China Statistics Press, 1999), pp. 81–82.

late period of the Cultural Revolution and before the start of reform and opening up, the student enrollments of primary, junior, and senior high schools in China all reached a peak. In the early stage of the reform and opening-up, these enrollments all went down instead of going up. It took another 20 years or even longer to see another peak. Some people may be critical that the education level back then was not high enough, as some high schools were so-called "capping" or irregularly upgraded schools, namely, some primary schools were upgraded to junior high schools, and junior high schools to senior high schools. But at least a large number of people received basic education, and education was greatly popularized.

Allowing people to live healthy and well educated is not only the purpose of the development, but health and knowledge also improve the quality of human capital, which in turn stimulates the economic growth.[37] Without the foundation laid in the first three decades, where did China's high-quality labor force who made great contributions to the reform and opening-up come from? Giovanni Arrighi, an Italian economist, sociologist, and renowned world-systems thinker, used a wealth of comparative data to prove that the secret of China's rapid economic growth after reform and opening-up lies in that its labor force is of better quality than that in other developing countries.[38]

## *Material Infrastructure*

In addition to the political and social infrastructures, prosperity and strength also require a certain material infrastructure.

### *Based on Agriculture*

The first point of the material infrastructure is to take agriculture as the basis, which was a slogan put forward after the founding of New China.

In the early stage of New China, China was an agricultural country, and its economic development was based on agriculture to solve the problem of feeding the population first. To this end, China did many things then, the most prominent could be summarized in three matters: the first was the large-scale construction of water conservancy projects, the second was

---

[37] Please consult the New Growth Theory represented by Paul Romer and Robert Lucas.

[38] Giovanni Arrighi, *Adam Smith in Beijing: Lineages of the Twenty-First Century* (London: Verso, 2007).

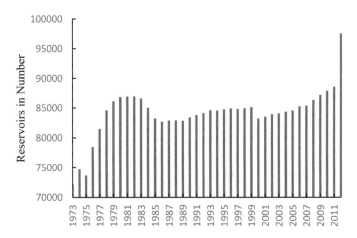

Fig. 3.12 Number of reservoirs in China (*Source* Ministry of Water Resources of the People's Republic of China, *China's Water Conservancy Statistics Yearbook*, Statistical Database of Chinese Economic and Social Development)

to carry out effective irrigation, and the third was to increase the grain output.

**Large-Scale Construction of Water Conservancy Projects**

At a time when mechanized sci-tech means were at a relatively low level, agriculture was an industry at the mercy of the elements. Without water, no problem could be solved, and to solve the water problem, it is necessary to build water conservancy facilities, including reservoirs. Before the founding of New China, there were very few reservoirs in the country, only around 1,200 nationwide. After the founding of New China, a large-scale construction of water conservancy projects was launched, with many reservoirs built. By the beginning of reform and opening up, some 87,000 reservoirs were already built up in China. For a long period of time after the reform and opening up, the number of reservoirs in China did not grow, but fell, because some reservoirs were abandoned and could no longer work due to long disrepair. Therefore, one pole of the total number of reservoirs was reached in the early days of reform and opening up, and the other pole was not reached until the last 10 years or so (see Fig. 3.12).

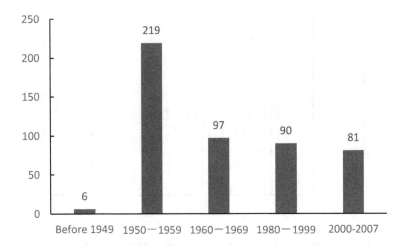

**Fig. 3.13** Construction of large reservoirs 1949–2007 (*Source* Ministry of Water Resources of the People's Republic of China, *China's Water Conservancy Statistics Yearbook*, Statistical Database of Chinese Economic and Social Development)

If we focus on the large reservoirs only, then up to the new wave of reservoir construction surging in 2008, there were 493 of them nationwide, of which only 6 were built before 1949, nearly half (219) were built in the 1950s, and 97 were built in the 1960s and 1970s. A total of 171 reservoirs were built in the 28 years from 1980 to 2007 (see Fig. 3.13). In other words, the overwhelming majority of large reservoirs were built before the reform and opening up (including Danjiangkou, Gezhouba and Liujiaxia reservoirs and hydropower stations). It was really remarkable to build so many reservoirs before the reform and opening up. When the country renewed the efforts to build reservoirs in the last 10 years or so, the spending was often at hundreds of billions and trillions yuan (in 2011–2013 alone, the cumulative investment from the water conservancy fund of the government finance amounted to 1,326.1 billion yuan). In contrast, the construction of reservoirs in the old days mainly depended on manpower, on self-reliance, on enthusiastic zeal and highly effective organization, while the capital investment from the state was not much.

*Effective Irrigation*

Now let's have a look at the capital construction of farmland. To irrigate the farmland, it won't do to just have the reservoirs built up, as the water won't automatically flow into the fields. Work must be done to dig ditches, build irrigation facilities and level the land, which is known as the capital construction of farmland. One indicator to measure the level of capital construction of farmland is the area of effective irrigation. Figure 3.14 shows that the effective irrigation area in 1952 was about 20,000,000 hectares, and by the beginning of reform and opening up, it had reached about 45,000,000 hectares, more than double the 1952 figure. The 1950s and the latter period of the Cultural Revolution were two periods witnessing rapid growth of effective irrigation areas. In the first decade after the family contract responsibility system was implemented, the effective irrigation area not only did not grow, but even decreased a little bit, because once the opportunity to mobilize a large number of manpower was lost, the capital construction of farmland became a very labor-consuming and costly project. It was only after 1990 that the area of effective irrigation began to expand again.

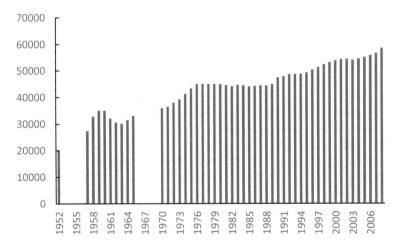

**Fig. 3.14** Area of effective irrigation (unit: 1,000 hectares) (*Source* Ministry of Water Resources of the People's Republic of China, *China's Water Conservancy Statistics Yearbook*, Statistical Database of Chinese Economic and Social Development)

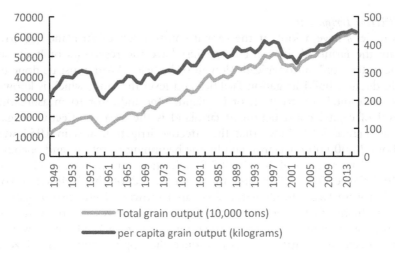

**Fig. 3.15** Total grain output and per capita grain output (*Source* Department of Comprehensive Statistics of National Bureau of Statistics, *China Compendium of Statistics 1949–2008*, *China Statistics Yearbook*, Statistical Database of Chinese Economic Social Development)

**Increase Grain Output**

Water conservancy construction and capital construction of farmland promoted agricultural production, which was directly reflected in the changes in total grain output and per capita grain output. As indicated in Fig. 3.15, after the founding of New China, the total grain output increased first, but then declined after the Great Leap Forward, and thereafter maintained a sustained growth by and large, which was followed by a downslide in the late 1990s, and the growth picked up again, which has sustained for about 10 consecutive years by now. The per capita grain output is a similar case, the real growth was not very quick after the reform and opening up and after the family contract responsibility system was implemented, but it was a relatively flat growth with some fluctuations, which might be some distance away from many people's imagination. In the early days of the reform and opening up, the grain problem or the problem of feeding the Chinese people was largely solved already.

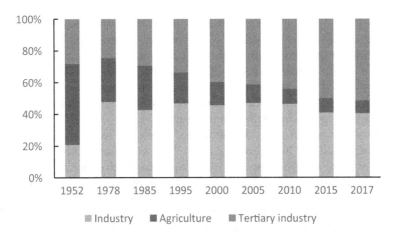

Fig. 3.16 Shares of industry, agriculture and tertiary industry in national economy (*Source* Department of Comprehensive Statistics of National Bureau of Statistics, *China Compendium of Statistics 1949–2008*, *China Statistics Yearbook*, Statistical Database of Chinese Economic Social Development)

*Led by Industry*

Old China was a typical agricultural country. On the eve of the founding of New China, Mao Zedong described China's economic structure as such: "China still has scattered and individual agriculture and handicrafts, constituting about 90 percent of her entire economy; this is backward, this is not very different from ancient times -- about 90 percent of our economic life remains the same as in ancient times."[39] If the Chinese economy was to take off, there must be an industrial revolution in the first place. When did China's industrial revolution take place? Fig. 3.16 gives an unequivocal answer: It by and large took place during the first three decades of the New China. In 1952, agriculture accounted for more than 50% of GDP and industry for about 20% of the national economy; and by 1978, the share of agriculture had shrunk to below 30%, and the tertiary industry had also dropped to less than 25%, but the share of industry in the national economy had risen sharply to about 48%. This indicates

---

[39] Mao Zedong, Mao Zedong: *Report to the Second Plenary Session of the Seventh Central Committee of the Communist Party of China* (March 5, 1949), *Selected Works of Mao Tse-tung*, Vol. IV (Peking, China: Foreign Languages Press, 1961), p. 367.

that the development of national economy in the first three decades was indeed led by industry. After the reform and opening up, the industry maintained this status in the national economy for a long time, that is, it accounted for more than 45% of the national economy. If an industrial revolution did take place in China, it must have taken place in the first three decades, transforming the entire economic structure of the country from agriculture to industrial manufacturing.

With a review of many key industrial products, such as crucial basic industrial products like steel, pig iron, crude coal, and electricity generation, we will find that the growth of their production in the first three decades actually outpaced that in the following 30 years. Only the growth rate of light industrial products was faster in the next 30 years than in the first 30 years (see Table 3.4). Therefore, the point that the industrial revolution took place in the first three decades is based on facts of many aspects.

*Establishment of Integrated Industrial System*
In the first three decades of the New China, three systems were also established throughout the country, all of which were crucial and essential to the subsequent development.

The first is an independent and relatively integrated industrial system covering nearly all sectors, including the heavy industry, national defense industry, and high-tech industry, such as electronics, aviation, aerospace, and nuclear energy. The establishment of such a system was a dream of the Chinese leaders at the time. Mao Zedong pointed out in March 1949, before the New China was founded, that "the problem of establishing an independent and integrated industrial system will remain unsolved and it will be finally solved only when our country has greatly developed economically and changed from a backward agricultural into an advanced industrial country."[40] His dream was largely realized by the end of the 1970s. In the early 1980s, the World Bank released a three-volume research report on China's economy, noting that few developing countries were able to establish a fairly integrated industrial system, but China made it.[41]

The second is the national economic system. In 1963, at a meeting of the Drafting Committee on the Industrial Development, Zhou Enlai

[40] Ibid., p. 369.

[41] World Bank, *China: Socialist Economic Development, Vol. 1, The Economy, Statistical System, and Basic Data* (Washington, DC: World Bank, 1983), p. 12.

Table 3.4 Growth rate of major industrial products

| Products | 1949 | 1952 | 1978 | 2008 | 1978/1952 | 2008/1978 |
|---|---|---|---|---|---|---|
| Crude steel (10,000 tons) | 15.8 | 135.0 | 3178.0 | 50092.0 | 23.5 | 15.8 |
| Pig iron (10,000 tons) | 25.2 | 193.0 | 3479.0 | 47067.0 | 18.0 | 13.5 |
| Coal (100 million tons) | 0.3 | 0.7 | 6.2 | 27.9 | 9.3 | 4.5 |
| Electricity | 43.1 | 72.6 | 2565.5 | 32560.0 | 35.3 | 12.7 |
| Crude petroleum oil (10,000 tons) | 12.1 | 43.6 | 10405.0 | 18973.0 | 238.6 | 1.8 |
| Cement (10,000 tons) | 66.0 | 286.0 | 6524.0 | 140000.0 | 22.8 | 21.5 |
| Plain glass (10,000 weight cases) | 108.0 | 213.0 | 1784.0 | 55185.0 | 8.4 | 30.9 |
| Sulfuric acid (10,000 tons) | 4.0 | 19.0 | 661.0 | 5132.7 | 34.8 | 7.8 |
| Soda ash (10,000 tons) | 8.8 | 19.2 | 132.9 | 1881.3 | 6.9 | 14.2 |
| Caustic soda (10,000 tons) | 1.5 | 7.9 | 164.0 | 1852.1 | 20.8 | 11.3 |
| Chemical fertilizers (10 000 tons) | 2.7 | 18.1 | 869.3 | 6012.7 | 48.0 | 6.9 |
| Metal-cutting machine tools (10,000 units) | 1582.0 | 13734.0 | 183200.0 | 500000.0 | 13.3 | 2.7 |
| Motor vehicles (10,000 sets) | – | – | 14.9 | 934.6 | | 62.7 |
| Cloth (100 million m) | 18.9 | 38.3 | 110.3 | 710.0 | 2.9 | 6.4 |
| Cigarettes (100 million pieces) | 160.0 | 265.0 | 1182 | 22199 | 7.4 | 18.8 |
| Refined sugar (10,000 tons) | 19.9 | 45.1 | 227.0 | 1449 | 5.0 | 6.4 |
| Salt (10,000 tons) | 298.5 | 494.5 | 1953.0 | 5953.0 | 3.9 | 3.0 |

Source Department of Comprehensive Statistics of National Bureau of Statistics, *China Compendium of Statistics 1949–2008*, *China Statistics Yearbook*, Statistical Database of Chinese Economic Social Development

pointed out, "The term of 'industrial country' is incomplete, and it is more complete to say to establish an independent national economic system than just saying an independent industrial system. The Soviet Union focused on industrialization only, but neglected agriculture." What is the national economic system? He explained, "The national economic system includes not only industry, but also agriculture, commerce, science and technology, culture and education, and national defense." As the Premier, Zhou Enlai set the target at the time to "basically establish an independent national economic system through the three-year transition from 1963 to 1965 and the 10-year program for 1966–1975."[42] Such a system was already established before the reform and opening up.

The third is the transportation system consisting of railways, highways, inland shipping, and civil aviation. The system at that time certainly could not match what we have today, but at least under the circumstances China had established such a transportation system.

The three systems built a solid material infrastructure for the modernization drive in the next 40 years. Many people assume that the economy did not grow much in the first three decades, and the economic growth occurred mainly in the later four decades. But a review of the statistics indicates that this is not the case. The economic growth in the first 30 years indeed shows a curve of steep ups and downs, yet the average annual growth rate was not low, at nearly 8% (see Fig. 3.17). An average annual growth rate exceeding 7.5% for a period of 30 years looks fairly good in the perspective of today, which could almost look down on any other economy globe wide. Of course, the pace of economic growth after the reform and opening-up even more quickened, and the growth curve has become relatively smoother since the early 1990s, without violent fluctuations, indicating a better ability to exercise macroeconomic control.

## Summary

What is the relationship between the New China's first 30 years and following 40 years? I'm afraid some people may not be willing to accept our own assessment, so let's see how two of the outside watchers have to say about it.

---

[42] Zhou Enlai, *Principles and Targets of the Development of National Economy, Selected Articles on Economy by Zhou Enlai* (Beijing: Central Party Literature Press, 1993), p. 519.

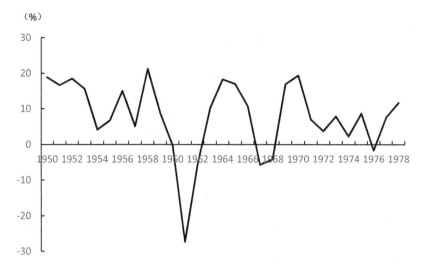

Fig. 3.17 Economic growth rate of China, 1950–1978 (%) (*Note* The figures for 1949–1952 refer to the growth rate of national income, and those since 1953 refer to the growth rate of GDP. *Source* Department of Comprehensive Statistics of National Bureau of Statistics, *China Compendium of Statistics 1949–2008*, *China Statistics Yearbook*, Statistical Database of Chinese Economic Social Development)

The first is Amartya Sen, an internationally renowned Indian scholar and Nobel Laureate in Economics. In fact, some of his statements are often quoted by some people in China, the mostly cited is his criticisms of the famine in China after the Great Leap Forward. Here's what he said about the New China's first three decades: "Living conditions in China at the time of the political transformation in 1949 were probably not radically different from those in India at that time. Both countries were among the poorest in the world and had high levels of mortality, undernutrition, and illiteracy."[43] He forgot to mention that China's case was actually even worse than India's. He went on to say that before the Chinese reforms, "the relative standings" of India

---

[43] Jean Dreze and Amartya Sen, India: *Economic Development and Social Opportunity* (Clarendon Press, 1996), p. 58.

and China "had been decisively established"[44] because China's achievements in the fields of elementary education and primary health care were dramatic and remarkable. Therefore, he concluded, China's "accomplishments relating to education, health care, land reforms, and social change in the pre-reform period made significantly positive contributions to the achievements of the post-reform period. This is so in terms of their role not only in sustaining a high life expectancy and related achievements, but also in providing firm support for economic expansion based on market reforms."[45] It should be pointed out that here he ignores China's political achievements, such as political independence and self-reliance, national unification and social stability mentioned before.

This is an Indian scholar's view. He also criticized some of China's policies, but when he made the general calculation, he could see that without the foundation laid in the previous three decades, it would be hard to achieve the glory of the next few decades, because no high-rises could be built on the sand beach.

The second scholar may be less known in the mainland. His name is Y. Y. Kueh, a senior economist in Hong Kong who is in his late 80s and has long retired. He produced two books, one in English and the other in Chinese. The title of the English book is interesting—the chief title may not be so attractive, *China's New Industrialization Strategy,* but the subtitle is striking—*Was Chairman Mao Really Necessary?*[46] Anyone familiar with the studies of socialist political economy probably knows that as early as 1964, Alec Nove, a British expert on Soviet economy, published a book titled *Was Stalin Really Necessary?*[47] Since then, many books and papers discussing the economic history of the Soviet Union have used similar expressions. Y. Y. Kueh also used this expression, but his answer was unambiguously positive—without the foundation laid in the Mao Zedong era, there would be no way to make the following achievements.

Another book in Chinese by Y. Y. Kueh is simply entitled *Not to Forget Mao Zedong: An Alternative View from a Hong Kong Economist,*

---

[44] Ibid., p. 65.

[45] Ibid., p. 58.

[46] Y. Y. Kueh, *China's New Industrialization Strategy: Was Chairman Mao Really Necessary?* (Cheltenham: Edward Elgar, 2008).

[47] Alec Nove, *Was Stalin Really Necessary?* (New York: Routledge, 2011).

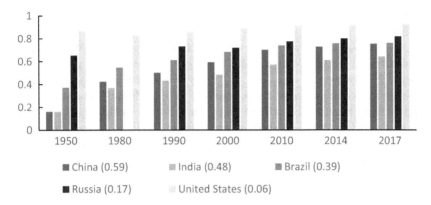

**Fig. 3.18** Comparison of HDI in five countries (*Note* The figure after each country is related to the added value of its HDI from 1950 to 2014. *Source* Data of 1950 are from Nicolas Crafts, *Globalization and Growth in the Twentieth Century*, IMF Working Paper No. 00/44 (March 1, 2000); data of 1980–2014 are from the UNDP webpage http://hdrstats.undp.org/indicators/14.html)

which was published by Oxford University Press in 2010.[48] Before that he published an essay in the journal of the New Asia College of the Chinese University of Hong Kong, also entitled *Not to Forget Mao Zedong*. In this article, he mentioned that China's thriving national strength today is due to "Mao's Path" and "Deng's Road." Mao Zedong's Path and Deng Xiaoping's Road are not two ways separated at a fork, but one carrying on the other; and they cannot be cut away, without "Mao's Path" there would be no "Deng's Road," or "Deng's Road" will get to a dead end. Only by following the path opened by Mao Zedong can we walk on the road pointed out by Deng Xiaoping.[49]

In recent years, the United Nations Development Program's Human Development Index (HDI) is often used as a composite indicator of the level of social development in various countries. As indicated in Fig. 3.18, in 1950, China's HDI was one of the lowest in the world, at only 0.16, on

---

[48] Y. Y. Kueh, *Not to Forget Mao Zedong: An Alternative View from a Hong Kong Economist* (Hong Kong: Oxford University Press, 2010).

[49] Y. Y. Kueh, *Not to Forget Mao Zedong: On Mao's Historical Role in Reform and Opening-up and in China's Peaceful Rise*, *New Asia Life*, Vol. 36, No. 5 (2009).

par with India. By 1975, China's HDI had raised to 0.53, far surpassing India's 0.42.

A high-rise towering into the sky starts from the ground, with the most critical point being to lay a solid foundation. The first 30 years of the New China were the years of foundation laying. It is arduous and time-consuming to lay a foundation, and the people doing the foundation-laying work may not be able to enjoy the comfort of the high-rise right away. But without the solid foundation laid in the first 30 years, it would be impossible to see the magnificent group of high-rises towering from the ground in the latter four decades.

CHAPTER 4

# Exploration: From New China's First 30 Years to Next 40 Years

"A specter is haunting Europe – the specter of communism," wrote Marx and Engels. When the *Manifesto of the Communist Party* was first published in German in 1848, the Communist League was still a secretive organization whose influence was confined to Britain, France, and other European countries. Half a century later, by the end of the nineteenth century, this "specter" appeared on the vast land of China. Another half a century later, by the mid-twentieth century, socialism had become a torrent sweeping the globe. The Communist Party of China, with communism as its ultimate goal, had seized the national power at this time, and the Chinese nation had begun to move toward socialism vigorously. One more half a century later, by the end of the twentieth century, once flourishing socialism had fallen to an unprecedented low ebb, and some people even boldly asserted that the history had ended as capitalism was the only way out for human society, and there was no any other choice.

For more than 30 years, there has been an uproar of "market fundamentalism." Its promises are simple and tempting: as long as the property rights are privatized, the decision-making power handed over to private business owners seeking to maximize their own interests, and government interventions are minimized, the "invisible hand" of the market will continuously create inexhaustible wealth, and the "trickle-down effect" will ultimately benefit everyone.

However, just as Karl Polanyi pointed out, "the idea of a self-adjusting market implied a stark utopia. Such an institution could not exist for any length of time without annihilating the human and natural substance of society; it would have physically destroyed man and transformed his surroundings into a wilderness."[1] At the end of the twentieth century, while the "Washington Consensus" was spreading wantonly, the divide between the poor and rich countries and between the poor and rich people grew wider and wider, compelling the Latin American countries with the widest poor-rich divide to turn left one after another. By the beginning of the twenty-first century, the impairment of "market fundamentalism" had become so obvious that even some of its conscientious believers could bear it no more. In a column article on October 16, 2007, Mr. Lam Shan-muk, the founder of *Hong Kong Economic Journal* who had written political and economic commentaries for more than 30 years, began to reflect on himself for "being a blind believer of the free market while young... seeking economic benefits in everything, and holding that the sole function of the enterprise is to pursue maximized profits for its shareholders."[2] On April 28, 2008, he published another column article, reiterating his "regret for confidently upholding the capitalist system in the past" because he had seen "too many inequitable means and frauds, and some theories that were thought to be 'universally applicable' cannot stand the test of reality." He earnestly pleaded that "China should not go capitalism thoroughly" and believed that "socialism can indeed maintain social equity."[3]

Shortly thereafter, a severe economic crisis spread from the United States to the world, and large corporations, as symbols of capitalism, faced the ill fate of bankruptcy one by one. From Iceland to Ireland, from Australia to Japan, from the United Kingdom to the United States, governments were forced to lend a hand and nationalize banks, insurance companies, and automobile manufacturers under government trusteeship. No wonder a *Newsweek* cover story exclaimed: "We're all socialists now!"[4]

---

[1] Karl Polanyi, *The Great Transformation* (Boston: Beacon Press, 2001), pp. 1–2.

[2] Lam Shan-muk, More Humanity from Enterprises to Build a Harmonious Society, *HK Economic Journal* (October 16, 2007).

[3] Lam Shan-muk, Expectations on the Rich and China in Food Crisis, *HK Economic Journal* (April 28, 2008).

[4] Jon Meacharm and Evan Thomas, *We Are All Socialists Now*, *Newsweek* (February 16, 2009).

"When the seas are in turmoil, heroes are on their mettle." Although the world economic crisis also dragged down its economy, China's economic growth rate in 2008 was as high as 9.65%, and its average annual growth rate remained at 9.86% over the next three years. Despite a slowdown since 2012, China's economy has maintained a positive growth and become the locomotive of the global economic recovery. In such a striking contrast, it is of extraordinary significance to re-examine the direction and path China has adhered to.

## EXPLORATIONS IN THE 30 YEARS PRE-REFORM

On the eve of its founding, Mao Zedong pointed out the future direction for the New China, that is, "to achieve socialism and communism through the people's republic, to abolish classes and enter a world of Great Harmony."[5] In his view, only socialism could save China, so that "ours will no longer be a nation subject to insult and humiliation," and "we have stood up."[6]

After the founding of New China, Mao Zedong repeatedly stressed that our general objective was to "build a great socialist country," "to accomplish socialist industrialization and the socialist transformation and mechanization of agriculture"[7] and to "change China's backwardness in economy, science and culture, and rapidly reach the advanced level of the world."[8] In 1957, he summed up this objective clearly as "to build a socialist state with modern industry, modern agriculture and modern science and culture."[9] In order to achieve this goal, it was necessary to

---

[5] Mao Zedong, *On the People's Democratic Dictatorship—In Commemoration of the Twenty-Eighth Anniversary of the Communist Party of China* (June 30, 1949), *Selected Works of Mao Tse-tung*, Vol. IV (Peking, China: Foreign Languages Press, 1961), p. 414.

[6] Mao Zedong, *The Chinese People Have Stood Up!* (September 21, 1949), *Selected Works of Mao Tse-tung*, Vol. V (Peking: Foreign Languages Press, 1977), p. 17.

[7] Mao Zedong, *On the Draft Constitution of the People's Republic of China* (June 14, 1954), *Selected Works of Mao Tse-tung*, Vol. V (Peking: Foreign Languages Press, 1977), pp. 145–146.

[8] Mao Zedong, *Socialist Revolution Aims at Liberating the Productive Forces* (January 25, 1956), *Works of Mao Zedong*, Vol. VII (Beijing: People's Publishing House, 1999), p. 2.

[9] Mao Zedong, *Speech at the Chinese Communist Party's National Conference on Propaganda Work* (March 12, 1957), *Selected Works of Mao Tse-tung*, Vol. V (Peking: Foreign Languages Press, 1977), p. 423.

develop productive forces vigorously first. China was still poor and backward in the 1950s, when Mao Zedong attached great importance to the development of productive forces. He pointed out: "Han Yu[10] wrote an article titled *Eliminating Poverty*, and we should write our article of eliminating poverty. It will take decades for China to eliminate the devilish poverty."[11] He also reminded the people all over the country, "What can we make at present? We can make tables and chairs, teacups and teapots, we can grow grain and grind it into flour, and we can also make paper. But we can't make a single motor car, plane, tank or tractor."[12] He held that it would take three five-year plans, or about 15 years, to lay a foundation, and it would take about 50 years, or ten five-year plans, to build a prosperous and strong China. Of course, as a socialist country, "this is the common prosperity and common strength, shared by everyone, including the landlord class as well."[13]

Since the direction was clear, after the rehabilitation period of the national economy from 1949 to 1952, Mao Zedong began to explore a path of socialist transformation suitable to China's reality.

### Explorations in Ownerships

As Table 4.1 indicates, in 1952, the public economy's share in the national economy was not big, with the non-public economy still dominating. The socialist transformation was to turn the individual ownership of agriculture and handicrafts into the socialist collective ownership, and turn the capitalist ownership of private industry and commerce into the socialist ownership by the whole people, so that the public ownership of the means of production should become China's only economic basis.

---

[10] Han Yu (768-824) was a prose writer, poet and government official of the Tang Dynasty (618-907) known as "comparable in stature to Dante, Shakespeare or Goethe" for his influence on the Chinese literary tradition.—*Translator.*

[11] Mao Zedong, *Talk with Leaders of National Democratic Construction Association and All-China Federation of Industry and Commerce* (December 7, 1956), *Works of Mao Zedong*, Vol. VII (Beijing: People's Publishing House, 1999), pp. 167–173.

[12] Mao Zedong, *On the Draft Constitution of the People's Republic of China* (June 14, 1954), *Selected Works of Mao Tse-tung*, Vol. V (Peking: Foreign Languages Press, 1977), p. 146.

[13] Mao Zedong, *Speech at the Forum on Socialist Transformation of Capitalist Industry and Commerce* (October 29, 1955), *Works of Mao Zedong*, Vol. VI (Beijing: People's Publishing House, 1999), pp. 495–496.

Table 4.1  Shares of different economic sectors (Unit: %)

| Year | State-owned economy | Public economic | | Non-public economy | |
|---|---|---|---|---|---|
| | | Collective economy | | Capitalist economy | Individual economy |
| | | Cooperative economy | Public–private joint management | | |
| 1952 | 19.1 | 1.5 | 0.7 | 6.9 | 71.8 |
| 1957 | 33.2 | 56.4 | 7.6 | 0.0 | 2.8 |
| 1978 | 56.2 | 42.9 | | | 0.9 |
| | | 33.9 | | | |
| | | 8.0 | | | |
| 1997 | 41.9 | | | 24.2 | |
| | | | | 61.0 | |
| 2005 | 31.0 | | | | |

*Source* National Bureau of Statistics, *Great Decade*, Beijing: People's Publishing House, 1959: 36; China News Agency, *Changes in Figures: State-owned Economy Stable in Status, Non-public Economy's Share Grows* (October 7, 2002); Li Chengrui, *A Preliminary Calculation of Shares of China's Public and Private Economy, Exploration*, No. 4 (2006)

To Mao Zedong, the objective of the socialist transformation was also to liberate the productive forces,[14] because only by solving the problem of ownership first could productive forces be liberated so as to blaze a trail for the development of new productive forces, and create social conditions for the great development of industrial and agricultural production.[15] In four years, China largely completed the socialist transformation in 1956. By 1957, the public economy had jumped to dominate the national economy.

Many people believe that China's socialist construction before 1957 was a complete copy of the Soviet model. This is a sheer misunderstanding. Mao Zedong was sober at this point by saying, "We are followers of Marxism, but we do not blindly copy Soviet experience. To

---

[14] Mao Zedong, *Socialist Revolution Aims at Liberating Productive Forces* (January 25, 1956), *Works of Mao Zedong*, Vol. VII (Beijing: People's Publishing House, 1999), p. 1.

[15] Mao Zedong, *Transition of the Revolution and the Party's General Line in the Transition Period* (December 1953), *Works of Mao Zedong*, Vol. VI (Beijing: People's Publishing House, 1999), p. 316.

do so would be a mistake. Our industrial and commercial transformation and agricultural cooperation differ with the Soviets'."[16] The Soviet Union adopted a policy of depriving the capitalists and even attempted to physically annihilate them, while China converted the private capital into public capital through redemptions by paying a fixed rate of interest in an attempt to transform capitalists into self-supported socialist workers. The Soviet Union collectivized its agriculture by commandist and arbitrary means and adopted a policy of thoroughly depriving and exterminating the rich peasants with violence, while China's agricultural cooperation was not that mandatory as in the Soviet Union, and the process was not that chaotic. The outcomes were certainly different: "In the several years after agricultural cooperation, their production decreased, but our production has increased."[17]

Although Mao Zedong wished to realize the whole people ownership of all the means of production someday, he made particular emphasis that the boundary between the two forms of socialist ownership, the public ownership by the whole people and the collective ownership, "must be clearly defined and not be confused." "The Soviet Union declared that the land is owned by the state, and we did not declare the state ownership of the land. Stalin did not sell tractors and other means of production to collective farms, we sold them to people's communes. So in our country, labor, land, and other means of production all belong to collective farmers and are collectively owned by people's communes. So the products are also collectively owned."[18] The Soviet Union declared

[16] Mao Zedong, *Instructions at a Discussion Meeting Attended by Some of the Delegates to the Second Session of the First Committee of the All-China Federation of Industrial and Commerce* (December 8, 1956), *Works of Mao Zedong*, Vol. VII (Paris: Foreign Languages Press, 2020), p. 371. Talking with a foreign guest in 1979, Deng Xiaoping also made it clear that "the socialist road of China is not the same as that of the Soviet Union. They were different from each other from the very start in that China's socialism had its own characteristics ever since the founding of the People's Republic." See *Selected Works of Deng Xiaoping*, Vol. II (Beijing: Foreign Languages Press, 1995), p. 238.

[17] Mao Zedong, *Instructions at a Discussion Meeting Attended by Some of the Delegates to the Second Session of the First Committee of the All-China Federation of Industrial and Commerce* (December 8, 1956), *Works of Mao Zedong*, Vol. VII (Paris: Foreign Languages Press, 2020), p. 371.

[18] Mao Zedong, *Talks on Stalin's Economic Problems of Socialism in the USSR* (November 9–10, 1958), Association of National History of the People's Republic of China, *Mao Zedong's Notes and Talks on the Socialist Political Economy* (Abridged) (Beijing: Association of National History of the People's Republic of China, 2000), p. 29.

that it had built up socialism in 1936. The next year, its state ownership had accounted for 99.97% of the total industrial sectors, and state-owned farming claimed 79.2% of the fixed funds in agriculture. Thereafter in the Soviet Union, this high concentration of the means of production to the state was never weakened but had been constantly enhanced.[19] But China was different. After 1956, although state-owned enterprises played an increasingly important role in the national economy, it was not until 1978 that their share in the national economy just turned more than half (see Table 4.1). In the same year, state-owned enterprises accounted for 77.16% of the total industrial output value, and collective enterprises for 22.14%. But in terms of the number of industrial enterprises, there were only 83,700 state-owned enterprises, against as many as 264,700 collective enterprises.[20] In addition, during the Great Leap Forward and latter period of the Cultural Revolution, China also vigorously fostered a new type of enterprises, namely, commune and brigade enterprises (renamed as township enterprises after 1984). In 1978, there were 1.52 million commune-brigade enterprises nationwide, with a total social output value of 49.1 billion yuan, accounting for 7.17% of national total social output value and 24.10% of the total rural social output value. These enterprises employed a total of 28.27 million workers, accounting for 9.2% of the total rural labor force.[21] Such a large number of enterprises made it difficult to implement the strict central plans in all types of enterprises throughout the country.

### *Explorations in Planning Economy*

If there were areas where the Soviet experience was copied before 1956, they were mainly in areas where the five-year plans were formulated. It was an extremely arduous task to advance the socialist industrialization on a large scale, involving a series of complex issues. Mao Zedong confessed: "... we have a set of experiences, general and specific policies and methods on politics, military affairs, and class struggle; but as for

---

[19] Zhang Jianqin, *A Comparative Study of Traditional Planning Economic System in China and the Soviet Union* (Wuhan: Hubei People's Publish House, 2004), pp. 131–133.

[20] Liu Guoguang and Dong Zhikai, Changes in Ownership Structure in the 50 Years of New China, *Contemporary China History Studies*, No. 5–6 (1999), pp. 27–28.

[21] Wang Fenglin, Origin and Development of China's Commune-Brigade Enterprises, *China Rural Survey*, No. 4 (1983).

socialist construction we have never done any in the past, and we still have no experience."[22] Since leaders in the early days of the New China were not familiar with socialist construction, the only way out was to learn from the "Big Brother" of socialism, the Soviet Union. China was set to formulate its first Five-Year Plan (1953–1957) in early 1951, making a total of five tries throughout the process. During the formulation, Mao Zedong dispatched a government delegation headed by Zhou Enlai, with Chen Yun and Li Fuchun as deputy heads, to the Soviet Union for study. Zhou Enlai and Chen Yun spent more than a month in the Soviet Union to conduct surveys, while Li Fuchun led the delegation to stay in the Soviet Union for as long as 10 months.[23]

Although the first Five-Year Plan was a product of learning from the Soviet Union, it was not a Soviet-style plan. Chen Yun, who presided over the formulation of the plan, said frankly: "The part concerning the state sector is based on sound calculations. Some other parts, however, are by no means reliable, such as those concerning agriculture, handicraft industry, and capitalist industry and commerce, which together make up a very large portion of the economy. These parts can only serve as 'indirect planning.' Because we have little experience in this area and because there are not enough data to rely on, the figures in these sections of the plan can only be tentative and subject to revision in practice."[24] And this plan, with its formulation beginning in 1953, was not officially adopted until July 1955 by the Second Session of the First National People's Congress. On November 9 and December 19 of the same year, the State Council issued orders requiring all localities and departments to implement the plan. By 1956, the targets set in the plan were already realized ahead of the schedule.[25] This indicates that it was not as rigid as the Soviet plan.

Mao Zedong, with his philosophy on the universality of contradictions and his observation of the first Five-Year Plan, did not believe in the strict

[22] Mao Zedong, *Talk at an Enlarged Working Conference Convened by the Central Committee of the Communist Party of China* (January 30, 1962), Extracted from *Peking Review*, No. 27, July 7, 1978.

[23] Yuan Baohua, Days and Nights of Negotiations in the Soviet Union, *Contemporary China History Studies*, No. 1 (1996), pp. 16–26.

[24] Chen Yun, *Explanatory Remarks on the First Five-Year Plan* (June 30, 1954), *Selected Works of Chen Yun*, Vol. II (Beijing: Foreign Languages Press, 1997), p. 244.

[25] Liu Suinian, *National Economy During the First Five-Year Plan Period* (Harbin: Heilongjiang People's Publishing House, 1984), pp. 17–19.

Soviet-style plans. When reading the Soviet Union's *Textbook of Political Economy*, he was most critical of Chapter 26, *The Laws Governing Planned and Proportional Development of the National Economy*. He held that "the existence of imbalance and disproportion will urge us to gain a better understanding of the objective laws. Even something trifle goes wrong, some people would feel it to be so disastrous that they shed bitter tears as if both their parents are dead, and this is not the attitude a materialist should have at all."[26] In this case, "plans often have to be revised because new imbalances appear."[27] Mao Zedong emphasized more on a holistic and balanced approach, "walking on two legs," and achieving several "concurrent promotions" (namely, concurrent promotions of industry and agriculture, of light and heavy industry, of large and medium-sized enterprises, of foreign and indigenous methods, and of central and local industries) in the premise of giving priority to the heavy industry. Under this guiding ideology, the second Five-Year Plan (1958–1962) was formulated, but no sooner was its implementation begun than it was upset by the Great Leap Forward on the heels of its formulation. The following major disproportions in the national economy created a situation in which the economic construction was unable to continue as originally planned, and the eight-character policy of "adjustment, consolidation, rounding out and upgrading" in the national economy had to be carried out in 1961. This adjustment sustained until 1965, delaying the start of the third Five-Year Plan until 1966.[28]

But the third Five-Year Plan (1966–1970) began when the Cultural Revolution broke out. In the first three years of the Cultural Revolution, it was hard to do any planning work. Although an annual plan was drawn up in 1967, it could not be circulated to the grass-roots level, so there was simply no plan made at all in 1968; and in 1969, with the exception of crude oil production, nearly all the other planned targets were not completed.[29]

---

[26] Association of National History of the People's Republic of China, *Mao Zedong's Notes and Talks on the Socialist Political Economy* (Abridged) (Beijing: Association of National History of the People's Republic of China, 2000), p. 73.

[27] Ibid., 71.

[28] Cong Jin, *Years of Zig-Zag Development* (Zhengzhou: Henan People's Publishing House, 1989), pp. 455–456.

[29] Wang Nianyi, *Years of Great Turmoil* (Zhengzhou: Henan People's Publishing House, 1989), pp. 356–361.

The fourth Five-Year Plan (1971–1975) targets were not issued until April 1971. By 1973, Mao Zedong held that the planning work was still not on the right track and that it was necessary to draw up the *Outline of the Fourth Five-Year National Economic Plan* (Draft Revision).[30]

All this indicates that the planning system in the Mao Zedong era was far less rigid than the Soviet system, and was always in the change. The cost of this changeableness, however, was the drastic fluctuations of economic growth.

A more prominent difference between China's planning system and that of the Soviet Union was the degree of its power decentralization. Mao was never in favor of the highly centralized Soviet-style planning system, mainly because he hated bureaucracy from his bones. As early as 1953, he opposed the practice that local industries handed over too much profit upward because it meant that "there will be too little investment left to expand re-production, which is not conducive to bringing the local initiative into play."[31] In his talk *On the Ten Major Relationships* in 1956, he repeatedly stressed that "it is far better to have the initiatives from both the central and local authorities than from one source alone. We must not follow the example of the Soviet Union in concentrating everything in the hands of the central authorities, shackling the local authorities and denying them the right to independent action."[32] In February 1958, he put forward an idea of "republic with powerless monarch" in China.[33] After that, whenever he had the chance, he would push hard for decentralization. The first time was in 1957–1958, when the central government massively decentralized financial, planning, and corporate management powers.[34] After 1961, due to the setback of the Great Leap Forward, China resumed centralized and unified management

---

[30] Shi Yun and Li Danhui, *The "Continuing Revolution" Hard to Be Continued: From Criticizing Lin to Criticizing Deng* (Hong Kong: Chinese University of Hong Kong Press, 2008), pp. 243–247.

[31] Mao Zedong, *Speech at the Enlarged Meeting of the Political Bureau of the CPC Central Committee* (July 29, 1953), *Works of Mao Zedong* (Beijing: People's Publishing House, 1999), p. 289.

[32] Mao Zedong, *On the Ten Major Relationships* (April 25, 2956), *Selected Works of Mao Tse-tung*, Vol. V (Peking: Foreign Languages Press, 1977), p. 292.

[33] Bo Yibo, *Recollections of Some Important Decisions and Events*, Vol. II (Beijing: CPC Central Party School Press, 1993), pp. 796–797.

[34] Hu Angang, *The Political and Economic History of China (1949–1976)* (Beijing: Tsinghua University Press, 2008), pp. 247–251.

of the national economy and regained the powers decentralized a few years before under the auspices of Liu Shaoqi and Chen Yun. For Mao Zedong, however, to take the powers back was only a stopgap measure to get rid of the temporary difficulties. Once the economy turned for the better, he was determined to break the Soviet-style central planning system again. In March 1966, Mao Zedong once again put forward the slogan of "republic with powerless monarch" at the Political Bureau meeting in Hangzhou, criticizing the central authorities for overstepping in taking powers back and instructing that all the reclaimed powers should be returned to the local authorities. In his words, "everything, including both personnel and facilities, should be returned."[35] Yet the Cultural Revolution which broke out a few months later postponed his plan of power decentralization. In the early 1970s, when the situation had just stabilized, Mao Zedong once again launched a power decentralization. This time, he demanded that the management powers over all the enterprises "suitable" to local management should be decentralized to the local authorities, even those large enterprises like the Angang (the Anshan Iron and Steel Complex), Daqing Oilfield, Changchun First Automobile Works, and Kailuan Coal Mine were no exception. At the same time, the fiscal revenue and expenditure power and material management power were also decentralized once again.[36]

Later, Zhou Enlai and Deng Xiaoping appropriately strengthened the central government's dominance, but by the end of the Cultural Revolution, China was already a fairly decentralized country, very different from the Soviet-style, highly centralized planned economic system.[37] An important manifestation of this difference lies in that the goods under the central unified distribution were much less than in the Soviet Union. The Soviet Union divided the goods into three categories according to the authoritative permission of their allocation, namely, "fund like or capitalized products" with their distribution permission belonging to the State Planning Commission, "centralized planning products" with their

---

[35] Zhao Dexin, *Economic History of the People's Republic of China: 1967–1984* (Zhengzhou: Henan People's Publishing House, 1989), pp. 42–43.

[36] Shi Yun and Li Danhui, *The "Continuing Revolution" Hard to Be Continued: From Criticizing Lin to Criticizing Deng* (Hong Kong: Chinese University of Hong Kong Press, 2008), pp. 225–232.

[37] Thomas P. Lyons, *Economic Integration and Planning in Maoist China* (New York: Columbia University Press, 1987), pp. 213–218.

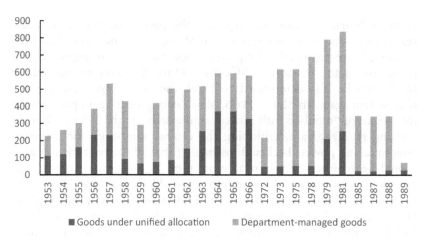

**Fig. 4.1** Varieties of goods under unified allocation and department-managed goods (*Source* Li Jingwen, *Direction of Reform on China's Goods Management System, Research on Economics and Management*, No. 1 (1980), pp. 56–62; Zhang Jianqin, *A Comparative Study of Traditional Planning Economic System in China and the Soviet Union* [Wuhan: Hubei People's Publishing House, 2004], p. 217)

distribution permission withheld by the central ministries, and "non-centralized planning products" with their distribution permission at the republics. In the early 1950s there were as many as 2,370 varieties of "fund like products" in the Soviet Union and the share of "non-centralized planning products" was very small. China also divided the goods into three categories according to the authoritative permission of their allocation, namely, "goods of unified allocation" which were uniformly allocated by the National Planning Commission, "department-managed goods" allocated by the central ministries and commissions, and "Category 3 goods" allocated by local authorities.[38] As Fig. 4.1 indicates, toward the end of the Cultural Revolution, there were only a total of 217 varieties of goods under unified allocation and department management. In addition, the local governments had felt the benefits from several times of decentralization, and they might not always be that compliant to fulfill

---

[38] Zhang Jianqin, *A Comparative Study of Traditional Planning Economic System in China and the Soviet Union* (Wuhan: Hubei People's Publishing House, 2004), p. 217.

the national allocation targets, and some even went so far as to refuse to sell their local goods to other parts of the country at the state allocation price.[39]

### Explorations in Breaking "Bourgeois Rights"

In the early 1950s, Mao Zedong's exploration of the socialist road focused on ownership, after the mid-1950s, his study on China's road began to shift to the planning system, and in the late 1950s, he set for the exploration in yet another aspect, namely, breaking the "bourgeois rights" and changing the interpersonal relationships.[40]

In fact, as early as 1957, Mao Zedong raised the point that although the socialist transformation in the ownership of the means of production had been completed, "the transformation of man had been unfinished."[41] In the following year, when commenting on Stalin's *Economic Problems of Socialism in the USSR*, he pointed out further that "after the question of ownership was basically solved through the socialist transformation, people's equal relations generated in labor production will not occur naturally. The existence of bourgeois rights is bound to hinder the formation and development of such equal relationship from all aspects. The bourgeois rights existent in the interpersonal relations must be broken. For example, strict hierarchy, arrogance from high ranking, being divorced from the people, treating people unequally, getting along not by ability but by seniority and administrative power, relationships between officials and people and between the leading and the led becoming like the cat-and-mouse relationship and the father-and-son relationship, and all these things must be eradicated and thoroughly wiped out. After they are

---

[39] Zhao Dexin, *Economic History of the People's Republic of China: 1967–1984* (Zhengzhou: Henan People's Publishing House, 1989), pp. 60–62.

[40] Hu Qiaomu, *Chairman Mao Was Pursuing a Type of Socialism* (June 9, 1980), *Hu Qiaomu's Talks on the History of the Chinese Communist Party* (Beijing: People's Publishing House, 1999), pp. 70–72.

[41] Mao Zedong, *Notes and Editing on the Article This Is Socialist Revolution on the Political and Ideological Front* (September 15, 1957), *Mao Zedong's Manuscripts Since the Founding of the People's Republic of China*, Vol. VI (Beijing: Central Party Literature Press, 1999), p. 579.

eradicated, they will re-emerge, and with their regeneration it is necessary to eradicate them again."[42] At that time, the means he used to break the "bourgeois rights" was to carry out rectifications and experiments, criticize hierarchy, send cadres down to grass-roots units or rural areas, and encourage officials to participate in labor, workers to participate in management, and reform the unreasonable rules and regulations. The subsequent socialist education movement in urban and rural areas throughout the country from 1963 to 1966 was also aimed at solving this problem. But to him, these measures were not enough to break the "bourgeois rights" and eliminate the danger of "capitalist restoration."

The May 7 Directive could be regarded as a declaration of Mao Zedong's ideal in his later years, from which we can see what Mao Zedong envisioned was a horizontal or flat society which should have gradually eliminated the division of labor, commodities, and the three major gaps between workers and peasants, between urban and rural areas, and between manual labor and mental labor, with the objective to achieve all-round equality between people in labor, culture, education, and political and material life. The criticisms of the "capitalism roaders" in the early stage of the Cultural Revolution, and the support for the "new things" like the May 7 cadre schools, educated youth going to the countryside, revolutionary model theatrical works, worker-peasant-soldier students going to and managing the institutions of higher learning, propaganda teams of workers and poor and lower-middle peasants, barefoot doctors, cooperative medical care system, management combing the old, middle-aged and young people, and combing workers, cadres and intellectuals in the latter period of the Cultural Revolution, all can be seen as the way to realize his ideal.

In short, Mao Zedong's exploration of the socialist road focused on three aspects: One was on the issue of ownership, and China did not focus too much on pure and pure large state-owned enterprises, but created millions of small and medium-sized enterprises under collective ownership. Another was on the issue of planning, and China did not carry out a centralized planning system, but decentralized to a great extent the fiscal revenue and expenditure power, planning power, and material management power to local authorities at all levels. The third was on the issue

---

[42] Association of National History of the People's Republic of China, *Mao Zedong's Notes and Talks on the Socialist Political Economy* (Abridged) (Beijing: Association of National History of the People's Republic of China, 2000), pp. 40–41.

of "bourgeois rights," and a strict hierarchy did not take shape in China, but equality of people in economic, social, political, and cultural status was promoted in various ways, of course with the exclusion of the "class enemies."

With regard to the history of exploring the socialist road in the first three decades, Deng Xiaoping pointed out, "Despite our errors, in the past three decades we have made progress on a scale which old China could not achieve in hundreds or even thousands of years."[43] Angus Madison, who has studied world economic growth over a long run, agreed with Deng Xiaoping: The New China's economy made great progress as compared with the previous 100 years in spite of its political and economic isolation, hostile relations with the West from 1952 to 1978, confrontation with both the United States and the Soviet Union, as well as wars with South Korea and India. His estimate of China's GDP growth rate was well below official data, but even according to his data, China's GDP trebled during that period, per capita real product rose 82% and labor productivity by 58%. The economic structure was historically transformed. In 1952, industry's share of GDP was about one-third of that in agriculture. By 1978, it was nearly equal to the agricultural share.[44]

### *Achievements of Explorations in the First 30 Years*[45]

Compared with the Soviet-style system, the existence of millions of small and medium-sized enterprises in China, the relatively integrated industrial systems in various places, and the decentralized planning system created favorable institutional conditions for the market competition after the reform and opening-up. In addition, despite twists and turns, the Mao Zedong era not only achieved a fairly rapid economic growth rate (see Fig. 4.2), but also laid a solid foundation both in "hardware" and "software" for the high-speed post-reform economic growth.

---

[43] Deng Xiaoping, *Upholding the Four Cardinal Principles* (March 30, 1979), *Selected Works of Deng Xiaoping*, Vol. II (Beijing: Foreign Languages Press, 1995), p. 176.

[44] Angus Maddison, *Chinese Economic Performance in the Long Run: 960-2030 AD* (OECD, 2007), p. 59. But Maddison's calculation that industry's share of GDP in 1952 was "one seventh" of that in agriculture was mistaken, which the author corrected with data from the National Bureau of Statistics.

[45] For more detailed discussion please consult Chapter 3 of this book.

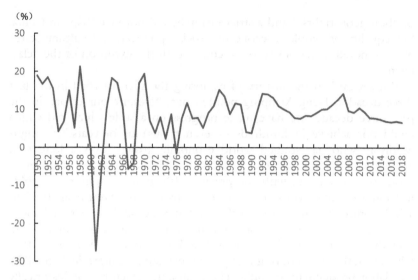

**Fig. 4.2** China's GDP growth rate, 1949–2018 (%) (Table 3] *Source* Data for 1953–2004 are from National Accounts Department of National Bureau of Statistics, *Data of Gross Domestic Product of China 1952–2004* [Beijing: China Statistics Press, 2007: Growth rate of GDP; data for 2005–2008 are from National Bureau of Statistics, *China Statistical Abstract 2009* [Beijing: China Statistics Press, 2009], p. 22)

In terms of "hardware," the Mao era established an independent and relatively integrated industrial system (including the national defense industry system) and national economic system for China, and a transportation network consisting of railways, highways, inland navigation, and civil aviation, which created favorable conditions for the economic takeoff in the 1980s. What's more, during this period, a great deal of human and material resources were put into harnessing large rivers and lakes, building embankments against flood in a total length of more than 200,000 kilometers and some 87,000 reservoirs, greatly mitigating the disasters of droughts and floods that ravaged the country for millenniums. The large-scale capital construction of farmland was carried out, dramatically increasing the ratio of irrigation area from 18.5% in 1952 to 45.2%

in 1978, essentially guaranteeing the demand for feeding and clothing 1 billion Chinese people.[46]

In terms of "software," the land reform, socialist transformation, and various measures to restrict "bourgeois rights" turned China into a relatively egalitarian society, with no powerful "distributional coalitions" existing.

For the economic growth, this "soft" infrastructure is as important as the "hard" one. Without the solid foundation in both the "soft" and "hard" aspects laid in the first three decades, it would be hard to achieve the post-reform economic takeoff.

## Explorations in the 40 Years Post-reform

Although the first three decades reversed a century of growth failure, and secured the kind of economic takeoff that had evaded previous regimes,[47] at the start of reform and opening-up, China was still a poor country. Out of the 790 million rural dwellers nationwide in 1978, 250 million lived below the poverty line (with the per capita annual income less than 100 yuan), equivalent to 30.7% of the total rural population. And the national average per capita annual income of rural residents that year was merely 133.6 yuan, while the average per capita annual income of urban residents was no more than 343.4 yuan.[48] This situation was clearly far from the ideal of socialism, and as Deng Xiaoping put it, "True, we are building socialism, but that doesn't mean that what we have achieved so far is up to the socialist standard."[49]

### *Explorations in Economic Reform*

After Mao Zedong's death, Deng Xiaoping made a new exploration of the socialist road on the basis of summing up the positive experiences

---

[46] Hu Angang, *The Political and Economic History of China (1949–1976)* (Beijing: Tsinghua University Press, 2008), pp. 524–530.

[47] Martin Jacques, *When China Rules the World: The Rise of the Middle Kingdom and the End of the Western World* (London: Penguin Group, 2009), p. 99.

[48] National Bureau of Statistics, *China Statistical Abstract 2009* (Beijing: China Statistics Press, 2009), pp. 109, 111.

[49] Deng Xiaoping, *Selected Works of Deng Xiaoping*, Vol. III (Beijing: Foreign Languages Press, 1994), p. 223.

and negative lessons in the first three decades. In order to remove the ideological barriers to the next step of exploration, Deng Xiaoping first emphasized emancipating the minds and seeking truth from facts from 1978 to 1980; emphasized that both Marxism and Mao Zedong Thought should also have to develop, otherwise they will become rigid. This was like a different tune played with the same skills as Mao Zedong advocated getting rid of the shackles of the Soviet model. Deng Xiaoping pointed out in particular, "We must emancipate our minds and we should do so even in answering the question as to what socialism is."[50] Like Mao Zedong, Deng Xiaoping also regarded the exploration of the socialist road as an open process; and he confessed on several occasions, "We summed up our experience in building socialism over the past few decades. We had not been quite clear about what socialism is and what Marxism is[51];" and "we are still trying to figure out what socialism is and how to build it."[52]

But one thing was clear from the very beginning: "We do not want capitalism, but neither do we want to be poor under socialism. What we want is socialism in which the productive forces are developed and the country is prosperous and powerful."[53] Since "poverty is not socialism," the main task of socialism is to develop productive force so that the material wealth of society will keep growing and the people's life will get better and better.

In order to promote the development of productive forces, Deng Xiaoping started to advocate for some people and some places to get rich first in 1980. Also to promote the development of productive forces, China began to explore how to combine the planning with the market on the basis of socialism under Deng Xiaoping's leadership. In 1981, the Sixth Plenary Session of the Eleventh Central Committee of the

---

[50] Deng Xiaping, *To Build Socialism We Must First Develop Productive Force* (April–May 1980), *Selected World of Deng Xiaoping*, Vol. II (Beijing: Foreign Languages Press, 1995), p. 311.

[51] Deng Xiaoping, *Reform Is the Only Way for China to Develop Its Productive Force* (August 28, 1985), *Selected Works of Deng Xiaoping*, Vol. III (Beijing: Foreign Languages Press, 1994), p. 141.

[52] Deng Xiaoping, *We Shall Draw on Historical Experience and Guard Against Wrong Tendencies* (April 30, 1987), *Selected Works of Deng Xiaoping*, Vol. III (Beijing: Foreign Languages Press, 1994), p. 225.

[53] Deng Xiaoping, *We Can Develop a Market Economy Under Socialism* (November 26, 1979), *Selected Works of Deng Xiaoping*, Vol. II (Beijing: Foreign Languages Press, 1995), p. 235.

Communist Party of China proposed to "carry out a planned economy on the basis of public ownership, while market playing an auxiliary role," which marked a breakthrough in the traditional concept of the planned economy completely rejecting any role of market forces. In 1984, the Third Plenary Session of the 12th CPC Central Committee proposed that "socialist economy is a planned commodity economy based on public ownership," highlighting the inherent unity of planning and market. In 1992, Deng Xiaoping put forward more clearly the concept of "socialist market economy."[54] Since then, the market has gradually replaced the planning as the basic mechanism for the allocation of major factors of production in China.

For socialism, there is no doubt about the necessity and importance of developing the productive forces, but after all, the development of productive forces is not a watershed between socialism and capitalism, and the market is not something unique to socialism. So aside from practicing market economy and developing the productive forces, what are the most essential characteristics of socialism? Deng Xiaoping held that its first characteristic was public ownership, including the ownership by the whole people and collective ownership. At the onset of reform and opening-up, he stressed that we must stick to our basic systems, "that is, the socialist system and socialist public ownership, and we must never waver in doing so. We shall not allow a new bourgeoisie to come into being."[55] Beginning from 1980, he ceased to emphasize pure and pure public ownership, but rather to keep the public ownership in the dominant position so as to leave sufficient space for the development of non-public economy. In 1985, he said, "We allow the development of individual economy, of joint ventures with both Chinese and foreign investment and of enterprises wholly owned by foreign businessmen, but socialist public ownership will always remain predominant."[56] Indeed, the publicly owned sector of economy still accounted for more than 90 percent of the total at

---

[54] Literature Research Office of the CPC Central Committee, *Chronicles of Deng Xiaoping (1975–1997)*, Vol. II (Beijing: Central Party Literature Press, 2004), p. 1347.

[55] Deng Xiaoping, *Carry Out the Policy of Opening to the Outside World and Learn Advanced Science and Technology from Other Countries* (October 10, 1978), Selected Works of Deng Xiaoping, Vol. II (Beijing: Foreign Languages Press, 1995), p. 144.

[56] Deng Xiaoping, *Unity Depends on Ideal and Discipline* (March 7, 1985), Selected Works of Deng Xiaoping, Vol. III (Beijing: Foreign Languages Press, 1994), p. 116.

that time.[57] Even when in his talks during his now famous southern tours in 1992, the public ownership still dominated in Shenzhen, a rising city at the forefront of reform and opening-up, with foreign investment accounting for only a quarter of the total.[58] Up to 1997, when Deng Xiaoping passed away, the public ownership still occupied three-quarters of the national economy (see Table 4.1).

Deng Xiaoping held that the second characteristic of socialism was common prosperity. To him, should China turn on the capitalist road, "capitalism can only enrich less than 10 percent of the Chinese population; it can never enrich the remaining more than 90 percent" and "most of the people would remain mired in poverty and backwardness."[59] He stressed, "One of the features distinguishing socialism from capitalism is that socialism means common prosperity, not polarization of income. The wealth created belongs first to the state and second to the people; it is therefore impossible for a new bourgeoisie to emerge. The amount that goes to the state will be spent for the benefit of the people, a small portion being used to strengthen national defense and the rest to develop the economy, education and science and to raise the people's living standards and cultural level."[60] He explained, "In encouraging some regions to become prosperous first, we intend that they should inspire others to follow their example and that all of them should help economically backward regions to develop. The same holds good for some individuals." At the same time, he warned, "If our policies led to polarization, it would mean that we had failed; if a new bourgeoisie emerged, it would mean that we had strayed from the right path."[61]

[57] Deng Xiaoping, *Reform Is the Only Way for China to Develop Its Productive Force* (August 28, 1985), *Selected Works of Deng Xiaoping*, Vol. III (Beijing: Foreign Languages Press, 1994), p. 142.

[58] Deng Xiaoping, *Excerpts from Talks Given in Wuchang, Shenzhen, Zhuhai and Shanghai* (January 18–February 27, 1992), *Selected Works of Deng Xiaoping*, Vol. III (Beijing: Foreign Languages Press, 1994), p. 361.

[59] Deng Xiaoping, *Building a Socialism with a Specifically Chinese Character* (June 30, 1984), *Selected Works of Deng Xiaoping*, Vol. III (Beijing: Foreign Languages Press, 1994), p. 73.

[60] Deng Xiaoping, *Bourgeois Liberalization Means Taking the Capitalist Road* (May and June 1985), *Selected Works of Deng Xiaoping*, Vol. III (Beijing: Foreign Languages Press, 1994), p. 129.

[61] Deng Xiaoping, *Unity Depends on Ideal and Discipline* (March 7, 1985), *Selected Works of Deng Xiaoping*, Vol. III (Beijing: Foreign Languages Press, 1994), p. 116.

Deng Xiaoping said similar words time and again on many occasions, just to theoretically distinguish socialism from capitalism. But throughout the 1980s, his focus was always on how to carry out the market reform, how to speed up opening to the outside world, how to promote the development of non-public economy, and how to motivate some people and some areas to get rich first.

Noticeably, after Deng Xiaoping delivered those talks during his southern tours in 1992, there was a change in the focus of his attention. On the one hand, he was more concerned about keeping the public ownership dominant. While reviewing the draft report to the 14th National Congress of the Communist Party of China, he began to re-introduce the idea of "two leaps," namely, after the family contract responsibility system was carried out for a period, the rural areas should still take the road of collectivization and intensive farming. In his words, "The socialist economy takes the public ownership in the dominant position, and so is agriculture, which will ultimately take the public ownership in the dominant position."[62] On the other hand, he was more concerned with common prosperity. In his conversation with his younger brother Deng Ken in 1993, he sighed: "How to achieve prosperity for the 1.2 billion people, how to distribute the wealth after they get rich, all these are big problems. The problem has come out, but it is more difficult to solve this problem than to solve the problem of development. … A small number of people have acquired so much wealth, while the majority of the people have got little, if things keep going like this, something serious will happen one day. Inequity in distribution could lead to polarization, which will lead to the explosion of problems at certain point. This problem must be solved. In the past, we talked about getting developed first. Now in retrospect, there are no fewer problems after getting developed than we used to have when we were yet to develop."[63] These two changes indicate that Deng Xiaoping's understanding of the nature of socialism deepened. He once assumed that so long as the pie was made bigger, the 1.2 billion people could eventually achieve common prosperity. But now he came to realize that even with rapid economic growth, most people might not necessarily benefit from it. Only by adhering to the socialist direction and

---

[62] Literature Research Office of the CPC Central Committee, *Chronicles of Deng Xiaoping (1975–1997)*, Vol. II (Beijing: Central Party Literature Press, 2004), pp. 1349–1350.

[63] Ibid.

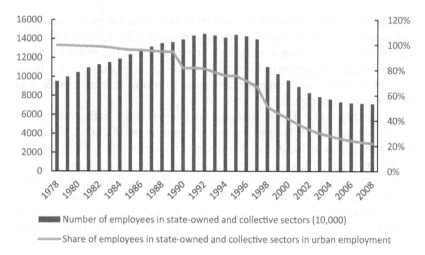

**Fig. 4.3** Employment in urban units of public ownership (*Source* National Bureau of Statistics, *China Statistical Abstract 2009* [Beijing: China Statistics Press, 2009], p. 45)

the basic socialist system would it be possible to "use all kinds of means, all kinds of methods and all kinds of programs to solve these problems."[64]

The domination of public ownership was already shattered when Deng Xiaoping was still alive. The individual business, private economy, and foreign-funded economy developed rapidly, and there emerged mixed ownerships in which different ownerships took each other's shares mutually. Yet at that time the non-public economy was regarded only as a "necessary supplement" to the public ownership, while the existing enterprises of public ownership did not change their nature. This is clearly indicated in Fig. 4.3: Although the share of employees in publicly owned sectors in the urban employment decreased from 99.8% in 1978 to 71.6% in 1996, the absolute number of employees in publicly owned sectors increased from 94.99 million to 142.6 million during the same period.

The major change in the configuration of ownerships took place after the death of Deng Xiaoping. Among the reports at the Party congresses, no one put as much ink on the reform of ownership as the one at the 15th CPC National Congress in 1997. The report at the 15th CPC National

[64] Ibid.

Congress put forward new interpretations of both "public ownership" and "the dominant position of public ownership." "Public ownership" includes not only the traditional state- and collectively owned sectors, but also the state- and collective-controlled shareholding system, joint-stock cooperative system, and collective economy that features in the main the association of laborers in labor and capital. "The dominant position of public ownership" is interpreted as "public assets dominate in the total assets in society and state-owned sector controls the life-blood of the national economy and plays a leading role in economic development." On the other hand, in some localities and industries, public assets do not have to be in dominance, for industries and sectors that do not control the life-blood of the national economy, the state-owned economy does not have to be dominant. In this sense, in the premise that "public ownership" is held "in the dominant position," even if the state-owned sector and the collective economy account for a smaller proportion of the economy, it will not affect the socialist nature of China.

The restructuring of existing public-owned enterprises became the focus of the ownership reform after the 15th CPC National Congress. Such slogans for invigorating large enterprises while relaxing control over small ones, encouraging mergers, standardizing bankruptcy procedures, diverting laid-off workers and providing them with re-employment opportunities, and downsizing for efficiency became popular. By 2005, 85% of state-owned small and medium-sized enterprises and even more collective enterprises had been involved in the restructuring, and a large number of them went bankrupt and vanished, but more of them became private enterprises.[65] Of the 2,524 state-owned and state-controlled large backbone enterprises whose combined net assets accounted for two-thirds of those of the country's state-owned enterprises, 1,331 or 52.7% of them were restructured into joint-stock enterprises with diversified shareholders.[66] Meanwhile, the originally collective-owned township enterprises also changed their nature, as 95% of the 1.68

---

[65] Li Rongrong, *Further Advance Restructuring of State-owned Assets Management and Reform of State-owned Enterprises, Achieve Institutional Innovation and Sustainable Development of SOEs: Speech at China's Reform Summit* (July 12, 2005), http://www.sasac.gov.cn/n1180/n3123702/n3123987/3125287/3188291.html.

[66] Zhao Zhuoyuan, *Retrospect and Prospect of the Restructuring of State-owned Enterprises Over 30 Years* (February 3, 2008), http://finance.sina.com.cn/economist/jingjixueren/20080203/11264487740.shtml.

million township-village enterprises nationwide had reformed property rights system in various forms by 2006, with 200,000 of them becoming shareholding enterprises and joint-stock cooperative enterprises, and 1.39 million becoming individual private enterprises.[67] After several years of restructuring, the proportion of state and collective input in the total paid-in capital of the enterprise legal entities nationwide fell to 56% by the end of 2004.[68] By 2005, the share of the public economy in the national economy fell to 39% (see Table 4.1); and by 2007, the share of state-owned, state-controlled, and collective industrial enterprises in the total industrial output value fell to 32%, while the share of employees in state-owned and collective sectors in the total urban employment fell to 24.3%.[69]

Compared with the Mao Zedong era and Deng Xiaoping era, tremendous changes have taken place in China's ownership structure: public sectors in the economy have drastically shrunk, and its forms have been diversified. This apparently has departed far from the "traditional socialism" model. Nevertheless, the public sectors in China still surpass most countries in the world by far. And China's *Constitution* stipulates that mineral resources, waters, forests, mountains, grassland, unreclaimed land, beaches and other natural resources, and land in the cities are owned by the state; land in the rural and suburban areas is owned by collectives except for those portions which belong to the state in accordance with the law. This makes China more "socialist" than most countries in the world. In the process of reform, there have always been people at home and abroad who either overtly advocate "privatization," or covertly wave the banner of "anti-monopoly" with the attempt to completely eliminate the remaining public economic sectors so as to chop down the socialist banner

---

[67] Zhao Yue, *Past and Present of Township Enterprises*, CCTV China Finance News (April 23, 2007), http://cctve.com/program/cbn/20070424/102108/shtml.

[68] Leading Group Office of State Council for First National Economy Census and National Bureau of Statistics of the People's Republic of China, *Communique on Major Data of First National Economic Census* (No. 1) (December 6, 2005), http://news.xinhuanet.com/fortune/2005-12/06/content_3883969.htm.

[69] National Bureau of Statistics, *Report No. 3 on 30 Years of Reform and Opening Up: Major Adjustments on Economic Structure in Ever Optimization and Upgrading* (October 29, 2008), http://www.stats.gov.cn/tjfx/ztfx/jinggkf30n/t20081029_402512864.htm.

in China.[70] The 17th, 18th, and 19th CPC National Congresses successively reaffirmed the commitment to the two "irresolutions" put forward at the 16th CPC National Congress, namely, "unswervingly consolidate and develop the public sector of the economy", "unswervingly encourage, support, and guide the development of the non-public sector of the economy" This has disappointed them considerably.[71]

### Explorations in Political Reform

Reform and opening-up involve not only economic process, but also political process, as well as adjustments (intentional) and changes (unintentional) in the distribution of resources among social groups. Over the past 40 years, on the one hand, we can say that China's political system has been changing every day; on the other hand, we can say that China's politics has remained essentially the same despite tens of thousands of changes. Between what has changed and what has remained unchanged, China has always been exploring a new political path.

*Political Direction of Economic Reform: Always Focusing on the Improvement of Well-Being of the Overwhelming Majority of the People*

Since the founding of New China, the Communist Party of China, Chinese governments at all levels, and Chinese people have always been exploring a socialist road that is suitable to their national conditions and their stage of development. In retrospect of the past 70 years, China has crossed two historical stages of development and is on its way of the third historical stage and approaching the fourth one (see Fig. 4.4). No

---

[70] A research fellow for Asian economy of the Heritage Foundation, a conservative organization in the United States, wrote a paper in 2009 criticizing that "since the present Communist Party leadership took power, fresh market-oriented liberalization has been minor. Such policies have been wound down and supplanted by renewed state intervention. In privatization, prices and even foreign trade and investment, the PRC was heading away from the market… privatization was … explicitly reversed." See Derek Scissors, *Deng Undone*, April 29, 2009 and Liberalization Review, May 4, 2009, http://www.heritage.org/about/staff/derekscissorspapers.cfm.

[71] In 2019, Nicholas R. Lardy, a senior research fellow of the Peterson Institute for International Economics, published a book titled *The State Strikes Back: The End of Economic Reform in China?* (Washington, DC: Peterson Institute for International Economics, 2019).

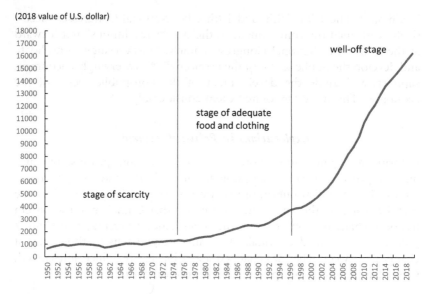

**Fig. 4.4** Historical stages in China's development (2018 value of U.S. dollar) (*Source* The Conference Board, Total Economy Database, April 2019, http://www.conference-board.org/data/economydatabase/TED1)

matter in what historical stage, the socialist China has always focused on improving the well-being of the overwhelming majority of the people.

The first stage can be called the "stage of scarcity," which began from the founding of New China and continued until 1978. At the constant international US dollar price in 2018, China's GDP per capita climbed from around 666 US dollars continuously up in this stage, but remained below 1,500 US dollars.[72] It is called the "stage of scarcity" because the economic development in this stage remained at a low level, with the output enough only to sustain people's basic subsistence. The main domestic contradictions at this stage were those between the people's demand for building an advanced industrial country and the reality of a backward agricultural country (industrialization), and between the

---

[72] As calculated at the constant US dollar price of 2018, the per capita GDP may look rather high. But whether compared with other economies in the same period or with China's own history, it still could indicate the dynamics of the change.

people's need for rapid economic and cultural development and the situation in which current economy and culture could not satisfy the people's need (education and health).

In order to develop the economy under the condition of extremely limited surplus, China adopted the socialist model of public ownership plus planned economy at this stage, so as to concentrate the limited surplus for the development of key industries and key social undertakings in priority. At the same time, when the per capita income was very low and people were generally poor at the stage of scarcity, the only way to maximize the social welfare under those conditions was to ensure the basic subsistence of the overwhelming majority of the people. Since the per capita income was enough only to maintain basic subsistence, a slight inequity in the distribution could deprive some people of the guarantee for their basic subsistence. Therefore, China at that time paid great attention to equity in its distribution policy, often issuing coupons to supply daily necessities in fixed rations, while promoting the coverage of basic medical care and basic education for the whole people, which laid the foundation from both the "hard" and "soft" aspects for the next step of development. This is the Chinese-style socialism 1.0 in the Mao Zedong era.

The second stage is called the "stage of adequate food and clothing," which lasted throughout 1979–2001. In 1979, China's GDP per capita exceeded 1,500 US dollars, marking China's entry into the "stage of adequate food and clothing." At this stage, the per capita income was sufficient to maintain people's subsistence, and the way to maximize the social welfare was to break the "iron rice bowl" and take away the "big pot of rice" on the one hand so as to promote rapid economic growth, trying as much as possible to "let some people and some areas get rich first" before improving the income and consumption level of the vast majority of the people; and on the other hand to alleviate and mitigate poverty, with the focus on helping people at the bottom of society get rid of poverty and solve the problem of food and clothing. This is exactly the quintessence of Chinese-style socialism 2.0.

From 1979 to 2001, China's GDP grew at an average annual rate of 9.6%, about two percentage points higher than in the previous three decades. As an oversized and super-complex economy with a population of more than one billion, China's high-speed growth for more than 20 years in a row was unprecedented in human history and a veritable miracle. If people were not so well fed and clothed during the stage of scarcity, then with per capita income gradually increasing from 1,500 US dollars to 5,000 US dollars in the stage of adequate food and clothing, the overwhelming majority of Chinese were already able to eat more and more nutritiously and dress more and more decently.

Perhaps what is more commendable is China's achievements in poverty alleviation, as evidenced by data provided later.

Of course, there are flaws in the Chinese-style socialism 2.0. In order to pursue the highest possible economic growth rate, China once neglected social equity, workers' rights and interests, public health, medical security, ecological environment, and national defense construction to a considerable extent in this stage, rendering a series of grave consequences, with people generally feeling insecure, unequal and uncomfortable.

In 2002, China's GDP per capita crossed the benchmark of 5,000 US dollars and the country entered the "well-off stage" and planned to achieve the goal of building a well-off society in an all-round way by 2020.

If the increase in private income and consumption levels in the stage of adequate food and clothing contributed to the improvement of social welfare, then after entering the well-off stage, the increase of private income and consumption levels was no longer the main driving force for the improvement of overall social welfare, and their marginal positive correlation with the improvement of social welfare began to decline, or even turn to its opposite.[73]

It was on this basis that John Kenneth Galbraith, a famous Harvard economist, published a book *The Affluent Society* as early as 1958. He sharply observed that America's affluence at the time was only the affluence of private goods and services, while public goods and services were actually deficient. Although many American families owned private houses, cars, refrigerators, washing machines, television sets, and air conditioners, even in New York City, which the United States is proud of, Galbraith saw that "the schools are old and overcrowded. The police force is inadequate. The parks and playgrounds are insufficient. Streets and empty lots are filthy, and the sanitation staff is underequipped and in need of men. Access to the city by those who work there is uncertain and painful and becoming more so. Internal transportation is also overcrowded, unhealthful and dirty. So is the air. Parking on the streets

---

[73] Huang Youguang, *Efficiency, Equity and Public Policies* (Beijing: Social Sciences Academic Press, 2003).

should be prohibited, but there is no space elsewhere."[74] In Galbraith's view, certain balance must be sought between private goods and services and the supply of public goods and services. Or it would be pointless to increase private products and services. For instance, "an increase in the consumption of automobiles requires a facilitating supply of streets, highways, traffic control and parking space. The protective services of the police and highway patrols must also be available, as must those of the hospitals."[75] In order to achieve this balance, and in order to further improve the level of social welfare, Galbraith stressed that, after entering the affluent stage, a society must substantially increase its investment in public goods and services. Galbraith's advice, however, did not have much impact in the United States.

In 1998, in his introduction to the 40th anniversary edition of *The Affluent Society*, Galbraith lamented, "My case is still strong. The government does spend money readily on weaponry of questionable need and on what has come to be called large corporate welfare. Otherwise there is still persistent and powerful pressure for restraint public outlay. In consequence, we are now more than ever affluent in our private consumption; the inadequacy of our schools, libraries, public recreation facilities, health care, even law enforcement, is a matter of daily comment. ... In civilized performance it has lagged even further behind the private sector, as it is now called."[76]

The socialist China should be able to do better and has indeed done quite well.

With the solution of the problem of providing adequate food and clothing to more than a billion people stabilized, the Chinese-style socialism 3.0 began to focus on the supply-side structural reform, in an attempt to respond to the requirement of private consumption for better quality and more diversified products and services.

More importantly, as the relationship between the increase of private income and consumption and the improvement of social welfare began to decline, the Chinese-style socialism 3.0 pays more attention to issues concerning the "public" and "society," and continuously explores how to expand inputs in those sectors which could effectively improve welfare of

---

[74] John K. Galbraith, *The Affluent Society* (Boston: Mariner Books, 1998), Chapter 17.
[75] Ibid.
[76] Ibid., p. 5.

the majority of the people (such as public housing, public security, public transportation, ecological protection, public health, public education, infrastructures, culture and art, and science and technology). Specifically, after the problem of "clothing" and "food" was largely solved, China has paid more attention in recent years to the problem of improving "housing" (livable) and "travel" (smooth); and after the problem of private food, clothing, housing, and travel was solved by and large, China has paid more attention in these years to solving the problems of public consumption (safety, ecology, and health), human security and social equity.

Since the increase of private income and consumption levels will become less related to the improvement of welfare, it is necessary to put redistribution of income high on the agenda of the government. The Chinese-style socialism 3.0 also pays more attention to narrowing the interregional and urban-rural disparities.

At the same time, the Chinese-style socialism 3.0 had been committed to eradicating absolute poverty before the end of 2020 in unprecedented endeavors. On the basis of building a well-off society in an all-round way by 2020 and achieving the goal for the first centenary (the 100th anniversary of the Communist Party of China), China will enter the fourth historical stage—the stage of building a powerful country: On the basis that socialist modernization is basically realized by 2035, the nation will go on with the endeavor to build China into a modern socialist country that is prosperous, strong, democratic, culturally advanced, harmonious and beautiful by 2050. There is no doubt that the Chinese-style socialism 4.0 will still focus on the further improvement of well-being of the overwhelming majority of the people.

*Stakeholders of Reform: Benefit the Most Possible People, and Impair the Least of Them*
In economic perspective, reform is viewed more from its overall benefits—growth and efficiency; but from a political point of view, even if the whole country has gained overall, the reform is bound to render both the benefitted and the impaired. The benefitted or impaired persons in the absolute sense refer to the rise or fall of the absolute level of their well-beings; and the benefitted or impaired in the relative sense mean that the gains of certain social groups might be greater or smaller than those of others. The question is how to manage and resolve the distribution of the gains and losses of reform among different social groups. If the work is

not done well, social conflicts incurred by improper distribution of benefits are likely to disrupt the reform process and drag down the economic growth.

In retrospect, in the late 1980s and early 1990s, when the East European countries and the Soviet Union began their transition to capitalism, everyone knew that this process would be painful for many people. Ralf Dahrendorf of the London School of Economics, for example, described the transition from socialism to capitalism as crossing a deep and wide "valley of tears." Professor Jeffrey Sachs of Harvard University, "the father of shock therapy," told the people of the Soviet Union and East Europe that even if the reform should result in deteriorating their living, they had no other choice, because any other option was nothing more than a "halfway-done" reform, which was doomed to failure. He compared the transition from socialism to capitalism to crossing a trench, and he quoted a Russian proverb as saying, "You can't jump a trench in two steps." In other words, the option was either not to jump, or clench your teeth to cross it in one step no matter how painful. The "valley of tears" or the "trench," the subtext of these metaphors is that once you cross over it, the paradise of the world is on the other side. This is a kind of thinking that focuses on reform only, regardless of the life or death of the stakeholders of reform, and it is a kind of thinking that however dearly the cost is to pay will not matter, even if many people will fall into the abyss in the reform process.

China's reform has been gradual, trying to make economic reform a win–win game instead of a zero-sum one. Over the past 40 years, China's economic reform has always sought to maximize the benefitted and minimize the impaired. In this regard, China has three experiences.

First, China has been carrying out a gradual reform rather than administering a "shock therapy." As there are too many uncertainties in the reform process, if the "shock therapy" is adopted, the impair rendered may be enormous and irreversible, but the gradual reform approach can stop the damage in time and find an alternative path.

Second, at any stage of reform, ways must be found to benefit the overwhelming majority of the people and avoid impairing them or compelling them to make sacrifices. Whenever this approach is adhered to, the economic reform would be going relatively smoothly; and whenever there is deviation from this approach, the economic reform would bump into thorny problems. Every time a reform measure impaired the interests of most people or a significant proportion of them, the reform would be blocked. For example, the high inflation in the mid-to-late 1980s and the high unemployment rate in the mid-to-late 1990s both affected social stability and undermined the public confidence and support for the next step of reform. This has become a profound lesson for those in power to bear in mind.

Finally, if the reform benefits the nation overall and improves the welfare level of the entire country, then the beneficiary groups will still gain even if they have to compensate the groups impaired. Such compensation, however, will not be realized spontaneously, the compensation must be made to the impaired through taxes levied and transfer payments made by the government. In case the government is not so willing or capable of doing so for a moment, a backlash from the people will force the government to realize it (the cost of stability and unity). For instance, the ownership reform on state-owned and collective enterprises carried out in the mid-1990s resulted in tens of millions of workers laid-off and unemployed. As compensation, starting from July 1, 1999, the state substantially increased the income of people in the middle and low-income brackets in urban areas, which included raising the basic living allowances for laid-off workers of state-owned enterprises, unemployment insurance benefits, and minimum living standard guarantee for urban residents by 30%; increasing the wages of employees in-service and pensions of retirees of government-affiliated institutions; uplifting the pension standard for retirees of state-owned enterprises; paying back pension entitlements for retirees of state-owned enterprises covered by the overall government plan; and increasing allowances for some of the objects of the preferential treatment policies like disabled service people and family members of revolutionary martyrs and service people. To implement these measures, the state's fiscal expenditure increased by more than 54 billion yuan, benefiting more than 84 million people nationwide. In 2002, the central government proposed the establishment of a minimum income guarantee system (*Dibao*) and issued one document after another urging all the localities to make sure that all those who should be covered by the system are covered: in 2002 the *Dibao* system covered more than 20 million people, and its coverage thereafter has remained at 22–23 million. Systematic social policies began to roll out after 2003, from the reconstruction of rural cooperative medical care to the comprehensive medical insurance, to the extension of old-age insurance to rural and urban residents, and finally to the emergence of a great leap forward in social protection.

*Path of Reform: Groping for Steppingstones While Crossing the River*
Everyone seems to know that the path of reform in China is to "grope for steppingstones while crossing the river." Some people dismiss that it is a low-level decision-making method to "grope for steppingstones while crossing the river," which is not so rational, scientific and considerate as the "topmost-level design." Actually this is not the case. Reform is always full of unknown variables, and all those involved in it, including policymakers and experts, are confined to limited rationality and unable to foresee all possible scenarios and the possible consequences of their own actions, and therefore they are unable to make the absolutely best options. All they can do is just to handle the utmost pressing issues in priority, and eventually find a solution not necessarily the best but satisfactory to the most people through constant process of trial and error and comparisons of different options.

As a country with a vast geographical area, a large population, and uneven internal development, China's reform is especially complex, because many policies are hard to be formulated and implemented uniformly in a "one-size-fitting-all" way, and a unitary or undifferentiated approach may not be able to solve the problems of all localities (provinces, cities, counties), so more variables have to be taken into consideration. Over the past few decades, China has come up with a set of practices that allow, encourage, and even require the local authorities to take actions that suit their local circumstances and actively seek different solutions to the same problems and transform internal differences into piloting areas for exploring new paths for reform. That is exactly why China over the past 40 years has crossed numerous institutional and policy hurdles in its transition that outsiders considered insurmountable. The reform of the retirement system of leading officials, wage reform, price reform, reform of state-owned enterprises, restructuring of the banking system, reform of the financial system, the issue of the army and law enforcing personnel engaged in business operation, the issue of agriculture, rural areas and farmers, the reform of the housing system, the reform of the education system, and the reform of the medical system, all these were once regarded as a "treacherous pass," where one slight misstep may cause a holistic disaster. But now in retrospect, one could not help but utter a sign that "amidst incessant wailing of monkeys on either bank, my skiff darted past ten thousand mountain peaks."

Many people assume that it is very simple to "grope for steppingstones while crossing the river," but that is not true. Many other countries may be unable to manage to do so even if they want to learn to "grope for steppingstones while crossing the river," because some features unique to China's political system have enabled the country to be apt to "grope for steppingstones while crossing the river." These features are as follow:

First, the institutional arrangement is thus that decision makers are very sensitive to emerging problems, difficulties, and imbalances, and consciously feel obliged to respond.

Second, decision makers are convinced that the way to find solutions to policy and institutional problems is only through learning from practice and piloting, rather than copying foreign experience or fashionable theories.

Third, in the premise of political unity, decentralized decision-making is allowed in a considerable number of fields, thus creating institutional conditions for exploring different ways to solve problems to the maximum extent through decentralized practice and piloting. In other words, the institutional framework fosters rich and diversified sources of learning, without losing overall coordination.

Fourth, for new things emerging from practice and piloting, decentralized horizontal diffusion of their application is allowed or encouraged, especially in the early stage of decision-making, while centralized vertical diffusion is promoted.

These experiences apply not only to the current situation, but also to China entering the stage of building a powerful country.

### *Achievements of Exploration in the 40 Years Post-reform*

World-amazing achievements have been made in the exploration of the socialist road in the 40 years after reform and opening-up.

First, the pace of economic growth has quickened. From 1979 to 2018, China's GDP grew at an average annual rate of 9.44%, faster than the rate of 7.86% in the previous three decades. The "Four Little Dragons of Asia" acclaimed before are all small economies, the largest of which is South Korea, with a population of no more than 40 million at the time, about a medium-sized province in China. The population of Japan in its high-speed growth period was only about 100 million, about the size of the largest province in China. As a super large and super-complex economy with a population of more than one billion, China's high-speed growth for 40 consecutive years was unprecedented in human history and will probably never occur again, which is an out-and-out miracle.

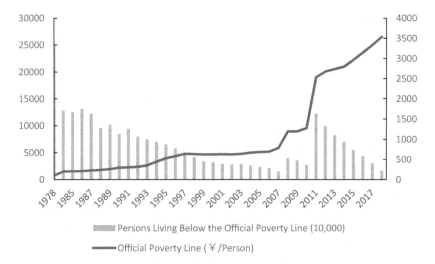

Fig. 4.5 Poverty of rural dwellers (*Source* Comprehensive Statistics Department of National Bureau of Statistics, *China Statistical Yearbook; China Statistical Abstract*; Statistical Database of Chinese Economic Social Development)

Second, the economic growth has become steadier. As well indicated in Fig. 4.2, the economic fluctuations in the last 40 years were not as frequent and violent as in the previous 30 years. Especially after 1992, the economic growth curve has become smoother, whether the rise or fall is no longer steep up or down, marking a significant progress of the Chinese government in macroeconomic management.

Third, the number of people living in poverty has been significantly reduced. As Fig. 4.5 indicates, the Chinese government has constantly lifted the poverty threshold over the past 40 years, from the initial 100 yuan to 2,300 yuan (at the constant price in 2010). Even so, the rural poverty rate fell from 30.7% in 1978 to 1.7% in 2018.[77] If measured by the World Bank poverty standards, China's achievements in poverty alleviation are even more remarkable. From 1981 to 2004, the absolute number of poor fell from 652 to 135 million, a decline of over half a

---

[77] National Bureau of Statistics, *Rural Population Living in Poverty Reduced by 13.86 Million* (February 15, 2019), http://www.stats.gov.cn/tjsj/zxfb/201902/t20190215_1649231.html.

billion people. Over the same period, the absolute number of poor in the developing world as a whole declined by only 400 million. In other words, but for China there would have been no decline in the numbers of poor in the developing world, but there would be a rise. No wonder a World Bank report admired China that "a fall in the number of poor of this magnitude over such a short period is without historical precedent."[78]

Of course, there were inevitably detours in the exploration during the last four decades. Especially in the 1990s, some people seemed to accept, intentionally or unintentionally, the "trickle-down theory" advocated by "neoliberal" economists, believing that as long as the economy continued to grow, everyone would eventually benefit from it, then all the other problems would be easily solved sooner or later. Under the guiding ideology of "giving priority to efficiency with due consideration to equity,"[79] in order to pursue the highest possible economic growth rate, they would rather sacrifice equity, employment, workers' rights and interests, public health, medical insurance, ecological environment, and national defense construction, resulting in a chain of serious problems. By the late 1990s, some of the problems had become alarming, and despite sustained economic growth, the mass of workers and farmers were enjoying less and less welfare guarantee. Large-scale laid-offs and unemployment, and expensive schooling and medical services reduced numerous people to a bitter feeling of deficient economic and social security. Against this background, those groups whose interests were impaired or who did not benefit much from the previous reform ceased to support the newly introduced market-oriented reforms unreservedly. On the contrary, they became full of misgivings about any move labeled with "market" and "reform," for fear of getting hurt again.

---

[78] Poverty Reduction and Economic Management Department East Asia and Pacific Region of World Bank, *From Poor Areas to Poor People: China's Evolving Poverty Reduction Agenda—An Assessment of Poverty and Inequality in China* (2009), p. iii.

[79] The concept of "giving priority to efficiency with due consideration to equity" was initiated by a research team on the Reform of Social Equity and Social Security System headed by Zhou Weimin and Lu Zhongyuan, whose main report was published in the No. 2 issue of *Economic Research Journal* in 1986, entitled *Giving Priority to Efficiency with Due Consideration to Equity: Balance to Prosperity*. *The Decision of the CPC Central Committee Regarding a Number of Issues Concerning the Establishment of a Socialist Market Economy* adopted at the Third Plenary Session of the 14th CPC Central Committee in 1993 officially used the phrase of "giving priority to efficiency with due consideration to equity," which was sustained at the 15th CPC National Congress.

At a time when people generally felt that China's reform had reached the point where it must revamp, decision makers at the central level began to reflect earnestly on Deng Xiaoping's warning: "If polarization occurred... The contradictions between various ethnic groups, regions, and classes will become sharper and, accordingly, the contradictions between the central and local authorities would also be intensified. That would lead to disturbances."[80] The 16th CPC National Congress held at the end of 2002 tried to re-interpret the implication of "giving priority to efficiency with due consideration to equity," using the term of "paying more attention to efficiency in primary distribution and paying more attention to fairness in redistribution."[81] But the harsh reality of the disparity between the rich and the poor indicated that attention should also be paid to inequality in primary distribution (like the income gap between bosses, managers and cadres on the one side and ordinary workers on the other), and it would be far from enough to rely solely on redistribution levers like taxation for readjustments.[82] The Third Plenary Session of the 16th CPC Central Committee in October 2003 continued to use the term "giving priority to efficiency with due consideration to equity," but its weight was much diluted by the concept of "people-oriented" "scientific concept of development." The Fourth Plenary Session of the 16th CPC Central Committee held in September 2004 simply abandoned the term of "giving priority to efficiency with due consideration to equity."[83] In October 2005, the *Communist Party of China Central Committee's Proposal on the Eleventh Five-year Program on National Economy and Social Development* adopted at the Fifth Session of the 16th CPC Central Committee went further to propose that in the future China should "pay more attention to social equity and enable

---

[80] Deng Xiaoping, *Seize the Opportunity to Develop the Economy* (December 24, 1990), *Selected Works of Deng Xiaoping*, Vol. III (Beijing: Foreign Languages Press, 1994), p. 351.

[81] Jiang Zemin, Report at the 16th National Congress of the Communist Party of China (November 18, 2002), http://www.china.org.cn/english/features/49007.htm.

[82] Liu Guoguang, Place "Giving Priority to Efficiency" to Where It Belongs, *Economic Information Daily* (October 15, 2005).

[83] *Communique of the Fourth Plenary Session of the 14th Central Committee of the Communist Party of China* (September 19, 2005).

the whole people to share the fruits of reform and development."[84] At the 17th CPC National Congress, the standard term had changed to that "a proper balance will be struck between efficiency and equity in both primary distribution and redistribution, with particular emphasis on equity in redistribution."[85]

Starting from 2002, the Chinese government also began the work to establish and consolidate a system of social assistance and social insurance covering all the urban and rural residents (including free nine-year compulsory education, minimum subsistence guarantee, basic old-age pension, basic medical care, insurance systems for unemployment, work injury and maternity, etc.), which has progressed faster than ever before, greatly substantiating what Deng Xiaoping conceived on "common prosperity." If China had only economic policies but no social policies from 1978 to the late 1990s, at the turn of the century we saw that social policies had prevailed in China. Without a government sticking to the socialist direction, without a basic economic system with the public ownership in dominant position, it would be impossible for such a historic "great transformation" to come by in just a few years, and this "great transformation" itself has constituted an important step in China's exploration of the socialist road.[86]

## Summary

By 2019, the New China had gone through 70 years. There is no denying that after 70 years we are still in want of a perfect solution as to how to build an ideal socialist society; all we have is but a direction, that is, to liberate and develop the productive forces, greatly increase the material wealth of the whole society, eradicate exploitation and oppression, eliminate polarization, achieve social equity and justice, and gradually establish "a community of free individuals" without class antagonism, "a society

---

[84] *The Communist Party of China Central Committee's Proposal on the Eleventh Five-Year Program on National Economy and Social Development*, Xinhuanet (Ocotober 18, 2005).

[85] Hu Jintao, *Hold High the Great Banner of Socialism with Chinese Characteristics and Strive for New Victories in Building a Moderately Prosperous Society in All Respects* (October 15, 2007).

[86] Wang Shaoguang, Great Transition: China's Bidirectional Movements Since the 1980s, *Beijing: Social Sciences in China*, No. 1 (2008), pp. 129–148.

in which the full and free development of every individual forms the ruling principle."[87] Historical experience tells us that the most important thing in building socialism is not whether there is a detailed blueprint, but whether there is a clear vision of the direction of socialism, whether there is the wisdom not to believe "history has ended," whether there is the courage to move unyieldingly toward the future of socialism, and whether there are the guts to constantly explore new paths to realize the socialist ideal.

Over the past 70 years, while adhering to the socialist direction, China has been persevering in its exploration of the socialist road suited to its national conditions. Of course, China went through detours in both the first 30 years and the next 40 years. But as long as it is exploration, how possible is it not to take a detour at all? The point is that China's leaders have never believed in fallacies like "the end of history" or in any so-called "universal" model "applicable all over the world." Instead, they have focused more on learning from practice and piloting, obtaining the necessary experiences and lessons, "carrying on those suitable and changing or modifying those not," and constantly adjusting policy objectives and tools to respond to always changing circumstances.[88]

It is precisely because China's exploration of socialist road has "followed the mandate of heaven and complies with the popular wishes of the people," the country has made brilliant achievements no matter in the first 30 years or in the next 40 years, writing another version of *Eliminating Poverty* that is far more fascinating than Han Yu's article of the same title centuries ago. In terms of the comprehensive economic and social development, China's human development indicator was among the "very low" in 1950, less than one-third of that of the Soviet Union; but by 2014, China's HDI had entered the "upper-middle" ranks, only one step away from the "Big Brother" in the old days. Over the past 70 years, China's HDI has risen rapidly by 0.56, far higher than other countries, evidencing that it is a right choice to adhere to the socialist direction.

---

[87] Karl Marx, *Capital*, Vol. I (Moscow, USSR: Progress Publishers, online edition, 2015), pp. 51, 417.

[88] Wang Shaoguang, Mechanism of Learning and Adaptability: Revelation of Vicissitudes in China's Rural Cooperative Medical Care System, *Beijing: Social Sciences in China*, No. 6 (2008), pp. 111–133.

There are still many problems in China today, with many serious challenges confronting it, but as long as the direction of socialism is adhered to, the road ahead is bound to become wider and wider.

CHAPTER 5

# Steering: From Planning to Programming

In the 70 years since the founding of New China, a system has always followed the form like a shadow that is the five-year planning (or programming).[1] Has the system been working well? The answer is crystal clear with the help of the charts and data provided in the first three chapters. As Angus Maddison calculated, until the beginning of the nineteenth century, China was still the largest economy in the world, larger than 30 Western European countries put together, not to mention the United States, which had fewer than 20 states at the time. But since then, mired in both internal and external troubles, China's share in the global economy had kept declining, to the bottom of the valley when the New China was founded.[2] Having gone through a catastrophic century and more, this ancient civilization that was once splendid witnessed the establishment of the People's Republic of China in 1949, and began its epic rejuvenation ever since.

After the founding of the People's Republic, the fundamentally changed China began to embark on the road of rise. Despite a poor economic foundation and harsh external environment, China's economy in the Mao Zedong era, notwithstanding some twists and turns, achieved

---

[1] For the convenience of the account, the term Five-Year Plan used in this book refers in general to either "five-year plan" or "five-year program".

[2] Angus Maddison, *Statistics on World Population, GDP and Per Capita GDP, 1–2008 AD*, http://www.ggdc.net/MADDISON/Historical_Statistics/vertical-file_02-2010.xls.

a remarkable growth rate. Since 1978, China's economy has been advancing triumphantly for more than 40 years, with its share in the global economy climbing all the way up, calculated by exchange rate surpassing Italy in 2000, France in 2005, Britain in 2006, Germany in 2008, and Japan in 2010, and now settling down to rank second in the world economy.

If calculated by purchasing power parity, China's gross economic volume actually already exceeded Japan's as early as 1992. Likewise, if calculated by purchasing power parity, as estimated by Arvind Subramanian, an Indian economist at the Peterson Institute for International Economics, "China's index of overall economic dominance overtook that of the United States around 2010."[3] The International Monetary Fund (IMF) was not as optimistic, but the data it provided also revealed that in 1980, China's share in the world economy was merely 2.19%, against the United States' share of one-third, more than 10 times that of China. Since 1980, China's share in the global economy has been climbing all the way up, while the United States' share has gradually declined, with the amplitude of fluctuation ever greater. The IMF predicted in 2012 that by 2017, the global share of China's economy would rise to 18.3%, while the global share of the U.S. economy would drop to 17.9%.[4] That would be a historic turning point: the United States would lose its leading position since 1871, and China would return to the throne of the world's largest economy. For a long time to come, although China's per capita income will remain lower than that of the United States, and it still has to struggle to catch up, the significance of this historical turning point should not be underestimated.

Why was the Old China before 1949 unable but the New China after 1949 able to make it? Why is it that the New China not only made it in the 40 years post-reform but has always been able to make achievements throughout the 70 years? There are many colorful chapters in the China story, and here we will focus on one of them: how China has been based on the current circumstances to plan the future.

The device for China to project future trends and priorities is its medium- and long-term plans (or programs) for the national economic

---

[3] Arvind Subramanian, *Eclipse: Living in the Shadow of China's Economic Dominance* (Washington, DC: Peterson Institute for International Economics, 2011), p. 9.

[4] IMF World Economic Outlook Database (2012), http://www.imf.org.external/pubs/ft/weo/2012/02/weodata/download.aspx.

and social development that are turned out regularly, often in a five-year cycle. The five-year planning is almost the same age as the New China, as the country began to prepare its first Five-Year Plan in 1951. Since then, with the only exception of the 1963–1965 adjustment period, 13 five-year plans have been formulated and implemented, becoming a cycle of policies at five-year intervals. It best illustrates how the New China's political system has sustained and been carried on for the long run with constant adjustments and innovations, and it also serves as the most vivid testimony of how the New China's policy-making system has experienced setbacks and zigzags but has made continuous improvements and progress anyway.

## Planning Well for Decision Made, Action Taken with Success Secured

Compared with various other plans, medium- and long-term national economic and social development planning could be regarded as "mankind's most ambitious collective enterprise."[5]

What is unique about humans on this planet compared with other animal species? With a little thinking, we could realize that one of the key differences between humans and other animals is their ability to plan for the future. Although some animals seem to share this ability (such as black bears living in seclusion for winter and birds building nests), biological studies have found that other animals' seemingly pre-planning activities are just the result of instinct, instead of the result of conscious planning. And humans cannot do without planning in their daily life, from planning the dinner for this evening to planning the next vacation, from planning family finance to planning the life for children. In more striking contrast to other animals' behavior, "building skyscrapers and launching rockets require an extraordinary amount of forethought."[6] Not only do modern people have the ability to plan for the future, but the pyramids of Egypt, Stonehenge in Britain, and Roman Colosseums that remain on the Mediterranean coast, all demonstrate the extraordinary human ability to plan for the future. Aside from the amazing monolith engineering wonders, ancient people also created one fascinating

---

[5] A. F. Robertson, *People and State: An Anthropology of Planned Development* (New York: Cambridge University Press, 1984), p. 1.

[6] Daniel D. Chiras, *Human Biology: Health, Homeostasis, and the Environment*, 3rd ed (Sudbury, MA: Jones and Bartlett Publisher, 2005), p. 11.

systematic engineering miracle after another, such as Athens' Acropolis, Peru's Machu Picchu, China's Great Wall, Dujiangyan irrigation and flood control project, nine ancient capitals, Grand Canal, and Turpan's karez water tunnels, and so on.

Entering modern times, humans began the attempts to think about planning the development direction for the whole society. Friedrich List, a German economist, was perhaps one of the pioneers in this regard. Although he did not explicitly use the term "economic planning" or "planned economy," his famous book, *National System of Political Economy* (published in 1841), clearly implied it. One of his famous sayings is: "It is true that experience teaches that the wind bears the seed from one region to another, and that, thus waste moorlands have been transformed into dense forests; but would it on that account be wise policy for the forester to wait until the wind in the course of ages effects this transformation? Is it unwise on his part if by sowing and planting he seeks to attain the same object within a few decades? History tells us that whole nations have successfully accomplished that which we see the forester do?"[7] These words directed against the market supremacy advocated by Adam Smith in *The Wealth of Nations*, and List meant to justify government intervention in the economy and steering the development in theory.

Likewise, when talking about the new social system in the future, Marx repeatedly mentioned the necessity for planned regulation on economy, but did not use the term "economic plan" or "planned economy."[8] For instance, in Volume III of *Capital*, Marx envisioned that a future socialist society consists in "socialized man, the associated producers, rationally regulating their interchange with Nature, bringing it under their common control, instead of being ruled by it as by the blind forces of Nature;

---

[7] Friedrich List, *National System of Political Economy* (London: Longmans, Green and Co., 1909), p. 93.

[8] Engels held that there was certain planning in capitalism. When criticizing the draft *Social-Democratic Program* in 1891, he wrote: "Capitalist production by *joint-stock companies* is no longer *private* production but production on behalf of many associated people. And when we pass on from joint-stock companies to trusts, which dominate and monopolize who branches of industry, this puts an end not only to private production but also to planlessness." See Engels, *A Critique of the Draft Social-Democratic Program of 1891*, https://www.connexions.org/CxArchive/MIA/marx/works/1891/06/29.htm.

and achieving this with the least expenditure of energy and under conditions most favorable to, and worthy of, their human nature."[9] However, Marx's vision for planned regulation in the future new society was still very abstract. His advice was that what the future socialist society should do "depends of course entirely on the given historical conditions in which one has to act. But this question is in the clouds and therefore is really the statement of a phantom problem...".[10]

In the history of economic thought, Lenin was perhaps the first to propose the concept of "planned economy." In his 1906 essay *The Land Question and the Fight for Freedom*, he asserted, "Exploitation can be completely abolished only when all the land, factories, and tools are transferred to the working class, and when large-scale socialized and planned production is organized."[11] At this point, he was yet to elaborate on the connotation of "planned production" or economy.

A few years later, a German named Walther Rathenau came up with his own theory of planned economy.[12] Rathenau is almost forgotten today, but Friedrich August von Hayek remembered well: "I was especially influenced—in fact the influence very much contributed to my interest in economics—by the writings of a man called Walther Rathenau, who was an industrialist and later a statesman and finally a politician in Germany, who wrote extremely well. ... and he had become an enthusiastic planner."[13] Rathenau had published a number of articles outlining a model of planned economy while Hayek was still a teenager. Although his theory was full of endogenous dynamics, not perfect and self-consistent, his contempt for liberalism was unquestionable. No wonder some people called him "a pioneer of the planned economy."[14]

---

[9] Karl Marx, *Capital*, Vol. III (NY: International Publishers, 1968), p. 593.

[10] Karl Marx, *Marx to Domela Nieuwenhuis*, February 22, 1881, *Marx and Engels Correspondence* (International Publishers, 1968).

[11] Lenin, *The Land Question and the Fight for Freedom* (May 19, 1906), *Lenin Collected Works*, Vol. 10 (Moscow, 1965), pp. 436–439.

[12] *Encyclopedia Britannica* does not mention his theoretical contribution in this regard at all in his entry.

[13] *Nobel Prize-Winning Economist, Friedrich A. von Hayek*, Oral History Program, University of California at Los Angeles, 1983 (interviews with Hayek conducted on October 28 and November 4, 11, and 12, 1978), p. 11.

[14] W. O. Henderson, *Walther Rathenau: A Pioneer of the Planned Economy, Economic History Review*, Vol. 4, No. 1 (1951), pp. 98–108.

The start of World War I offered a chance for Rathenau's concept to become a reality.[15] Following his proposal, the Prussian War Ministry, the highest administrative agency in the German army, set up a new raw material section centralizing the requisition and allocation of key raw materials up to 300 varieties at most, even including every kind of manure in farmers' horse and cattle stalls to satisfy the demand of military production.[16] In addition to production plans, Germany also established wartime food companies, central feed bureau, central potato bureau, wartime animal fats and vegetable oil management committee, central fruit and vegetable bureau, wartime food bureau, imperial cereals bureau, imperial garment bureau, and other agencies, to bring people's basic consumer needs into the government planned management.[17] In fact, during World War I, not only Germany, but other Western countries also organized the national production of war materials in a planned manner. An economic historian, for example, called the U.S. economy at that time "a totally planned economy."[18]

After the October Revolution, Lenin confessed, "We know about socialism, but knowledge of organization on a scale of millions, knowledge of the organization and distribution of goods, etc.—this we do not have. The old Bolshevik leaders did not teach us this. The Bolshevik Party cannot boast of it in its history. We have not done a course on this yet."[19] Lenin was deeply impressed by Germany's wartime planned approach to steering the direction of economic development, which considerably

[15] Fritz Redlich, *German Economic Planning for War and Peace*, The Review of Politics, Vol. 6, No. 3 (Jul, 1944), pp. 315–335.

[16] R. R. Palmer, Lloyd Kramer and Joel Colton, *A History of the Modern World* (NYC: McGraw-Hill Companies, 2006). Nial Ferguson, *Paper and Iron: Hamburg Business and German Politics in the Era of Inflation, 1897–1927* (Oxford: Cambridge University Press, 1995).

[17] Karl Dietrich Erdmann, *Handbook of the German History*, 8th Edition, Vol. IV, *The Age of World Wars* (Stuttgart: Union-Verlag, 1959).

[18] Murray N. Rothbard, *War Collectivism in World War I*, in Ronald Radosh and Murray N. Rothbard, eds., *A New History of Leviathan* (New York: E.P. Dutton & Co., Inc., 1972), p. 66.

[19] Lenin, *Report on the Immediate Tasks of the Soviet Government at the Session of All-Russia Central Executive Committee* (April 29, 1918), *Collected Works of Lenin*, 4th English Edition, Vol. 27 (Moscow: Progress Publishers, 1972), pp. 279–313.

influenced his elaboration on his own theory of planned economy.[20] In turn, Lenin's theory later influenced the practice of the Soviet planned economy during the war communism period and Stalin era. Marxist historian Eric Hobsbawm asserted: "...Soviet ideas of planning were originally inspired by, and to some extent based on, what the Bolsheviks knew of the German planned war economy of 1914–1917."[21] Non-Marxist historian Edward Hallett Carr held a similar view: "Historically, Friedrich List preceded Marx as the father of the theory of planning; Rathenau, who organized the first modern planned economy in Germany of the first world war, preceded Lenin, whose approach to the problem of planning in Soviet Russia was consciously based on the German precedents."[22]

When Lenin was alive, Soviet Russia formed the State Electrification Commission in 1920 and at the end of that year launched its first national economic recovery and development plan. In February 1921, Soviet Russia established the State Planning Commission. A few years later, the commission began to formulate an annual plan with "tentative figures." After Lenin's death, the Soviet Union (established in 1922) began to implement its first Five-year Plan in 1928. Before World War II, its first three five-year plans (1928–1940) were very successful, with GDP growing at a record rate of 5.3% annually, and industrial output increased at 11% annually. This was a remarkable performance at that time, enabling the Soviet Union to jump from an agricultural country into a world industrial power in a short period of time.[23]

When the New China was founded, the Soviet Union had entered the ending period of its fourth Five-Year Plan for the postwar recovery. Those were years when the economic planning was sweeping the world. The planning was so popular that British economist Arthur Lewis declared in his 1949 book *The Principles of Economic Planning*: "There are no longer any believers in *laisser-faire*, except on the lunatic fringe. ...The truth is

---

[20] Ren Xiaowei, *Germany's Planned Economy in World War I and Its Influence on Lenin: The Historic Origin of the Soviet Model of Planned Economy*, Issues of Contemporary World Socialism, Vol. 3 (2007).

[21] Eric Hobsbawm, *The Age of Extremes: The Short Twentieth Century, 1914–1991* (London: Abacus, 1995), p. 46.

[22] Edward Hallett Carr, *The Bolshevik Revolution 1917–1923*, Vol. 2 (New York: Macmillan, 1952) p. 363.

[23] Robert C. Allen, *Farm to Factory: A Reinterpretation of the Soviet Industrial Revolution* (Princeton: Princeton University Press, 2003), p. 153.

that we are all planners now."[24] At that time and in some years thereafter, not only did the Soviet Union and the socialist countries of East Europe carry out the all-round planning system,[25] but some vintage Western capitalist countries (like the Netherlands, France, Sweden and Norway) introduced the concept of planning in varying manners in the economic and social development.[26] Japan comprehensively restored its wartime controlled economy immediately after the war, and even as it switched to a "market economy" in 1949, it initiated the *Secondary Recovery Plan* (1949–1953). Since then, the Japanese government has sustained its long-term economic planning to this day, beginning with the *Five-Year Economic Self-Support Plan* drawn up in December 1955. This means that "Japan's economy, although counted as a market economy, contains elements introduced from the basis of war-time planning and controlled economy in its institutional foundation."[27] Some Japanese scholars simply called their economic system "planned economy."[28] Countries of the Third world (like India, Malaysia, Indonesia and Egypt) were all the more not to lag behind, setting up planning departments in their governments and launching development plans.[29] South Korea and China's Taiwan among the "Four Little Dragons of Asia" are examples of them.[30]

---

[24] Arthur Lewis, *The Principles of Economic Planning* (NY: Routledge Taylor & Francis Group, 2010), p. 14.

[25] Marie Lavigne, *The Socialist Economies of the Soviet Union and Europe* (New York: International Arts and Sciences Press, 1974).

[26] Stephen S. Cohen, *Modern Capitalist Planning: The French Model* (Berkeley: University of California Press, 1977).

[27] Yasushi Yamanouchi, J. Victor Koschmann and Ryuichi Narita, *Total War and "Modernization", Cornell East Asia Series 100* (New York: Cornell University East Asia Program, 1998), Cited from Feng Wei, *Total War and Formation of Three Features in Modern Japan's Economic System—New Trends in the Research on Japan's Economic History in Recent Years, Historical Research*, Vol. 5, No, 157 (2004).

[28] Takahashi Kamekichi, *Fundamental Cause of Japan's Post-war Economic Leap* (Shenyang: Liaoning People's Publishing House, 1984), p. 10.

[29] Albert Waterston, *Development Planning: Lessons of Experience* (Baltimore: Johns Hopkins University Press, 1979).

[30] Tibor Scitovsky, *Economic Development in Taiwan and South Korea: 1965–1981, Food Research Institute Studies*, Vol. XIX, No. 3 (1985), pp. 215–264; Tun-Jen Cheng, Stephan Haggard & David Kang, *Institutions and Growth in Korea and Taiwan: The Bureaucracy, The Journal of Development Studies*, Vol. 34, No. 6 (1998), pp. 87–111.

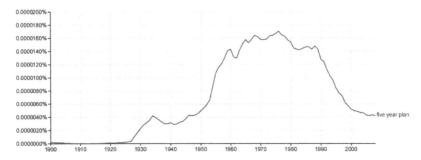

**Fig. 5.1** Frequency with which English phrase "five-year plan" appears in Google Book Ngrams 1900–2000

Of the more than 30 million books scanned by Google, the frequency with which the English phrase "five-year plan" appears at different historical times can be regarded as an indicator of the importance attached to this institutional arrangement globe wide. As Fig. 5.1 indicates, the first turning point at which people's interest in the concept of planning was kindled came in 1928, when the Soviet Union began to implement its first Five-Year Plan. In the following 50 years except for the period around World War II, the passion for five-year planning gradually grew and culminated in the mid-to-late 1970s. At that time, only a handful of economies were going against the tide: the United States, Switzerland, Liechtenstein, and Hong Kong of China, who did not have national plans.[31] Against this background, it may not be surprising that the New China began to draw up and implement its five-year plans shortly after it was founded. It was not until the late 1970s that the concept of five-year planning began to show a declining tendency, with a steep downslide after 1990, most notably because of the transition of the Soviet Union and East European countries one by one: they gave up the public ownership and economic planning and transited to capitalist system.

Then how effective is the economic planning? The case in 1980, when the concept of economic planning had culminated and began to decline but the transition in swarms was yet to come up, may serve as an illustration. Figure 5.2 lists the ranking of GDP per capita and the ranking of the Human Development Indicator (HDI) of each economy in the

---

[31] A. F. Robertson, *People and State: An Anthropology of Planned Development*, p 7.

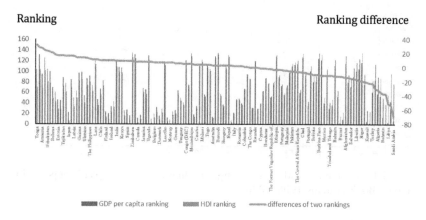

**Fig. 5.2** GDP per capita and HID rankings in each economy, 1980 (*Source* UNDP, 2010 Report Hybrid-HDI data of trends analysis, http://hdrundp.org/en/media/2010_Hybrid-HDI-data.xls)

year of 1980 and lists the differences between the two rankings. The first ranking can be used to measure the level of economic development, while the second can be used to measure the extent to which a society satisfies the basic human necessities. If one economy's two rankings are equal, i.e., the difference of its two rankings is zero, that means the first ranking determines the second, but its socio-economic system itself does not have the capacity to improve human well-being. This was the case in Hong Kong of China, which followed a "free economic system" at that time. If the difference between the two rankings is a positive value, it means that even if the level of economic development is not high, the socio-economic system could do something in improving human well-being, which was the case in China. The greater the positive value, the more obvious the institutional superiority. If the difference between the two rankings is a negative value, it means that, even at a high level of economic development, the socio-economic system may drag down the improvement of human well-being, which was the case in Saudi Arabia. The greater the negative value, the more obvious the institutional inferiority.

In Fig. 5.2, almost all the top 30 countries and more with the biggest positive difference values of the two rankings carried out economic planning (especially those socialist countries), and among them were most populous countries accounting for a large proportion of the global population. This evidences that whatever other problems the economic planning might incur, its credit in satisfying the basic human necessities cannot be denied.

By the 1980s and 1990s, the concept of planning was no longer that popular. Prior to the Soviet Union's collapse at the end of 1991, the 70-year-old State Planning Commission was annulled in April that year. Around that time, countries that had been carrying out economic planning all changed the way to abandon the five-year planning and switch to the so-called free market economy. It was in this context that Francis Fukuyama, a Japanese-American who worked in the policy planning unit at the U.S. State Department, boldly asserted that the socialist central planning mechanism had failed and "history has ended," and liberal capitalism would be the only evolutionary direction of the "universal history" of mankind.[32] However, such an overbearing conviction that capitalism was sure to prevail was just a flash in the pan.

Those "transition countries" divorced from the socialist track were not all in a merry state. At the beginning of their transition, someone already predicted that these countries would inevitably lead through a bitter journey of "valley of tears" before things got better.[33] But no one expected that the "valley of tears" would be so deep and so long. Figure 5.3 shows how GDP per capita in the countries in transition varied. Of the 28 Soviet-European countries in transition, only five had their GDP per capita barely restored to the pre-transition level within 10 years; and 17 countries managed to restore their GDP per capita to the pre-transition level in 17 to 20 years, with a whole generation of people desolated. What was worse, up to the 30th year of transition in 2019, there were still four countries, Moldova, Georgia, Serbia, and Ukraine, where GDP per capita was yet to recover to the pre-transition level, and people were still struggling in the "valley of tears." Among them, Ukraine's GDP per capita in 2019 was less than three-quarters of what it was before the transition, and even if everything goes well, it may take it several more decades to recover to the 1989 level. For these countries, the cost of transition was that they had to endure a recession many times worse than the Great Depression of the 1930s,

---

[32] Francis Fukuyama, *The End of History? The National Interest*, Vol. 16 (Summer 1989), pp. 3–18; Francis Fukuyama, *The End of History and the Last Man* (New York: Free Press, 1992).

[33] Ralf Dahrendorf, *Europe's Vale of Tears, Marxism Today* (May 1990), pp. 18–23.

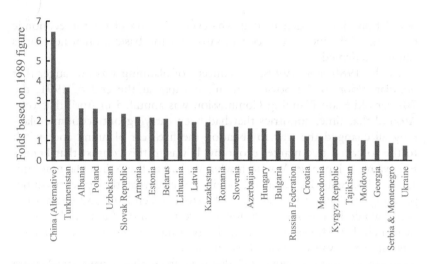

**Fig. 5.3** Variation of GDP per capita of countries in transition, 1989–2019 (calculated at 2018 international US dollar) (*Source* The Conference Board, Total Economy Database, April 2019, http://www.conference-board.org/data/economydatabase/TED1)

which is probably extremely rare in human history. Moreover, there was widespread criminalization in many transition countries, with drastically increasing inequality and declining life expectancy which was rarely seen in peace time of the mankind, leading to millions of premature deaths.[34] By contrast, China's performance can be described as superb. In 1989, China's GDP per capita was way lower than that of the 28 countries in transition; but by 2019, China had surpassed about half of them in GDP per capita.

In a paper reviewing the rise and fall of planning concept in 2007, Michael Ellman, a Dutch scholar spending years studying the Soviet planning system, concluded: If the planning mechanism is not perfect, "markets on their own could not be relied on to generate attractive

---

[34] David Stuckler, Lawrence King and Martin McKee, *Mass Privatization and the Post-Communist Mortality Crisis: A Cross-National Analysis*, Lancet, Vol. 373, No. 9661 (2009), pp. 399–407.

outcomes."[35] Meanwhile, in the backyard of the United States where the Washington Consensus went rampant, the peril of "market fundamentalism" has become so obvious that Latin American countries began to "turn left" in swarms. By 2008, a severe economic crisis spread from the United States to the world, and large corporations as symbols of capitalism were facing bankruptcy one after another. As a last resort, governments from Iceland to Ireland, from Australia to Japan, from the United Kingdom to the United States, all stepped in to nationalize banks, insurance companies, and the auto industry. To this, a *Newsweek* cover story exclaimed, "We are all socialists now!".[36]

In economic and social development, to draw medium- and long-term plans implies a disbelief in that the market is omnipotent, and a belief in that the future can be managed to some extent. It is indeed very difficult to forecast the future, because there are too many variables that affect the future while it is neither possible nor necessary to accurately predict every detail of the future. In this sense, Hayek was undoubtedly right to assert that it is impossible for mankind to command full and accurate details about the present and the future in time.[37] But one step further may turn the truth into a fallacy. The impossibility "to command full and accurate details about the present and the future in time" does not mean a complete incapability to comprehend the present and the future. Suppose we are completely unable to understand the present, then how could Hayek criticize the socialist theory and practice in reality? Suppose it is completely impossible to understand the future, then how could Hayek's followers believe that the "invisible hand" of free market can lead human society to the best outcome forever? As long as the present and the future is knowable to some extent, the planning is possible; as long as the planning is possible, it is necessary to make plans, so as to clear the direction of struggle, and endeavor to maximize the well-being of people under conditions of resource scarcity.

---

[35] Michael Ellman, *The Rise and Fall of Socialist Planning*, in S. Estrin, G. Kolodko & M. Uvalic (eds) *Transition and Beyond: Essays in Honor of Marriot Nuti* (Basingstoke: Palgrave Macmillan, 2007), p. 31.

[36] Jon Meacham and Evan Thomas, *We Are All Socialists Now*, Newsweek (February 6, 2009).

[37] F. A. Hayek, *The Fatal Conceit: The Errors of Socialism* (Chicago: University of Chicago Press, 1988).

Chinese scholars are familiar with Janos Kornai's criticisms of the traditional socialist planning system, but I'm afraid they are not quite aware of his real thinking about planning. Kornai thought it foolish to pour the baby out with the bath water. In his autobiography published in 2006, his consideration on the prospect of planning is worth citing in length:

> I think it is regrettable that the failure of the communist system should have discredited the idea of planning. Not just Hungary's National Planning Office but the Soviet Gosplan and the central planning apparatus in every former socialist country were dissolved. The ranks of planners have thinned and planning institutes have lost influence outside the former Soviet bloc as well. You do not need to be a Communist or accept Marxist thinking still to see possibilities in planning on the national economic level. The undertaking would require computations that went beyond the bounds of one or two fiscal years and tried to survey consistently the development alternatives before a country. Such planning need not lead to a document full of instructions for the actors in the economy. It would be enough to compute alternative development paths for politicians and for other decision makers to think about and use as background in their discussions -- rather as Ragnar Frisch, Jan Tinbergen,[38] and the French planners of the 1960s envisaged when they recommended *indicative* planning (compatible with the market economy) instead of the *imperative* planning of a communist economy. Perhaps one day, when the dire memories of old-style planning under a communist system have vanished, the idea of planning may enjoy a renaissance.[39]

---

[38] Norwegian Lagnar Frisch and Dutchman Jan Tinbergen won the first Nobel Prize in Economics in 1969. Their respective studies have both contributed to introducing econometric models into government economic planning. In fact, the two concepts of "econometrics" and "macroeconomics" were introduced into economics by Frisch. The two of them also vigorously advocated and promoted economic planning in their respective country. Frisch is regarded as a key figure in introducing planning into Norway. See Arild Saether and Ib E. Eriksen, *Ragnar Frisch and the Post-war Norwegian Economy*, Econ Journal Watch, Vol. 11, No. 1 (January 2014), pp. 46–80. Tinbergen served as director of the Nethelands Bureau for Economic Policy Analysis from 1945 to 1955 and chairman of the United Nations Committee on Development Planning from 1965 to 1972. See Daniel B. Klein and Ryan Daza, *Jan Tinbergen*, Econ Journal Watch, Vol. 10, No. 3 (September 2013), pp. 660–666.

[39] Janos Kornai, *By Force of Thought: Irregular Memoirs of an Intellectual Journey* (Cambridge, MA: The MIT Press, 2006), p. 157.

In his new book *Dynamism, Rivalry and Surplus Economy: Two Essays on the Nature of Capitalism* published in early 2014, Kornai was no longer entangled with the problems of traditional socialism characterized by shortage, but tried to address the challenges faced by capitalism characterized by surplus. In order to solve the problem of supply–demand balance in the capitalist economy, Kornai did not blindly advocate the "invisible hand" as some "market fundamentalists" did, but said sincerely:

> Let me propose what may seem anachronistic: the application of medium and long-term planning. Not the failed socialist system of imperative planning, but updated forms of indicative planning on the lines of those once used in France. After requisite experimentation, this may contribute to better coordination of new capacity and expected demand, and perhaps deter the heads of large corporations from undertaking mammoth investments that only increase the idle capacity in their industries further.[40]

"When the seas are in turmoil, heroes are on their mettle." Unlike other countries in transition, there is no need for the idea of planning to enjoy a renaissance in China, because it has never vanished but just has been modified. Although China declared in 1992 to shift from a planned economy to a socialist market economy and renamed the State Planning Commission the National Development Planning Commission in 1998 and the National Development and Reform Commission in 2003, the disappearance of the word "planning" does not mean to throw away the five-year planning.[41] As Jiang Zemin put it in 1992, "From the very beginning, socialist economies have been planned; everyone knows this perfectly well, and they will not be confused about whether planning has been eliminated just because the term 'planned' is not used in the formulation."[42] To date, China has implemented 13 five-year plans or five-year programs, of them five were formulated and implemented after the transition to a socialist market economy. Although the world economic crisis

---

[40] Janos Kornai, *Dynamism, Rivalry and Surplus Economy: Two Essays on the Nature of Capitalism* (New York: Oxford University Press, 2014), p. 137.

[41] Hu Angang, Yan Yilong and LvyJie, *From Imperative Planning for Economy to Strategic Program for Development: Path to Transition of China's Five-year Planning (1953–2009)*, China Soft Science, Vol. 8 (2010), pp. 14–24.

[42] Jiang Zemin, *Concerning China's Establishment of a Socialist Market Economy* (June 9, 1992), *Selected Works of Jiang Zemin*, Vol. 1 (Beijing: Foreign Languages Press, 2010), p. 192.

that erupted in 2008 also put a drag on China's economy, the socialist China's economy continued to grow at a pace ahead of other countries, and China is worthy to be the locomotive of the global economic recovery.[43]

China's five-year plans (or programs) can be regarded as the "compass" of its economic and social development, and as the framework guiding specific economic and social policies. It is no exaggeration to say that the road to China's economic miracle is paved with a string of five-year plans or programs. More and more foreign observers have come to realize it. After a visit to China, Andy Stern, a senior fellow at Columbia University, wrote an article at the end of 2011, praising China's capacity to develop a more superior economic model, with the bright spot being its ability to plan for the future. At the end of the article, he expressed the hope to see that the United States would also have "a forward-looking, long-term economic plan."[44] His article drew widespread attention and discussion in the United States, as Stern served as president of a major U.S. labor union and was an Obama insider. It is interesting to note that this article was published in the *Wall Street Journal* which is heavily pro-business with a libertarian color, while its Chinese edition put the article into Chinese under the headline: "China has a planned economy, so should the United States." This, I am afraid, might attempt to mislead readers deliberately.

Suppose Stern may have misjudged because he didn't know China well, James McGregor is arguably a "China hand." McGregor was a reporter of *the Wall Street Journal* and a chief executive of Dow Jones & Company in China in the early 1990s, later he became chairman of the American Chamber of Commerce in China and chairman of APCO Worldwide's greater China region, dealing with China for more than 30 years. In his book *No Ancient Wisdom, No Followers: The Challenges of Chinese Authoritarian Capitalism*,[45] McGregor repeatedly referred to China's 12th Five-Year Plan and reminded readers of how important China's five-year planning would be. To him, "One key thing we can learn from China

---

[43] Sun Yuting and Gao Sheng, *China Exceeded the U.S. in Contribution to the World Economic Growth in the Past Decade*, Chinanews.com, 2010-10-30.

[44] Andy Stern, *China's Superior Economic Model: The Free-Market Fundamentalist Economic Model Is Being Thrown Onto the Trash Heap of History*, Wall Street Journal (December 1, 2011).

[45] James McGregor, *No Ancient Wisdom, No Followers: The Challenges of Chinese Authoritarian Capitalism* (Prospercta Press, 2012).

is setting goals, making plans, and focusing on moving the country ahead as a nation." Chinese "have taken the old five-year plans and stood them on their head. Instead of deciding which factory gets which raw materials, which products are made, how they are priced, and where they are sold, their planning now consists of 'how do we build a world-class silicon-chip industry in five years? How do we become a global player in car-manufacturing?'".[46]

Orville Schell, Arthur Ross Director of the Center on U.S.-China Relations at the Asia Society in New York, may know China better than McGregor. He has been studying China since the 1960s, published nine books on China, and served as dean of the Berkeley Graduate School of Journalism at the University of California, and is one of the most famous "China hands" in the United States. Despite his criticisms of China on many issues, he fully agreed with McGregor on this point: "I think we have come to realize the ability to plan is exactly what we are missing in America. We can't make a one-year plan, much less a five-year plan. Some of us have begun to understand that is a great danger to us." Then why is this ability to plan is missing in America? The observation from Robert Engle, winner of the 2003 Nobel Memorial Prize in Economic Sciences, hit the nail on the head: When China is planning for the future with wonderful five-year plans, Americans are merely planning for the next election.[47]

This touches on deeper institutional problems. In 2012, Ann Lee, a successful Chinese-American career woman who had gone through challenging experiences in American financing business for years and was a visiting professor to Peking University, published a book titled *What the U.S. Can Learn from China*? She argued that the American political system has turned the country into a "short-term-oriented society" since American politicians' top concerns are how to get enough votes in the next election. They cross verbal swords all day long and quarrel endlessly, which looks extraordinarily bustling, but they are careless about the country's long-term development direction, and they are unable to reach consensus on major strategic issues. By contrast, the leadership of the Communist Party in China has guided its officials to avoid short-sighted

---

[46] Bill Powell, *Five Things the U.S. Can Learn from China*, Time (November 12, 2009), http://content.time.com/time/magazine/article/0,0171,1938734,00.html.

[47] Chen Weihua, *Time for US to Make Plans for the Future*, China Daily (November 18, 2011), http://www.chinadaily.com.cn/opnion/2011-11/18/content_14115844.him.

campaign mentality but focus on long-term strategic planning, so that the precious time and resources are not wasted in endless campaigning. In Ann Lee's words, "The debate over whether democracy needs one, two, three, or more parties to achieve proper representation of the public interest misses the bigger question — what conditions are required to create a system that will be the most proactive in planning for a sustainable future for the greatest number of people?"[48] What's more, in an election campaign, politicians often make big and empty promises that are nicknamed "election promises" so as to get as many votes as possible. Such "promises" are neither serious nor prudent, which are hard to come true, and cannot be counted at all.[49] But the medium- and long-term plans are different. They mean that the government takes the initiative to give the public objective benchmarks to measure its performance. With these objective benchmarks, the public is less likely to forget them and can also see whether government officials keep their promises, and the government will spur on itself to move in the direction set in the plan.[50] Toward the end of the book, Ann Lee appealed, "Talk alone is not enough. An action plan must be drawn up. Whether it's a 5-year plan or a 25-year plan, a roadmap must exist and hold groups accountable for achieving agreed-upon milestones that are both meaningful and measurable."[51] Ian Bremmer, president of Eurasia Group, the world renowned political risk research and consulting firm, concluded the *Forward* he wrote for Lee's book with these words: "...the sometime excesses of our system remind us that short-term tactical thinking too often replaces sound long-term planning– both in Washington and on Wall Street. What can the U.S. learn from China? Plenty."[52]

---

[48] Ann Lee, *What the U.S. Can Learn from China: An Open-Minded Guide to Treating Our Greatest Competitor as our Greatest Teacher* (San Francisco: Berrett-Koehler Publishers, Inc. 2012), p. 90.

[49] See the entry of "election promise" on Wikipedia.

[50] Ann Lee, *What the U.S. Can Learn from China: An Open-Minded Guide to Treating Our Greatest Competitor as our Greatest Teacher* (San Francisco: Berrett-Koehler Publishers, Inc. 2012), p. 117.

[51] Ibid., p. 201.

[52] Ibid., p. xi.

## Preparedness Ensures Success, Unpreparedness Spells Failure

The above account of necessity and importance of planning in economic and social development does not mean that the plan should be all-inclusive, involving every detail of people's lives; nor does it mean that the plan will be error-free and deviation-free; much less to mean that, as long as there is a plan, economic and social development will unfold on its own orderly. In other words, the necessity and importance of a plan lies not in a plan that is formulated, but in the planning itself. In both Chinese and Western languages, "plan" can be either a verb or a noun. The "plan" as a noun is the result of "planning" as a verb. "Plan" as a noun refers to a program previously drawn up, which is important, but what really matters is "planning" as a verb, that is, the intention and ability to plan for the future. As for the differentiation between the two words, the late British Prime Minister Winston Churchill had a saying well to the point: "Plans are of little importance, but planning is essential." In fact, Churchill who had experienced World War II had another saying: "We may have taken decisions which will prove to be less good than we hoped, but at any rate anything is better than not having a plan."[53] In Churchill's view, the "plan" as a noun should not be used to bind people, but to guide their conducts. In his words, "the best generals are those who arrive at the results of planning without being tied to plans."[54] Here the necessity and importance of planning are preset.

Helmuth Karl Bernhard von Moltke, Prussian field marshal and chief of staff of the German army for 30 years, had a similar take: "The plans are nothing but the planning is everything." Dwight David Eisenhower, who served as the Allied commander in Europe during World War II, allegedly often quoted Moltke as saying so and routinely told associates, "Relying on planning, but never trust plans."[55] This deeply impressed Nixon, who later served as president of the United States, only he was not clear that the quote was from Moltke.[56]

---

[53] Richar M. Langworth, ed., *Churchill by Himself: The Definitive Collection of Quotations* (New York: Public Affairs, 2008), p. 492.

[54] Ibid., p. 214.

[55] Even Thomas, *Ike's Bluff: President Eisenhower's Secret Battle to Save the World* (Back Bay Books, 2013), p. 44.

[56] Richard Nixon, *Six Crises* (New York: Simon & Schuster, 1990), p. 247.

Moltke, Churchill, and Eisenhower were all outstanding military strategists. Also a great military strategist, Mao Zedong clearly understood the necessity and importance of planning. One of his famous sayings is, "'Preparedness ensures success and unpreparedness spells failure', there can be no victory in war without advance planning and preparations."[57] In fact, the importance of planning is not confined to the military strategic domain, it is equally important in the economic and social development. The United States does not have the capacity to plan for medium- and long-term economic and social development, but this did not stop Timothy Franz Geithner, former U.S. Secretary of the Treasury, from coming to realize that "Plan beats no plan." He repeated this phrase in his new book *Stress Testing: Reflections on Financial Crises*.[58]

The planning is essential and important not because the plans made could accurately predict every step toward the future. Individuals who have drawn up their career plans are often likely to be disappointed, enterprises that have formulated their marketing plans probably often find that the business performance is not desirable, research teams that have come up with their research plans may often hit the wall, and cities that have drawn up their urban plans may see unapproved construction projects. But can this prove that career planning, marketing planning, scientific research planning, and urban planning are unnecessary at all? Obviously not! Imagine that without planning, would these individuals, enterprises, research teams, and cities get any better off?

Likewise, countries that have formulated economic and social development plans may never achieve their goals 100%. Actually, it would not be hard for a country to achieve all the preset metrics in case there are not many metrics in the plan it has made while each one is not set very high. But the planning would be meaningless by doing so. That's why no country that makes plans for economic and social development would act that way. Instead, they would set the planning metrics at a height that cannot be reached unless through considerable efforts. That's what the practice China has taken. As Fig. 5.4 indicates, since the implementation of the first Five-Year Plan began in 1953 up to 2010 when the 11th Five-Year Plan was completed, China never fulfilled all its planned metrics

---

[57] Mao Zedong, *On Protracted War* (May 1938), *Selected Works of Mao Tse-tung*, Vol. II (Beijing: Foreign Languages Press, 1965), p. 168.

[58] Timothy F. Geithner, *Stress Test: Reflections on Financial Crises* (New York: Crown, 2014).

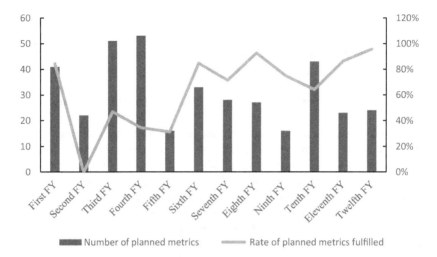

**Fig. 5.4** Quantity of planned metrics and their fulfillment rate *(Note* The fulfillment rate of planned metrics refer to the ratio of the number of metrics fulfilled (at and above 100%) and the overall number of planned metrics. *Source* Yan Yilong, *Metrics Governance: Visible Hand of Five-Year Planning*, Beijing: China Renmin University Press, 2013: 293–295; 326–340)

100%. Yet I'm afraid no one could jump to the conclusion based on this chart that China's economic and social development may have been equally amazing or even better without medium- and long-term planning. Such counter-factual assumptions can neither be proven true nor proven false, they at best are just expressions of emotions and positions. Despite the vicissitudes of the world over the past few decades, China has never given up its medium- and long-term planning, and although the implementation of the resulted plans has not been all that satisfying, the perseverance in formulating the medium- and long-term plans to ensure that China moves forward in the predetermined direction is one of the secrets of China's success.

The previous studies on China's five-year planning tended to focus the attention on how the planned metrics were fulfilled (so did the studies of the Soviet five-year planning). Fulfillment became a criterion to measure if the plan succeeded and a basis for debating whether the planning was necessary. This way of thinking was actually based on an unspoken assumption that the noun "plan" weighs more than the verb "plan." As mentioned above, this assumption is seriously misleading. The logic of the above-mentioned way of thinking should be reversed, and our focus should be on planning rather than resulted plans. Focusing on the starting point and formation process of the plan enables us to see different aspects of the planning study.

First, focus on planning is helpful to highlight its strategic characteristics.

Planning must proceed from strategic height, and what draws people's attention in the resulted plans are often those operational details (such as planned metrics, their breakdowns, and roadmaps for the implementation of the plans). To formulate a medium- and long-term plan, the focus must be put on the overall situation, including the two major overall status-quos of current domestic and international situations, the new happenings, new changes, and new features that have emerged in them, as well as the uncertainties and unstable elements that have emerged or may arise at home and abroad. The formulation of medium- and long-term plans must also focus on the long term, not only to see the present and forecast the next three to five years, but also to look ahead to the next 10 to 20 years of development.[59] And the so-called strategic height is focusing on two subjects from the overall and long-term perspectives: Where to go? How to get there? This requires grasping the complex phenomena in all aspects on the one hand, and simplifying the complexity to focus on the key on the other hand. Only by doing so can the medium- and long-term plan drawn up be able to "pull up the head rope of a fish net and open all its meshes" (*Master Lvy's Spring and Autumn Annals*,[60]) and guide all regions and departments across the country to develop at different stages in the future.

Second, focus on planning is helpful to highlight its dynamic nature.

Planning is bound to be a dynamic process, which cannot be finished overnight, but requires many parties to go through multiple rounds of interaction before it could take shape. Yet the resulted plan is often static, in meticulous sequence, and seems to be achievable by following it step by step. Of course, different planning concepts may lead to different

---

[59] Starting from the formulation of the first Five-Year Plan, China has prepared longer-term plans like 10-year and 20-year plans while drawing up every Five-Year Plan.

[60] *Master Lvy's Spring and Autumn Annals* is an encyclopedic Chinese classic compiled at the end of the Warring States period (475–221 BC) under the patronage of LvyBuwei (291–235 BC), chancellor of the Qin State. – *Translator.*

planning processes and result in different types of plans. Suppose people involved are rational, capable of not only fully possessing the information, but also scientifically handling the relevant information, the planning process may rely heavily on specialized agencies, experts, and professional planners, and the process may be full of technical analysis, model building, and data calculations. With the belief that it is possible to draw up a perfect plan, such a plan may be lengthy in writing, complex in content, with many metrics, very detailed conceptions, and very strict demands. Conversely, suppose people involved (including so-called experts) are at best with limited rationality, not only incapable of fully possessing the information, but also unable to systematically and comprehensively process the relevant information, then the planning process will be more open, allowing more interactions between the parties. Such a planning philosophy does not believe in "perfect planning," and the plan formulated under its guidance may be much shorter, much more concise, with far fewer metrics, much more generalized conceptions, and much more moderate demands. More importantly, under the latter philosophy, the planning process does not stop at the moment when the resulted plan comes out, but continues until the end of its implementation. This is because no matter how perfect the resulted plan is, it will not be exactly in line with reality, and all the military commanders know that "no plan survives contact with the enemy." In the same logic, once put into implementation, the economic and social development plan has to be adjusted in time according to the actual development in the due course. Therefore, planning and plan implementation are not two absolutely different stages, and it is more important to move in the direction specified in the plan than rigidly fulfilling the planned metrics.

Third, focus on planning is helpful to highlight its feature of learning.

As mentioned above, during the process of implementating the plan is subject to necessary adjustments, which in itself is learning by doing. The planning is continuous, as the completion of one plan period ushers in the next plan period. There might be successful experiences and lessons of mistakes in every plan period, while experiences and lessons from other countries may also be worth taken as enlightenment for our own country. Learning from the experiences and lessons of our own country and other countries is conducive to constantly adjusting the philosophy, way, content and implementation path of the planning. As Fig. 5.4 indicates, throughout the first to the fifth Five-Year Plan periods, China's fulfillment rates of planned metrics fluctuated dramatically; but the fulfillment rates in general improved after the sixth Five-Year Plan period, with the fluctuations narrowed to a small range. This is where the learning feature of planning has functioned.

Finally, focus on planning to see if countries are willing and capable to draw up plans is also helpful to gain an in-depth understanding of different political and economic systems.

**Whether willing to do planning.** In our personal life, some people like to make a plan before doing something, while others prefer to go with the flow. This reflects different attitudes toward life. When it comes down to the economic and social development, some countries consciously formulate a comprehensive medium- and long-term plan, considering it is the best way to achieve national prosperity and popular strength quickly with limited resources; other countries believe that it is completely unnecessary for the government to coordinate and make plans, as the interaction of rational individuals based on maximizing their own short-term interests could lead to the maximization of long-term social benefits; still other countries do not replace or even deny the role of government with the decisive role of the market in the allocation of resources, nor do they replace or deny the decisive role of the market in the allocation of resources with better playing the government's role, but simultaneously use both the "invisible hand" and the "visible hand." These differences can reveal the ideological features of different political and economic systems, which cannot be simply revealed by the binary method of either socialism or capitalism.

**Whether capable to do planning.** In some political and economic systems, even if many people wish their country to draw up a medium- and long-term plan, they may not be able to do so. The key here is whether the intersections of different decision-making entities in the decision-making system are "veto points" or points of consultation, coordination, or agreement.

Some systems emphasize individual values, competition, and check and balance, setting multiple veto points in the decision-making process, or allowing the presence of multiple veto players. In such a system, different participants tend to pursue the maximization of their own interests, and maneuver among various political groupings and hold each other back to find ways rejecting the proposals put forward by other participants for this end. Special interest groups could play like fish in the water in such a system, and through hijacking the decision-making process by influencing the veto players, they could prevent any policies likely to impair their interests from rolling out, even if the policies benefit the majority of people. What is special about the American system, for example, is that it is full of veto players. Obviously, in the course of policy formation, the more the veto players, the less likely the policy changes will take place, with one person exercising the veto power at one node and the policy change proposal will nip in the bud. This institutional arrangement with widespread veto points makes it hard to produce incremental adjustments on general policies, and even harder to make major policy changes, not to mention the medium- and long-term plans for a wide range of economic and social development.[61] Because of this, Francis Fukuyama, the Japanese-American scholar who once advocated "history has ended," bitterly called the American political system a "vetocracy."[62]

Other systems are different, which emphasize collective values, cooperation, and consensus, trying to set the intersections of the parties in the decision-making process as "contact points," "input points" and "deliberation points" rather than "veto points." In this system, different participants can only go by expressing their views fully, consulting again and again, high-level coordination, and agreeing to differ before finally reaching a policy consensus that blends the views of all parties. There is not much room for special interest groups to play in such a system, they can participate in decision-making, but it is difficult for them to influence or hinder the decision-making process according to their will. This mechanism is conducive to the formation of medium- and long-term plans for economic and social development. China is a model of

---

[61] Charles E. Lindblom was the first who noticed that the American system was special in that it was veto power studded. See Charles E. Lindblom, *Still Muddling, Not Yet Through*, Public Administration Review, Vol. 39, No. 6 (1979), pp. 520–521. Ellen M. Immergut was the first to use the concept of "veto points." See her *Institutions, Veto Points, and Policy Results: A Comparative Analysis of Health Care*, Journal of Public Policy, Vol. 10, No. 4 (1990), pp. 391–416. George Tsebelis used the phrase "veto players" the most systematically, with his representative works *Veto Players: How Political Institutions Work* (Princeton: Princeton University Press, 2002).

[62] Francis Fukuyama, *Oh for a Democratic Dictatorship and not a Vetocracy*, Financial Times (November 22, 2011), http://www.ft.com/intl/cms/s/0/d82776c6-14fd-11e1a2a6-00144feabdc0.html/#axzz28PC8kNpJ.

such institutional arrangements.[63] Even Fukuyama had to admit: "The most important strength of the Chinese political system is its ability to make large, complex decisions quickly, and to make them relatively well, at least in economic policy."[64]

China undoubtedly has the willingness, capacity, and experience to formulate medium- and long-term plans, which has been verified by the history of the past few decades. It is one of China's great institutional advantages. What is admirable is, while advancing its medium- and long-term plans, China has constantly absorbed nutrients from its own and other countries' experiences and lessons, constantly modified and revised the strategic direction of the plans in accordance with changes in reality, constantly adjusted the strategic positioning of the plans, and constantly changed the ways the plans are formulated, so that it has evaded the dogmatist and rigid institutional defects in the Soviet-style planned economy.

From the first to the fifth Five-Year Plan, the focus of China's planning was on determining and adjusting the strategic direction of the plans. For instance, the first Five-Year Plan highlighted the industrial sequence in the planning (with priority given to the development of heavy industry); the second Five-Year Plan highlighted the growth metrics of the plan (with the planned metrics set in three accounts: the first covered the national planned metrics that must be fulfilled; the second referred to the national plan metrics expected to be fulfilled, or that must be fulfilled by localities;and the third account included the planned metrics expected to be fulfilled by localities); and the third Five-Year Plan highlighted the spatial layout of the plan (a comprehensive deployment was made on the first, second and third lines while speeding up the construction on the third line). Each shift in the strategic direction of planning implied that lessons were drawn from the previous period to a certain extent. For instance, after the first Five-Year Plan was formulated, Mao Zedong proposed "to adjust properly the ratio between investment in heavy industry on the one hand and in agriculture and light industry on the other in order to bring about a greater development of latter." Also in the late stages of the second Five-Year Plan period through his last years, Mao Zedong

---

[63] Wang Shaoguang and Fan Peng, *Chinese-style Consensus Decision-making: "Opening Door" and "Running-in"* (Beijing: China Renmin University Press, 2013).

[64] Francis Fukuyama, *US Democracy Has Little to Teach China*, Financial Times (January 17, 2011).

emphasized time and again that it was necessary to "make allowances" in planning. Yet another example was that the fifth Five-Year Plan reduced the ratio of the investment in the third line construction and readjusted its specific content.

From the sixth to the ninth Five-Year Plan, the focus of China's planning work shifted to readjusting the plan's own strategic positioning (also referred to its position in the socialist economic system). If the previous plans were all-round and imperative, then the space for such all-round and imperative planning gradually shrank thereafter, giving way step by step to indicative planning and market regulation: first with the recognition of the positive role of the market (1978), then with the proposal of the "principle that the planned economy is in dominance and market regulation plays an auxiliary role" (1982), followed by the proposal of "organic combination of planning regulations and market regulations" (1984), and finally with the endowment of the market the "basic role" (1992) and "decisive role" (2013) in resource allocation. In 35 years, China has changed from practicing a planned economy to "put into practice a socialist market economy" (amendment to the *Constitution*), the scope and content of the market role have continuously expanded, while the *National Economic Plan* was replaced by the *National Economic and Social Development Plan*, which later was replaced by the *National Economic and Social Development Program*.

## Summary

In English, the Chinese term *Guihua* (规划) does not differentiate from *Jihua* (计划) and both mean "plan" or "planning".[65] In Chinese, the two terms are similar in meaning, but the former is used more for relatively comprehensive and long-term development plans. In this sense, the Five-Year Plan and Five-Year Program are literally not much different.[66] However, the national five-year programs we formulate now

---

[65] The Translator has taken the liberty to use "program" or "programming" for *Guihua* so as to make a difference from "plan" or "planning" as *Jihua*.

[66] In fact, the term "program" has long been used, such as the *Twelve-Year National Long-Term Program for Science and Technology Development (1956–1967)* made in the mid-1950s, the *Fifteen-Year Long-Range Vision*, the *Ten-Year Program for Science and Technology (1963–1972)*, the *Long-Term Program for Agriculture*, *Draft Outline of the Seven-Year Program for Elementary and Secondary Education and Vocational Education*

are substantially different from the pre-reform five-year plans. On the one hand, in terms of the breadth of coverage, the five-year programs are more comprehensive and inclusive than the five-year plans, involving not only economic development but also social progress; focusing not only on public sectors but also on non-public ones. On the other hand, in terms of the depth of coverage, the five-year programs are more macro and strategic, focusing mainly on structural issues like industries, regions, urban and rural areas, land use, social services, and ecological environment protection, emphatically putting forward the direction and missions of economic and social development, and corresponding development strategies and measures, instead of focusing on guiding the micro-activities of enterprises. The five-year programs still play the role of resource allocation, especially in strategic areas such as land, energy, and network industries (like communication, transportation, electricity, telecommunications, finance, and the Internet); but in most areas, the market role in the allocation of resources is basic and decisive. There are still metrics in the five-year programs, but their nature has changed significantly: after the Ninth Five-Year Plan, there have been no clearly imperative metrics, in their stead are predictive and indicative metrics. Although beginning with the 11th Five-Year Plan, constraining metrics were reintroduced, the objects of constraints are no longer the enterprises but governments at all levels. As the *Outline of the Eleventh Five-Year Program for National Economy and Social Development* and the *Outline of the Twelfth Five-Year Program for National Economy and Social Development* put it, China has persevered in formulating the Five-Year Plans mainly to "clarify national strategic intention, identify government work emphasis, and guide market behavior"; such a program is "a grand blueprint for China's economic and social development in the next five years, the common guideline for all ethnic groups in China as well as the

---

*(1964–1970)*, the *Long-Term Program for Industry and Transport* China was set to draw up in the 1960s, the *Development Program for National Agricultural Mechanization (Draft)* made in the early 1970s, the *Outline of the Ten-Year Program for the Development of National Economy (1976–1985)* made in the mid-1970s, the *Ten-Year Program for the Development of National Economy (1981–1990)* made in the early 1980s, and a ten-year program made while formulating the eighth Five-Year Plan. However, the term "program" was not used in the *Fifteen-Year Long-Range Vision* prepared in the 1950s.

important basis for the government to carry out economic adjustment, market supervision, social administration and public service."[67]

---

[67] The *Outline of the Eleventh Five-Year Program for the National Economy and Social Development of the People's Republic of China* (adopted by the Fourth Session of the 10th National People's Congress on March 14, 2006); the *Outline of the Twelfth Five-Year Program for the National Economy and Social Development of the People's Republic of China* (adopted by the Fourth Session of the 11th National People's Congress on March 14, 2011).

CHAPTER 6

# Pillar: State-Owned Enterprises and Industrialization

The greatest change in China's economy in the 70 years since the founding of the People's Republic is the achievement of industrialization, with its level constantly rising. In this process, state-owned enterprises (SOEs) played a crucial role. This chapter is to discuss the relationship between SOEs and industrialization, which is more of an account of what changes have taken place in China' economy and industry and how SOEs have contributed to them over the past 70 years with large amounts of data, instead of merely giving a theoretical analysis.

What is industrialization? The *Modern Chinese Dictionary* defines Industry as "productive undertakings that apply natural material resources to produce the means of production and means of living or process various kinds of raw materials."[1] Industrialization refers to the process of transformation from traditional agricultural to modern industrial society, or the gradual evolution of modern industry featuring machines, which step by step dominates the national economy. Here "modern" is added to preceding "industry," because industry also contains traditional handicraft undertakings, and it cannot be counted as industrialization if the industry stays in the stage of handicraft manufacturing.

There are four indicators to judge whether a society has entered industrialization.

---

[1] *Modern Chinese Dictionary*, 7th edition, p. 449.

© CITIC Press Corporation 2021
S. Wang, *China's Rise and Its Global Implications*,
https://doi.org/10.1007/978-981-16-4341-5_6

The primary indicator is the structural change. The first is whether the composition of national economy has changed, what is the share of agriculture, industry, and tertiary industry. The second is to see whether the manufacturing of the means of production within the industrial sectors has expanded. Here the so-called means of production refer to things that cannot be directly consumed for eating, drinking, wearing, and using, but other things that need to be manufactured to produce those consumption goods. The production of things directly consumable for eating, drinking, wearing, and using belongs to the light industry, and the production of other things that cannot be directly consumed belongs to the heavy industry. To examine the change of industrial structure, it is necessary to pay attention to the variation of light and heavy industry share. For either light or heavy industry, it is also necessary to see the structure of its products, whether they have upgraded and if the technology involved has advanced.

The second indicator is the growth of quantity. This includes the growth of total output of production and per capita output. The variation in quantity is apparently related to the growth rate of economy.

The third indicator is the improvement of efficiency. That is the time, labor and raw materials involved in producing the same product. In professional terminology, efficiency implies both labor productivity and total factor productivity.

The fourth indicator is the geographical distribution. Is the industrialization concentrated in a particular region within a country, or extended to other regions? Is the industrialization achieved on certain small spots or realized nationwide? This should be an indicator for industrialization that cannot be neglected.

Before the New China was founded, Comrade Mao Zedong expressed his two aspirations for China's industrialization, which were embodied in two of his quotes. One quote is from his report to the Seventh National Congress of the Communist Party of China in 1945: "When the political system of New Democracy is won, the Chinese people and their government will have to adopt practical measures in order to build heavy and light industry step by step over a number of years and transform China from an agricultural into an industrial country."[2] That is to say, his first

---

[2] Mao Zedong, *On Coalition Government* (April 24, 1945), *Selected Works of Mao Tse-tung*, Vol. III (Peking, China: Foreign Languages Press, 1965), p. 303.

aspiration was to "transform China from an agricultural into an industrial country."

The second quote is from Chairman Mao's report to the Second Plenary Session of the Seventh Central Committee of the Communist Party of China in 1949: "… the problem of establishing an independent and integrated industrial system will remain unsolved and it will be finally solved only when our country has greatly developed economically and changed from a backward agricultural into an advanced industrial country."[3] His second aspiration was that China should not only become industrialized, but also establish an independent and integrated industrial system on its own land and become "an advanced industrial country."

Now let's check the New China's accomplishments with data and see if Mao Zedong's two aspirations came true around the time of his death.

Two days before the founding of New China, on September 29, 1949, the First Plenary Session of the Chinese People's Political Consultative Conference adopted *The Common Program of the Chinese People's Political Consultative Conference* which functioned as an interim constitution. Article 28 of the *Common Program* defines the mission of state-owned economy: "State-owned economy is of a socialist nature. All enterprises relating to the economic lifeline of the country and exercising a dominant influence over the people's livelihood shall be under the unified operation of the state. All state-owned resources and enterprises are the public property of all the people and are the main material basis on which the People's Republic will develop production and bring about a prosperous economy." What should be noted is that it mentions not only "state-owned" but also "state-operated." Since such "state-owned" economy "under the unified operation of the state" is "a public property of all the people," for a long time we used to call the state-owned economy the "economy under the ownership of the whole people."

Article 35 of the *Common Program* puts forward the mission of industrialization: "In order to lay the foundation for the industrialization of the country, the central point of industrial work should be the planned, systematic rehabilitation and the development of heavy industry, such as mining, the iron and steel industry, power industry, machine-making industry, electrical industry and the main chemical industries, etc." Here it

---

[3] Mao Zedong, *Report to the Second Plenary Session of the Seventh Central Committee of the Communist Party of China* (March 5, 1949), *Selected Works of Mao Tse-tung*, Vol. IV (Peking, China: Foreign Languages Press, 1961), p. 369.

underlines the importance of giving priority to the development of heavy industry. It is clear that the *Common Program* is not simply a political statement but it has a rich content, making a specific plan of China's path to industrialization.

This chapter is of three parts. The first part is about the starting point of the New China. Unless making the starting point clear, it is hard to understand what achievements have been made in the following seven decades. The second part addresses how China was "transformed from an agricultural to an industrial country" and how "an independent and integrated industrial system" was established in the first 30 years of the People's Republic, so Mao Zedong's two aspirations came true. The third part talks about how China advanced from an industrial country into an industrial power in the latter 40 years. The role the state-owned enterprises played in the entire historic course of the 70 years will go through all the three parts.

## New China's Starting Point

The New China's starting point will be reviewed in four aspects, economy, industry, capital, and SOEs. This section is to proceed from economy and end in the discussion of SOEs. The next two sections will reverse to start from SOEs before discussing about capital, industry, and economy.

### Starting Point in Economy

Our discussion of the New China's starting point in economy will begin with an analysis of its structural features, and then we'd take a look at its quantitative features.

Structurally, China in 1949 was a backward agricultural country. Of a population of more than 500 million, only about two million were engaged in industrial work. The total industrial output value accounted for merely some 10% of the national aggregate economic volume. China at the time lagged far behind even the relatively backward pre-revolution Russia, not to say to compare with Western Europe and the United States. And Russia already had its industry taking a share of 43% in its aggregate economic volume in 1913 before the First World War. China was even more backward in terms of basic industries.

Figure 6.1 presents the shares of traditional and new economy in the total industrial and agricultural output value. Apart from agriculture, the

Fig. 6.1 Shares of traditional and new economy in the gross industrial and agricultural output value (*Source* Xu Dixin and Wu Chenming, *History of the Development of Chinese Capitalism*, Vol. III [Beijing: People's Publishing House, 2003], p. 756)

so-called traditional economy here also includes the backward handicraft undertakings. As the figure indicates, in 1920, China's new economy (modern industries and public utilities excluding agriculture and handicraft undertakings) accounted for merely 7.37% of the total industrial and agricultural output value, which rose to but 13.37% in 1936. By 1949, when the new economy in Northeast China were added in, the share of new economy nationwide grew to 17%, while the remaining more than 80% was traditional economy, mainly agriculture. If we look at the modern sectors composed of manufacturing industry, mining, and public utilities only, their shares were even smaller. Take 1933 for example, they perhaps accounted for only 3.4% of net gross domestic product (GDP), really a very tiny piece in the economy.

By 1952, China's national economy overall had surpassed the level in 1936, the country's highest before World War II, when the share of new economy rose to 26.6%. Figure 6.2 presents a more detailed analysis of the composition of GPD in that year, from which we could see that the primary sector took 51% of the entire GDP, while industry, construction, transport, warehouse storage, and postal service added up to take about one quarter, and other services and wholesale and retail businesses

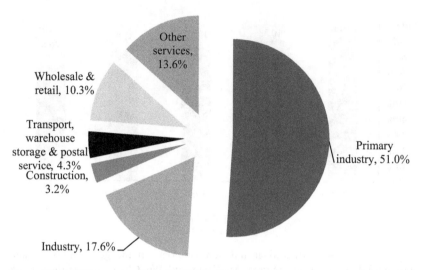

**Fig. 6.2** GDP composition in 1952 (*Source* National Bureau of Statistics, *China Compendium of Statistics 1949–2008*; *China Statistical Yearbook*; Statistical Database of Chinese Economic and Social Development)

together took about another one quarter. In general, China at the time was still a typical agricultural country.

Table 6.1 indicates that India was a bit more advanced than China in economic structure during the 1949–1950 period, as the proportions of its industrial and service employees in the total employment were higher

**Table 6.1** Comparison of China and India's economy

| Economic indicators | China | India |
| --- | --- | --- |
| Per capita GDP (2018 Constant Price US$) | 666 | 930 |
| Agriculture's share in GDP | 59% | 51% |
| Large-scale manufacturing industry & public undertakings in GDP | 9% | 6% |
| Agricultural employees in total employment | 77% | 72% |
| Industrial employees in total employment | 7% | 11% |
| Employees of service industry in total employment | 16% | 17% |

*Source* Data of GDP per capita are from The Conference Board, Total Economy Database, April 2019, https://www.conference-board.org/data/economydatabase/TED1; other data are from Ashwani Saith, "China and India: The Institutional Roots of Differential Performance" *Development and Change*, 2008 (5)

than those of China, while the proportion of people engaged in agriculture was lower. As India enjoyed a better climate and natural environment than China, it led China in GDP per capita by one-third. Both were poor countries at the time, but China was even poorer.

China lagged behind not only India in terms of GDP per capita, but also remained in a low status as compared with many other countries in the world. Data of the World Bank date back to 1960 only, but data of the Conference Board began in 1950. The database of the Conference Board collected data from 126 countries in 1950. Excluding the extreme exceptions of three oil countries in the Gulf, China ranked seventh from the bottom in a top-down sequence of GDP per capita level, that is, it was among the most backward countries in the world. That was the starting point in our economy.

### *Starting Point in Industry*

The New China's starting point in industry was so low that it is hard for people to imagine today.

The Old China's industry was dominated by handicraft workshops, with very little mechanical industry. What the handicraft workshops produced were not agricultural but industrial goods, which were almost entirely handmade. Such a mode of production may have existed for several hundred or even several thousand years. With low production, inferior quality, and few varieties, it could by no means match the modern industry. In 1933, the output value of China's handicraft undertakings accounted for 73% of the total industrial output value, while the output value of its modern mechanical industry occupied only 27% of the total.

Even in the mechanical industrial sector, most production was semimechanical, half done by machines and half by manual labor, with very low per capita productivity and backward technology. When we talk about the number of patents today, they are counted by ten or hundred thousand or even by million. But in the period from 1912 to 1936, China's annual average number of patents was 11, indicating how backward its technology was.

In terms of structure of industrial sectors, most of them produced consumer goods, or daily necessities directly consumable for eating, drinking, wearing, and using, which accounted for 70% of the total industrial output value. The share of means of production took only 30% of the industrial output value. At that time, the famous manufacturers in China were only yarn mills, flour mills, and match factories.

In terms of geographical distribution, the majority of modern industrial enterprises were concentrated in the coastal areas of East China, particularly in Shanghai. Only a handful of big inland cities like Chongqing and Wuhan were tinged with a few modern factories. One could hardly see any sign of modern industry in the hinterland of China.

The factories in China then were few in number and small on scale. When the New China was founded in 1949, there were a total of 123,000 private industrial firms, of which only 14,800 hired ten or more workers. Such relatively larger private industrial firms accounted for 12% of the total (see Table 6.2). In other words, in accordance with the standard of the time, firms hiring ten people or more were considered sizable enterprises. By the standard of today, they were just a bit larger than self-employed businesses. In 1949, China's private industrial firms employed a total of 1.644 million workers, of whom 925,000 worked in factories hiring 10 or more people. All the firms added up to claim a net asset value of 2 billion yuan, with a total output value of less than 7 billion yuan. Among them, the firms hiring ten or more people registered a total net asset value of about 1.4 billion yuan, with a total output value of some 4.66 billion yuan.

The private industry and commerce showed a good momentum of development after the founding of New China. By 1953, the private industrial firms nationwide increased to 150,000 in number, but still not large on scale. There were only 167 enterprises with an employment of

Table 6.2 Private industry in 1949

|  | All private industrial firms | Private firms hiring 10 or more people |
|---|---|---|
| No. of factories | 123,165 | 14,780 |
| No. of workers | 1,643,832 | 925,477 |
| Net asset value(hundred million yuan) | 20.08 | 14.056 |
| Total output value(hundred million yuan) | 68.28 | 46.635 |

*Source* Unless noted by specific sources, all other data used in this chapter are based on a databank that the author compiles from various sources

500 and more, accounting for 0.1% of the total. By contrast, the enterprises hiring 500 people and more in Russia accounted for 54% of the total before the October Revolution in 1917, when Russia was considered to be a backward country compared with Europe and the United States. China could not even match the Old Russia, let alone comparing with other countries. As early as 1907, there were already as many as 580 factories hiring 1,000 people and more in Germany.

There were few factories hiring 500 workers or more in China in 1950, even the firms hiring 50 people or more were not many, only taking 3.74% of the total. Although there was a marginal increase in the number of firms hiring ten and more workers after the founding of New China, they nevertheless accounted for less than one-third of the total, and 60% of them were still using hand tools. The remaining 70% of industrial firms were just handicraft workshops hiring fewer than 10 workers, and few of them were installed with modern power equipment and able to have their products shaped and produced in massive batches in a standardized way. It is not hard to imagine how backward such a mode of production could be.

In 1953, China's industrial firms using machines were mainly in the light industry rather than in the heavy industry, of which workers and output value in the food and textile industries accounted for more than half of the total. The heavy industry at the time was mainly fuel industry, like coal mining, with its products mainly used for direct consumption to meet the urban dwellers' need of boiling water and cooking, although they could also be used to produce the means of production.

The backward industrial structure is directly embodied in the backward product structure. Table 6.3 lists the major industrial products at the early stage of New China, their maximum annual outputs before 1949, and those in 1952. We could decipher a lot of messages in this table, but here I'd only make three points.

First, the structure of industrial products was quite primitive. The top six were light industrial products indispensable in people's daily consumption, and the seventh to ninth product, crude coal, crude oil and electricity, were products of the heavy industry, but they were mainly used for people's direct consumption. The rest were heavy industrial products mainly used as the means of production. Young people today may not know that in those years, most industrial goods were often preceded by a word "foreign" or "imported" (*Yang*). Yarn fabrics were called "foreign textiles," and cloth was called "foreign" or "imported" cloth, so

**Table 6.3** Output of major industrial products at early stage of New China

| Name | Unit | Peak year before 1949 | | Index (with peak year before 1949 as 100) | |
|---|---|---|---|---|---|
| | | Year | Output | 1949 | 1952 |
| Yarn | 10,000 tons | 1933 | 44.5 | 73.5 | 147.4 |
| Cloth | 100 million meters | 1936 | 27.9 | 67.7 | 137.3 |
| Match | 10,000 pieces | 1937 | 860 | 78.1 | 105.9 |
| Crude salt | 10,000 tons | 1943 | 392 | 76.3 | 126.3 |
| Sugar | 10,000 tons | 1936 | 41 | 48.8 | 109.8 |
| Cigarettes | 10,000 cases | 1947 | 236 | 67.8 | 112.3 |
| Crude coal | 100 million tons | 1942 | 0.62 | 51.6 | 106.5 |
| Crude oil | 10,000 tons | 1943 | 32 | 37.5 | 137.5 |
| Electricity | 100 million KWHs | 1941 | 60 | 71.7 | 121.7 |
| Steel | 10,000 tons | 1943 | 92.3 | 17.1 | 146.3 |
| Pig iron | 10,000 tons | 1943 | 180 | 13.9 | 107.2 |
| Cement | 10,000 tons | 1942 | 229 | 28.8 | 124.9 |
| Plate glass | 10,000 TEUs | 1941 | 129 | 83.7 | 165.1 |
| Sulfuric acid | 10,000 tons | 1942 | 18 | 22.2 | 105.6 |
| Soda ash | 10,000 tons | 1940 | 10.3 | 85.4 | 186.4 |
| Caustic soda | 10,000 tons | 1941 | 1.2 | 125 | 658.3 |
| Metal cutting machines | 10,000 units | 1941 | 0.54 | 29.6 | 253.7 |

as to differentiate from the "indigenous yarn" and "indigenous cloth." Match was called "foreign fire," cigarette was "imported smoke," sweets were "foreign sugar,"[4] kerosene was "foreign oil," kerosene lamps were "foreign oil lamps," and cement was "foreign powder." Even the most neglected iron nails were called "foreign nails." Nearly every industrial product with the slightest modern feature was identified as "foreign." The word "foreign" implies that either the good was imported or it was modeled after an imported one.

Second, the output of industrial goods at the time was very low. If we divide the maximum annual outputs of the top six consumer goods by the

---

[4] The author grew up in Wuhan, where a breakfast snack was known as "cupcake with foreign sugar," just ordinary sweetened cake made of rice flour and yeast. But since it used sugar, it was called "cupcake with foreign sugar."

then population (about 500 million) to get a per capita output, how little would the yarn, cloth, salt, and sugar be? Everyone with an elementary schooling could make the calculation. As for the steel production, the maximum yearly steel output before 1949 appeared in 1943, at 923,000 tons, which dropped to 158,000 tons in 1949, 17.1% of the 1943 figure. Although the steel production in 1952 surpassed that of 1949, it was merely 1.35 million tons, on average only 2.4 kg for every Chinese. The same was true of power generation, as the electricity generated in a single day today is three times the maximum annual capacity generated before 1949 in China! (Table 6.4)

Third, three years after the founding of New China, the production of major industrial products in the country had comprehensively surpassed the highest production before 1949 by big margin.

Aside from backwardness, China's industry was concentrated in the eastern coastal areas which occupy less than 12% of the country's land territory. There were mainly two big blocks, one was in Shanghai, and the other was in the northeast, plus cities of Tianjin, Qingdao, Guangzhou, Nanjing, and Wuxi. Except for Wuhan and Chongqing, there was hardly

Table 6.4 Comparison of major industrial products between China and India in 1949

|              | Unit               | China    | India    | Times over China |
|--------------|--------------------|----------|----------|------------------|
| Steel        | 10,000 tons        | 15.8     | 137      | 8.67             |
| Pig iron     | 10,000 tons        | 25.2     | 164      | 6.56             |
| Sugar        | 10,000 tons        | 19.9     | 118      | 5.9              |
| Cement       | 10,000 tons        | 66       | 186      | 2.82             |
| Sulfuric acid| 10,000 tons        | 4        | 10       | 2.5              |
| Crude oil    | 10,000 tons        | 12.1     | 25       | 2.08             |
| Yarn         | 10,000 tons        | 32.7     | 61.5     | 1.88             |
| Cloth        | 100 million meters | 18.9     | 34.6     | 1.83             |
| Electricity  | 100 million KWHs   | 43.1     | 49       | 1.14             |
| Crude coal   | 100 million tons   | 0.3      | 0.3      | 1                |
| Crude salt   | 10,000 tons        | 298.5    | 202      | 0.68             |
| Caustic soda | 10,000 tons        | 1.5      | 0.6      | 0.4              |
| Cigarettes   | 10,000 cases       | 160      | 44       | 0.28             |
| Soda ash     | 10,000 tons        | 8.8      | 1.8      | 0.2              |
| Population   | 10,000             | 54,167.0 | 35,051.0 | 0.65             |

any modern industry in the inland areas. In frontier regions inhabited by ethnic minorities, there was almost no sign of modern industry.[5]

Therefore, China's industry then lagged far behind other parts of the world measured in whatever indicators.

### Starting Point in State Capital

It needs capital input to develop industry and modern economy. As mentioned in previous chapters, western countries started their industrialization by colonialism, slave trade, and slave system to plunder "the first pot of gold" for their primitive accumulation of capital. It was impossible for the New China to do the same for its capital accumulation. Not only was it impossible for it to do so, but it was confronted with many layers of blockade imposed by western imperialist powers, who tried to strangle us by every means in an attempt to choke the New China to death. The New China could only rely on itself to accumulate capital.

To examine the accumulation of capital before the founding of New China, we may borrow the "capital system" used by Xu Dixin and Wu Chengming in Volume III of the *History of the Development of Chinese Capitalism* as a framework for analysis. This system divides capital into the industrial capital, transportation capital, industrial capital II, commercial capital, and financial capital. Industrial capital covers sectors of modern manufacturing, public utilities of water and electricity supplies, and all mining and smelting (including those using indigenous methods) industries. Transportation capital covers sectors of railway, highway, shipping, civil aviation, postal service, and telecommunication. Industrial capital II[6] is the sum of industrial and transportation capital. Commercial capital covers the capital required for primary transactions of market commodities. Financial capital includes all the new and old forms of monetary businesses, but not investment companies.[7]

---

[5] Wang Haibo, *History of New China's Industrial Economy*, October 1949–1957 (Beijing: Economy & Management Publishing House, 1994), p. 1.

[6] In the original Chinese text, the term is "产业资本." And there is no other English equivalent for "产业" than "industry" or "industrial," the same as "工业." After consulting the author, "industrial capital II" is used for "产业资本" to differentiate from "industrial capital" (工业资本) and hopefully make it less confusing.—*Translator*.

[7] Xu Dixin and Wu Chengming, *History of the Development of Chinese Capitalism*, Vol. III (Beijing: People's Publishing House, 2003), pp. 735–736.

In the Old China, whatever category of the capital in this system, it came from three sources: foreign capital, state bureaucratic capital, and domestic private capital. Table 6.5 describes the situation of the five categories of capital in these three kinds in the period of 1947 to 1948.

We could see that the scale of industrial capital at the time was very small, with the foreign capital, state bureaucratic capital, and domestic private capital adding up to no more than 3.71 billion yuan (on the 1936 monetary value) by 1948. Even plus the transportation capital of 2.84 billion yuan, the entire industrial capital II was about 6.55 billion yuan. Yet the commercial capital and financial capital totaled 7.7 billion yuan. In other words, the volume of industrial capital II at the time was less than the volume of commercial capital and financial capital put together. The sum total of the four categories of capital was a little more than 14.2 billion yuan, averaging about 26 yuan for every Chinese. In fact,

Table 6.5 Composition of Capital Volume, 1947–1948 (Unit: Fiat money100 million yuan in 1936 value)

|  | Foreign capital | State Bureaucratic capital | Domestic Private capital | Total |
| --- | --- | --- | --- | --- |
| Industrial capital | 6.2446 | 15.9874 | 14.8492 | 37.0812 |
| % | 16.84% | 43.11% | 40.05% | 100.00% |
| Transport capital | 1.0968 | 26.0205 | 1.3007 | 28.418 |
| % | 3.86% | 91.56% | 4.58% | 100.00% |
| Industrial capital II | 7.3414 | 42.0079 | 16.1499 | 65.4992 |
| % | 11.21% | 64.13% | 24.66% | 100.00% |
| Business capital | 1.5348 | 0.3 | 36.4 | 38.2348 |
| % | 4.01% | 0.79% | 95.20% | 100.00% |
| Finance capital | 2.2888 | 34.4 | 2.029 | 38.7178 |
| % | 5.91% | 88.85% | 5.24% | 100.00% |
| Total capital volume | 11.165 | 76.7079 | 54.5789 | 142.4518 |
| % | 7.84% | 53.85% | 38.31% | 100.00% |

Source Sorted out based on Chapter 7 Development level of Chinese capitalism in Vol. III of *History of Development of Chinese Capitalism* compiled by Xu Dixin and Wu Chengming, People's Publishing House, Beijing, 2003

the 14.2 billion yuan was not all the domestic capital. The foreign capital refers to the investment of the United States, Britain, and other western countries in China. With the 1.1 billion yuan of foreign capital deducted, the domestic capital was just 13.1 billion yuan, averaging 24 yuan per Chinese.

The state bureaucratic capital took the lion's share in the domestic capital at the time, about 7.67 billion yuan, including mainly the capital of Kuomintang-operated enterprises, whose main source was the capital confiscated from three fascist countries Japan, Germany and Italy, and Chinese traitors after the victory of Anti-Japanese War in 1945. The state bureaucratic capital was concentrated in two sectors of transportation and financing businesses, respectively accounting for 91.56% in the former and 88.85% in the latter, both in absolute domination. Even its share in the industrial sectors (43.11%) was not so high, it was still higher than the foreign capital (16.84%) and domestic private capital (40.05%).

After decades of development, the scale of private national capital was still small before the founding of New China, amounting to 5.46 billion yuan, accounting for only 38.3% of the total capital volume. Moreover, of the over 5 billion yuan of private capital, there was only 1.61 billion yuan of industrial capital II, taking less than 30% of the total, and more than 70% of the private capital was concentrated in non-production sectors, namely, commercial and financing, particularly commercial. The 1.61 billion yuan of private industrial capital II implies that on average one Chinese had only three yuan of investment, hardly to shoulder the weight of industrializing China. Table 6.5 makes it clear that on the eve of the founding of New China, the state bureaucratic capital took the biggest share in the industrial capital II directly related to industrialization, which accounted for about two thirds of this category of capital. It was apparently unrealistic to expect the private capital to be responsible for China's industrialization.

In terms of time latitude, the composition of industrial capital II had constantly changed from the 1911 Revolution to the eve of the founding of New China. Before the First World War (1911–1914), the total capital volume nationwide was about 1.788 billion yuan. Thirty years later in 1947–1948, it grew to 6.55 billion yuan, three times the original (see Table 6.6). We will see later in the 30-odd years from 1952 to 1984, how many folds the New China's total capital volume had increased. By comparison, we will see how far we can go by following the old path of Old China.

**Table 6.6** Variation of total volume of industrial capital II in 35 years up to the founding of New China (Unit: fiat money, 100 million yuan, 1936 value)

| Sum | 1911–1914 | 1920 | 1936 | | 1947–1948 |
|---|---|---|---|---|---|
| | | | Northeast included | Northeast not included | |
| Foreign capital | 10.22 | 13.30 | 57.18 | 19.59 | 7.34 |
| Domestic capital | 7.66 | 12.49 | 42.73 | 35.87 | 58.16 |
| State bureaucratic capital | 4.78 | 6.70 | 22.25 | 19.89 | 42.01 |
| Domestic private capital | 2.88 | 5.80 | 20.48 | 15.97 | 16.15 |
| Total capital volume | 17.88 | 25.79 | 99.91 | 55.46 | 65.50 |

In the 30-odd years from the 1911 Revolution to the founding of New China, the share of domestic private capital in the industrial capital II increased, 5.6 times more in 1947–1948 than in 1911–1914. The increase seems to be significant, but because the starting point was rather low (288 million yuan), it reached merely some 1.61 billion yuan one or two years before the founding of New China. During the same period, foreign investment first rose but then dropped, and the 1947–1948 figure was less than 72% of the 1911–1914 figure.

Throughout these years, the state bureaucratic capital had the biggest increment. Around the time of the 1911 Revolution, the bureaucratic capital was small, at 478 million yuan, about one quarter of the industrial capital II. Up to the eve of the founding of New China, it had grown to 4.201 billion yuan, 8.8 times of the original. A very important factor here was the victory of the Anti-Japanese War. Most of the foreign capital in China before October 1949 was the Japanese capital, which was mainly in Northeast China. After the victory of the Anti-Japanese War, part of the Japanese capital was taken away by the Soviet Union, who later returned some of it; but the majority of the Japanese capital was taken over by the Kuomintang government and became the bureaucratic capital. That is why the bureaucratic capital took the biggest share of China's industrial capital II in 1947–1948, accounting for two thirds of the total (Table 6.7).

**Table 6.7** Shares of items of industrial capital II in its total volume in 35 years up to the founding of New China (Unit: %)

| Share | 1911–1914 | 1920 | 1936 Northeast included | 1936 Northeast not included | 1947–1948 |
|---|---|---|---|---|---|
| Foreign capital | 57.16 | 51.56 | 57.23 | 35.33 | 11.21 |
| Domestic capital | 42.84 | 48.44 | 42.77 | 64.67 | 88.79 |
| Bureaucratic capital | 26.76 | 25.96 | 22.27 | 35.87 | 64.13 |
| Private capital | 16.08 | 22.48 | 20.5 | 28.8 | 24.66 |
| Total capital volume | 100 | 100 | 100 | 100 | 100 |

*Source* Sorted out based on Chapter 7 Development level of Chinese capitalism in Vol. III of *History of Development of Chinese Capitalism* compiled by Xu Dixin and Wu Chengming, People's Publishing House, Beijing, 2003

In summary, by the time before the New China was founded, imperialist capital in China accounted for 11.21% of China's industrial capital II, the domestic capital took 88.79%. Of the 88.79% taken by the domestic capital, the bureaucratic capital took 64.13%, and the private capital occupied 24.66%. This was mainly because the Japanese capital which accounted for 87% of the foreign capital was confiscated by the Kuomintang government after the end of the Anti-Japanese War and became the bureaucratic capital, thus greatly increasing the KMT government's capital share. This was actually a good thing. When meeting the Soviet Union's representative Artem Ivanovich Mikoyan at Xibaipo of Hebei Province in February 1949, Chairman Mao said, to certain extent KMT created favorable conditions for the development of China's industry. Why? Because "Japan and KMT made capital concentrated to the state, for instance, the northeast accounted for 53% of China's industry, of which 47% was taken by the state, and 6% was privately owned." So "the major part of China's industry was in the hands of the state."[8] In other words, the KMT government confiscated the enemy assets and

---

[8] Shen Zhihua and Cui Haizhi, *Mao Zedong's First Direct Contact with the Soviet Communist Party Leaders, Declassified Archives about Mikoyan's Visit to Xibaipo, International History Studies on the Cold War*, Vol. XVIII (Beijing: International Knowledge Press, 2015), p. 388.

nationalized them, which in effect created a favorable condition for the New China. In fact, when the Communist Party took over the power, the state-owned share was already quite big, especially in the industrial sectors.

### *Starting Point in SOEs*

Why did the New China vigorously develop state-owned enterprises when it was newly founded?

First of all, the state ownership was then the trend of the times, which could be reviewed from four aspects.

First, nationalization was a consensus of various political parties and political and cultural elites in modern China. Sun Yat-sen advocated for "developing the state capital but regulating the private capital." In his perspective, "China cannot be compared with foreign countries, and it is not enough to regulate capital only. Since foreign countries are rich and China is poor, there is production surplus in foreign countries while China witnesses underproduction. Therefore in China we should not regulate the private capital only, but also develop the state capital."[9] Weng Wenhao and Qian Changzhao, two important leaders of the National Resources Commission of the KMT government, also held that three principles must be followed in developing China's economy: One is that modernization in the main is industrialization, which China's construction must center on. The second principle is that the industrialization must center on the construction of heavy industry. And the third principle is that the construction of heavy industry must center on the state-owned undertakings.[10] This was not only the view of KMT officials, but intellectuals also believed so, even the pro-West returned students in the United States shared this view. In spring of 1948, the Chinese Students' Christian Association in North America conducted a Gallup-type poll among Chinese students in the United States, which found that "college students in the

---

[9] Sun Yat-sen, *The Three Principles of the People, The Livelihood of the People* (August 10, 1924), *The Completed Works of Sun Yat-sen*, Vol. IX (Beijing: Zhonghua Book Company, 1986), p. 391.

[10] Wu Zhaohong, *The National Resources Commission as I know*, Industry and Business Group, Committee for Studies on Cultural-Historical Literature under the National Committee of the Chinese People's Political Consultative Conference, *Recollections of the National Resources Commission of the KMT Government* (Beijing: Chinese Literature and History Press, 1988), p. 106.

States now stand for socialism as the far-reaching basic economic policy," and 51.5% of the poll respondents held that the heavy industry and public utilities should be operated by the state in China's industrialization, while 6% of them even believed that the light industry should also be operated by the state. Only less than 5% of the respondents stood for complete private ownership.[11] There is an abundance of evidence in this regard, and the list is endless.

Second, nationalization was a consensus of various countries after World War II. Take China's neighbor—the postwar Korea—for example, despite the vast ideological differences between the north and the south, most intellectuals, journalists, and political parties believed that the system of planned economy was the best option for Korea. The most radical right-wing Independent Party, the most radical left-wing Communist Party, and the most conservative Democratic Party in Korea all agreed to this. Even An Jae-hong, the Civil Administrator appointed by the United States Army Military Government in Korea, was no exception.[12]

Actually Korea was only part of the worldwide trends. At the time, almost all the developing countries in Asia, Africa, and Latin America were taking this path. So did the old fashioned capitalist countries in Europe. As early as one year after Russia's October Revolution, the *British Labor Party Rule Book* put forward a clear aim in Clause IV to pursue the common ownership of the means of production and the best obtainable system of popular administration and control of each industry and service. Shortly after the end of World War II, the ruling Labor Party began to push for the economic nationalization. In 1946, the Bank of England and all the airliners were nationalized, and the National Health Service was established. In 1947, all the telecommunication companies came under the ownership of the state, and the National Coal Board was created. In 1948, the railways, canals, road transport and electrical companies were nationalized. In 1951, the iron and steel industry and petroleum oil refinery were nationalized.[13] Up to the mid-1980s, public sectors still took a big proportion in the European countries' investment, 65%

---

[11] Mo Rujian, A Political Poll on Chinese Students in America, *Observation*, Vol. 4, No. 20 (1948).

[12] Tae-Gyun Park, Different Roads, Common Destination: Economic Discourses in South Korea during the 1950s, *Modern Asian Studies*, Vol. 39, No. 3 (July 2005), pp. 661–682.

[13] Martyn Sloman, *Socializing Public Ownership* (London: Palgrave Macmillan, 1978).

in Austria, 55% in France, 25% in Britain, and 20% in West Germany.[14] It was not until the end of the 1980s when the wave of privatization began to surge. In 1988, the World Bank published a three-volume *Techniques of Privatization of State-Owned Enterprises*, which claimed that at least 83 countries had begun the attempt of privatization, according to its statistics.[15] It should be pointed out that the Soviet Union and most of the East European countries were yet to start privatization at that time. This report by the World Bank indicates from a negative perspective as to what breadth and depth the nationalization had once reached in various countries in the world, including countries not in the socialist bloc.

Third, the influence of the Soviet mode. The New China was to build socialism, but it had no experience in doing so. The only socialist model it could learn from at the time was that of the Soviet Union. Since the Soviet Union's socialism was built on the basis of state ownership, China was bound to be influenced. But the ownership China later adopted varied from the Soviet Union in form. In China, the collective ownership took a bigger share, and a large number of state-owned enterprises in China were local SOEs, which were not under the direct control of the central government.

Fourth, the tradition of public-administered economy of the liberated areas. Another difference between China and the Soviet Union is that the establishment of new economic and political system was not begun in the Soviet Union until after the victory of revolution, whereas the Communist Party of China had possessed vast stretches of bases long before the founding of New China. The CPC had already established some public-administered economic entities in those bases and accumulated operation experiences.

State-owned enterprises began to appear after the founding of New China, and they were from at least five sources: (1) various kinds of public-administered enterprises created in the liberated areas; (2) public enterprises taken over from the KMT government's National Resources Commission and those operated by KMT governments at various levels; (3) foreign enterprises seized or taken over; (4) private enterprises that

---

[14] Steve H. Hanke, *Europe's Nationalized Industries*, The Free Market (April 1985).

[15] Rebecca Cantoy-Sekse and Anne Ruiz Palmer, *Techniques of Privatization of State-Owned Enterprises*, Vol. III, *Inventory of Country Experience and Reference Materials*, World Bank Technical Paper, No. WTP 90 (Washington, DC: The World Bank, 1988).

went through socialist transformation; and (5) newly established SOEs after the founding of New China.

There are a lot of qualitative historical materials about the first group of SOEs, but there are very few quantitative statistics, so it is hard to calculate the total capital volume of this group.[16]

The second group were public enterprises taken over from the KMT government's National Resources Commission and those operated by local KMT governments. At the early stage of the New China, it was the biggest source of SOEs, but its relative importance declined later. According to historical records, in the financial sector, the New China took over the "four banks, two bureaus and one treasury" (namely, the Bank of China, Bank of Communications, Farmers Bank of China, Central Bank, Postal Savings and Remittance Bureau, Central Trust Bureau, and Central Cooperative Treasury), plus more than 2,400 banks under the local bank systems at provincial and municipal levels, and government shares in the banks jointly run by government and business. In the commercial sector, it took over a dozen monopolizing trading companies such as the Chinese Tea Company, China National Petroleum Corporation, China National Salt Industry Corporation, China Silk Corporation, and China Import & Export Corporation. In the transport sector, it took over all the transport enterprises under the KMT Ministry of Transportation and Communications and China Merchants. In the industrial and mining sector, it took over 2,858 industrial and mining enterprises with 1.29 million employees, including 750,000 workers on the production line. In 1951, the shares and properties of the former officials of KMT government, its national economic institutions, of former enemy governments and their expatriates, and of KMT war criminals, traitors, and bureaucratic capitalists in private or public enterprises were also returned to the People's Government.[17]

In today's perspective, the scale of SOEs left behind by the KMT government was very limited. But back in those days it was significant

---

[16] Wang Haibo, *History of New China's Industrial Economy*, October 1949–1957 (Beijing: Economy & Management Publishing House, 1994), pp. 72–84.

[17] Wu Taichang and Wu Li, et al., *A Historical Analysis of China's State Capital* (Beijing: China Social Science Press, 2012), p. 261; Li Ding, *Socialist Transformation of China's Capitalist Industry and Commerce* (Beijing: Contemporary China Publishing House, 1997), p. 40; Xu Dixin and Wu Chengming, *History of the Development of Chinese Capitalism*, Vol. III (Beijing: People's Publishing House, 2003), p. 717.

to seize the state bureaucratic capital. Prior to the founding of New China, the bureaucratic capital accounted for two thirds of all the industrial capital II of the country, which occupied 80% of the fixed assets of the nation's industrial, mining, and transport industries, plus a dozen monopolizing trading companies. With the confiscation of bureaucratic capital, the state-owned economy gathered most of the modernized industries in the national economy, controlling the most advanced and powerful part of the social productive forces, and thus establishing its dominant position in the national economy. With this single move, the fixed assets of state-operated industries occupied 80.7% of the total industrial fixed assets of the country.[18] The output value of the state-owned industries accounted for 26.2% of the national total industrial output value, and 41.3% of the output value of the big industries of the country.[19] The state-owned economy had gained absolute advantage in the key areas of industry, and nearly 100% of the transport sector was held by SOEs, so was the banking sector (see Table 6.8).

The third group were foreign enterprises seized or taken over. There were 1,192 foreign-funded enterprises nationwide at the time when the New China was founded, with total assets of 1.21 billion yuan and 126,000 employees, which were mostly held by British or American capital. The new government did not confiscate these enterprises. After the Korean War broke out, the US government announced on December 16, 1950 that Chinese public and private assets within the US jurisdiction were to be placed under control, and Britain immediately followed suit. The Chinese government was forced to take corresponding measure and issued the order on December 28 to put all the US government and private enterprises within the borders of the People's Republic under control to check over, and freeze all the American public and private bank savings in China. While they were not confiscated, once deprived of the privileges they used to enjoy, most British and American-funded enterprises fell into a state of collapse. By 1953, foreign enterprises declined to 563 in number, with assets of 450 million yuan and 23,000 employees

---

[18] Party History Research Center of the CPC Central Committee, *History of the Communist Party of China*, Vol. II (Beijing: History of Chinese Communist Party Publishing House, 2010), p. 33.

[19] Wang Haibo, *History of New China's Industrial Economy*, October 1949–1957 (Beijing: Economy & Management Publishing House, 1994), p. 106.

**Table 6.8** SOE share in major industrial products in 1949

| Industry | % | Transport | % |
|---|---|---|---|
| Electricity | 67 | Railway | 100 |
| Crude coal | 68 | Highway | 100 |
| Crude Oil | 100 | Shipping | 100 |
| Pig iron | 92 | Shipping fleet (tonnage) | 45 |
| Steel | 97 | **Banking** | **%** |
| Non-ferrous metals | 100 | Total capital volume | 59 |
| Cement | 68 | | |
| Spindles (equipment) | 40 | | |
| Looms (equipment) | 60 | | |
| Cotton Yarn | 53 | | |
| Sugar | 90 | | |

Source Xu Dixin and Wu Chengming, *History of the Development of Chinese Capitalism*, Vol. III (Beijing: People's Publishing House, 2003), p. 730; Wang Haibo, *History of New China's Industrial Economy*, October 1949–1957 (Beijing: Economy & Management Publishing House, 1994), p. 106

left. There was another kind of foreign enterprises, which were the properties in Dalian and Changchun Railway handed over to China by the Soviet Union in 1950–1952. The two kinds of enterprises funded by Europe/United States and the Soviet Union, even put together, were not many in number, which were not an important source of Chinese SOEs and played but a limited role in expanding China's national economy.[20]

The fourth group were private enterprises that had gone through socialist transformation. Many people now have a misunderstanding of this, taking it for granted that most of China's SOEs came from the confiscation of private enterprises. This is totally wrong. When China accomplished the socialist transformation in 1956, the private shares of the country's enterprises under public–private partnerships (PPP) totaled 2.42 billion yuan (about one billion US dollars at exchange rate of the time), of which there was 1.69 billion yuan of industrial private shares from 88,800 enterprises with 1.31 million employees and a total output value of 7.27 billion yuan. Of the 2.42 billion yuan of private shares, Shanghai alone claimed 1.12 billion yuan, nearly half of the national total.

[20] Wang Haibo, *History of New China's Industrial Economy*, October 1949–1957 (Beijing: Economy & Management Publishing House, 1994), p. 110.

The majority of the capitalists at that time were not very rich, because the 2.42 billion yuan investment was owned by 1.14 million people; of whom about 860,000 were designated as "capitalists" and entitled to take fixed dividend from their shares. Dividing the 2.42 billion yuan by 860,000 people, the average investment per capitalist was less than 3,000 yuan. Of course, the majority of the 860,000 capitalists were able to invest far less than 3,000 yuan, who should be counted as small business owners at best. The socialist transformation was not aimed at confiscating the capitalists' properties but allowed these investors to have yearly fixed dividend of 5% of their shares, known as the "fixed interest." Most of the principals invested were very limited, so was the fixed interest. Many people's monthly fixed interest could even hardly afford a package of cigarettes. Therefore, they pleaded at the time, "I don't want the label of capitalist, so please don't give me any more fixed interest." But the government did not listen to them. Not until in 1979 did the government decide to rid the label of more than 700,000 of them, saying their capital was too small to be counted as capitalists. Nowadays many people are misled by some lousy soap operas, assuming that capitalists before the founding of New China all lived in fancy mansions and rode luxury limousines. Such capitalists did exist, but they were as scarce as morning stars in the sea of Chinese population. In this case, the transformation of private industry and commerce was not an important source of socialist SOEs either, but only a tiny part of them.

The fifth group were the newly established state-owned enterprises after the founding of New China. In the whole process of public–private partnership, as far as industry was concerned, the total amount of private shares was only 2.42 billion yuan. In contrast, during the First Five-Year Plan period (1953–1957), the investment within the state budget amounted to 53.12 billion yuan, and together with the extra-budgetary investment, the state capital construction investment amounted to 58.85 billion yuan, which was 24.3 times the amount of private shares in the public–private partnership.[21]

In summary, of the five sources of SOE assets in China, the largest share came from the last category, namely, new state investment, which was used to build new SOEs, increase capital in existing SOEs, and inject

---

[21] Wu Taichang and Wu Li, et al., *A Historical Analysis of China's State Capital* (Beijing: China Social Science Press, 2012).

capital into public–private partnerships; the second source was the confiscation of enterprises run by the KMT government at all levels; the other three sources were rather less important.

State-operated and PPP industrial enterprises were superior to private industries not only in production scale and technology, but also in funding, raw materials supply, and products marketing. Table 6.9 presents the labor productivity of workers in various types of industrial enterprises. It indicates that SOEs also led their private counterparts in production efficiency from 1950 to 1954. After 1950, PPP enterprises and SOEs were always far ahead of private enterprises in efficiency. This was also an important reason for the popular support for nationalization at the time: If the state ownership was more efficient, why not nationalized?

Through the socialist transformation of capitalist industry and commerce and with large-scale investment in SOEs, tremendous changes took place in the structure of China's economic ownerships by 1957. From Table 6.10 one could see that state-owned economy accounted for merely 19.1% of the national economy in 1952, which grew to one-third by 1957. During the same period, the share of capitalist economy dwindled from 6.9% to zero, while that of self-employed or private businesses dropped from 71.8 to 2.8%. Meanwhile, cooperative economy, or what we call collective economy later, witnessed the most rapid growth, with its share jumping from 1.5 to 56.4%. This indicates that Chinese socialism varied greatly from Soviet socialism in terms of ownership, as we had a large amount of collectively owned enterprises of the socialist or public nature, whereas in the Soviet Union the SOEs were in domination.

Table 6.9 Labor productivity of workers in Industrial Enterprises Nationwide (Unit: Yuan/Per Capita/Year)

|  | 1949 | 1950 | 1951 | 1952 | 1953 | 1954 |
| --- | --- | --- | --- | --- | --- | --- |
| PPP | 3,515 | 4,257 | 6,553 | 9,297 | 10,880 | 13,401 |
| SOEs | 4,933 | 6,218 | 7,118 | 7,919 | 8,894 | 10,218 |
| Cooperative | 6,436 | 7,003 | 7,671 | 8,415 | 8,557 | 9,165 |
| Private |  | 4,357 | 5,928 | 6,801 | 7,848 | 7,222 |
| Total | 4,839 | 6,037 | 7,087 | 8,049 | 9,016 | 10,372 |

Source Wu Taichanga and Wu Li, et. al., *A Historical Analysis of China's State Capital* (Beijing: China Social Science Press, 2012)

Table 6.10 Structural changes in ownerships 1952–1957 (Unit: %)

| Year | State-owned economy | Cooperative economy | PPP economy | Capitalist economy | Individual economy |
| --- | --- | --- | --- | --- | --- |
| 1952 | 19.1 | 1.5 | 0.7 | 6.9 | 71.8 |
| 1953 | 23.9 | 2.5 | 0.9 | 7.9 | 64.8 |
| 1954 | 26.8 | 4.8 | 2.1 | 5.3 | 61 |
| 1955 | 28 | 14.1 | 2.8 | 3.5 | 51.6 |
| 1956 | 32.2 | 53.4 | 7.3 | 3.0 | 4.1 |
| 1957 | 33.2 | 56.4 | 7.6 | 0 | 2.8 |

*Source* Institute of Economics of Chinese Academy of Sciences and Central Administration of Industry and Commerce: *Statistics Summary of Socialist Transformation of Private Industry and Commerce of the People's Republic of China (1949–1957)*, October 1958

So far we have discussed the starting point of New China from four aspects: economy, industry, capital, and SOEs. In whatever aspect, this starting point is very low. Starting from such a low starting point, every step forward should not be easy. It was indeed an arduous course to transform China from an agricultural to an industrial country as the industrial foundation, human resources, capital, and experience were all insufficient. Today there are many poor countries in the world that do not know how to make the economic leap. In fact, when the New China started, it was even more difficult than them. Only if we choose the right path can we enter the new epoch!

## From an Agricultural to an Industrial Country, 1949–1984[22]

As early as before the end of Anti-Japanese War, Mao Zedong was already mapping out the blueprint for the New China's future development. In his perspective, the New China "cannot be consolidated unless it has a solid economy as its base, a much more advanced agriculture than at present, and a large-scale industry occupying a predominant position in

---

[22] The reason is simple to end this period in 1984: Although it is generally to deem the start of reform and opening as in 1978, it was not until after the *Decision of the Central Committee of the Communist Party of China on Reform of the Economic Structure* was adopted at the Third Plenary Session of the 12th CPC Central Committee at the end of 1984 did the focus of reform and opening-up shift from rural areas to cities.

the national economy, with communications, trade and finance to match." To this end, after the founding of New China, "the Chinese people and their government will have to adopt practical measures in order to build heavy and light industry step by step over a number of years and transform China from an agricultural into an industrial country."[23]

Mao Zedong was fully aware that to realize this goal of economic development, the primary task was to create "a China that is independent, free, democratic and united" politically, because "in semi-colonial, semi-feudal and divided China, many people have for years dreamed of developing industry, building up national defense, and bringing well-being to the people and prosperity and power to the nation, but all their dreams have been shattered." The history of the 105 years up to then had brought this important point home to the Chinese people, which was, "Without independence, freedom, democracy and unity it is impossible to build industry on a really large scale. Without industry, there can be no solid national defense, no well-being for the people, no prosperity or strength for the nation."[24]

With the founding of the People's Republic of China, "a China that is not colonial or semi-colonial but independent, not semi-feudal but free and democratic, not divided but united" came into being, laying solid political foundation for creating "a China that is not poor and weak but prosperous and strong"[25] (see Chapter 3 of this book for more details).

After the founding of New China, Mao Zedong was more concerned about the question of China's path to industrialization, that is, the "relationship between the growth of heavy industry, light industry and agriculture." He believed that "it must be affirmed that heavy industry is the core of China's economic construction. At the same time, full attention must be paid to the development of agriculture and light industry."[26]

---

[23] Mao Zedong, *On Coalition Government* (April 24, 1945), *Selected Works of Mao Tse-tung*, Vol. III (Peking, China: Foreign Languages Press, 1965), p. 303.

[24] Mao Zedong, *On Coalition Government* (April 24, 1945), *Selected Works of Mao Tse-tung*, Vol. III (Peking, China: Foreign Languages Press, 1965), pp. 302–303.

[25] Mao Zedong, *On Coalition Government* (April 24, 1945), *Selected Works of Mao Tse-tung*, Vol. III (Peking, China: Foreign Languages Press, 1977), p. 302.

[26] Mao Zedong, *On the Correct Handling of Contradictions Among the People* (February 27, 1957), *Selected Works of Mao Tse-tung*, Vol. V (Peking: Foreign Languages Press, 1965), p. 419.

With heavy industry at the core was an experience learned from the Soviet Union. Mao Zedong pointed out, "In transforming China from a backward, agricultural country into an advanced, industrialized one, we are confronted with many strenuous tasks and our experience is far from being adequate. So we must be good at studying." He especially stressed that "we must be good at learning from our forerunner, the Soviet Union."[27] This was because "the Soviet experience in construction is fairly complete." However, by "complete" he meant "it includes the making of mistakes. No experience can be considered complete unless it includes the making of mistakes."[28]

To learn from the Soviet experience does not mean to copy it blindly. "To copy, it is necessary to be analytical, not to copy rigidly, which means no independent thinking and forgets the lessons of dogmatism in history." "The Soviet experience is one side, and China's practice is another, which are the unity of opposites. We should only accept everything good in the Soviet experience and reject what is bad."[29] The Soviet Union's log-sided development of heavy industry to the neglect of light industry and agriculture resulted in imbalanced development of agriculture, light and heavy industry. In Mao Zedong's perspective, this was a serious lesson that must be taken as a warning. He firmly believed that in thinking about China's path to industrialization, it was crucial to proceed from China's reality, that is, from the basic condition that China was a big agricultural country, and from the need to satisfy the people's demand for material and cultural life, so as to explore a path to industrialize China different from the Soviet Union.

Why did he stress that "full attention must be paid to the development of agriculture and light industry" at the same time when the heavy industry was taken as the core? Mao Zedong gave a detailed enunciation in *On the Correct Handling of Contradictions among the People*: "… agriculture must develop along with industry, for only thus can industry secure raw materials and a market, and only thus is it possible to accumulate more funds for building a powerful heavy industry. Everyone knows

---

[27] Mao Zedong, *Opening Address at the Eighth National Congress of the Communist Party of China* (September 15, 1956), Foreign Languages Press, Peking, 1956.

[28] Mao Zedong, *Be Activists in Promoting the Revolution* (October 9, 1957), *Selected Works of Mao Tse-tung*, Vol. V (Peking: Foreign Languages Press, 1977), pp. 490–491.

[29] Mao Zedong, *Talks at Chengdu Conference* (March 1958), *Collected Works of Mao Zedong*, Vol. VII (Beijing: People's Publishing House, 1999), p. 336.

that light industry is closely tied up with agriculture. Without agriculture there can be no light industry. But it is not yet so clearly understood that agriculture provides heavy industry with an important market. This fact, however, will be more readily appreciated as gradual progress in the technical transformation and modernization of agriculture calls for more and more machinery, fertilizer, water conservancy and electric power projects and transport facilities for the farms, as well as fuel and building materials for the rural consumers. ... the entire national economy will benefit if we can achieve an even greater growth in our agriculture and thus induce a correspondingly greater development of light industry. As agriculture and light industry develop, heavy industry, assured of its market and funds, will grow faster. Hence what may seem to be a slower pace of industrialization will actually not be so slow, and indeed may even be faster."[30]

In short, Mao Zedong saw two possible approaches to the development of heavy industry, "one is to develop agriculture and light industry less, and the other is to develop them more. In the long run, the first approach will lead to a smaller and slower development of heavy industry, or at least will put it on a less solid foundation and when the overall account is added up a few decades hence, it will not prove to have paid. The second approach will lead to a greater and faster development of heavy industry and, since it ensures the livelihood of the people, it will lay a more solid foundation for the development of heavy industry."[31] To give priority to the development of agriculture was a major characteristic of Mao Zedong's thinking on China's path to industrialization. Later on, he summarized this thinking as planning the national economy in the sequence of agriculture, light industry, and heavy industry.[32]

The path was settled, but every step forward had to be explored, with strenuous efforts paid. Exploration is bound to take a detour. Since it is "exploration," it is impossible to be free of mistakes, let alone that

---

[30] Mao Zedong, *On the Correct Handling of Contradictions Among the People* (February 27, 1957), *Selected Works of Mao Tse-tung*, Vol. V (Peking: Foreign Languages Press, 1965), p. 419.

[31] Mao Zedong, *On the Ten Major Relationships* (April 25, 1956), *Selected Works of Mao Tse-tung*, Vol. V (Peking: Foreign Languages Press, 1965), p. 286.

[32] Mao Zedong, *Eighteen Questions Discussed at Lushan Conference* (June 29, July 2, 1959), *Collected Works of Mao Zedong*, Vol. VIII (Beijing: People's Publishing House, 1999), p. 78.

China was engaged in an unprecedented epoch-making great exploration. Some people who assume they are wise only in hindsight are fastidious about the path covered by our forerunners, feeling that so many mistakes were made in the first 30 years and the period seemed to be pitch-dark. This only reveals that they are stunted mentally. From one's birth to adulthood, nobody knows how many times the person may have said something wrong and tumbled. Should a baby be not allowed to prattle in learning to speak or stumble in learning to walk, he may have to stay in his swaddling wrap forever. Is it possible for a big and poor agricultural country like China, who was confronted with blockade and embargo imposed by world powers, not to take some detours and make some mistakes in its exploration of a path to industrialization? This is even beyond the capacity of God! Despite some missteps, China has done it, and the Chinese people have 10,000 reasons to be proud of it!

### *Growth of SOEs*

When the socialist transformation of industry and commerce was completed in 1957, there were about 50,000 state-owned industrial enterprises around the country (see Fig. 6.3). During the Great Leap Forward in the following year, such enterprises exploded to 120,000 in number, a peak unprecedented and never to be duplicated. Starting from 1959, the number of industrial SOEs began to decline and hit the bottom at about 45,000 by 1964, even fewer than in 1957. Then a revival began, and by the late 1970s and early 1980s, the number of industrial SOEs rebounded to about 85,000, which was a quarter of the number of collective industrial enterprises (about 350,000) in the same period.

And the employment of industrial SOEs was not quite sizable, which just exceeded 5 million in 1952, and skyrocketed to 23 million during the Great Leap Forward period. So many people flooded into cities all at once and became commodity grain consumers, which went beyond the capacity of agricultural production at the time. During the three-year period of "adjustment, consolidation, filling-in and improvement," a large number of industrial enterprises closed down, suspended operation, merged with others or shifted to different lines of production, and the industrial SOEs' employees were streamlined by half, with some 11 million left. The industrial SOE employment jumped back after 1964 and exceeded 35 million in the early 1980s.

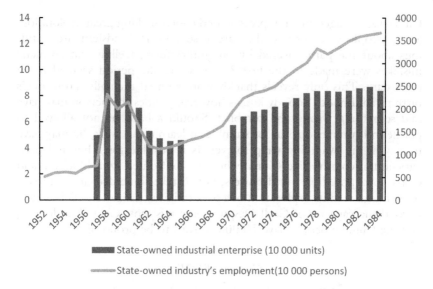

**Fig. 6.3** Number and employment of state-owned industrial enterprises (*Note* Unless otherwise noted, all the data of figures and tables in this and the next section are sourced in the *Statistical Database of China's Economic and Social Development* on the China National Knowledge Infrastructure [CNKI])

While the number of employees of state-owned industrial enterprises grew, the urban employed population was also growing rapidly at the same time, from less than 25 million in 1952 to more than 120 million in 1984. In this case, except for the period of Great Leap Forward, the proportion of state-owned industrial employees never exceeded one-third of the urban employed population.

State-owned industrial enterprises were not large in number, and their employees did not take a big proportion of the urban employed population, which could lead people to the misconception that SOEs did not play a big role in industry and the entire national economy. In reality, the opposite is true, and it is clear as indicated in Fig. 6.4.

As Fig. 6.4 indicates, except for the period of Great Leap Forward and the early stage of the Cultural Revolution, both China's national and SOEs' total industrial output values maintained a rapid growth. Even with the 1952 (instead of 1949) figure as reference, the former grew by nearly 29 folds, and the latter by more than 36 folds. SOEs accounted for

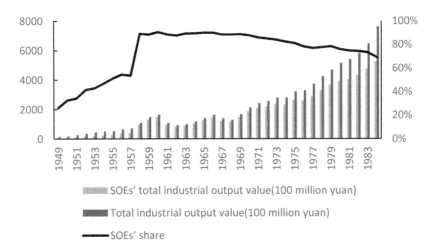

**Fig. 6.4** SOEs' contribution to industrial growth, 1949–1984

merely 26.3% of the total industrial output value when the New China was just founded, but that share rose to more than 50% when the socialist transformation was completed. The Great Leap Forward drove the SOEs' share up further to about 90%, which then sustained till the end of the 1960s. In the 1970s, "five small industries" (namely iron and steel, coal mining, machinery, cement and fertilizer) operated by commune and brigade enterprises (later known as township and village enterprises or TVEs) were on the rise, when the SOEs' share gradually went down, but it was still over 70% in the early 1980s. This indicates that although SOEs were limited in number and employment, they made great contributions to industry and played a key role in advancing China's industrialization.

In recent years, some people have been spreading the idea that when it comes to SOE, its efficiency must be low. This has misled many people who are not clear about the issue. Table 6.9 already makes it clear that SOEs were superior to private enterprises in efficiency in the period of 1949–1954. Table 6.11 illustrates that throughout 1949 to 1984, SOEs' overall labor productivity constantly went up. If the overall labor productivity of SOEs in 1952 is taken for 100, it went up to 336.3 in 1984, a more than threefold increase.

As the industrial output and labor productivity of SOEs continued to rise, the profits they generated and the taxes they paid also rose, to higher

**Table 6.11** Improvement of overall labor productivity of state-owned industrial enterprises (Counted at the constant price of 1970)

| Year | Overall labor productivity (yuan/person/yr) | Index (based on the 1952 figure) |
|---|---|---|
| 1949 | 3,016 | 72.1 |
| 1952 | 4,184 | 100 |
| 1957 | 6,362 | 152.1 |
| 1965 | 8,979 | 214.6 |
| 1980 | 12,080 | 288.7 |
| 1984 | 14,070 | 336.3 |

and higher levels every few years. In 1952, the two items (profits and taxes) added up to no more than 3 billion yuan, which topped 100 billion yuan by 1984, an increase of nearly 34 times (see Fig. 6.5). During this period, the government imposed "unified collection and unified expenditure" on SOEs, i.e., all profits of SOEs were paid to the state, all losses were compensated by the state, and the cost of reproduction was audited and allocated by the finance department of the state. Therefore, the profits and taxes realized by SOEs were their contributions to the state treasury.

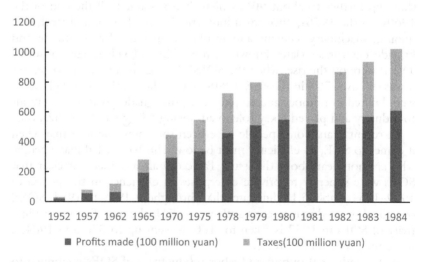

**Fig. 6.5** Profits and taxes made by state-owned industrial enterprises, 1952–1984

## Growth of State Capital

Capital is vital to backward countries in their economic development. Without capital, there is no way to invest; without investment, it is impossible to expand production; and without expanded production, it is hard to develop economy. Where did their capital come from for the capitalist countries' early development? Chapter 2 of this book cited a paragraph from Marx's *Capital*, in which he said the primitive accumulation of capital in western capitalist countries "depend in part on brute force," namely, at the cost of slave trade, slavery, colonialism and ruthless exploitation and oppression of people in their own countries.

The New China could not rely on external expansion to accumulate capital. Not only that, it had to guard against imperialist intervention all the time. In this circumstance, it could only rely on itself for capital accumulation. As mentioned in the previous section, in the 35 years before the founding of New China, the total amount of industrial capital II increased by less than 4 times. For comparison, in the 35 years after the founding of New China, that is, from 1949 to 1984, the original value of industrial fixed assets increased 47.71 times. Where did this money come from? Almost entirely from domestic capital! Where did the domestic capital come from? Mainly by the state financial resources! Where did the state financial resources come from? Mainly through the accumulation contributed by SOEs! The following figures are the evidence.

In 1952, the investment of state fixed capital was 4.356 billion yuan; in the following 8 years, it grew rapidly; by 1960, it reached 41.658 billion yuan, almost 10 times as much as in 1952. After the setback of the Great Leap Forward, the level of investment fell sharply, but it was still higher than that in the early years of the founding of New China. Over the next decade, state fixed capital investment fluctuated, never exceeding the level of 1960. With the passing of the stormy period of the Cultural Revolution, state capital investment began to climb up after 1968. In 1971, it exceeded the 1960 level; in 1984, it exceeded the 100 billion mark, reaching 118.52 billion yuan, more than twice as much as in 1960 (see Fig. 6.6).

Another noteworthy point in Fig. 6.6 is the proportion of state fixed assets investment in the total social fixed assets investment. From 1952 to 1980, only the units under ownerships by the whole people were within the statistical scheme of fixed asset investment. That's why the statistical data available now all indicate that the composition of total social fixed

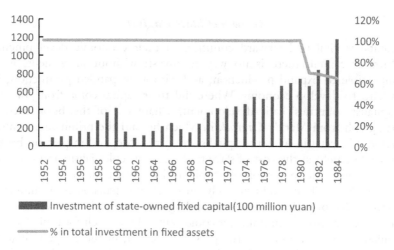

**Fig. 6.6** Rapid growth of state-owned fixed capital investment, 1952–1984

asset investment was 100% of state fixed capital investment. It was not until after 1981 when the fixed asset investment in collective economy, self-employed or private businesses and other businesses appeared in the statistical data. There was surely some fixed asset investment by collective economy from 1952 to 1980, but its share in the total fixed asset investment could not be big, probably around 5 to 10%.[33] There is no doubt that state fixed asset investment then occupied the dominant share in the total fixed asset investment.

Where did the fund of state fixed asset investment come from? Fig. 6.7. illustrates that there were four sources. From 1953 to 1957, the "government financial allocation" largely accounted for more than 60%. Prior to 1966, the share of government financial allocation was often up to 80% or more. The second largest source was the fund "self-raised and from other investments" by SOEs. After 1964, "domestic loans" became a new funding source for state fixed asset investment, but its share was too tiny to speak of. Its importance did not become apparent until after 1980, as by then pilot practice of replacing government financial allocation with

---

[33] Based on the 1980 data, it is estimated that state economy took 74.59 billion yuan in the total fixed asset investment that year, while collective economy claimed 4.6 billion yuan.

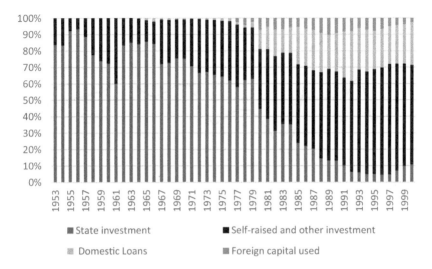

**Fig. 6.7** Funding sources shares in state-owned economy's fixed asset investment, 1953–2000

bank loans was already being carried out. "Foreign capital" first emerged in 1977, but its share remained low, around 5%, up to 1984. Foreign capital had to wait until after 1992 when Deng Xiaoping's talks during his inspection tour to South China were released to enter China on large scales and become a fresh force in fixed asset investment.

China was a poor country in the first 30 years of the People's Republic. It was not easy for such a poor country to spend so much money on investment. There was a saying describing such practice of being frugal in food and clothing, minimizing the consumption for investment at that time, which goes, "tightening the belt for construction."

For an understanding of how the Chinese government and people exhausted their efforts to keep the construction going at that time, take a look at Fig. 6.8. When speaking of investment in those years, the official statistical yearbooks used to use a term "state financial resources," which is no longer in use. "State financial resources" refer to funds disposable by the government. Specifically, state financial resources are the sum total of the overall state budgetary revenue and extra-budgetary revenue. Figure 6.8 depicts the share of state-owned institutions' fixed asset investment in the state financial resources. In the 32 years from 1953 to 1984,

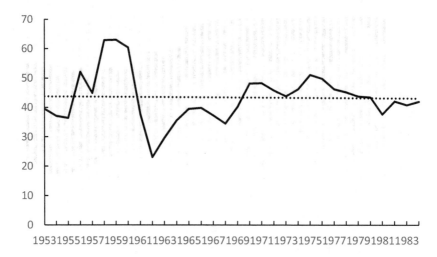

**Fig. 6.8** Share of state-owned institutions' fixed asset investment in state financial resources, 1953–1984

the peak value of the proportion was 63% (in 1959), while the bottom value was 23.1% (in 1962), with the average value at 43.4%. In other words, about 43% of China's annual financial resources were put into the newly increased fixed asset investment. Here we could see how hard the Chinese people and the Chinese government struggled in those years.

Some people may wonder where the money of state financial resources came from. The reply to this question should be made with the help of Fig. 6.9. Divided by economic types, there were four sources for the state financial resources, namely, economies under the ownerships of the whole people, collective, self-employment, and others. Figure 6.9 shows that at the time of the founding of New China, the majority of financial revenue came from private economy, namely, "self-employed businesses" and "others." But by 1952, 60% of the financial revenue came from the whole people ownership. After the completion of the socialist transformation of industry and commerce, the whole people ownership accounted for more than 80% of the financial revenue, which sustained till 1984. That is to say, the money of state financial resources came mostly from SOEs, and once the state acquired the money, it was mostly put into the state-owned economy as investment of fixed assets, thus forming a benign cycle.

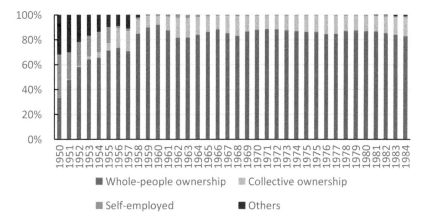

**Fig. 6.9** Shares of various sources in state financial revenue, 1950–1984

There are idioms in China: gather the sand into a tower, gather the armpit into a fur. Many a little really makes a mickle. This benign cycle operated continuously for 30 years, and the effect of accumulation day after day and month after month was amazing: The original value of fixed assets of state-owned industry grew from 14.8 billion yuan in 1952 to 517 billion yuan in 1984 (see Fig. 6.10), and the foundation of state-owned industry became ever more solid.

One does not have to master a profound knowledge of economics to perceive that investment and consumption are a pair that one's loss is the other's gain. The things produced within a year were in a certain quantity, if more of them were put into investment, those for consumption would be less, vice versa. The effect of accumulation over several decades could be surprising. For a family, it is better to be frugal on food and expenses and be industrious and thrifty in managing house affairs than to spend money without restraint and squander in consumption. It is also true for a country.

In 1982, American economist Wilfred Malenbaum published a paper, in which he made a comparison of modern economic growth between China and India. Remarkable differences already revealed in their growth at that time, why? Malenbaum thought the reason was simple: India's annual investment rate was often 10% lower than China's, or even less. With the extra investment equivalent to 10% of GDP, how much could

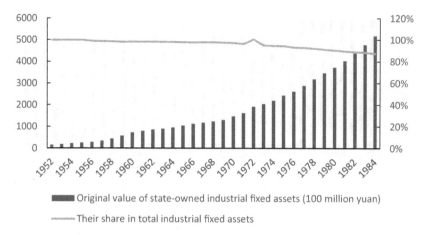

Fig. 6.10 Original value of state-owned industrial fixed assets and their shares, 1952–1984

the cumulative money be over several decades? The cumulative investment gap over the years resulted in China's economic growth rate leading India by far. In other words, in advancing industrialization, China temporarily gave up the current consumption but greatly promoted the rapid growth of overall well-being in the end.[34] To put it in an iconic way, at the initial stage of industrialization, China took the way of forced march. A forced march certainly poses an overwhelming challenge to one's immediate physical proficiency and will, but it was exactly this way that enabled China to come to the fore from behind.

### Growth of Industry

Thanks to the state investment in large amount, China's industry grew in a skyrocketing way in the first 30 years of the People's Republic, which is embodied in following aspects.

First, industrial added value grew rapidly. Industrial added value is the total value of goods and services produced by an industry, after deducting

---

[34] Wilfred Malenbaum, Modern Economic Growth in India and China: The Comparison Revisited, 1950–1980, *Economic Development and Cultural Change*, Vol. 31, No. 1 (October 1982), p. 66.

the cost of goods and services used in the process of production. It is the ultimate outcome of industrial production embodied in form of money within a reporting period. China's industrial added value in 1949 was less than 12 billion yuan, which then went up rapidly afterwards. Even during the first few years of the 1960s after the failure of Great Leap Forward, there was more than 30 billion yuan every year, about three times of the 1949 level. During the three years in the Cultural Revolution which witnessed the sternest situation, namely, in 1967, 1968, and 1976, the growth of industrial added value dropped slightly, but in other years it retained the momentum of rise. By 1984, China's industrial added value reached 281.59 billion yuan, 23.5 times of the 1949 level.

In addition, industrial added value is part of GDP, reflecting the contribution of industrial sectors to gross domestic product. In 1949, industrial added value accounted for only 17.6% of GDP. Its contribution to GDP was less than agriculture, and also than services. By the mid-1970s, China's industrial volume expanded tremendously, and its share in GDP had exceeded 40%, becoming the biggest contributor to GDP among the sectors of national economy.

Then the internal composition of industry became more modernized. Total industrial output refers to the entire goods produced by industrial enterprises in a certain period embodied in money. To review the development level of a country's industry, it is necessary not only to look at the gross output, but also to check its internal composition. In the early years of the New China, the country's industrial sectors were not only small on scale, but the composition of their products was dominated by simple consumption goods. In 1952, output value of the two industries of textile and food alone accounted for half of the total industrial output. This situation began to change in 1957, when the two industries' share dropped by 10%. By 1984, their share declined further by more than 10%. On the other hand, shares of electricity, metal metallurgy, petroleum, chemical, and machine-building industries increased greatly, and these modern industrial sectors had accounted for more than half of total industrial output in 1984 (see Table 6.12).

People usually classify the various industries within the industry into two categories, "light industry" and "heavy industry." The former refers to industries supplying consumption goods for daily life and manufacturing hand tools, whereas the latter refers to industries providing the means of production for various sectors of the national economy. In this perspective, about three-quarters of China's total industrial output

**Table 6.12** Changes in internal composition of gross output by industry (Unit: %)

| Year | 1952 | 1957 | 1984 | Comparison of 1984 vs 1952 |
|---|---|---|---|---|
| Textile industry | 27.5 | 20.4 | 15.4 | −12.1 |
| Food industry | 24.1 | 19.7 | 12.3 | −11.8 |
| Forest industry | 6.5 | 5.8 | 1.8 | −4.7 |
| Sewing industry | 4.4 | 4.4 | 2.5 | −1.9 |
| Paper-making industry | 2.2 | 2.2 | 1.3 | −0.9 |
| Leather industry | 1.4 | 1.3 | 0.9 | −0.5 |
| Cultural and art products | 2 | 2.1 | 2.2 | 0.2 |
| Coal and coking industry | 2.4 | 2.9 | 2.8 | 0.4 |
| Building materials | 3 | 3.2 | 4.1 | 1.1 |
| Electricity | 1.3 | 1.7 | 3.4 | 2.1 |
| Metallurgy | 5.9 | 8.5 | 8.3 | 2.4 |
| Other industries |  | 2.6 | 3.4 | 3.4 |
| Petroleum | 0.5 | 1.1 | 4.8 | 4.3 |
| Chemical | 4.8 | 6.8 | 11.8 | 7 |
| Machine-building | 11.4 | 16.9 | 25 | 13.6 |
| Total | 100 | 100 | 100 |  |

were light industry when the People's Republic was newly founded. The composition of total industrial output changed rapidly afterwards, as the share of heavy industry exceeded 30% in 1951. Then it exceeded 40% in 1955, topped 50% in 1959, and climbed to the peak value of 66.7% in 1960. After the Great Leap Forward, the share of heavy industry declined, swinging between 50 to 55% from the 1960s to the 1980s.

Heavy industry is the material basis on which the expanded social production is realized, and its importance goes beyond saying. Taking the historical context in which China existed into consideration, there were at least another four important reasons for giving priority to developing heavy industry. One reason was that China was confronted with very stern external situation, and it was a must to develop defense industry. Defense industry belongs to heavy industry, which is not consumable for eating, drinking, or even for daily use. But China had to be prepared for the worst, and must produce guns and artilleries, tanks, and atom bombs. The second reason was that it must rely on heavy industry to advance the growth of railway, highway, inland shipping, ocean shipping, and aviation. Without a modern transportation network, it was impossible for economies in various regions of China to get interconnected and develop coordinately. The third reason was that it would not do to rely on manual labor to develop light industry but on machines. So the machinery used by light industry itself had to be manufactured by heavy industry. The fourth reason was that the development of agriculture could not depend on traditional manual labor and animal stock, but it needs fertilizer, pesticides, electricity, agricultural machinery, and water conservancy facilities, which all call for heavy industry. After the rural reform, agricultural production increased, which some people attributed to the practice of household contract responsibility system. However, if fertilizer, pesticides, electricity, agricultural machinery, and water conservancy facilities remained at the level before the founding of New China, it would not have worked even if the household contract responsibility system was carried out for 100 times, I'm afraid.

As a part of heavy industry, electrical or power industry is the backing for the entire modern industry. In 1949, China's electricity generation was a pitiful 4.3 billion KWHs. Throughout the 1950s, the annual growth rate of China's electricity generation exceeded 26%, and grew 10 folds by 1959. In 1984, China's electricity generation reached 377 billion KWHs, 87.7 times of the 1949 level, jumping to rank 6th in the world, with even its fraction surpassing the 1949 figure.

Such jump in fact was not confined to electricity. By 1984, China's many major industrial products already ranked among the world's top ones in terms of output (see Table 6.13). Among them cotton cloth ranked first in the world. China produced 1.89 billion meters of cotton cloth in 1949, averaging two and one-third meters for every Chinese.

Table 6.13 Variations in output ranking of major industrial products in the world

| Name | 1949 | 1957 | 1965 | 1984 | 2000 | 2016 |
| --- | --- | --- | --- | --- | --- | --- |
| Steel | 26 | 9 | 8 | 4 | 1 | 1 |
| Coal | 9 | 5 | 5 | 2 | 1 | 1 |
| Crude oil | 27 | 23 | 12 | 6 | 5 | 5 |
| Electricity | 25 | 13 | 9 | 6 | 2 | 1 |
| Cement | | 8 | 8 | 2 | 1 | 1 |
| Fertilizer | | 33 | 8 | 3 | 1 | 1 |
| Cotton cloth | | 3 | 3 | 1 | 2 | 1 |
| Chemical fiber | | 26 | | 4 | 1 | 1 |

**Table 6.14** Geographical distribution of industrial production, 1952–1984 (Unit: %)

| Proportion | Gross industrial output | | Light industry | | Heavy industry | |
| --- | --- | --- | --- | --- | --- | --- |
| | Coastal | Inland | Coastal | Inland | Coastal | Inland |
| 1952 | 69.4 | 30.6 | 71.5 | 28.5 | 65.5 | 34.5 |
| 1957 | 65.9 | 34.1 | 66.3 | 33.7 | 65.6 | 34.4 |
| 1962 | 63.8 | 36.2 | 66.6 | 33.4 | 61.3 | 38.7 |
| 1965 | 63.1 | 36.9 | 67.3 | 32.7 | 58.8 | 41.2 |
| 1970 | 63.1 | 36.9 | 68.2 | 31.8 | 59.3 | 40.7 |
| 1975 | 61 | 39 | 64.1 | 35.9 | 58.6 | 41.4 |
| 1984 | 59.8 | 40.2 | 64.9 | 35.1 | 54.8 | 45.2 |
| Variant of 1984 vs 1952 | -9.6 | 9.6 | -6.6 | 6.6 | -10.7 | 10.7 |

In 1984, China produced 13.7 billion meters of cotton cloth, more than seven times of the 1949 output, plus the 735,000 tons of chemical fibers, about 20 meters of cloth for every Chinese. On November 22, 1983, the Chinese government issued a notice in the name of Ministry of Commerce: Beginning from December 1 of that year, ration coupons on cloth and cotton were temporarily exempted nationwide and cotton cloth and cotton were to be supplied in sufficiency. Ration coupons on cloth would be no longer issued starting from 1984. That marked the end of the era when China's textiles were in restricted supply and that the problem of "clothing" for the whole country was basically solved.[35]

Next, the geographical distribution of industrial production became more balanced. Either in the overall review of total industrial output, or to look at breakdowns of light and heavy industry, we could see that proportions of coastal provinces fell while those of inland provinces rose (see Table 6.14). This indicates that the capacity of industrial production had expanded all over the country rather than concentrated on a few spots.

Lastly, a complete independent industrial system was established. In 1980, a World Bank delegation visited China for the first time, resulting in a three-volume report. What struck the mission was "Almost the

---

[35] Yuan Qiao, *"Clothing and Covering" China: 60 Years of China's Textile Industry*, Sohu Finance 2009–10-23. http://business.sohu.com/20091023/n267672597.shtml.

entire range of modern industry has been built up, but with particular emphasis on those making capital equipment. Thus although in many respects China's industrial structure is similar to other developing countries (the share of textiles, for instance, is quite close to that of India), the share of machinery and metal products is not much smaller than in the industrialized market economies – which is particularly striking in view of the low level of China's consumer durables production. As a result, China is now largely self-sufficient in capital goods (less than 10% are imported)."[36] Thus even foreign experts had to acknowledge that although China was still a poor country, it had already realized one aspiration of Chairman Mao: Build up an independent and integrated industrial system, which laid a solid material foundation for the then and later economic development.

### Growth of Economy

The economic growth could be reviewed from four respects, namely, growth rate of economy, economic structure, employment structure, and income level. The first two were already mentioned in Chapter 3.

Many people have a wrong impression that the GDP growth rate was stagnant before the reform and opening-up, and only after the reform and opening-up did it start to grow rapidly. Figure 3.17 shows us that this is not the case at all. From 1950 to 1978, the average annual growth rate of GDP was close to 8%. Counted from 1950 to 1984, it was 8.09%, and even the average annual growth rate of per capita GDP reached 6.08%. No matter in which historical stage it is put and with which economy it is compared, the New China's economic performance in its first 35 years was quite prominent, just slightly below that of the 35 years after the reform and opening-up.

In view of the evolution of economic structure, Chairman Mao's another aspiration also came true in the first 35 years of the New China, that is, China was transformed from an agricultural into an industrial country. If we define the Industrial Revolution as the process by which the share of industry (or the secondary industry with construction) in the national economy changed from irrelevant to a mainstay, then China's Industrial Revolution took place during this period. At the time when

---

[36] World Bank, *China: Socialist Economic Development*, Vol. I, *The Economy, Statistical System, and Basic Data* (Washington, DC: World Bank, 1983), p. 12.

the New China was just founded, the share of the secondary industry in the national income was barely 13%, while the primary industry claimed as high as 68.4%. China then was a typical agricultural country. In 1952, the secondary industry's share in GDP exceeded 20%, which went beyond 30% in 1958, 40% in 1970, and 45% in 1975 and sustained at the level for a long time. By 1984, it is safe to say that China had already achieved initial industrialization.

In conclusion, around the time when Chairman Mao passed away, both of his wishes were largely fulfilled.

However, in view of employment structure and income level, China then was still distant from modernization, and had a long way to go.

Although the secondary industry's added value took a big share in GDP to reach 45%, its employees accounted for a low proportion in the total employment: 7.4% in 1952, which once reached 26.6% in 1958, followed by a process of sharp decline and slow rise to come to 19.9% in 1984. Employees of service or tertiary industry did not claim a big share either, at 9.1% in 1952 and once accounted for 18.4 in 1960. There was also a process of sharp decline and slow rise after 1960, and the proportion was 16.1% in 1984. Employees of secondary and tertiary industry in 1984 put together accounted for 36% of the total employment. That means people engaged in agriculture or primary industry at the time still claimed 64% of the total employed population. In this sense, the industrialized China still had a leg trapped in traditional agriculture.

As for per capita national income, on the one hand a considerable progress was made in this respect, but on the other hand, it was still at a low level. According to statistical data published in the mid-1980s, China's per capita national income in 1949 was merely 66 yuan. In the first dozen years of the New China, it continuously went up. Except that it showed a downslide in two years following the Great Leap Forward and three years during the Cultural Revolution, the income went up steadily in all the other years. By 1984, the per capita national income reached 549 yuan, 8.32 times of the 1949 level. In the first 35 years of the New China, the average annual growth rate of per capita national income was 7.1%, which was quite high and brought about earthshaking changes (see Fig. 6.11). It is only because of the low starting point, even after 35 years of rapid growth, with the per capita income at the level of 550 yuan in 1984, China was still a poor country in the world. In other words, after strenuous efforts over several decades, China had passed through

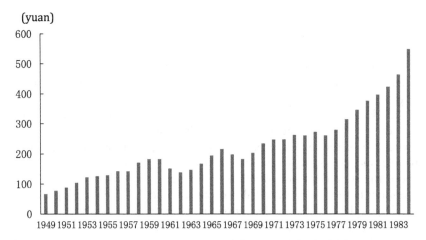

Fig. 6.11 Per capita national income, 1949–1984 (*Source* Department of National Economy Statistics of National Bureau of Statistics: *Compendium of National Income Statistics 1949–1984*, Beijing, China Statistics Press, 1987, p. 10)

the scarcity or starvation stage, but in the early 1980s, it just entered the subsistence stage (see discussions in Chapter 4 of the book).

## From Industrial Country to Industrial Power, 1985–2019

In 1982, the National People's Congress adopted the fourth *Constitution* of the New China. It "confirms the achievements of the struggle of the Chinese people of all nationalities and defines the basic system and basic tasks of the state in legal form," and is described by constitution scholar Xu Chongde as "the general statute for governing the country and the state in the new historical period of China."[37]

The *Constitution* deals with industrialization and state-owned enterprises. It declared that "the socialist system" was "established," and "major successes have been achieved in economic development. An independent and fairly comprehensive socialist system of industry has in the main been established." Paragraph 7 of the *Preamble* establishes that

---

[37] Xu Chongde, *Constitutional History of the People's Republic of China* (Fuzhou: Fujian People's Publishing House, 2005), p. 477.

the basic task of the nation in the years to come "is to concentrate its efforts on socialist modernization," and "to modernize industry, agriculture, national defense and science and technology step by step." That is to say, although China had become an industrial country, the industry overall was not advanced enough, and it needs to modernize industry step by step so as to become an industrial power.

Article 6 of the *Constitution* stipulates that "the basis of the socialist economic system of the People's Republic of China is socialist public ownership of the means of production, namely, ownership by the whole people and collective ownership by the working people." Article 7 is about the state economy, which goes further to stipulate that "the state economy is the sector of socialist economy under the ownership by the whole people, it is the leading force in the national economy. The state ensures the consolidation and growth of the state economy."

The *Constitution* has undertaken five revisions since it was adopted in 1982, and Paragraph 7 of the *Preamble* was revised four times. But the task "to modernize industry, agriculture, national defense and science and technology step by step" has remained never changed. Revisions of the *Constitution* are mostly related to the economic system, some directly concerning SOEs. For instance, the 1993 amendment changed "the state economy" into "the State-owned economy," and the 1999 amendment added a paragraph to Article 6: "In the primary stage of socialism, the state upholds the basic economic system with the dominance of the public ownership and the simultaneous development of an economic system of diverse forms of ownership, and upholds the distribution system with the dominance of distribution according to work and the coexistence of diverse modes of distribution." That means at the current stage and in long period to come the socialist economic system could not be very pure, but could only uphold the dominance of the public ownership. It would not do to demand exercising public ownership only but reject all the other forms of ownership. Apart from operating multiple forms of ownership, modes of distribution were also adjusted, that is, while upholding the dominance of distribution according to work, other modes of distribution, including distribution according to capital, were allowed to exist.

With the amendments to the *Constitution* over the past 30 years and more, SOEs, capital, industry, and economy all experienced changes that thoroughly remolded them.

## SOEs Grow Stronger

State-owned enterprises have gone through multiple rounds of reforms since China began to reform and open up in 1978, of which the major reforms have always related to the Third Plenary Sessions of different Central Committees of the Communist Party of China.

At the end of 1978, the Third Plenary Session of the 11th CPC Central Committee put forth to "adjust the relationship between the state and enterprises in terms of responsibility, power and interests." Reforms of SOEs from 1978 to 1984 focused on their external relations, such as their relations with government finance and banks. Major reform measures rolled out during this period included "replacing government financial allocation with loan" and "substituting tax payment for profits." The state used to execute "unified revenue and expenditure" on enterprises, who relied on state financial allocation for investment, technical renovation and other funding. Now it was no longer allocated freely, but changed to bank loans, for which the enterprise had to pay the capital stock and accrued interest. That is what "replacing government allocation with loan" means. "Substitution of tax payment for profits" means that enterprises used to hand over their profits to government finance with little to retain, and now they no longer had to hand over the profits but pay tax according to law, and the after-tax profits were at the disposal of enterprises. Both reform measures aimed to expand the enterprises' autonomy and stimulate their and workers' enthusiasm.

At the end of 1984, the Third Plenary Session of the 12th CPC Central Committee adopted the *Decision of the Central Committee of the Communist Party of China on Reform of the Economic Structure*. After that, from 1984 to 1993, the focus of SOEs reform shifted to their internal relations. A popular saying at the time went that "contract has entered the city." That is, the mentality of household contract responsibility system in rural areas was applied to the reform of enterprises. At that time, the idea was simple, thinking that the factory would be more efficient and profitable if the factory director or manager, workshop supervisor, and team leader was contracted layer by layer. The specific approach was to expand enterprises' autonomy in production and management step by step, and to promote the system of factory director/manager responsibility. But in reality it's not that simple. After all, modern industry is very different from small production in rural areas.

At the end of 1993, the Third Plenary Session of the 14th CPC Central Committee adopted the *Decision of the Central Committee of the Communist Party of China on Some Issues Concerning the Establishment of the Socialist Market Economic Structure*. Then, from 1994 to 2013, the guiding concept of SOE reform tilted to changing the operating mechanism of SOEs and establishing the modern corporate system. During this period, the state-owned Assets Supervision and Administration Commission was set up, but what was more influential was to apply the principle of "grasp the big and let go of the small." A large number of small- and medium-sized SOEs were restructured in various forms of regrouping, joint venture, merging, joint-stock holding, leasing, contracted operation, selling and bankruptcy, which had tens of millions workers of SOEs and collective enterprises laid off or diverted to other posts, who were directly pushed into markets.

At the end of 2013, the Third Plenary Session of the 18th CPC Central Committee adopted the *Decision of the CPC Central Committee on Major Issues Concerning Comprehensively Deepening Reforms*. From that time to the present, the guiding concept of SOE reform has been led by managing the capital and pushing SOEs for mixed ownership reform.

Each step of these few rounds of reforms made extremely profound impact on SOEs. Through the historical data presented in Fig. 6.12, we could still feel the striking shock of the momentum and vehemence of that impact.

Figure 6.12 depicts the trajectory of the three sources of state revenues during the period 1950–2010. The first source is enterprises' revenue, that is, profits submitted to state finance by enterprises. The second is various taxes, or taxes paid by enterprises and individuals to state finance. The third is other, which includes various non-tax financial earnings. Shares of three are in a relationship that one's loss is the others' gain. Even completely ignorant of finance, a look at Fig. 6.12 will notice a trendy change beginning from 1978, that is, the share of enterprise revenue diminished while that of various taxes increased. At first, the change was gradual, with a little gain or diminishment every year. By 1985, a cliff fall appeared, when the share of enterprise revenue shrank to nickel. After 1993, enterprise revenue completely vanished, various taxes almost became the only form of financial revenue. The entire evolution was the process in which "substitution of tax payment for profits" was carried out in enterprises step by step: Before this reform, enterprises handed over profits to government finance, with little to retain, but after the reform,

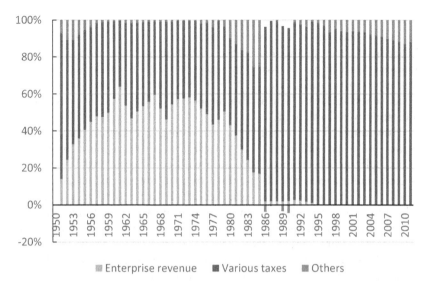

**Fig. 6.12** Breakdown shares in state financial revenue, 1950–2010

they paid taxes following regulations and the left-over profits were at their own disposal. The purpose of this reform is to shatter the soft budget constraint, which on the one hand gives companies a stronger incentive to generate profits, and on the other hand forces them to be more careful in the use of their profits.

"Substitution of tax payment for profits" left more money to enterprises, but "replacing government allocation with bank loans" deprived them of the privilege to get money easily from state finance. From the previous Fig. 6.7 we could see that up to 1979, two thirds of the money SOEs used for fixed asset investment came from the "state investment." Reformists believed that such a system relying on "state investment" could seduce enterprises into "investment hunger," who would try every means to vie for "state investment" as much as possible, without taking investment effect into consideration. As Fig. 6.7 illustrates, the share of "state investment" in the sources of state-owned economy's fixed asset investment declined rapidly after 1979, which dwindled to as small as about 5% in the mid-1990s. Replacing it were enterprises' "self-raised fund and other investments," namely, the profits that "substitution of tax payment for profits" allowed enterprises to retain. Meanwhile, "domestic loans" suddenly rose like a new force, becoming an important source of SOEs' fixed asset investment. Loans are very different from "state investment" from financial allocation, which must be repaid with accrued interest. Since it is necessary to repay the capital stock with accrued interest for investment from bank loans, enterprises have to consider cost-effectiveness seriously. This is also the purpose of "replacing government allocation with bank loans."

However, reform measures of expanding enterprises' autonomous power and responsibility such as "substitution of tax payment for profits" and "replacing government allocation with bank loans" led to an unexpected consequence: the distribution of total investment in fixed assets tilted to coastal areas in the east. Actually it is not hard to understand why. In the past, total investment in fixed assets was carried out according to the national plan, and balance among regions could be adjusted by the lever of "state investment." Now investment to a great extent became an enterprise's independent act. Enterprises in eastern coastal areas claimed advanced equipment, high-level management and better trained workers, plus a geographical location with matching components easily available, nearby markets for products, and convenience for import and export. As compared with enterprises in central and western regions, "substitution of tax payment for profits" allowed enterprises in the east to retain more profits, and "replacing government allocation with bank loans" made it easier for them to get bank loans. As a result, investment slowly inclined to coastal areas in the east. Figure 6.13 illustrates this clearly: In the early 1980s, only about half of total investment in fixed assets was in the east, but the share rose to about two thirds by the early 1990s. The consequence of the concentration of investment in the east and investment scarcity in the central and western regions was that regional gap was gradually widened.[38]

Both "substitution of tax payment for profits" and "replacing government allocation with bank loans" can be regarded as reform measures aimed to smash "the big pot of rice," or terminate the egalitarian practice of everybody eating from the same big pot. Probably it is relatively easy to smash "the big pot of rice," but it is rather hard to shatter "the

---

[38] Hu Angang, Wang Shaoguang, and Kang Xiaoguang, *Report on China's Regional Gap* (Shenyang: Liaoning People's Publishing House, 1995); Wang Shaoguang and Hu Angang, *China: Political Economics of Uneven Development* (Beijing: China Planning Press, 1999).

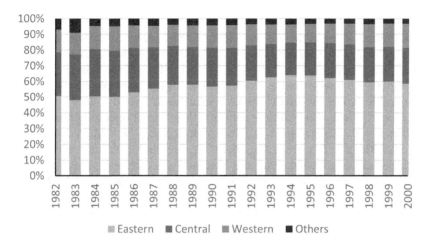

Fig. 6.13 Geographical distribution of total investment in fixed assets

iron rice bowl," or guaranteed job and income regardless of work performance. From the mid-1980s to early 1990s, all the reforms with attempt to shatter "the iron rice bowl" were not quite successful. As early as 1986, the State Council issued four regulations on reforming the labor system in SOEs, marking that the government began to push forward the labor contract system, and would no longer offer "iron rice bowl" to the new recruitments of SOEs. In the same year, the Standing Committee of the National People's Congress (NPC) adopted the *Enterprise Bankruptcy Law of the People's Republic of China (For Trial Implementation)*, which went to effect two years later, amid sustained disputes. It was not until 2006, 20 years later, that the NPC Standing Committee adopted the *Enterprise Bankruptcy Law of the People's Republic of China*. From the late 1980s to the early 1990s, few SOEs went bankrupt. By the end of 1991 and early in 1992, there was a nationwide wave of "smashing the three irons" in SOE reforms. The "three irons" refer to "iron rice bowl," "iron wage," or permanent pay irrespective of productivity, and "iron armchair" or lifetime job tenure for officials. Some places even raised the slogan of "smashing the three irons with three irons," namely, smashing "the iron bowl, iron wage and iron armchair" with the iron heart, iron face, and iron wrist. The slogan was loud, but the impedance was so great and the iron proved too hard to smash. It came to an abrupt end in a few months. In 1993, the Third Plenary Session of the 14th CPC Central Committee adopted the *Decision of the CPC Central Committee on Some Issues Concerning the Establishment of the Socialist Market Economic Structure*, clearly pointing out that the core task in SOE reform was to establish a modern enterprise system. And it put forth the principle of "grasp the big and let go of the small": "As for small-sized state-owned enterprises, in general, some could exercise contract operation or operation by leasing, others could be regrouped as joint-stock holding, or sold to collectives or individuals." But from Fig. 6.14 we can find that after 1993, the number of state-owned industrial enterprises and their employment did not decline but continued to grow, the former increased by 13,000 and the latter by 3.4 million people. This indicates that the policy design for reform or the policy announcement on its own could bring about but very limited changes.

What really led SOEs to smash "the iron rice bowl" was actually a historical turning point created by state-owned enterprises themselves. For many years China's economy was always a shortage economy, as most of commodity goods, including daily necessities, could not satisfy the whole people's demand. However, by the early 1990s, a new phenomenon emerged. In late 1990, He Xin, a scholar at the Chinese Academy of Social Sciences, was keenly aware that the main

**Fig. 6.14** Number of state-owned industrial enterprises and their employment

economic problem facing China was no longer "demand over supply" but overproduction.[39] Many economists at the time dismissed his belief as "nonsense," because according to famous Hungarian economist Janos Kornai, socialist economy was bound to be the economy of shortage. These economists firmly insisted that China's economy was still the one of shortage with no surplus at all.

Nevertheless, theory could outdo the reality. By the mid-1990s, surplus appeared in more and more sectors, and the buyer's market prevailed over the seller's market. In 1999, the Institute of Industrial Economics under the Chinese Academy of Social Sciences compiled the *Report on China's Industrial Growth*, which carried a striking subtitle: *China's Industry that Bids Farewell to the Shortage Economy*. It formally declared that "since the mid-1990s, significant changes have taken place in China's industrial products and supply–demand relations, with a shift from severe shortage to relative surplus, and the industrial growth turning from supply-side constraint to demand constraint."[40]

It should be noted that the farewell to the shortage economy was achieved when state-owned enterprises still overwhelmingly dominated the industrial sector. In the mid-1990s, the number of state-owned industrial enterprises and their employment both reached the peak value, and the profits of state-owned enterprises reached an unprecedented level (over 160 billion yuan). SOEs and collective enterprises still accounted for more than 70% of total industrial output value, and there were not many private and foreign enterprises at that time. Accordingly, we can say that the farewell to the shortage economy was a historic turning point created by state-owned enterprises.

Laozi said, "Disaster lurks within good fortune, good fortune follow upon disaster." This is indeed true. Once we bid farewell to the shortage economy, competition intensified, and it became difficult to make profits. The last straw that broke the camel's back was Asian Financial Crisis. Starting from the second half of 1997, the growth rate of foreign trade

---

[39] He Xin, *On the World Economic Situation and Problems of Chinese Economy: Talks with Prof. S of Economics from Japan* (December 11, 1990), He Xin, *China's Revival and the Future of the World* (Part I) (Chengdu: Xichuan People's Publishing House, 1996), p. 134.

[40] Institute of Industrial Economics, *Report on China's Industrial Growth—China's Industry that Bids Farewell to the Shortage Economy* (Beijing: Economy and Management Publishing House, 1999).

exports fell sharply, and it did not resume a sustained growth until 2002, five years later. On the one hand, there is a surplus in the domestic market, on the other hand, it is difficult to sell things abroad, or the growth rate of exports is very low. With the dual pressures overlaying, the profit of state-owned enterprises (including collectively owned enterprises) declined sharply (from 166.73 billion yuan in 1993 to 21.37 billion yuan in 1998), the proportion of loss-making SOEs expanded rapidly (from 22.7% in 1992 to 53.5% in 1999), and the bankruptcy cases increased dramatically.[41] As a result, the number of state-owned industrial enterprises and the number of state-owned employees both fell precipitously. Figure 6.14 illustrates this clearly. It was in this context that the "iron rice bowl" was eliminated.

If the collective enterprises' employees are added to the work force of SOEs, then the total employment dropped from 140 to 70 million in the 10 years after the mid-1990s, a decrease of about half. In such a short period of time, so many people were laid off, unemployed or had to take early retirement, which almost affected every urban family in China but without provoking massive social unrest. This could be a miracle in the world. Such a dearly cost led to the rebirth of SOEs through the fire. As indicated in Fig. 6.15, after hitting the bottom in 1998, SOEs' profitability began to recover rapidly, and their profits reached 3,387.77 billion yuan by 2018, 20.3 times of the peak value before SOE reform (1993). Meanwhile, the proportion of profit-making SOEs also began to rise, maintaining at around 55% for the past ten years and more.

After the number of state-owned industrial enterprises fell to the bottom in 2011, the constant downward trend of the previous 16 years came to an end, and it was increased by about 2,000 enterprises. After 2005, the decline momentum in SOEs' employment also eased (see Fig. 6.14). Although it is true that SOEs have lost their former dominant position in terms of these two indicators, from another perspective, SOEs have become stronger and more powerful. The annual profits they created rose to an unprecedented high, so did assets of state-owned and

---

[41] In the early 1990s, there were only several tens of bankruptcy cases closed by Chinese courts a year, which later increased to several hundred a year, and after 1994, there were several thousand a year. By around 2001 they reached the peak value of 9,110 cases. See the *Summary of Studies on China's Cross-Border Bankruptcy Cases* compiled by the Guangdong Provincial High People's Court. It should be noted that bankruptcy cases closed by the courts were only the tip of the iceberg of the actual number of bankruptcies.

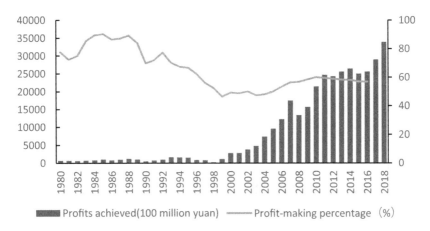

**Fig. 6.15** Profit volume and profit-making percentage of SOEs, 1980–2018

state-holding industrial enterprises, which jumped from 8.05 trillion yuan in 1999 to 42.5 trillion yuan in 2018, at an average annual growth rate of 9. 8% (see Fig. 6.16).

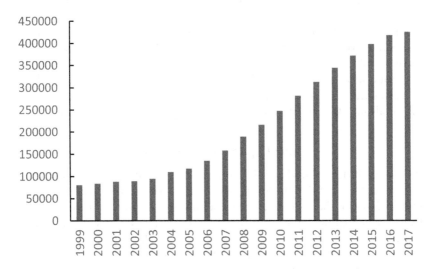

**Fig. 6.16** Total assets of state-owned and state-holding industrial enterprises, 1999–2017 (Unit: 100 million yuan)

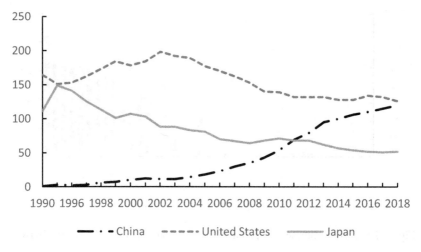

Fig. 6.17 Number of Chinese, United States, and Japanese enterprise in the Fortune 500 list

Against this backdrop, more and more SOEs entered the Fortune 500 list. In 1990, the only enterprise in China entering the list was a state-owned company. Over the past 30 years, the number of Chinese companies on the list has soared (see Fig. 6.17). By 2018, 120 Chinese companies were listed among the Fortune 500, far ahead of Japan and second only to the United States' 126. If the trend of the previous 30 years sustains, it should be a matter of a few years when China surpasses the United States. Of the 120 Chinese companies on the list, 83, or about 70%, are state-owned.

### *State Capital Grows Stronger*

Although SOEs went through a rebirth-like transformation, state fixed asset investment did not shrink, but continued to grow. Yes, since the mid-1990s, the share of state fixed asset investment in total investment of fixed assets dwindled a lot, but the volume of state fixed asset investment was not what it used to be, growing more than 20 times (see Fig. 6.18). More importantly, state fixed asset investment was not only a means to expand the state-owned economy, but also a means to carry out macroeconomic control. A closer look at Fig. 6.18 will find that in 1998 after the

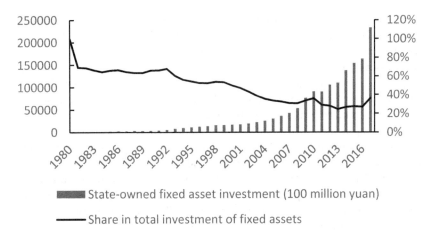

**Fig. 6.18** State-owned fixed asset investment and share, 1980–2017

Asian Financial Crisis and in 2009 after the outbreak of the world financial crisis, the growth rate of state fixed asset investment was much higher than in the average year. Figure 6.18 also illustrates that after China's economic growth rate slowed in 2013, the proportion of state fixed asset investment in total investment of fixed assets stopped falling but stabilized and rebounded, especially when the economic growth rate slipped to 6.7% in 2016, the proportion expanded about 10%. This may come as a surprise to some people. In fact, the reason for this rebound is that, in the context of insufficient motivation for investment in society, it is necessary for the government to use state investment to stimulate economic growth. This evidences the necessity and importance of the government control over a certain scale of state investment in socialist China.

Perhaps even more surprising to many is that from 1952 to 1984, there were eight years when state-owned fixed asset investment declined; but in the period of 1985–2017, there was only two years when such decline happened (1989 and 2011). In the previous period, state fixed asset investment grew at an average annual rate of 16.1%, and in the latter period, the average annual growth rate of state fixed asset investment was 18 1%, two percentage points higher than in the previous period.

While restructuring SOEs, the growth rate of state fixed asset investment did not slow down, and the cumulative original value of fixed assets of state-owned industries also grew rapidly, from less than 600 billion yuan in 1985, to top 1 trillion yuan in 1989, and exceeded 10 trillion yuan in 2007. By 2016 it was close to 30 trillion yuan. That was an increase of 49.3 times in these years (see Fig. 6.19). The original value of fixed assets reflects the enterprise's investment in fixed assets and its scale of production and equipment level. It is clear that the overall production scale and equipment of state-owned industry had jumped over several steps and come to a new high ground.

The proportion of original value of state-owned industrial fixed assets in the original value of overall fixed assets of independent accounting industrial enterprises nationwide declined by nearly half in the past 30 years. In the early 1980s, state-owned industry was outstanding alone in the country's independent accounting industrial enterprises' original value of fixed assets, but after more than 30 years of reform, private and foreign-funded industries had grown a lot, and the share of state-owned industries shrank accordingly, stabilizing at 45% after 2014. In this sense, SOEs to date still occupy the leading position in China's industrial economy.

The state capital has grown stronger, but now it is investing in a very different direction than before. Following the two principles of "advancing or retreating in flexible maneuver, being clear of what to do and what not," and "advancing to be productive and retreating but in good order," the Chinese government has in recent years accelerated the pace of layout and restructuring of the state-owned economy along

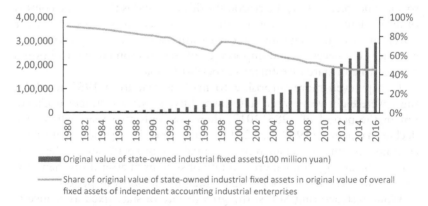

**Fig. 6.19** Original value of state-owned industrial fixed assets and share, 1980–2016

two lines: competitive industries and strategic and monopolistic industries. In competitive industries, the state-owned economy only selectively retains a small number of SOEs, otherwise it chose to shrink the front in accordance with the market-oriented principle, stepping out, retreating fully and withdrawing enough, trying the best possible to create a broad market space for the development of private capital and private economy. However, in the important industries and key areas concerning national security and lifeline of the national economy, state capital investment has retained the vigor, while at the same time relaxing access to the industry, guiding social capital and private capital to enter, improving the competitiveness of the competitive businesses of relevant industries, and improving the quality and efficiency of their operation.

Table 6.15 shows that "advancing or retreating in flexible maneuver, being clear of what to do and what not" is no longer just a policy guideline but has become a reality to a considerable extent. China's industry is divided into three main lines, namely, "mining," "manufacturing" and "electricity, thermal power, gas and water production and supply," which are further subdivided into 50 major categories, 509 secondary categories, and 5,090 small categories.[42] If we look at the composition of "real capital" in various industrial sectors, we will find that the share of "state capital" in some areas is higher, while in other sectors shares of "collective capital," "legal person capital," "individual capital," "Hong Kong, Macao and Taiwan capital," or "foreign capital" are higher. Paid-in capital is the actual capital received by the enterprise from investors. Using the benchmark of whether the share of state capital in paid-in capital in each sector is greater than 45%, Table 6.15 highlights the broad categories of investment priorities for state capital. We see that in the "mining industry" line, state capital dominates three major categories, namely, "coal mining, dressing and washing," "oil and gas extraction," and "ferrous metal mining." Of the many categories in the "manufacturing" line, only three are dominated by state capital, namely, "tobacco manufacturing," "oil processing, coking and nuclear fuel processing," and "railways, ships, aviation, aerospace and other transport equipment manufacturing." And the entire line of "electricity, thermal power, gas and water production

---

[42] State Administration of Quality Supervision and Inspection of the People's Republic of China and the State Standards Commission, *Industry Categorization of National Economy*, GB/T 4754–2017 [S/OL] http://www.state.gov.cn/tjsj/tjbz/201709/P02 017009408910690353.pdf.

**Table 6.15** State capital dominated sectors, 2016

| Mining | Timber processing and wood, bamboo, vane, palm fiber, straw produces | Special equipment manufacturing |
|---|---|---|
| Coal mining, dressing, & washing | Furniture manufacturing | Automobile |
| Oil & gas extraction | Paper-making & paper products | Railways, ships, aviation, aerospace, & Other transport equipment |
| Ferrous metal mining & dressing | Printing & record medium reproduction | Electrical machinery & equipment |
| Non-ferrous metal mining & dressing | Cultural, educational, arts, sports, & recreational goods | Computer, telecommunication, & other electronic equipment |
| Non-metallic mining & dressing | Oil processing, coking, & nuclear fuel processing | Instruments & meters |
| Other mining | Raw chemical materials & chemical products | Other manufacturing |
| **Manufacturing** | Manufacturing of medical products | Comprehensive use of waste resources |
| Agricultural & side-line food Processing | Chemical fiber | Metal products, machinery, & equipment repair |
| Food manufacturing | Rubber & plastic products | **Electricity, thermal power, gas & water production and supply** |
| Liquors, beverages, & fine tea | Non-metal mineral products | Electricity, thermal power production, & supply |
| Tobacco manufacturing | Ferrous metal smelting & rolling processing | Gas production & supply |
| Textile industry | Non-ferrous metal smelting & rolling processing | Water production & supply |
| Garments & apparel | Metal products | |
| Leather, furs, feather and Their products & shoe-making | General equipment manufacturing | |

and supply industry" is dominated by state capital. It is clear that these state capital dominated industries are precisely the important industries and key areas concerning national security and lifeline of the national economy, while other sectors are competitive industries. "Being clear of what to do and what not" is no empty talk, it has become a reality.

### Industry Grows Stronger

Led by SOEs and driven by the input of state capital, China's industry as a whole has made rapid progress over the past 70 years. As compared with the years before the founding of New China, China's industry today can be said to be a far cry from the past. A look at the changes in the ranking of major industrial products in the world in Table 6.13 could reveal that by the turn of the century, China already ranked first in the world in the production of steel, coal, cement, fertilizer, and chemical fiber. By 2016, China had ranked first in the output of products in seven major categories except crude oil due to limitations by natural resources endowment.

Table 6.13 presents only a few major products of China's industry. In fact, of the world's more than 500 major industrial products, China has secured the global first ranking in the production of more than 220 products. In 1990, China's manufacturing sector accounted for 2.7% of the global total, ranked ninth in the world. It moved up to claim 6% and rank fourth in the world in 2000. In 2007 its share increased to 13.7%, ranking second in the world. In 2010 its share climbed up further to 19.8%, outgoing the United States to rank first in the world. Since then, China's manufacturing industry has staying in the first rank for many years in a row.[43] By 2017, China had accounted for 28.8% of the global manufacturing value added.[44]

Power generation can be taken for a microcosm of China's industrial development. Figure 6.20 is a comparison between China and the United States in power generation since 1949. In 1949, China's electricity generation was merely 1.5% of that of the United States. It was not until 1975 that China's electricity generation was equal to 10% of that generated in the United States. In the following years up to 2000, China chased after the United States at a rate of about one percentage point more every year. In 2001, China generated up to 40% of the United States'. In the next nine years, China entered a frog-jumping catch-up phase, increasing

---

[43] Jia Tao, *A Few Features of Global Manufacturing and China's Response*, Economic Herald, July 2018.

[44] Zhuo Xian and Huang Jin, *Whither the Manufacturing Posts: Change and Analysis of China's Employment Structure*, Caijing, September 2019.

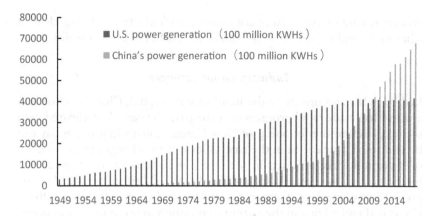

**Fig. 6.20** Comparison of power generation between China and the United States, 1949–2018 (*Source* US data are from US Energy Information Administration, Annual Energy Review, http://www.eia.gov/totalenergy/data/annual/index.php)

by six or seven percentage points every year. Thus, by 2010, China had overtaken the United States as the world's No. 1 in electricity generation. Over the past nine years, China has made even more rapid progress. In 2018, China generated 63% more electricity than the United States.

Power generation grew rapidly, so did China's overall industry. In 1990, China ranked 32nd in the world as measured by the United Nations Industrial Development Organization's Competitive Industrial Performance Index (CIP). In the following years China moved up at least one place in the ranking on average each year. China surpassed South Korea in 2015 to rank fourth in the world. In 2016 (according to the latest data released in 2019) overtook the United States to rank third; and China was the only developing country among the top 10 economies. In that year, China scored 0.3764, a difference of 0.0234 with second-ranking Japan (with a score of 0.3998), which is a very small gap. Days could be numbered when China overtakes Japan in terms of the Competitive Industrial Performance index. There is still a big gap between China and No. 1, Germany (with a score of 0.5234), it should be the goal of China's industry in the next decade to catch up with Germany.[45]

The Competitive Industrial Performance Index is a comprehensive index that can also be broken down into some other sub-indices, which can be used to judge the level of industrial development of countries from different angles (see Table 6.16). The "share in GDP" measures the weight of manufacturing in each country's economy. In China, "the share of manufacturing value added in GDP" is as high as 0.32, higher than in Ireland, South Korea, Germany and Japan, and even higher than in other countries. And "the share of manufacturing exports in total exports" reached 0.96, second only to South Korea's 0.97, but higher than all other economies.

The Global Share index measures the impact of different countries' manufacturing on global economy. We see that China leads other nine economies by far, both in terms of "impact on world manufacturing value added" and "impact on world manufacturing exports," highlighting China's position as a major manufacturing power in the world.

The above two types of indicators both measure the magnitude of the manufacturing industry in various countries, they clearly show that today's China is a well-deserved world industrial power.

However, the third category of indicators, "share of medium and high technology activities" reveals the shortcomings of China's industry. What these indicators measure are not the "quantity" of various countries' industry but its "quality." Table 6.16 shows that in terms of "medium and high-tech value-added share in total MVA" (Manufacturing Value Added Index), China lags behind the other nine economies, and in terms of "medium and high-tech manufacturing export share in total manufacturing export," China ranks far lower than the other five industrial powers: the United States, Switzerland, Germany, South Korea, and Japan, although it scores slightly higher than Ireland, Italy, the Netherlands, and Belgium. Similarly, measured in MVA per capita, the gap between China and the other nine economies is also quite big. Being able to rank in the top 10 by the global Competitive Industrial Performance index signifies that China has joined the club of industrial powers, but compared with the stronger and the more powerful, we are not the

---

[45] United Nations Industrial Development Organization, *The Competitive Industrial Performance, Biennial CIP Report*, Edition 2018 (March 2019), https://www.unido.org/sites/default/files/files/2019-05/CIP_Report_2019.pdf.

**Table 6.16** Top 10 economies' CIP index and sub-indexes, 2016

| | Germany | Japan | China | USA | South Korea | Switzerland | Ireland | Belgium | Italy | Netherlands |
|---|---|---|---|---|---|---|---|---|---|---|
| CIP ranking | 1 | 2 | 3 | 4 | 5 | 6 | 7 | 8 | 9 | 10 |
| CIP score | 0.52 | 0.4 | 0.38 | 0.37 | 0.37 | 0.32 | 0.32 | 0.28 | 0.27 | 0.27 |
| Share in GDP | | | | | | | | | | |
| Share of MVA in GDP | 0.21 | 0.19 | 0.32 | 0.11 | 0.29 | 0.18 | 0.3 | 0.14 | 0.14 | 0.11 |
| Share of manufacturing exports in total exports | 0.89 | 0.9 | 0.96 | 0.74 | 0.97 | 0.68 | 0.95 | 0.89 | 0.92 | 0.85 |
| Global Share Index | | | | | | | | | | |
| Impact on world manufacturing value added | 0.06 | 0.09 | 0.24 | 0.16 | 0.03 | 0.01 | 0.01 | 0.01 | 0.02 | 0.01 |
| Impact on world manufacturing exports | 0.1 | 0.05 | 0.17 | 0.08 | 0.04 | 0.02 | 0.01 | 0.03 | 0.04 | 0.03 |
| Share of medium and high-tech | | | | | | | | | | |
| Medium and high-tech value added share in total MVA | 0.61 | 0.56 | 0.41 | 0.48 | 0.64 | 0.65 | 0.54 | 0.5 | 0.43 | 0.49 |

| | Germany | Japan | China | USA | South Korea | Switzerland | Ireland | Belgium | Italy | Netherlands |
|---|---|---|---|---|---|---|---|---|---|---|
| Medium and high-tech manufacturing export share in total manufacturing export | 0.74 | 0.81 | 0.59 | 0.66 | 0.76 | 0.71 | 0.56 | 0.55 | 0.56 | 0.56 |
| MVA index | | | | | | | | | | |
| Manufacturing value added per capita | 0.48 | 0.45 | 0.11 | 0.3 | 0.36 | 0.69 | 1 | 0.31 | 0.25 | 0.27 |
| MVA index in global share | 0.26 | 0.38 | 1 | 0.65 | 0.12 | 0.04 | 0.03 | 0.02 | 0.1 | 0.03 |
| Share of MVA index in GDP | 0.6 | 0.54 | 0.91 | 0.32 | 0.82 | 0.52 | 0.86 | 0.39 | 0.41 | 0.3 |
| Share of medium and high-tech in MVA | 0.79 | 0.72 | 0.53 | 0.61 | 0.81 | 0.83 | 0.69 | 0.63 | 0.55 | 0.62 |
| Industrialization index | 0.69 | 0.63 | 0.72 | 0.47 | 0.82 | 0.68 | 0.78 | 0.51 | 0.48 | 0.46 |

*Source* United Nations Industrial Development Organization, The Competitive Industrial Performance Index 2018, https://stat.unido.org/database/CIP%202018

strongest as yet. "The revolution has not yet succeeded, comrades still need to make efforts." It is our glorious mission to make still further progress and turn our country into an even stronger industrial power.

### *Economy Grows Stronger*

In the modern world, a weak industry means a weak economy, and a strong industry leads to a strong economy. Backed by an ever-stronger industry, China today has become one of the world's largest economies.

Figure 6.21 illustrates that when the New China was founded, as such a large country (with a quarter of the world's population), its total GDP (in purchasing power parity terms) accounted for only 4.2% of the world total, while the United States was the undisputed dominant power at the time, accounting for 26.4% of the world's GDP. Although they went through the bloody and bitter Second World War, other old imperialist and colonialist countries were still like a centipede that does not topple over even if dead. Then the Western Europe, the United States, and Australia together accounted for as high as 35.8% of the world total.

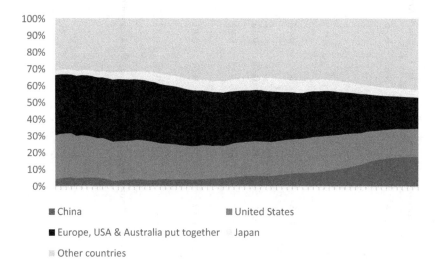

**Fig. 6.21** Countries' GDP share in global total, 1950–2019 (*Source* The Conference Board, Total Economy Database, April 2019, https://www.conference-board.org/data/economydatabase/TEDI)

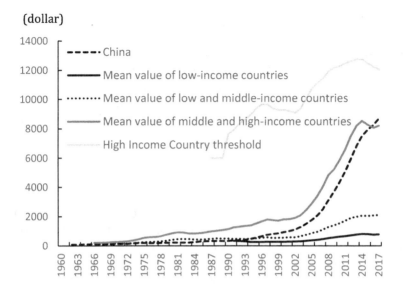

Fig. 6.22 China: Toward high-income economy

Seventy years have passed, changes in the world economic landscape can be described as "earth-shaking:" China's GPD share in the global total has increased to 18%, four times that of Japan, and surpassing the share of the United States (16. 8%), and only one step away from the share of Western Europe, the United States, and Australia combined (18. 4%).

The expansion of China's economy as a whole is beneficial to all the Chinese. According to the World Bank's classification, China had always been among the low-income countries, and in 1949, China was among the lowest in the "low-income economies." In 1999, China finally graduated from the "low-income countries" and joined the group of "lower-middle-income economies." In 2010, China entered a higher category of "upper-middle-income economies."[46] Fig. 6.22 depicts with the World Bank data how, since 1960, China's per capita national income has gone step by step beyond the mean value of low-income countries (1991), the mean value of lower-middle-income countries (1995), and the mean value of upper-middle-income countries (2016). At present,

---

[46] World Bank: Classifying Countries by Income 2019, http://databank.worldbank.org/data/download/site-content/OGHIST.xls.

China is moving toward the goal of high-income economy. It is worth noting that the high-income threshold is not constantly raised. In fact, the high-income threshold set by the World Bank in 2019 is lower than it was eight years ago. Based on the trends of the past decade or so, it is highly probable that China will enter the ranks of high-income countries in the next five years or so. If this does happen, the world economic map will be very different: for the first time in human history, the population living in high-income countries will exceed the population living in low-income countries.

## Summary

The contribution of state-owned enterprises to China's industrialization can be summarized in four sentences: They advanced China's transformation from an agricultural into an industrial country; they drove China's transition from a shortage economy to a surplus economy; they helped transform China from an industrial country to an industrial power; and they control the lifeline of the national economy and lead the economic development.

CHAPTER 7

# Direction: From Economic to Social Policies

The Third Plenary Session of the Eleventh CPC Central Committee convened at the end of 1978 started a great historic transformation. With that, the Communist Party of China discarded the obsolete principle and line of "taking class struggle as the key link" and shifted the focus of its work to socialist modernization.

## TAKE ECONOMIC CONSTRUCTION AS THE CENTRAL TASK

Starting from 1978 until the mid-1990s, China arguably had only economic policies but no social policies. Throughout these years, "giving priority to efficiency" was the guiding ideology of everything, the government had consistently adhered to taking economic growth as the central task, trying to seize every opportunity to accelerate the economic development and solve all the problems in the process of economic development. Development was regarded as the unquestionable priority goal. In these years of great economic development, although when talking about "giving priority to efficiency," the phrase of "with due consideration to equity" would be added, in practice, governments at all levels (including the central government) focused their attention more on economic development or economic growth, and the "due consideration" was often neglected. In order to pursue efficiency or the maximization of the overall economic growth rate, not only was it hard to give due consideration to equity, but also to ecological environment and national defense construction. Such neglect was probably because of three reasons as follow:

- There did exist the problem of inefficiency brought about by "iron rice bowls" and "big pot of rice" before the reform. The proposal of "giving priority to efficiency with due consideration to equity" did not seem to contradict people's empirical judgment.
- In the 1980s, farmers' enthusiasm for production was at an all-time high following a significant increase in the purchase price of agricultural products and the introduction of the family contract responsibility system, and their income levels rose rapidly. As a result, both the gaps between urban and rural areas and between regions narrowed.
- Until the late 1980s, China's reform had been a win–win game, as everyone gained from it, with the only difference in that some people might gain a bit more, while others a bit less. In this case, even if the income gap within a region, a city, and a village widened, it was acceptable as long as the gap was not too big.

With the time going by, however, the one-sided emphasis on efficiency, development, and economic growth gradually exhibited its malicious consequence. Suppose the reform in the 1980s was a win–win game, the reform in the 1990s became more and more like a zero-sum game, in which some people gained at the expense of others' interests. By 1992, the urban–rural and regional disparities had exceeded the 1978 level. Thereafter the two disparities widened dramatically, especially the gap between the southeast coast and the middle and western regions greatly widened to an unprecedented extent.[1] Meanwhile, the income gap between various social segments within a city or a village widened rapidly. By the mid-1990s, China's overall Gini coefficient of income had risen to as high as 0.45, to the degree of fairly big income gap in accordance with internationally accepted standard.

More seriously, after the mid-1990s, employment in formal sectors (i.e., state-owned and urban collective sectors) dropped dramatically: with

---

[1] Hu Angang, Wang Shaoguang and Kang Xiaoguang, *Report on China's Regional Disparities* (Shenyang: Liaoning People's Publishing House, 1995); Wang Shaoguang and Hu Angang, *China: Political Economics of Uneven Development* (Beijing: China Planning Press, 1999).

the number of employees dwindling from 140 to 70 million in ten years, reduced by about half. Perhaps no country in human history had reduced its employed population in formal sectors on such a scale in such a short period. With a large number of people laid off and out of work, the issue of urban poverty came to the fore.

In rural areas, there was an oversupply of grain and other agricultural products in the late 1990s. "Low prices for grain hurt the farmers," which resulted in overall slow growth of farmers' incomes. In quite a lot of regions, farmers' incomes slid down instead of growing. And the problem of arbitrary collections of fees, unjustified financial levies, and indiscriminate fines that had long plagued China's rural areas further exacerbated, with farmers overburdened, which intensified contradictions between farmers and the government.

While enormous social wealth sprang up, various factors of social instability were on the rise quickly, rendering a feeling among the people up and down that China was facing layer upon layer of crises. How did such a serious problem of uneven development and income inequality come up while the overall national strength was greatly enhanced? One important cause was probably the one-sided adherence to "giving priority to efficiency." Yes, Deng Xiaoping once encouraged some regions and some people to get rich first. But he made it very clear that "the aim of socialism is to make all our people prosperous, not to create polarization. If our policies led to polarization, it would mean that we had failed."[2] He also warned, "If polarization occurred... The contradictions between various ethnic groups, regions and classes would become sharper and, accordingly, the contradictions between the central and local authorities would also be intensified. That would lead to disturbances."[3] By the late 1990s, there were more and more signs of disturbances. This led more and more people to realize that efficiency or development or economic growth, they were nothing more than means to improve the people's well-being, and the order should not be reversed with the pursuit of the means on top of the end. More precisely, the fruits of economic growth must be shared by the vast majority of the people, rather than enjoyed exclusively by

---

[2] Deng Xiaoping, *Unity Depends on Ideals and Discipline* (March 7,1985), *Selected Works of Deng Xiaoping*, Vol. III, (Beijing: Foreign Languages Press, 1995), p. 116.

[3] Deng Xiaoping, *Seize the Opportunity to Develop the Economy* (December 24, 1990), *Selected Works of Deng Xiaoping*, Vol. III, (Beijing: Foreign Languages Press, 1995), p. 351.

a handful of people; and the cost of economic reform must be shared among all sectors of society rather than shouldered by ordinary workers and farmers only.

Against this background, the Chinese government's policy orientation was starting to shift, with more efforts put to the "due consideration" to equity while adhering to "giving priority to efficiency," and the "due consideration" by this moment finally became substantiated.[4] By the time the Fourth Plenary Session of the 16th CPC Central Committee was held in 2004, the Central Committee eventually gave up the scheme of "giving priority to efficiency with due consideration to equity." If we say the Chinese government had only economic policies and no social policies in the first 20 years of reform and opening-up, after entering the twenty-first century, the Chinese government began to pay more attention to social policies and put more resources into this area.

The background against which social policies are rolled out is when social contradictions come to the foreground, yet this only explains that social policies would come out sooner or later, but not why they should come out early in the twenty-first century. Social policies are not just a matter of government declarations, every social policy has to be backed by sound financial support, without which the social policy is just a castle in the air. At the beginning of the twenty-first century, the Chinese government was able to turn more attention to social policies also thanks to the financial restructuring that greatly improved the state's extractive capacity, making it possible for the government to put more financial and other resources into this area. Starting in the early 1980s, the Chinese government's extractive capacity went all the way down to hit the bottom of the valley by the early 1990s. The budget for maintaining the national defense, public security, and routine operation of the government was seriously deficient, not to mention the support for social policies, which came to a very dangerous juncture politically.[5] Faced with huge risks, the Chinese government had to make major adjustments to the fiscal system in 1994.

Looking back at the past quarter of century, the tax-sharing reform, which was introduced that year, has apparently achieved unexpectedly

---

[4] Literature Research Office of the CPC Central Committee, *Chronicles of Deng Xiaoping Thinking* (Beijing: Central Party Literature Press, 1998), p. 453.

[5] Wang Shaoguang and Hu Angang, *Report on China's State Capacity* (Shenyang: Liaoning People's Publishing House, 1993).

great success: The government's consolidated fiscal revenue and expenditure (the combined budgetary revenue and expenditure, extra-budgetary revenue and expenditure, and social security fund income and expenditure) grew rapidly, soaring to nearly 28 trillion yuan from 700 to 800 billion yuan in 25 years, a 34–35-fold increase. As Fig. 7.1 indicates, the shares of consolidated fiscal revenue and expenditure in GDP have also changed dramatically. From 1978 to 1995, the shares fell from 30–40% to 16–17%. After the financial restructuring began to show its effect in 1994, the situation improved rapidly. By the end of 2018, the shares rebounded to around 30%. Although the share of China's fiscal revenue in GDP is still not high as compared with many developed countries and transition economies in Eastern Europe, this performance is quite considerable, at least compared with average developing countries.

If the Chinese government's failure to do anything in social policies in the 1990s was due to the fact that "a smart housewife cannot cook

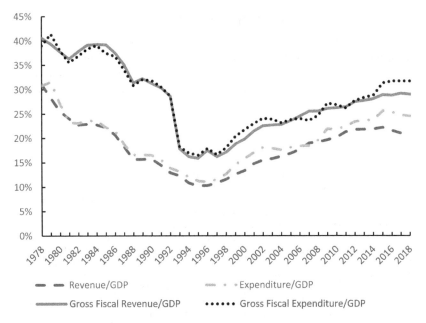

**Fig. 7.1** Shares of consolidated fiscal revenue and expenditure in GDP (*Source* Unless noted by specific sources, all the data used in this chapter are based on a databank the author compiles from various sources)

without rice," now the problem of the government's extractive capacity has been largely solved, which has laid the financial foundation for the implementation of social policies.

There might be a case for people to say that China was a "low-welfare" country around 2000.[6] But if there are people today who still assert that China is a country of "low welfare," "zero welfare", or even "negative welfare," it is groundless. The extensive data presented in this chapter suggest that a new great leap forward has occurred in China over the past 20 years: a significant increase in social protection. This new great leap forward has quietly brought about dramatic changes to Chinese society: on the one hand, it has curbed inequality from further worsening; on the other hand, it has created favorable conditions for reducing human insecurity. Without these two changes, it is only an empty word to let all people share the fruits of economic development, and it is only an empty word to adhere to and develop the socialist system.

## REDUCE INEQUALITY

In terms of the composition of income gap, China's income gap can be broken down into four components: income gap within urban areas, income gap within rural areas, income gap between urban and rural areas, and inter-regional income gap. Studies show that a large portion of

---

[6] "Welfare" here refers to welfare in the objective sense rather than in the subjective sense. It refers to social welfare rather than individual welfare. Social welfare is a very complex concept, and it is beyond the scope of this book to get involved in theoretical and methodological disputes related to it. However, no matter how social welfare is defined, it can be measured in terms of inputs (expenditures on social welfare) and outputs (like infant mortality and average life expectancy). In the literature on social welfare, the share of public social spending in GDP is often used as an indicator to compare countries' welfare level. See Adema W., P. Fron and M. Ladaique, *Is the European Welfare State Really More Expensive? Indicators on Social Spending, 1980–2012*; and a *Manual to the OECD Social Expenditure Database* (SOCX), OECD *Social, Employment and Migration Working Papers*, No. 124 (2011), http://dx.doi.org/10.1787/5kg2d2d4pbf0-en, p. 10. The author once used these data to verify that the problem of low-welfare existed in China's public health area around 2000. See Wang Shaoguang, *Crisis and Opportunity for Turn of China's Public Health, Comparative Studies*, Vol. 7 (2003), pp. 52–88. Of course, there are scholars who are reserved on using input indicators to measure welfare levels, like Gosta Esping-Anderson, *Decommodification and Work Absence in the Welfare State* (San Domenico, Italy: European University Institute, 1988), pp. 18–19.

China's overall income gap stems from regional and urban–rural disparities. Therefore, the key to narrow the overall income gap is to curtail the regional and urban–rural disparities.

### Narrow Regional Disparities

The major measure to narrow the regional disparities is the central government's increase in fiscal transfer payments to provincial regions, especially those in central and western parts of the country where the economy is relatively backward. Up to 1993, China's fiscal structure featured a system of "serving meals by separate kitchens" or dividing revenue and expenditure between the provincial authorities and holding each taking full responsibility for balancing their budgets. Such an institutional arrangement was in favor of the developed provinces along the southeast coast because their financial resources were relatively abundant and did not have to share much of their local taxes with other provinces. But for the central and western provinces with scarce financial resources, without external fiscal transfer payments, it was difficult for them to provide local residents with the same public services as those coastal provinces, still less the capacity to build infrastructures and invest in industrial projects as their coastal counterparts did. After the mid-1980s, regional disparities constantly widened, and one of the main reasons for that was the fiscal system whereby local authorities had to take nearly full responsibility for their finances.[7]

In 1994, the Chinese government made a major adjustment to the fiscal system, changing the system of holding local authorities fully responsible for their finances to a tax-sharing system. This reform fundamentally reversed the downslide trend of the "two shares"[8] that had gone on for 15 consecutive years, thereby strengthening the central government's fiscal extractive capacity and laying the institutional basis for it to increase the fiscal transfer payments to the needy provinces. Figure 7.2 makes it clear that since 1994, the central government's total fiscal transfer payments to the provinces have been growing rapidly; especially after 1999, it has almost taken one big step forward every year, reaching a

---

[7] Wang Shaoguang and Hu Angang, *China: Political Economics of Uneven Development* (Beijing: China Planning Press, 1999).

[8] The "two shares" refer to the share of the total government fiscal revenue in GDP and the share of central government fiscal revenue in the total fiscal revenue.

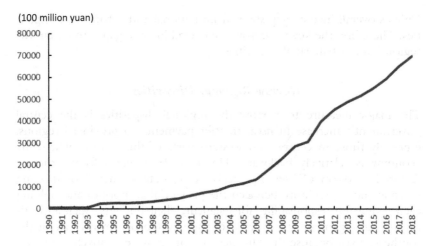

**Fig. 7.2** Central authorities' transfer payments to localities (100 million yuan)

level of nearly 7 trillion yuan by 2018, which was 128 times the total amount of fiscal transfers in 1993!

After the large-scale central fiscal transfers, the disparity in per capita financial resources between regions has been greatly reduced, alleviating the imbalance of financial income and expenditure between regions, and helping to equalize public services, as well as facilitating the coordinated development of all regions in the country.

Before the implementation of the tax-sharing system, there were significant differences in GDP growth rates among the four major economic blocks of the East, Central, West, and Northeast, with the eastern coastal provinces far ahead of others, leading to widening regional disparities. After 1994, growth rates of the economic blocks began to gradually converge.[9] In recent years, there has been a fundamental reversal in the pattern of GDP growth among China's provinces: GDP growth in the central and western provinces is generally higher than that in the eastern coastal provinces, resulting in the narrowing of regional disparities. Figure 7.3 shows that since 2002, the gap of GDP per capita between

---

[9] Research Team on China's Regional Coordinated Development of Development Research Center of the State Council, *Analysis of Changes and Causes in Regional Growth Patterns and Disparities in China*//Development Research Center of the State Council Survey and Research Report No. 138, (General No. 2653), July 14, 2006.

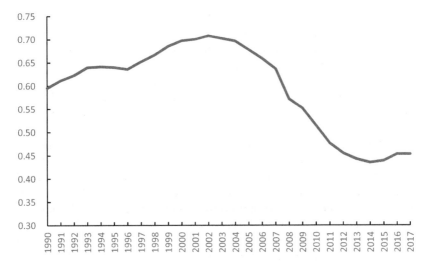

Fig. 7.3 Coefficient of variation of interprovincial GDP per capita

different provinces in China has shown a downward trend. The measurement for regional disparities in Fig. 7.3 is the coefficient of variation, and in fact, even if the measurement is switched to Thiel Index, Gini Coefficient or Atkinson Index, the downward trend in regional disparities is the same.[10] No one could deny it's a miracle that the regional disparities narrowed significantly in such a short period of time. Although quite a number of factors played a role in it, the merit of large-scale central fiscal transfer payments cannot be ignored.

### Narrow Urban–rural Disparities

It is known to all that the income gap between China's urban and rural areas has been relatively large. Compared with some other developing countries, China's national income gap is not the highest as measured by the overall Gini coefficient, but lower than some countries in Latin America and Africa; yet China's urban–rural disparities might be

---

[10] Masashi Hoshino, *Measurement of GDP Per Capita and Regional Disparities in China, 1979–2009*, paper presented at Workshop on Poverty and Inequality in China and India, March 13, 2012. Many other scholars made the same or similar conclusions as Professor Masashi Hoshino.

the largest in the world, which constitutes one of the most important characteristics in China's income distribution pattern.[11]

In order to narrow the income gap between rural and urban areas, the Chinese government has adopted two sets of strategies for rural residents in recent years: "taking less" and "giving more." "Taking less" is mainly embodied in the abolition of agricultural tax. Agricultural tax is one of the oldest levies, with its history dating back thousands of years. After the reform and opening-up, the share of agriculture in China's national economy kept declining, yet the share of various agricultural levies (including agricultural tax, taxes on special agricultural products, animal husbandry tax, farmland occupation tax and deed tax) in total fiscal revenue went up rather than down from 1986 to 1996. In 2004, the Chinese government announced that "all the taxes on special agricultural products other than those on tobacco should be rescinded and the agricultural tax should be rescinded within five years." But in fact, the target of rescinding the agricultural tax completely was achieved ahead of schedule by 2006.

With the task of "taking less" completed, the policy support for "giving more" has been continuously enhanced. In 1997, the central fiscal budgetary expenditure on agriculture, rural areas, and farmers (in 15 big categories including policy subsidies on agricultural products, expenditure on rural primary and secondary schools, and expenditure on rural health) was merely some 70 billion yuan.[12] After entering the twenty-first century, funds for such expenditures began to grow rapidly, which topped the 200 billion yuan benchmark in 2003 and the 1 trillion yuan benchmark in 2011, and exceeded 2 trillion yuan by 2018.

The two-pronged approach of "taking less" and "giving more" achieved obvious results. As Fig. 7.4 indicates, after the dramatic deterioration in the mid-1990s, the urban–rural per capita income and consumption gap has stabilized in a narrow range since 2003, with the urban–rural per capita consumption showing a downslide trend. What is more gratifying is that since 2010, the rural residents' income has grown

---

[11] UNDP, China Human Development Report 2005: Toward Human Development with Equity, http://chundp.org.cn/downloads/nhdr2005/c_NHDR2005_complete.pdf.

[12] Ding Xuedong and Zhang Yansong, *Policy on Financial Support for Agriculture, Rural Areas and Farmers: Analysis, Evaluation and Proposal, Public Finance Research*, 2005 (4).

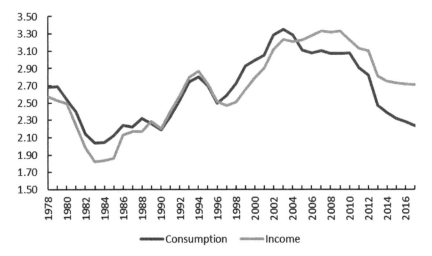

**Fig. 7.4** Urban–rural income and consumption gaps (rural areas as 1), 1978–2017

at a faster pace than that of urban residents for many consecutive years, and the income gap between urban and rural residents has also narrowed.

The regional and the urban–rural disparities are the main components of China's overall inequality. Since both of these gaps have been reduced or even narrowed, the trend of China's worsening overall inequality should have been curbed. Figure 7.5 indicates that the Gini coefficient, which reflects the level of inequality in overall income distribution, rose between 1996 and 2008 and then gradually fell down. Although the Gini coefficient of 0.467 in 2017 was still high, its continuous decline is what was rarely seen since the mid-1980s, which may herald a new era.[13]

---

[13] As early as in the beginning of 2010, a research by OECD had concluded that "overall inequality has ceased to increase in recent years, and may even have inched down." See *Richard Herd, A Pause in the Growth of Inequality in China? OECD Economics Department Working Papers*, ECO/WKP, 2010–4 (February 1, 2010). Another research report issued by OECD in 2012 came to the similar conclusion with this section, see OECD, *China in Focus: Lessons and Challenges* (Paris, OECD, 012), Chapter 2 Inequality: Recent Trends in China and Experience in the OECD Area, pp. 16–34.

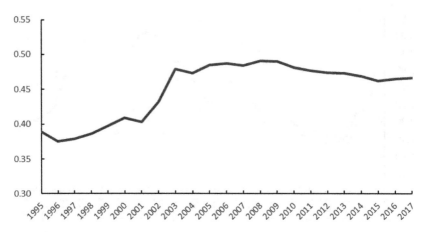

**Fig. 7.5** National Gini index in China, 1995–2017

## Reduce the Sense of Insecurity

Before the reform and opening-up, although incomes and living standards were not high in China, the "big pot of rice" and the "iron rice bowl" gave people a sense of security because the rural community and the urban units provided protection against various risks (such as unemployment, illness, and old age care). After the reform and opening-up, people's income and living standards were continuously improved. However, at the same time, the rural commune system and the urban work units were gradually dismantled, the "iron rice bowl" was broken, and the "big pot of rice" was taken away. Under this new structure, the middle and high-income groups are deeply threatened by various uncertainties and risks, not to mention the low-income groups. In the 1980s and 1990s, the Chinese government once mistakenly assumed that market-oriented reforms meant that individuals and families could and should bear such risks and thereby ignored its own responsibilities in this regard. After entering the twenty-first century, this situation began to change. As the government has introduced a series of social policies in the areas that are related to the welfare of the majority of people, including minimum living guarantee, medical insurance, work-related injury insurance, unemployment insurance, old-age security, housing security, etc., the scope of social protection has become more and more extensive, the level of protection has become higher and higher, and the protection system has become more and more consolidated.

### *Minimum Living Guarantee Scheme*

The minimum living guarantee scheme (*Dibao*) for urban residents was first established in Shanghai. In 1997, when the campaign of "downsizing for efficiency, laying off workers and repositioning redundant personnel" on a large scale was launched, the State Council issued the *Circular on the Establishment of a Minimum Living Guarantee Scheme for Urban Residents Across the Country*, and began to push the implementation of the urban *Dibao* system throughout the country, but local governments at various levels did not seem to feel the urge to carry it out at the time. In the following three years, the country's *Dibao* coverage expanded slowly. By 2000, only 4.03 million urban residents nationwide had received minimum living guarantee allowances. It was not until the next year when governments at various levels began to expand the minimum living guarantee coverage for workers in extreme difficulties in large and medium-sized state-owned enterprises, as urban poverty caused by massive and persistent layoffs in previous years began to stir up social order.[14] In 2002, the coverage was further expanded, and the central government demanded all the local authorities that the urban poor be insured to the fullest extent possible. By the end of that year, the total population covered by the urban *Dibao* system soared to 20.65 million. Over the following decade, the *Dibao*-covered population had fluctuated around 22 million, largely including all the eligible *Dibao* targets in cities and towns across the country. In recent years, with a large number of laid-off people entering retirement age and starting to take social security, the urban *Dibao* population has plummeted, with only about 9.94 million left in 2018 (see Fig. 7.6).

Urban poverty is troublesome, but the more serious problem of poverty is in rural areas. Before the twenty-first century, as rural poverty

---

[14] For instance, in September 2001, more than 1,000 laid-off and retired workers in Daqing City of Heilongjiang Province took to the streets for a demonstration; and in March 2002, more than 10,000 workers went to protest in Liaoyang City of Liaoning Province.

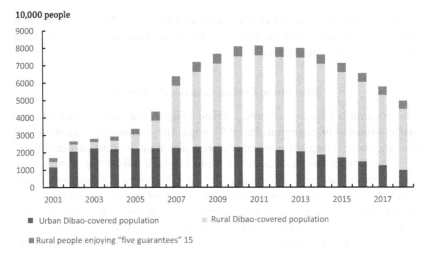

**Fig. 7.6** Urban and rural minimum living security coverage, 2001–2018 (10,000 people)

was still a widespread phenomenon, the focus of the Chinese government's rural poverty alleviation policy had to be on supporting the development of designated poor areas. This strategy of poverty reduction worked very well, lifting 500 million people out of poverty in China between 1981 and 2004.[15] After entering the twenty-firstcentury, the Chinese government began to turn its attention to the poverty population, including those living outside the designated poor areas.

Starting from 1997, some provinces and cities along China's eastern coast where conditions allowed began to set up a minimum living guarantee system for rural residents step by step. But it was not until 2004 that the central government asked localities where conditions permitted to explore the establishment of a minimum living guarantee system

---

[15] World Bank, *From Poor Areas to Poor People: China's Evolving Poverty Reduction Agenda – An Assessment of Poverty and Inequality in China* (Washington, DC: The World Bank, 2009), http://documents.worldbank.org/curated/en/2009/03/10444409/china-poor-areas-poor-people-chinas-evolving-poverty-reduction-agenda-assessment-poverty-inequality-china-vol-1-2-main-report.

for farmers.[16] After piloting work for three years, the State Council in 2007 explicitly required in the *Circular on the Establishment of a Rural Minimum Living Guarantee System Across the Country* that, a rural minimum living guarantee system should be established throughout the country within the year, covering all the eligible poor people in rural areas, with a focus on providing guarantees for rural residents living in chronic difficulties such as the sick, disabled, aged, feeble and infirm, and ensuring that the minimum living guarantee funds should be distributed to the household within the year.[17] This meant a transition from a mutual aid system within a peasant village to a support system funded by state financial resources, which was an epoch-making change in China's history. Consequently, the population covered by the rural *Dibao* system that very year surged to nearly 36 million, with a dramatic increase of nearly 20 million.[18] The rural *Dibao* coverage thereafter gradually expanded, if combined with the "household enjoying five guarantees" on collective and individual support, the total population covered reached 59 million by the end of 2013. After that, with the growing endeavor to alleviate poverty, the number of people in these two groups in the countryside also began to decline. By the end of 2018, the total population covered by the urban and rural *Dibao* system fell below 50 million (see Fig. 7.6).

*Medical Insurance System*

Before the reform and opening-up, there were three sets of medical care systems in China, namely, a public-funded or free medical care system for employees of government agencies, students and faculty of colleges and universities, and employees of public institutions; a labor insurance system for employees of state-owned enterprises and some collective enterprises; and a cooperative medical care system based on communes and brigades

---

[16] CPC Central Committee and State Council, *Opinion on Some Policies for Helping Farmers Increase Incomes* (December 2003, 31), http://www.gov.cn/test/2006-02/22/content_207415.htm.

[17] The establishment of rural minimum living security system is led by the local people's government, and operated by localized management, with appropriate subsidies from the central fiscal budget to areas with financial difficulties.

[18] Ministry of Civil Affairs, *Statistical Report on the Development of Civil Affairs Undertakings 2007* (May 2008, 26), http://cws.msa.gov.cn/article/tjbg/200805/20080500015411.shtml.

in rural areas. They provided the vast majority of urban and rural residents with affordable and equal basic health care.

In the early 1980s, with the people's commune system dissolved, the rural cooperative medical care system, which had been widely acclaimed internationally, collapsed soon. In urban areas, the large-scale ownership change of enterprises and laid-offs in the 1990s resulted in the withering of both free medical care and labor insurance systems. As a result, by the turn of the century, more than 80% of rural residents and more than half of urban residents were left without any medical insurance.[19]

In response to the public concerns about "inadequate and overly expensive medical services," the Chinese government began to promote the basic medical insurance system for urban workers in 1999. The new system covered retirees, allowing this relatively vulnerable group to enjoy basic medical security, but it no longer covered the beneficiaries' family members and relatives, nor did it cover the self-employed individuals, those working in informal sectors and the floating population (rural–urban migrants). Thus, although the new system developed quickly, by 2006 it covered only a quarter of the urban population, and if the floating population was taken into account, the actual coverage would be even lower.

With regard to the rural health crisis, the CPC Central Committee and the State Council issued the *Decision on Further Enhancing Health Services in Rural Areas* in October 2002, which explicitly put forward that "a new rural cooperative medical system" (abridged as NRCMS) should be gradually established, with the goal of "basically covering the rural population by 2010." To achieve this goal, the central government decided that, starting from 2003, fiscal budgets at various levels should subsidize the farmers participating in the NRCMS.[20] The NRCMS changed the nature of cooperative medical care, which was no longer a mutual aid organization based on village and township communities, but

---

[19] Center for National Health Statistical Information, Ministry of Health, *Analysis Report on the Third National Health Service Survey*, 2004, p. 85.

[20] CPC Central Committee and State Council, *Decision on Further Strengthening of Rural Health Work* (October 19, 2002).

a holistic rural medical insurance system organized, guided and supported by the government at a higher level of coordination.[21]

Despite these initiatives in response to the rural and urban health crisis, people are not satisfied with their strength and progress. In March 2005, a research group of the Development Research Center of the State Council published a 160-page report in the *China Development Review* run by the Center, which, titled *China's Health Care Reform: Evaluation and Recommendations*, sternly criticized the hitherto medical reform.[22] Four months later, the report caught the attention of the *China Youth Daily*,[23] which quickly provoked a sensation in the media, and initiated a topic disturbing the whole country for a period that "China's (hitherto) medical reform was basically unsuccessful," hence unveiling the prelude of a new round of medical care reform in China. Pushed by the public opinion and steered by the top decision-making level, the central government came up to the guiding ideology of "restoring the non-profit nature of public health and medical care, and increasing the government financial input" in 2006, officially initiating the policy-making work for the new medical care reform. Three years later, in March 2009, the CPC Central Committee and the State Council finally issued the *Opinions on Deepening Reform of the Medical and Healthcare System* and the *Plan for Reforming Key Areas of the Medical and Healthcare System (2009–2011)*, with the overall goal as "establishing and consolidating the basic medical and healthcare system covering all urban and rural residents and providing the people with safe, effective, convenient and inexpensive medical and healthcare services."

After the introduction of the new medical reform program, the coverage of urban and rural medical insurance expanded rapidly. For urban areas, the State Council issued the *Opinions on Solving Problems Concerning Rural Migrant Workers* in 2006, emphasizing the necessity to "urgently address the issue of medical insurance for migrant workers

---

[21] Zhu Qingsheng, *Promote the Construction of China's New Rural Cooperative Medical System*: Fifth Speech at Special Plenary Session on China at the 28th ISSA Global Conference (September 2004, 17).

[22] Research Group of Development Research Center of the State Council, *China's Health Care Reform: Evaluation and Recommendations*, China Development Review, 2005 (Supplement 1).

[23] Wang Junxiu, *Research Institution of the State Council Says China's Medical Care Reform Is Basically Unsuccessful*, China Youth Daily, July 2005, 29.

with serious illnesses." In the following year, the Chinese government also started a pilot program to provide urban residents with medical insurance, which covered infants, primary and secondary school students and other non-working urban residents. These two measures were aimed at solving the problem of medical insurance for people other than in-service workers in towns and cities. At the end of 2002, medical insurance covered less than 100 million urban residents; but by the end of 2012, the coverage had extended to about 600 million people (equivalent to about 90% of the 690 million permanent urban residents of the year), a six-fold increase in 10 years.

In rural areas, the participation of public finance has effectively promoted the rapid development of the NRCMS. With the continuous uplifting of the subsidy standards for the participation in the system by government budgets at all levels, the number of participants in the NRCMS has increased quickly, by 2008 it topped the 800 million mark, and stabilized at around 830 million in the next few years, basically realizing the 100% coverage.[24]

In this way, China built up the world's largest medical insurance network in a matter of a few years. In 2003, less than 15% of the country's population, or less than 200 million urban and rural residents nationwide were covered by some kind of medical insurance; but by 2012, the urban and rural health insurance networks covered more than 1.3 billion people.

In 2016, the State Council issued the *Opinion on the Integration of Basic Medical Insurance Systems between Urban and Rural Residents*, aimed to combine the medical insurance system for urban residents and the NRCMS after the "full coverage" of medical insurance was achieved in urban and rural areas so as to establish a unified basic medical insurance system for urban and rural residents based on the principle of "six unifications," namely, unifications of coverage, financing policy, benefit packages, lists of drugs and services, contract suppliers and fund management. The integration of urban and rural residents' basic medical insurance was completed by 2019.

While rapidly expanding the coverage, China's new medical care reform was also committed to reducing the out-of-pocket payment portion in the total cost of health care. Figure 7.7 indicates clearly the

---

[24] The government has also funded some low-income families in urban and rural areas to facilitate their participation in urban medical insurance or NRCMS, and provided the households impoverished due to illness among them with serious-illness relief.

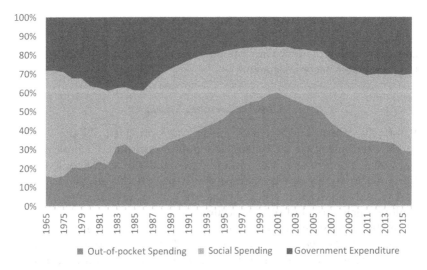

Fig. 7.7 Composition of China's total health cost, 1965–2018

significant changes in the field of health care financing. At the beginning of the twenty-first century, out-of-pocket spending once accounted for 60% of China's total health costs. In other words, individual residents shouldered the major burden of medical expenses at that time. People generally felt that the medical services were "overly expensive" then just because the government's function of providing public goods was weakened, and its responsibility to provide the people with healthcare security faded away in the last dozen years of the twentieth century. It is gratifying that in the dozen years since the new healthcare reform policy came out, there has been a striking reverse movement in health care: the share of government finance and health insurance payments has been increasing, while the share of individual spending has been decreasing. By 2018, the share of out-of-pocket spending in the total health cost had shrunk to 28.7%. It should be pointed out that, in terms of the share of out-of-pocket spending in the total health costs, China now is not only below the world average, but also lower than the average of high-income countries, closing to the average of European countries.[25]

---

[25] World Health Organization, Global Health Expenditure Database, 2019, https://apps.who.int/nha/database/Select/indicators/en.

Various indicators show that China is steadily moving toward the goal of "universal access to public health and basic medical services." For a large developing country with a population of more than 1.3 billion, this is a remarkable accomplishment!

### Old-Age Security System

Before the reform and opening-up, the State provided old-age security to the staff members of organs and public institutions, employees of state-owned enterprises in towns and cities, and workers of some collective enterprises through their respective units. The disintegration of the unit system and diversification of ownership structure prompted China to explore a new model of old-age security.

In 1997, the State Council issued the *Decision on the Establishment of a Unified Basic Pension System for Enterprise Employees*, marking the formal establishment of China's modern old-age pension system for workers in towns and cities. The basic old-age insurance system for urban employees (abridged as BOAI) initially covered only employees of state-owned or collective enterprises in the main, but its goal was to gradually extend to all enterprises and their employees in towns and cities, before extending to self-employed workers there. In the following dozen years, one of the key points in the building of China's old-age security system was to expand the BOAI coverage. After 1997, the population covered by the BOAI grew steadily, exceeding 200 million in 2007 and 400 million in 2017. Calculated on the basis of the urban employed population, the participation rate exceeded 70% in 2009 and 95% in 2018 (See Fig. 7.8). It should be pointed out that the BOAI coverage included rural migrant workers as well.

The bigger challenge in expanding pension coverage is how to include people outside the urban workforce, especially the rural population. Beginning from the early 1990s, some localities in China initiated explorations on how to carry out social endowment insurance in rural areas in different ways. Since only some areas were able to provide limited public financial subsidies, the rural pension insurance coverage hovered around 54 million for many years (see Fig. 7.8). This situation did not change until 2009. In order to fill in the long-standing institutional void of old-age security for rural residents and non-working urban residents, the central government decided to initiate a pilot program of New Rural Social Pension (abridged as NRSP) that year. Rural residents at and

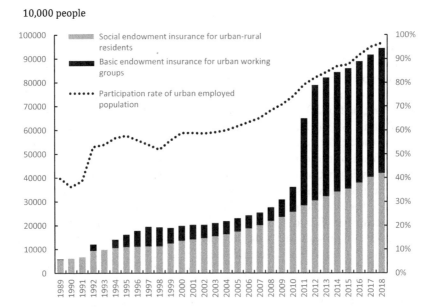

Fig. 7.8 Participation in China's endowment insurance (10,000 people)

above the age of 16 (excluding school students) and not covered in the basic pension insurance for urban working groups could participate in the NRSP on a voluntary basis at the place of their registered permanent residence. The NRSP system's most outstanding feature lies in that it makes it clear that the State is committed to "taking proper care for the elderly" with regard to farmers, which is embodied in the financial input from the government. The goal set at that time was to basically achieve the full coverage of eligible rural residents by 2020. The NRSP pilot program received favorable feedback from various social circles, which accelerated the pilot progress. By 2011, the pilot NRSP coverage had extended to 326 million rural residents.

In this context, the central government decided in 2011 to start carrying out the pilot program of social pension for urban residents (abridged as USP) from that year, adopting the same financial subsidy policy as the NRSP. Non-working urban residents at and above the age of 16 (excluding school students) who were not eligible to participate in the basic pension for urban workers could participate in the social pension for urban residents on a voluntary basis at the place of their registered permanent residence. The goal set at the time was to basically achieve the full coverage of social pension for urban residents by 2012.

From 2009 to 2011, government budgets at various levels allocated a total of more than 170 billion yuan to subsidize the two pension insurances in the three years, which was indeed majestic.[26] More importantly, in the first half of 2012, the central government decided to carry out the NRSP and USP work in an all-round way nationwide, namely, to basically achieve the full coverage of the social pension system within that year, much ahead of the originally expected schedule by 2020. At that point, it can be said that a social pension security system covering both urban and rural residents has been essentially established in China, and pension insurance for all is becoming a reality. This was yet another social security system covering all people following the urban and rural minimum living guarantee system and the basic medical care system, and is an important milestone in China's social security development.

As Fig. 7.8 indicates, the population covered by the NRSP, USP, and the original BOAI soared dramatically after 2010 to reach 943 million people by 2018. Considering that China's population at and above the age of 16 was about 1 billion, the participation rate of the social pension insurance system should be close to 95%.[27] China's social pension insurance system has undoubtedly become the largest one of its kind in the world.

### *Housing Security System*

At the beginning of reform and opening-up, housing conditions were not desirable whether in cities or in villages. In 1978, the urban per capita floor space of residential buildings was merely 6.7 square meters, while the rural per capita floor space was only 8.1 square meters. The focus of housing security at the time was to create conditions to improve the living environment for the vast majority of urban and rural residents.

---

[26] Wen Jiabao, *Speech at the National Work Conference on New Social Endowment Insurance for Rural and Urban Residents*, (October 2012, 12), http://politics.people.com.cn/n/2012/1013/c1024-19248968.html.

[27] Wang Baoan, *Earnestly Do a Good Job in Financial Guarantee for the Full Coverage of New Rural and Urban Residents' Social Endowment Insurance Systems*, China State Finance, 2012 (13).

Throughout the past 40 years, China's economy has grown rapidly, and the overall living conditions of urban and rural residents have improved dramatically. The homeownership rate of urban residents reached to more than 90%,[28] with the per capita floor space of residential buildings jumping to about 38 square meters. In rural areas, the homeownership rate was almost 100%, with the per capita floor space at 46 square meters (2018 data).[29]

However, after the residential housing began to be commercialized in 1998, the rapidly hiking housing prices became a stumbling block for a considerable number of urban residents to further improve their housing conditions. To address this problem, the Chinese government has adopted a multi-pronged approach to explore how to provide housing security to the people.

First, the government focused on people with stable employment in the formal sector and required all state organs, state-owned enterprises, urban collective enterprises, foreign-invested enterprises, urban private enterprises and other urban enterprises, public institutions, and their in-service employees to jointly contribute to the housing provident fund, which is deposited into individual provident fund accounts and used by the employees' families to solve their housing-related problems in the future. By the end of 2018, the number of employees who had contributed to the housing provident fund reached 144 million, with total contributions of 14.6 trillion yuan and total withdrawals of 8.8 trillion yuan.[30] The housing provident fund has helped hundreds of millions of working families realize their dream of a secure home.[31]

---

[28] National Bureau of Statistics, *Urban Residents' Incomes and Spending Grow Continuously Nationwide, with Living Quality Improved Remarkably* (March 2011, 7), http://www.stats.gov.cn/tjfx/ztfx/sywcj/t20110307_402708357htm; *CASS: Current Homeownership Rate Reaches 93.5%*, China News Website (December 2013, 25), http://finance.sina.com.cn/20131225/102517745814.shtml.

[29] *China's Residential Buildings: A Splendid Turn from "Dwelling Narrowness" to "Habitable Dwelling"*, Economic Information Daily, December 2018, 12, http://xinhuanet.com/2018-12/12/c_1123839239.htm.

[30] Wang Youling, *China's Total Deposit of Housing Fund Exceeds 14 Trillion Yuan by the End of 2018*, Xinhua News Agency (May 2019, 31), http://www.xinhuanet.com/fortune/2019-05/31/c_1124569932.htm.

[31] Wu Mengda and Fu Qing, *Three Questions to Housing Fund: Security, or Welfare?Fortnightly Chat* (January 2013, 15), http://news.xinhuanet.com/politics/2013-01/15/c_124231971.htm.

Second, in order to solve the housing problems of urban and rural social groups in destitute circumstances, the government finances the renovation of shantytowns in urban areas and dilapidated houses in rural areas, while helping nomadic herdsmen settle down.[32] The shantytowns mainly existed in mining areas, forest areas, reclamation areas, and also "urban villages" in various localities.[33] The subsidies on the renovation of dilapidated rural housing were mainly offered to households that were entitled to the five guarantees or the minimum living guarantee, households of impoverished people with disabilities and other poor households living in dilapidated housing.[34] The reason for helping nomadic herdsmen settle down was that up to 2000, there were still more than two million herdsmen in about 440,000 households in Tibetan areas in Qinghai, Sichuan, Gansu and Yunnan provinces, as well as in remote pastoral areas in autonomous regions of Tibet, Xinjiang and Inner Mongolia, who sustained the traditional nomadic living style, roaming with no permanent abode and enduring backward production and living conditions, vulnerable to the blows of natural disasters. The government launched a pilot nomadic settlement project in Tibet in 2001 and has increased the input in such projects since 2008.[35]

Finally, in order to meet the housing demand of low- and middle-income families in cities, the government rolled out policies to establish an indemnificatory housing system including affordable housing, housing with limited habitable space and price, low-rent housing, and public rental housing.

From 1994 to 2002, the indemnificatory housing system placed the affordable housing in dominance, supplemented with the low-rent housing. A rapid development of affordable housing was witnessed in this period, with its completed floor space taking a big share in the total floor

---

[32] "Renovation" often means rebuilding on the basis of original housing, not necessarily providing new houses.

[33] Du Yu, *Pace Up Renovation to Benefit More People: Leading Official of Ministry of Housing and Urban–Rural Development on Redevelopment of Run-down Areas*, Xinhua News Agency (September 2012, 8), http://www.gov.cn/jrzg/2012-09/28/content_2 235709.htm.

[34] Du Yu, *China Plans to Renovate Dilapidated Rural Housing for 3 Million Households in 2013*, Xinhua News Agency (February 2013, 15).

[35] National Development and Reform Commission, Ministry of Housing and Urban–Rural Development and Ministry of Agriculture: *12th Five-Year Plan for National Nomadic Population Settlement Project* (May 30, 2012).

space of commercial housing completed in the same period. But then the indemnificatory housing policy went astray in 2003. The State Council's *Circular on Promoting the Sustained and Sound Development of the Real Estate Market* issued that year changed the purpose of housing reform to: "gradually achieve the goal for the majority of families to buy or rent ordinary commercial housing; at the same time, to determine which income groups are entitled to affordable houses and low-rent houses according to the local conditions." This resulted in a steep decline in the construction of affordable housing and low-rent housing, which in effect thrust the vast majority of families in need of improved housing conditions into a market where house prices were soaring wildly.

This housing commercialization deviation began to be corrected in 2005, when the State Council issued a slew of documents to re-emphasize the construction of indemnificatory housing, and clearly put forward that in further improving the affordable housing system, the low-rent housing should be taken as the main channel to address the housing difficulties of low-income families. The government's efforts to correct the deviation gradually intensified in the following years. For instance, the State Council issued the *Opinions on Solving Housing Difficulties for Urban Low-Income Families* in August 2007, requiring that the solution of housing difficulties for low-income families in cities (including county seats) should be taken as important work to safeguard people's interests and an important part of the housing reform, and it put forward for the first time that the housing for rural migrant workers and other groups with housing difficulties should be gradually improved. In 2010, the focus of indemnificatory housing was adjusted once again, with the public rental housing becoming the main form of housing security.

The *Outline of the 12th Five-Year Plan* adopted in 2011 and the *Outline of the 13th Five-Year Plan* adopted in 2016 both set out more magnificent objectives in the area of indemnificatory housing projects, the former of which was over fulfilled, so is the latter expected. From 2006 to 2018, various indemnificatory housing projects solved the housing problem for a total of approximately 85 million households. Calculated on the basis that an average household has three members, China's indemnificatory housing policy benefited 250 million people, twice the population of Japan, equivalent to more than half of the population of the United States, almost equal to the combined population of Germany, Britain, France, and Italy (Fig. 7.9).

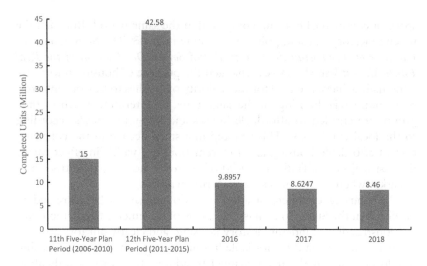

**Fig. 7.9** Units of indemnificatory housing completed, 2006–2018

*Other Securities*

The minimum living guarantee scheme, medical care, and old-age care apply to all people, while there are several other types of social security which apply only to the urban employed population (at least for the time being), namely, unemployment insurance, work-related injury insurance, and maternity insurance.

Before the reform and opening-up, the urban employed population held an "iron rice bowl," and there was no problem of unemployment. After the implementation of the labor contract system and the *Bankruptcy Law* in 1986, the phenomenon of state-owned enterprise employees being laid off and waiting for work emerged. At that time, the government focused only on the issue of "waiting for work insurance" for the employees of state-owned enterprises.[36]

In the mid and late 1990s, tens of millions of employees of state-owned and collective enterprises who had been holding the "iron rice bowl" were "laid off or repositioned as redundant personnel." Meanwhile, the rapidly

---

[36] For instance, the State Council issued the *Temporary Provisions on Employment-Pending Insurance for Employees of State-owned Enterprises* in 1986 and the *Regulations on Employment-Pending Insurance for Employees of State-owned Enterprises* in 1993.

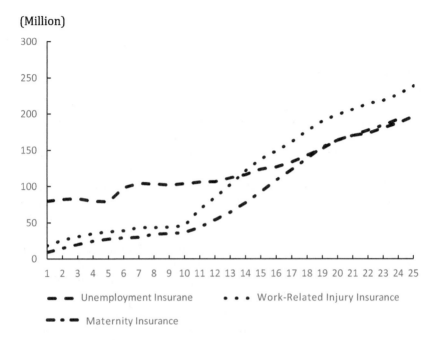

**Fig. 7.10** Participation of unemployment insurance, work injury insurance and maternity insurance, 1994–2018 (Million)

expanding non-public economy no longer provided any "iron rice bowl" from the outset. The development in both aspects protruded the problem of unemployment. In early 1999, the State Council issue the *Regulations on Unemployment Insurance*, which extended the coverage of unemployment insurance from state-owned enterprises to collective enterprises, foreign-invested enterprises, enterprises with funds from Hong Kong, Macao, and Taiwan, private enterprises and other enterprises and public institutions.[37] As Fig. 7.10 indicates, the enactment of the *Regulations on Unemployment Insurance* increased the participation of unemployment insurance from 79.28 million in 1998 to 104 million in 2000.

---

[37] It is up to the provincial-level government to decide whether social groups and their full-time employees, non-government non-profit institutions and their employees, urban self-employed industrial and commercial business owners and their employees should participate in unemployment insurance.

But after 2000, the development of unemployment insurance seemed to have lost the dynamics, and by the end of 2018, the unemployment insurance covered only 196 million people. The fatigue in the expansion of unemployment insurance is due to the fact that benefits from unemployment insurance are only slightly higher than that of the minimum living guarantee scheme for local residents, and its benefit period could last no longer than 24 months.[38] After the urban *Dibao* basically achieved the goal that all the eligible people were covered by the system, the life support function of the current unemployment insurance faded away. Since the unemployment insurance premiums are paid jointly by employers and their employees in accordance with state regulations, the insurance is unattractive to urban residents, while rural migrant workers in high mobility are even more reluctant to participate in the scheme.

The work injury insurance refers to the social insurance system in which workers acquire economic compensation and material assistance from the state and society for work-related injury, illness, disability, or death according to law. The work injury insurance follows the "no-fault compensation principle" and the premiums are paid by employers, and employees are not liable to pay them. Article 73 of the *Labor Law of the People's Republic of China*, which came into effect in 1995, provides that laborers shall be entitled to social insurance treatment in accordance with law in case they "become disabled during work or suffer occupational diseases." In order to implement the *Labor Law*, the Ministry of Labor issued on August 12, 1996 the *Measures for Industrial Injury Insurance for Employees of Enterprises (for Trial Implementation)*, which stipulated that the work injury insurance system shall be applied uniformly to all types of enterprises and their employees in China, and could be applied as reference to laborers in urban self-employed economic organizations. But there was little progress in work injury insurance in the next seven years. It was not until 2004 when the State Council promulgated the *Regulations on Work Injury Insurance* that a turning point came up. The newly increased participation in China's work injury insurance thereafter skyrocketed, from 45.75 million at the end of 2003 to 239 million by the

---

[38] Zhang Shifei, *China's Unemployment Security Policies*. Erin Wong Cheuk Ki, Teng Kuang-liang and Ngai Ngan-pun, *Social Policies of China's Mainland, Taiwan and Hong Kong: Theory and Practical Experiences* (Hong Kong: Chinese University Press, 2007), p. 288.

end of 2018, covering more than half of the urban employed population (see Fig. 7.10).

The maternity insurance was established to provide maternity subsidies, medical services, and maternity leave to working women and help them regain their working capacity and return to work. The maternity insurance premiums shall be paid by employers in accordance with State regulation, and employees are not liable to pay them. As Fig. 7.10 indicates, the maternity insurance lags behind all the other types of social insurance, with its participation not reaching 193 million until the end of 2017, slightly more than that of the unemployment insurance. This may have something to do with the fact that its beneficiaries are just a part of the employed population (women). In early 2019, the General Office of the State Council issued the *Opinions on the Comprehensive Promotion of the Integrated Implementation of Maternity Insurance and Basic Medical Insurance for Employees*, and the two types of insurance were merged into one by the end of that year.

## Summary

In 1989, Francis Fukuyama published *The End of History*, arguing that the "economic and political liberalism" carried out in the Western capitalist countries was the "end point of mankind's ideological evolution."[39] In 2009, the British Broadcast Company commissioned two pollsters to conduct a large-scale random sampling survey on 29,000 people in 27 countries (China included) around the world, which found Fukuyama's judgment to be false and completely untenable. According to the survey, dissatisfaction with "liberal capitalism" prevailed around the world, with an average of only 11% of the poll respondents in the 27 countries holding that the system worked well without any necessity for the government to intervene.[40] By contrast, an average of 23% of the polled believed that the capitalist system was fatally flawed and it had to be replaced by a new system. People holding this view accounted for 43% in France, 38% in Mexico, 35% in Brazil, and 31% in Ukraine. Among people of various countries, the most popular view was that the flaws with the capitalist

---

[39] Francis Fukuyama, *The End of History?The National Interest*, No. 16 (Summer 1989).

[40] The United States claimed the largest percentage of the poll respondents in favor of capitalism, at 25%.

system had to be corrected by reform and regulation, and that the direction of reform should be that the government must play a more active role in owning or directly controlling the country's major industries, redistribution of income and wealth, and business regulation.[41] In other words, "liberal capitalism" was unpopular.

Only in such a global context could one truly appreciate the significance in exploring the Chinese-style socialism 3.0. The Chinese have never believed in the end of history, they are still unremittingly exploring the socialist road; meanwhile, the Chinese people will never be complacent and conservative with what they have already achieved, but they will constantly probe on how to upgrade Chinese-style socialism through diversified practice and experiments after they have crossed the last stage of development.[42]

China had created brilliant Chinese-style socialism 1.0 and 2.0 in the "stage of scarcity" and "stage of adequate food and clothing," and made accomplishments that attracted worldwide attention. After entering the "stage of moderate prosperity," adequate food and clothing were no longer a main problem for the vast majority of Chinese. Chinese-style socialism 3.0 has significantly increased input in public goods and services, further improving the welfare level of the whole society. The large amount of data provided previously in this chapter have evidenced that China has indeed experienced an unprecedented great leap forward in social protection over the past two decades in order to realize the dream of common prosperity. To make this great leap forward apprehensible at one glance, Fig. 7.11 presents two sets of data for the 2000–2018 period: one is China's public spending on social protection[43] and the other is its share in GDP.

We could see that in less than 20 years, data of the first set increased from less than 600 billion yuan to nearly 14.3 trillion yuan, an increase of

---

[41] BBC, *Wide Dissatisfaction with Capitalism: Twenty Years after Fall of Berlin Wall*, November 9, 2009.

[42] Wang Shaoguang, *Learning Mechanism and Adaptability: Revelations of Vicissitudes of China's Rural Cooperative Medical Care System*, Social Sciences in China, No. 6 (2008), pp. 111–133.

[43] Public spending on social security = budgetary expenditure on social security (including social security and insurances of employment, medical care and housing) + expenditure on social insurance + social health expenditure − financial subsidies on social security fund. Note that this does not include the public education expenditure.

7 DIRECTION: FROM ECONOMIC TO SOCIAL POLICIES 283

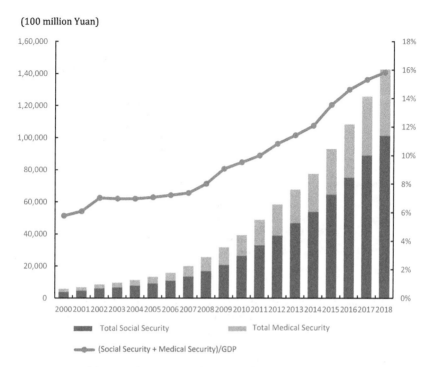

**Fig. 7.11** Public spending on social security (100 million yuan)

24.7 folds. Some people may argue that the high growth rate of this set of data was due to the rapid growth of China's economy in this period. This is true, as China's total economic volume did increase several times in this period, but the public spending on social protection did not just grow in tandem with GDP; rather it grew much faster than the already quickly growing GDP. This enabled the share of public spending on social protection in GDP to skyrocket from 5.77% in 2000 to 15.84% in 2018.

Figure 7.11 compares the present China with itself of more than ten years ago and illustrates the great leap forward China has experienced in social protection. This great leap forward is also evidenced through a comparison between China and other countries. Figure 7.12 compares the data from China and other countries and regions in terms of the share of public spending on social protection in GDP. In 2000, the proportion

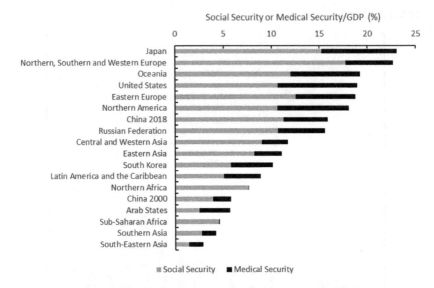

**Fig. 7.12** Share of public spending on social security in GDP (*Source* Chinese data are from a databank the author compiles from various sources; data for other countries are from International Labor Organization, *World Social Protection Report Data 2017–2019*, http://www.social-protection.org/gimi/gess/AggregateIndicator.action#expenditure)

of China's social spending in GDP was similar to that in Arab countries; but by 2018, China surpassed almost all developing countries and regions, and even South Korea and Russia, which were at a higher level of development than itself. Currently, China is behind only two kinds of economies in terms of the spending on social protection, namely, the developed economies of Europe and the United States and Japan, and the economies of the former Soviet Union and East Europe.

Thus, whether a longitudinal comparison with China's own past, or a cross-country comparison, both show indisputable fact that China has experienced a monumental great leap forward in social protection. People had good reason around 2000 to say that China was a "low-welfare" country, because China's public spending on social protection was really low at the time. But if these people still insist that China is a "low-welfare" country today, it is tantamount to claiming that the vast majority of the countries in the world are "low-welfare" countries. The question is, if the vast majority of them in the world are "low welfare" countries, how low is low, and how high is high? High and low are always relative, talking blindly about "high" and "low" without an objective standard measurement is no less than speaking nonsense irresponsibly.

Those in the West who are ignorant of China take it for granted that China is a "low-welfare" country, because the Western literature on social protection and welfare often regards competitive elections as a key factor in determining the breadth and strength of social protection, as if only with competitive elections could the government respond to the voters' cries, and only with the competitive elections introduced could essential conditions be constituted for strengthening social protection.[44]

Figure 7.12 tells us that such views are groundless. Otherwise, it cannot be explained why a large number of countries labeled "democracies" (such as India, the Philippines, Indonesia and South Korea, etc.) have lagged behind China in social protection. Since they cannot deny that China has improved its social protection level, those who think in the mainstream Western mentality would perhaps argue that the Communist Party of China has been doing this simply to stay in power. Of course, it is essential for every ruling political party to keep its political power, but if it is only for their selfish gain to maintain the regime, the rational option of those in power would be to raise social protection levels slowly,

---

[44] For instance, Nader Habibi, *Budgetary Policy and Political Liberty: A Cross-Sectional Analysis*, World Development, Vol. 22, No. 4 (1994), pp. 579–586; also see Peter Lindert (who is renowned in the Western academic world), *Growing Public: Social Spending and Economic Growth Since the Eighteenth Century*, Volume 1, the *Story* and Volume 2: *Further Evidence* (Cambridge: Cambridge University Press, 2004). However, aside from these mainstream views, there have been empirical studies that have led to some different conclusions. Some studies have found that the form of government is not related to the level of social security, such as Casey B. Mulligan, Ricard Gil, Xavier Sala-i-Martin, *Do Democracies Have Different Public Policies than Nondemocracies? The Journal of Economic Perspectives*, Vol. 18, No. 1 (2004), pp. 51–74. Some other studies have found that "totalitarian" countries, especially socialist countries, do better in social security at least in some aspects (like basic medical care, basic education) than other countries, like John R. Lott, Jr., *Public Schooling, Indoctrination and Totalitarianism*, The *Journal of Political Economy*, Vol. 107, No. 6, Part 2 (December 1999), pp. 127–157; Varun Gauri and Peyvand Kaleghian, *Immunization in Developing Countries: Its Political and Organizational Determinants*, Washington DC: World Bank, 2002. For various empirical studies on the relationship between political system and social security, please consult Stephan Haggard & Robert R. Kaufman, *Development, Democracy, and Welfare States: Latin America, East Asia, and Eastern Europe* (Princeton, NJ: Princeton University Press, 2008), *Appendix One Cross-National Empirical Studies of the Effects of Democracy on Social Policy and Social Outcomes*, pp. 365–369.

because there is no turning back once a certain level of social protection is in place. When the people are used to enjoy a certain degree of social protection, it would be hard or even impossible for them to accept retrogression. The "preservation of power" argument may be applied to those cases of slow, gradual expansion of social protection, but apparently it cannot explain China's great leap forward in social protection in the past decade or so.

In fact, once free from the shackle of the mainstream Western ideology, it is not difficult to explain this great leap forward. Social protection is an intrinsic need of human life,[45] and an ardent expectation of the broad masses of the Chinese people: everyone's access to "education, employment, medical service, elderly care, and housing" is an important part of the Chinese dream at the current stage. China was in a "low-welfare" state around 2000, but that was not as some people ascribed as an institutional feature of China. China's reform is a trial-and-error process, "neoliberalism" once influenced China's policy thinking, and reduced the country into a short nightmare of "market society" in the 1990s, resulting in the state of "low welfare." However, the "low-welfare" state also gave rise to a vigorous counter-movement thereafter.[46] The fact that a country with such a large population and such great internal differences has been able to push forward such a wide range of profound change in response to the people's wishes in such a short period of time since the beginning of the new century shows that China's political system is quite adaptable to the changing environment and quite responsive to the needs of the people. Today, there are still a lot of serious problems in various areas of social protection in China, and the people still have a very strong desire for further strengthening social protection. As long as this pressure sustains, as long as the adaptability and responsiveness of the Chinese system does not degrade, it can be expected that the Chinese dream is bound to become a reality step by step that benefits hundreds of millions of people in the future.

---

[45] For elaboration on such need, please see Karl Polanyi, *The Great Transformation: The Political and Economic Origins of Our Time* (Boston: Beacon Press, 2001).

[46] See Wang Shaoguang, *Great Transformation: Reciprocal Movements in China Since the 1980s*. Data show that the share of the public spending on social security in GDP fell to the bottom of the valley in the mid-to-late 1990s, when numerous state-owned and collective enterprises "reformed" their ownerships, several tens of millions of their workers were laid off, resulting in many of them and their family members thrown out of the social security network.

CHAPTER 8

# Leapfrogging: Striding from Middle Income to High Income

Over the past decade, a new term "middle-income trap" has entered into international parlance and drawn attention from economic scholars, news media, government officials, international organizations, and even the general public. Both Baidu Index and Google Trends have revealed that the attention to this term was growing after 2007 and has only declined since 2015. A search of two major repositories of English academic papers (Web of Science and EBSCOhost) and one major repository of Chinese academic papers (CNKI) reveals that research on the "middle-income trap" is still on the rise.[1]

In the domain of economic development research, "trap" is not a new word, as we are acquainted with such examples as "Malthusian trap," "Nelson's low-level equilibrium trap," and "poverty trap." Strictly speaking, a "trap" must have at least three characteristics: (1) a self-perpetuating or self-reinforcing mechanism; (2) in a constant steady state; and (3) difficulty to escape.[2]

In case there are any traps in the economic development, low income or poverty is a kind of trap for sure. Human history has lasted for 3 million years, but until about 200 years ago, the economic growth had

---

[1] Linda Glawe and Helmut Wagner, *The Middle-Income Trap: Definitions, Theories and Countries Concerned – A Literature Survey, Comparative Economic Studies*, Vol. 58, No. 4 (December 2016), pp. 507–538.

[2] Ibid., p. 512.

been extremely slow, with barely any change in per capita income, and the vast majority of people living in poverty, except for a very trifle few of the rich who lived on exploitation and oppression of others.[3] After the Industrial Revolution burst out in the second half of the eighteenth century, the "Great Divergence" emerged around the world, marked by the acceleration of economic growth in some countries and regions.[4] The Netherlands crossed the "lower-middle income" threshold from "low income" in 1827, perhaps the first in the world. In the following half a century, Britain (in 1845), Australia (in 1851), Belgium (in 1854), New Zealand (in 1860), the United States (in 1860), Switzerland (in 1868), Uruguay (in 1870), Denmark (in 1872), France (in 1874), Germany (in 1874), and Austria (in 1876) also successively joined the "lower-middle income" club.[5] The low-income trap or poverty trap clearly conforms to the above three characteristics, as it took millions of years for mankind to get rid of it, thus indeed an out-and-out trap.

But is there a "middle-income trap" in its strict sense? If we look back at the path the Western developed countries have covered (which are often forgotten today), it also seems to exist. The Netherlands, for example, crossed the "lower-middle income" threshold in 1827, but it did not join the "upper-middle income" group until 1955, 128 years later. The United States spent less time in the "lower-middle income" stage, still it took them 81 years (1860–1941) to make it.

For these countries, the further transition from the "upper-middle" to the "high income" stage was also difficult. It took 21 years for the United States (1941–1962), 19 years for Canada (1950–1969), 20 years for Australia (1950–1970), and 23 years for New Zealand (1949–1972) to perform it. In other words, all the Western developed countries once fell into the "middle-income trap" (including the two stages of middle-

---

[3] Robert William Fogel, *The Escape from Hunger and Premature Death, 1700–2100: Europe, America, and the Third World* (Cambridge: Cambridge University Press, 2004).

[4] Angus Maddison, *Contours of the World Economy 1–2030 AD: Essays in Macro-Economic History* (Oxford: Oxford University Press, 2007).

[5] Jesus Felipe, Utsav Kumara and Reynold Galope, *Middle-Income Transitions: Trapor Myth? Journal of the Asia Pacific Economy*, Vol. 22, No. 3 (2017), pp. 429–453. This study calculated GDP per capita at purchasing power parity (the 1990 international US dollar), those lower than 2,000 US dollar belong to the low-income category; those with 2,000–7,500 US dollars are in the lower-middle income group; with 7,250–11,750 US dollars are upper-middle income group; and at 11,750 US dollars or more are high-income group.

and upper-middle income) for some 100 years or even longer.[6] But after all, having experienced all kinds of hardships and ordeals, these countries eventually jumped out of the trap and entered the high-income stage.

The Western developed countries' experience may not necessarily be of universal value. Does the fact that they once fell into the "middle-income trap" mean that latecomer economies are bound to "follow the track of a previously overturned cart"? In an article published in the *Foreign Affairs* in 2004, Geoffrey Garrett, an Australian scholar teaching in the United States, put forth an argument that middle-income countries were in a plight of being squeezed from both sides: technically they could not compete with the rich countries, nor could they beat the poor ones in price. To support his argument, Garrett ranked the world's economies by GDP per capita in 1980, dividing them into three groups: top, middle, and low, and compared their growth by that measure over the subsequent 20 years (1980–2000). He found that the growth of the middle-income group (less than 20%) was slower than that of both high-income economies (about 50%) and low-income economies (more than 160%).[7] Three years later, in a lengthy report entitled *East Asian Renaissance: Ideas for Economic Growth*, two World Bank researchers cited Garrett's article and used the term "middle-income trap" for the first time.[8] In a few years, this concept suddenly exploded, and many people upon learning about it took it for granted that high-income economies had already been established, that it was relatively easy for low-income economies to "take off," and that only middle-income economies were likely to fall into the growth trap and it would be difficult for them to jump out of the pitfall.

In fact, neither Garrett nor the authors of the World Bank report have used the concept of "trap" in a strict sense, the former never mentioned the term at all, while the latter explained, in a reflective essay published 10 years later, that they originally meant only that middle-income economies could fall into a growth stagnation trap; not that middle-income economies were necessarily more likely to fall into a

---

[6] Jesus Felipe, Utsav Kumara and Reynold Galope, *Middle-Income Transitions: Trapor Myth? Journal of the Asia Pacific Economy*, Vol. 22, No. 3 (2017), pp. 429–453.

[7] Geoffrey Garrett, *Globalization's Missing Middle, Foreign Affairs*, Vol. 83, No. 6 (November/December 2004), pp. 84–96.

[8] Indermit Gill and Homi Kharas, *An East Asian Renaissance: Ideas for Economic Growth* (Washington, DC: World Bank, 2007), pp. 18–19, 68–69.

growth trap than low- and high-income economies; this "trap" existed at all income levels, from low to high income. They clarified that the "middle-income trap" was merely a term, a warning, and a device to spark a discussion of policy choices in middle-income economies, but the term of middle-income trap was neither rigorously defined nor supported by hard evidence.[9]

Middle-income economies have attracted a lot of attention from researchers in the early twenty-first century for two reasons.

First, compared with the early postwar period, the configuration of world economy had changed dramatically. Take the 124 economies with continuous data for example: in 1950, 80 of them were low-income economies, 41 were middle-income ones, and only 3 were high-income economies; but by 2013, the number of low-income economies fell to 37, and the number of high-income economies rose to 33, with the majority being middle-income economies, at 54.[10] The percentage of middle-income economies was higher particularly in Asia, claiming more than 95% of the population of the developing countries of the continent.[11]

Second, there existed a huge void in the existing economic theories. For understanding the growth problem in low-income economies (where about 1 billion people live), there is the Solow growth model; for understanding the growth problem in high-income economies (where another 1 billion live), there are endogenous growth theory; but there have been no satisfactory theories or models for understanding the development of middle-income economies (where the remaining 5 billion people live). That's why the two authors of the World Bank's 2007 report wrote ten years later that the "middle-income trap" is not so much a doomed fate for middle-income economies as it is an "ignorance trap" in economic theory.[12]

---

[9] Indermit Gill and Homi Kharas, *The Middle-Income Trap Turns Ten*, Policy Research Working Paper, No. 7403, World Bank, August 2015.

[10] Jesus Felipe, Utsav Kumara and Reynold Galope, *Middle-Income Transitions: Trap or Myth?* Table 1. Change in the Distribution of Economies by Income Categories, 1950–2013, p. 436.

[11] Germma Estrada, Xuehui Han, Donghyun Park, and Shu Tian, *Asia's Middle-Income Challenge: An Overview*, ADBE Economics Working Paper Series, No. 525 (November 2017), pp. 1–2.

[12] Indermit Gill and Homi Kharas, *The Middle-Income Trap Turns Ten*, p. 4.

If the originators of the "middle-income trap" have never used the "trap" concept in its strict sense, does it mean that such a trap is not existent at all? The data provided by Garrett were later proven not sufficient to be taken as evidence. Some scholars used updated data to recalculate the growth rates of various economies between 1980 and 2000 and found that the gap between middle-income and high-income economies was not as great as Garrett had described. If indicators different from Garrett's are used to divide the high, middle, and low economies, the gap would disappear completely.[13] So it's apparent that the selection of data and threshold measurements may seriously influence the conclusions of research. More importantly, even using Garrett's classification, middle-income economies grew at a higher rate than high-income economies, both in the 1990–2010 period and in the 1995–2015 period. That is to say, at one point in time, the trap may or may not appear to exist; but once switched to another point in time, there does not seem to be growth trap at all.[14]

The above-mentioned 2007 report of the World Bank provides no evidence for a "middle-income trap" at all. However, a diagram (see Fig. 8.1) in *China 2030: Building a Modern, Harmonious, and Creative Society* it published in 2013 was later cited widely by many as evidence of the existence of "middle-income trap." This diagram ranks the economies by their GDP per capita relative to the United States (in terms of purchasing power parity), dividing them into three types of economies: low, middle and high, in an attempt to tell readers that in 1960, there were already 101 middle-income economies in the world; yet by 2008 only 13 of them managed to enter the high-income rank.

However, a little scrutiny of this diagram reveals the fragility of its foundation.

First, it defines "middle income" too broadly to include all economies with per capita GDP equivalent to 5.2–42.74% of the United States level. As a result, there were only 12 low-income economies in the world in 1960, two of which were already on the middle-income threshold. By

---

[13] Garrett's approach to dividing the high, middle, and low income countries was very rough. Instead of using the absolute or relative income method commonly used in the academic circles, he simply ranked all countries according to their per capita income, calling the top 25% "high income countries," the bottom 30% "low income countries," and the remaining 45% "middle income countries."

[14] *The Economist, The Middle-Income Trap Has Little Evidence Going for It, The Economist*, October 7, 2017.

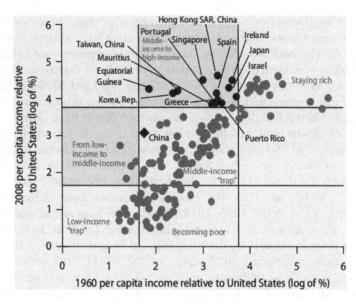

**Fig. 8.1** Evidence for "middle-income trap" (*Source* The World Bank, Development Research Center of the State Council, the People's Republic of China, *China 2030: Building a Modern, Harmonious, and Creative Society*, 2013:12)

2008, the number of low-income economies went up to more than 30, which is completely counterintuitive. What is even more inconceivable is that China was already ranked as a middle-income country in 1960, whereby a conclusion was drawn that it has mired in the "middle-income trap" ever since.

Second, of the 13 economies that had successfully crossed the "middle-income trap": Mauritius (with a population 1.26 million) and Equatorial Guinea (with a population of 740,000) actually remain "typical of developing economies;"[15] Israel has only 8.36 million people, while Hong Kong of China (7.4 million), Singapore (5.85 million), Ireland (4.84 million), and Puerto Rico (3.7 million) have even smaller populations,

---

[15] Following the World Bank's 2018 classifications of various economies, Mauritius never became a high-income economy, Equatorial Guinea had regressed to an upper-middle income one. See World Bank Data Team, *New Country Classifications by Income Level: 2017–2018*, July 1, 2017, http://blogsworldbank.org/opendata/edutech/new-country-classifications-income-level-2017-2018.

and Portugal and Greece have just barely more than 10 million people. All of them are small economies. Furthermore, back in 1960, Israel, Ireland, and Japan were already only inches away from the high-income border. Excluding these 10 economies, the "graduates" from the group of middle-income economies were just Taiwan of China, South Korea, and Spain. This conclusion is perhaps not what the drafters of this World Bank report wished to see.

Finally, low, middle, and high are relative concepts, and it is not unreasonable to use relative criteria, but it is important to note that the World Bank's reference for this chart is the GDP per capita of the United States. In other words, in this scatterplot, all those economies whose plots were higher in 2008 than in 1960 outpaced the United States in the growth of GDP per capita during the interim period; only those economies whose plots went lower registered a growth rate of GDP per capita lower than that of the United States. Calculated with data from 1950 to 2017,[16] the average annual growth rate of GDP per capita in the United States during this period was 2.05%, ranking in the middle or 52nd as compared with the other 100 economies with continuous data available, and only 7 economies registered a growth rate equal to or below zero. Unless it is concluded that the United States fell into a trap during these decades, there does not seem to be any reason to assert that the 51 economies with faster per capita GDP growth than the United States fell into some sort of trap: suppose the growth rate of the United States and these economies remained the same, it is only a matter of time before the latter approach and cross the high-income threshold, or even surpass the United States.

As mentioned earlier, those high-income countries of today were once stuck in the middle-income stage for a long time, but most of latecomers did not follow in their tracks. When people talk about middle-income countries, they often immediately think of those Latin American countries that fell into the "middle-income trap," as if the experiences of these few countries are the fate of all late-developing countries. Several countries in Latin America did reach the lower-middle-income stage very early, such as Uruguay (in 1870), Argentina (in 1890), Chile (in 1891), Venezuela (in 1925), Mexico (in 1942), Panama (in 1945), Colombia (in 1946), and Brazil (in 1958). So far, only Uruguay and Chile crossed the high-income threshold in 2012, and Argentina entered the high-income group only

---

[16] The Conference Board, Inc., Total Economy Database, 2018, https://www.conference-board.org/retrievefile.cfm?filename=TED_1_NOV2017.xlsx&type=subsite.

briefly, while the rest have remained in the upper-middle-income group. But Latin America is only one region of the world, and its experience is not necessarily representative.

Some studies indicate that, on the whole, the growth rate of the late-developing countries is generally faster than that of Western capitalist countries. Of the 124 economies with continuous data, 45 had completed the transition from lower-middle to upper-middle income by 2013, of which 36 had completed the transition in 1950 or earlier, and the remaining 9 made it after 1950. In the former group of economies, the Netherlands spent the longest time to complete the transition (128 years), and Israel spent the shortest time (19 years); and in the latter group, Costa Rica spent the most years (54 years) and China spent the shortest period (17 years).[17] If we put the 45 economies on a scatterplot, where the horizontal axis is the time of entry into the lower middle income (year) and the vertical axis is the length of the transition period (number of years), and then draw a regression line, we can clearly see that the two are negatively correlated, with a statistically significant slope of − 0.6, indicating that the later an economy entered the lower middle income, the shorter the transition period: the median of the transition period for the former group is 64 years, and the median of the transition period for the latter group is 28 years, less than half of the former group. When these 45 economies are examined together, the median transition period is 55 years (see Fig. 8.2).

Of these 45 economies, 30 (mostly in Europe and America) had completed the transition from upper-middle to high-income by 2013, of which 5 had made it in 1950 or before, and the remaining 25 completed the transition after 1950. In the former group of economies, New Zealand spent the longest period of time (23 years) to complete the transition, and Switzerland spent the shortest time period (14 years); and in the latter group, Argentina spent the longest time(41 years) and Hong Kong of China and South Korea spent the shortest time (7 years). If the 30 economies are put in one scatter diagram, a negatively correlated regression line of statistical significance can also be displayed, with a slope of − 0.24, indicating that the later an economy entered upper-middle income, the shorter the transition period: the median of the transition period for the former group is 20 years, and for the latter group it is

---

[17] The conclusion of this study does not necessarily comply with that of the World Bank.

# 8 LEAPFROGGING: STRIDING FROM MIDDLE INCOME TO HIGH INCOME

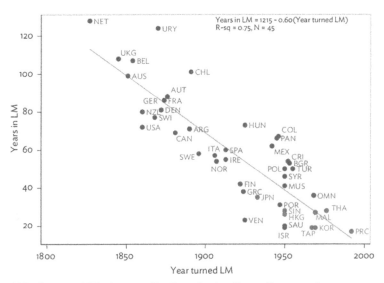

LM = lower-middle income, N = Sample size, R-sq = R-squared.

**Fig. 8.2** Year an economy turned lower-middle income and number of years it spent as lower-middle income (*Note* The line shown is obtained from the regression of the number of years in LM on the year the economy turned LM. The regression result is shown in the figure. Both the constant and the coefficient on "year turned LM" are statistically significant at the 1% level of significance. See Appendix Table 1 for the codes of each economy. LM = lower-middle income, N = Sample size, R-sq = R-squared. *Source* Jesus Felipe, Utsav Kumar, and Reynold Galope, Middle-Income Transitions: Trap or Myth? *Journal of the Asian Pacific Economy*, Vol. 22, No. 3 [2017], pp. 429–453)

14 years, while the median transition period for all the 30 economies is 15 years (see Fig. 8.3).[18]

An analysis of these 45 economies could help clarify the misconceptions in understanding the "middle-income trap." Some people may inadvertently use Japan and the "Four Little Dragons in Asia" as a benchmark for whether or not an economy falls into the "trap," as if the transition

---

[18] Jesus Felipe, Utsav Kumar and Reynold Galope, *Middle-Income Transitions: Trap or Myth?* If the years examined are confined to post-1960, different conclusions may be drawn, see Gemma Estrada, Xuehui Han, Donghyun Park, and Shutian, *Asia's Middle-Income Challenge: An Overview*, pp. 8–17.

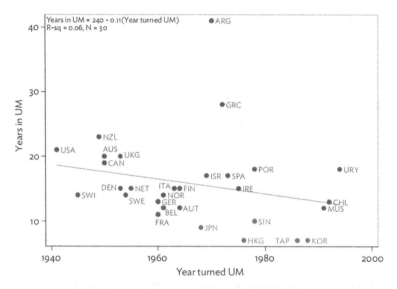

N = Sample size, R-sq =R-squared, UM = Upper-middle income.

**Fig. 8.3** Year an economy turned upper-middle income and number of years it spent as upper-middle income. (*Note* The line shown is obtained from the regression of the number of years in UM on the year the economy turned UM. The regression result is shown in the figure. The constant and the coefficient on "year turned UM" are statistically significant at the 5% and 10% level of significance, respectively. See Appendix Table 1 for the codes of each economy. N = Sample size, R-sq = R-squared, UM = Upper-middle income. *Source* Jesus Felipe, Utsav Kumar, and Reynold Galope, Middle-Income Transitions: Trap or Myth? *Journal of the Asian Pacific Economy*, Vol. 22, No. 3 [2017])

period longer than theirs would indicate the fall into the "trap." As a matter of fact, just as the Latin American countries are exceptional, so are these East Asian economies. European and American countries generally stayed in the middle-income stage (including the lower-middle and upper-middle-income stage) for a long time, but this did not impede them from eventually entering the high-income camp. The transition period for the late-developing economies is generally shorter than that of European and American countries, so what reason do we have to insist that those late-developing countries must fall into the trap? If one must set a time standard for falling into the trap (sustained steady state), I'm afraid it's necessary to examine whether an economy's transition from lower-middle to upper-middle income is longer than the 55 years, and whether the transition period from upper-middle to high-income is longer than the 15 years. Using these two yardsticks, one can certainly find examples of economies that have been in the lower-middle or upper-middle-income stage for a prolonged time (such as some but not all Latin American countries). However, more economies (such as most Asian countries and some African countries) have been forging ahead unremittingly although they are yet to transit to the next stage. Since it is not a high probability event to fall into the "middle income trap," it is totally unnecessary to make a fuss about it, assuming that the middle income is an obstacle difficult to stride over.[19]

China's rise is a majestic epic of the contemporary world. In 1950, when the New China was just founded, China was one of the poorest countries in the world. It lagged far behind even African countries known for their poverty and backwardness, not to say to compare with its neighboring countries and regions. Of the 25 African countries with data available at that time, 21 led China in terms of GDP per capita, and not a little but much higher. For instance, Angola's GDP per capita was 10 times that of China back then.[20] The first three decades of the new China laid a solid political, social, and economic foundation for the following four decades of reform and opening up. But even in 1978, China's per capita gross national income was still less than half of the average of low-income countries.

According to the World Bank data, China finally escaped from the poverty trap that had plagued Chinese for thousands of years and moved from the low to the lower-middle-income stage in 1999.[21] It was a historical event worth of volumes of writings that more than a billion people shook off poverty, but there are always some people in the world who want to see and predict that China will fall into the "middle-income trap." Will China get stuck in this trap? On the one hand, we should admit that

---

[19] A batch of latest empirical studies in recent years have all questioned the existence of "middle-income trap," their authors are from academic circles or international organizations (including the World Bank), who used different data and methods and covered different time periods, but the conclusions they have drawn are similar.

[20] The Conference Board, Inc., Total Economy Database, 2018.

[21] World Bank Data Team, *New Country Classifications by Income Level: 2017–2018*, July 1, 2017.

the transition from a middle-income to a high-income country is a special stage of economic development, more complicated than the transition from low income to middle income, and China will face challenges in all aspects during this stage. In this sense, the concept of "middle-income trap" could serve as a warning for the development of China at this stage. On the other hand, this book lists a large quantity of favorable conditions for China to cross the "middle-income trap," and we have every reason to believe that China is fully capable of striding over the "trap" and leapfrogging from the middle income to the high-income stage.

It has been 20 years since China entered the lower-middle-income stage in 1999. At this point, we are full of confidence that China will cross over the "middle-income trap" in the next 10 years and successfully join the ranks of high-income countries. This self-confidence of the Chinese people is by no means an illusory fantasy, but is well supported by solid data. According to the World Bank's classification criteria, China stayed in the lower-middle-income stage for only 12 years (1999–2011) before it entered the next stage of upper-middle income.[22] Another study cited earlier also shows that the number of years China spent on the transition from lower-middle to upper-middle-stage was the shortest as compared with any other economy with historical data.[23] In the history of world economic development over the past 100 years, the transition period from lower-middle to upper-middle income is generally longer than that from upper-middle to high-income stage: the median of the first transition period is 55 years, and the median of the latter is 15 years. Although China's economic growth rate has slowed down in recent years, it has still maintained a momentum of growth at medium–high rate. This gives us good reason to believe that China's transition period from upper-middle to high income will not exceed 15 years. In other words, starting from 2012 when China entered the upper-middle-income stage, the country will have completed its leapfrog to rank among the high-income countries by around 2025.

Actually, a number of provinces in China have provided examples of this successful leap. It is widely known that of China's 31 provinces, autonomous regions, and municipalities, 27 have a population of more

---

[22] Ibid.

[23] Jesus Felipe, Utsav Kumar and Reynold Galope, *Middle-Income Transitions: Trapor Myth?* p. 439.

than 15 million each, and with the largest three (Guangdong, Shandong, and Henan) having a population of about 100 million, a size in the world equivalent to a middle or large country. To judge whether China as a whole is capable of crossing over the middle-income stage, we can take a look at the performance of various provinces, autonomous regions, and municipalities first. As of 2015, two provinces and three municipalities in China (Jiangsu and Zhejiang provinces, and Shanghai, Beijing, and Tianjin municipalities) had already reached the high-income level, and among them the population size of Jiangsu and Zhejiang provinces exceeded that of South Korea, and Shanghai's population was larger than that of Taiwan. Meanwhile, Guangdong, Shandong, Liaoning and Fujian provinces, and Inner Mongolia Autonomous Region registered a GDP per capita exceeding 10,000 US dollars, close to the threshold of high income. The two groups of provincial regions add up to have a permanent residential population of 507.8 million, or 36.9% of China's total population (1.3746 billion people), equivalent to the total population of the European Union (509.6 million), and 1.58 times the population size of the United States (321.4 million). Since the regions that have successfully crossed the "middle income trap" and entered or approached the high-income stage claim more than one-third of China's population, there should be no problem for other provincial regions to jump over the middle-income level and move toward the high-income stage.[24]

So we have reason to say that the "middle-income trap" for China is a false proposition. Don't say that such a thing as the "middle-income trap" does not exist in the world at all, even if there is such a trap, the Chinese people will respond with a verse from a poem by Mao Zedong: "Idle boast the strong pass is a wall of iron, with firm strides we are crossing its summit."

It is absolutely not an easy job to realize the great rejuvenation of the Chinese nation. Since the end of World War II, there have been some "economic miracles" in the world, but they generally occurred in much smaller economies (like Sweden, Greece, and the former Yugoslavia), or they lasted no longer than 25 years (like Japan and Brazil). It is unprecedented in human history for a super large economy like China to achieve a sustained high-speed growth for 70 consecutive years. It is a great exploration that has never been experienced before, has no ready-made model

---

[24] Zhou Shaojie and Hu Angang, *China Leapfrogs the Middle-Income Trap* (Hangzhou: Zhejiang People's Publishing House, 2018).

to follow, and is extremely thrilling and exciting. China is like a gigantic vessel sailing at high speed in the sea without navigation signs, but in the face of surging waves and torrents, and perilous rapids and shoals, it constantly rides the wind and waves and forges ahead bravely.

Throughout the past 70 years, there have always been those, both at home and abroad, who thought they were wise enough to point fingers at our achievements and gloat over our setbacks. They have often asserted that China will not be able to cross this hurdle or that ditch, and from time to time they have gnashed their teeth and cursed the imminent collapse of the Chinese economy and the Chinese system. We hold a different position from theirs and look at issues in ways different from them. In our perspective, it could not be accidental for a large country with a population of more than 1 billion to sustain a rapid development for 70 years, nor can it be dismissed for any arbitrarily found reason, but there must be something right in China's socioeconomic and political systems. China's road does not depend on the experience of our ancestors, nor on the imported theories of some smart foreigners. Rather, it is contemporary Chinese themselves who discover such a brighter path by groping for steppingstones while crossing the river, wading out with one foot deep and one foot shallow. This is what makes the China story unique and fascinating!

"Despite the incessant cry of apes from both banks, my swift boat has already sailed through thousands of mountains." China, once a poor and weak "sick man of East Asia," has achieved a historic leapfrog, becoming a giant of the East with great vigor today, and will continue to make great strides forward in years to come.

# Appendix: A Look at the "Great Famine" from a Historical and Comparative Perspective

At the Nanning Conference on January 12, 1958, Mao Zedong told a story. During the Warring States period (475–221BC), a minister named Dengtu Zi in the State of Chu reported to King Xiang that a scholar named Song Yu was "beautiful, articulate, and lecherous," and he asked the king not to allow Song Yu to frequent his back palace. When he learned about it, Song Yu went to the King of Chu to defend himself: "My beauty was born of nature, my being articulate was learned from my teacher, and I'm not lecherous at all." He claimed that an ultimate beauty had seduced him for three years, but he was not taken in, which proved that he was not a man fond of sex. Song Yu then counterattacked Dengtu Zi, saying that Dengtu Zi loved his pockmarked and hunched-back wife so that he had five children from her. Song Yu said to the king, "Your Excellency should examine carefully who is really fond of sex." As a famous poet, Song Yu wrote this matter into a verse titled *Ode to Dengtu Zi's Lechery*, which was later taken into *Wen Xuan* or *Selections of Refined Literature*, the oldest surviving anthology of Chinese literature arranged by genre. Consequently, the love-dedicated Dengtu Zi became a symbol of lechery and misdemeanor, unable to recover to this day. On this Mao Zedong commented, "Song Yu finally won the case. His method was to 'attack a single point, maximize it and ignore the rest.' We can't do this."[1]

---

[1] Wu Lingxi, Recollections of Chairman Mao: *Fragments of Some Major Historical Events I Personally Experienced* (Beijing: Xinhua Publishing House, 1995), pp. 51–52.

When it comes to the history of New China, some people at home and abroad often take this method of "attacking a single point, maximizing it and ignoring the rest." The Great Leap Forward (1958–1960) and the subsequent "Great Famine" (1959–1961) are the subjects they hold in a tight grip. Whatever earthshaking accomplishments China has made in other areas, they would refer to the "Great Famine" to prove that "China's system is the worst in the world."

This Appendix is not to estimate the death toll of the "Great Famine," but to discuss how to view this famine from a historical and comparative perspective.

Why is the historical and comparative perspective so important? Let's start with a book about China's famine by Frank Dikötter, a Dutch professor at the University of Hong Kong. This book titled *Mao's Great Famine* is available in both English and Chinese. Both versions use pictures of starving people on their covers, which look tragic and heartbreaking.

The covers of both versions mislead people ignorant of the facts to believe that the pictures truly reflect the post-Great Leap Forward situation in China. But these two covers actually reflect the author's extremely irresponsible approach in his use of "evidence." The two pictures he used have nothing to do with the "Great Famine" of 1959–1961, as they were taken not after the Great Leap Forward, but in May 1946, featuring the starving people in Liling County of Hunan Province. Anyone familiar with the history of famine in China knows that famine was a common occurrence before the founding of New China, but in 1946 there was no famine worth mentioning. Yet even in such a year, there still appeared so many starving people. To use the famine victims in a normal year before the founding of New China as evidence of the "Great Famine" after the founding of New China is intentionally misleading on the one hand, and on the other hand, it can be seen as a comparison, that is, a comparison before and after the People's Republic was established.

There is one sentence in Dikotter's book that I think is correct: "Demographers distinguish between 'natural' and 'unnatural' deaths to tease out a rough estimate of how many people died prematurely as a consequence of famine." He added: "An average death rate is required in order to calculate 'extra' death figures. What would be reasonable?".[2]

---

[2] Frank Dikotter, *Mao's Great Famine: The History of China's Most Devastating Catastrophe, 1958–1962* (New York: Walker, 2010). This Frank Dikotter once published another

That's a pretty good question, but may not be easy to reply. Any book on the relationship between statistics and politics may talk about the use of average. Mark Twain is known to have a famous saying: "There are three kinds of lies: lies, damned lies, and statistics." There is an interesting book titled *How to Lie with Statistics*, which exposes how some people lie with statistical data. Chapter II of that book deals specifically with the issue of average, under the title *The Well-Chosen Average*. With "the word 'average' having a very loose meaning, it is a trick commonly used, sometimes in innocence but often in guilt by fellows wishing to influence public opinion or sell advertising space," the author wrote. "Often an average... is such an oversimplification that it is worse than useless,"[3] the author noted.

A book published in 2007 is titled *The Tiger That Isn't*.[4] The title of the book means that fiddling with numbers may look terrific, but in fact it is often just using number to bluff people. Chapter 5 of the book also focuses on averages, entitled *Averages: The White Rainbow*. What does that mean? People originally see seven colors in a rainbow: red, orange, yellow, green, cyan, blue, and violet, which present a colorful combination of spectrums; but if someone insists in making an average out of the rainbow, then all the colors turn white on average, which is colorless. That is, to analyze a rainbow by means of averaging, the rainbow is no longer a rainbow and becomes something meaningless. According to the author, averages play two tricks, one is to erase all the ups and downs of life and make it bland; and the other is to treat the average as "typical," "normal" or "reasonable" when it is not. Dikotter said a "reasonable" average is required, but the author of this book warned us to avoid regarding averages as "reasonable" and "normal."

Also worth mentioning is another book titled *The Fascination of Statistics: Insight into Current Research Problems and Findings*, already with a

---

book: *Narcotic Culture: A History of Drugs in China* (Chicago: University of Chicago Press, 2004), which intended to challenge the argument that "China was once a slave to opium" (Foreword of the 2016 edition) and emphasize the role of the consumption side in driving the formation of the drug market. Its subtext is that Lin Zexu's opium ban was completely unreasonable and the Opium War launched by Britain was just to uphold the "free trade.".

[3] Darrell Huff, *How to Lie with Statistics* (New York: Norton, 1954).

[4] Michael Blastland and Andrew Dilnot, *The Tiger That Isn't: Seeing through a World of Numbers* (London: Profile Books, 2007).

Chinese version available. Its Chapter 5 has an eye-catching title: *Manipulated Averages*.[5] The author went right to the heart of the matter by pointing out that "averages often blur the huge differences actually in existence because they completely cover up the dispersion of the averages ... There may be two different scenarios here: in one case, all these values are very intensively concentrated around the medians; and in another scenario, they are dispersed about rather than concentrated around the average. However, based on the average indicators solely, people could miss the difference between the two."

Just because the average has the function of simplifying complex realities, it is often cited by politicians and often appears in academic discussions, so we often see controversy triggered by averages. There was a joke that a party host introduced Bill Gates to the guests and announced the good news: Thanks to the presence of Gates, the average income of the attendees instantly rose by numerous folds. But does the good news make any substantial sense?

Back to Dikotter's question, in order to calculate the "extra" deaths from the "Great Famine," there must be a "reasonable" average death rate first. Then how do arrive at this "reasonable" average death rate? There are no more than two methods.

The first is to make historical comparisons to calculate the average death rate based on the mortality figures in the years prior to the famine. To do so, it is necessary to determine which years prior to the famine should be included. I see that some people directly used the death rate in 1957 as a "reasonable" average, while others averaged the data of 1957, 1962, and 1963. The key here is which years are chosen to average the data, this in itself is a political choice, because the choice of these years concerns the numerator and denominator.

The second method is to make cross-country comparisons to calculate the average death rate based on the mortality figures of cohort countries. The key in doing so is which countries should be included as comparable.

The calculation of the average death rate sounds simple, but actually it may not be so. If we put the death rates of Finland from 1751 to the present in a chart, we will see that the death rate of the country during the famine from 1866 to 1868 was close to 80 per thousand (see Fig. A.1), which is very high. The mortality rate from famines in China is generally

---

[5] Walter Kramer, *The Fascination of Statistics: Insight into Current Research Problems and Findings* (Springer Verlag, Hrsg.mit C. Weihs, 2019).

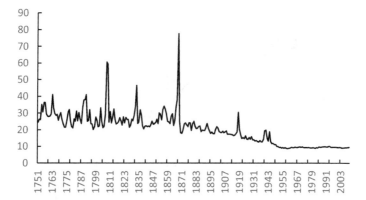

**Fig. A.1** Variation of average crude death rate: Finland (unit: ‰) (*Source*: Palgrave Macmillan Ltd., *International Historical Statistics* [Basingstoke: Palgrave Macmillan; April 2013])

not that high, around 40–50 per thousand. It is relatively easy to calculate the average death rate in Finland before the famine because the mortality rate in the years prior to the famine had fluctuated up and down without an apparent trend.

But switch to another country, like Germany, it is not the case. Germany experienced a famine from 1916 to 1918, leaving many people dead with the mortality rate climbing to 25 per thousand. But the death rate in Germany had declined continuously by big margins for long after 1877, so the mortality rate of 25 per thousand in 1916-18, although much higher than in previous few years, was lower than the normal rate prior to the outset of downslide trend (see Fig. A.2). Thus, it is not easy to calculate the average death rate for Germany, which depends on how many years are chosen to do the averaging.

Now turn to the example of Greece. Greece experienced a famine from 1941 to 1944, with a death rate exceeding 25 per thousand. In the years leading up to the famine, however, Greece's death rate had declined only for a short period of time (see Fig. A.3). In this case, how should the average death rate be calculated?

The case of the United States may be more complicated. At the time when the 1918 pandemic broke out, the mortality rate for Black Americans exceeded 25 per thousand, while for the Whites it was 18 per thousand (see Fig. A.4). But what is the "normal" average death rate?

**Fig. A.2** Variation of average crude death rate: Germany (unit: ‰) (*Source* Palgrave Macmillan Ltd., *International Historical Statistics* [Basingstoke: Palgrave Macmillan; April 2013])

**Fig. A.3** Variation of average crude death rate: Greece (unit: ‰) (*Source* Palgrave Macmillan Ltd., *International Historical Statistics* [Basingstoke: Palgrave Macmillan; April 2013])

Is it to calculate the "normal" using the death rates of the Blacks in the years leading up the pandemic, or using those of the Whites over the same period as a reference to the "normal," or to calculate the "normal" using the death rates of both Blacks and Whites in these years? If the latter two indicators are used, there would be simply too many extra deaths of

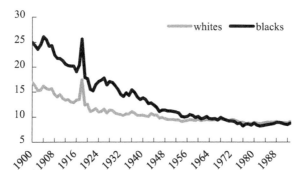

**Fig. A.4** Variation of average crude death rate: United States (unit: ‰) (*Source* Palgrave Macmillan Ltd., *International Historical Statistics* [Basingstoke: Palgrave Macmillan; April 2013])

the Blacks. In fact, the gap in the death rates between the Blacks and the Whites in the United States sustained until the late 1960s. People have every reason to come to a conclusion that, prior to the civil rights movement of the 1960s, the Blacks had continuously suffered massive extra deaths in the United States, that is, there were too many abnormal deaths.

The same happened in South Africa, where the mortality rate for the Whites remained at the level below 10 per thousand after 1935, but that for the Blacks initially approached to 25 per thousand. Although the death rate for the Blacks in South Africa gradually declined, it was still much higher than that for the Whites. This gap sustained until the 1980s–1990s before it became narrowed (see Fig. A.5). Suppose the death rate for the Whites in South Africa is "normal," then the Blacks there had suffered "abnormal deaths" on a large scale for a long time.

These examples of different countries indicate that it is not an easy thing to calculate a "reasonable" average death rate.

Back to China, official statistics reveal that the mortality rate went down drastically after the founding of New China, from 20 per thousand in 1949 to 11 per thousand in 1957, but suddenly rose again to 25 per thousand in 1960. Shortly after the "Great Famine," the mortality rate dropped below 10 per thousand (see Fig. A.6). The change was so dramatic in so short a period, how should the "normal" average death rate be calculated? This is not a simple question.

**Fig. A.5** Variation of average crude death rate: South Africa (unit: ‰) (*Source* Palgrave Macmillan Ltd., *International Historical Statistics* [Basingstoke: Palgrave Macmillan; April 2013])

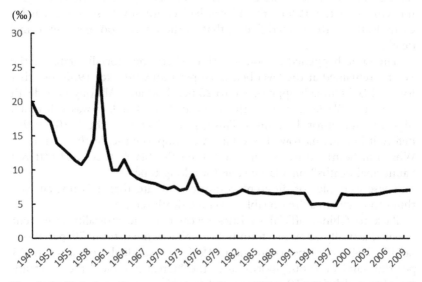

**Fig. A.6** Variation of average crude death rate: China (unit:‰) (*Source* National Bureau of Statistics, *China Statistics Yearbook* [every year])

The method of calculating the "normal" average was mentioned above. In the historical perspective, a comparison should be made with the past, such as the years prior to the Great Leap Forward, and that is what most researchers have done. But the comparison can also be made with the years before the founding of New China, because in fact Dikotter unintentionally but subconsciously implied that the situation in 1946 was similar to that of the "Great Famine." In the comparative perspective, a comparison should be made with other countries. Which countries should be compared with? India is probably the most comparable country. China can also be compared with the other least developed countries, because its level of development around 1960 was among the least developed countries, worse than India.

In comparing with the years prior to the Great Leap Forward, it is essential to remember what Amartya Sen warned in *Hunger and Public Action*, "It must, however, be remembered that since the Chinese mortality rates had come down sharply already prior to the famine, the 'extra death' estimates based on pre-famine mortality rates are in comparison with a pre-famine death rate lower than that of most poor countries in the world."[6] This sentence is placed in a footnote, not in the text. People who study the "Great Famine" love to quote Amartya Sen, but few of them seem to take notice of this sentence, yet it is this sentence that warns us that the "reasonable" average death rate required in calculating the "extra" mortality rate is not easy to determine.

China's crude mortality rate was 20 per thousand in 1949 and dropped to 11 per thousand in 1957, in just eight years. So, how many years does it generally take for the crude mortality rate to drop from 20 to 11 per thousand elsewhere? Please see Table A.1.

Table A.1 indicates that even in developed countries, it may take a very long time to reduce the crude mortality rate from 20 to 11 per thousand, with the shortest period being 41 years and the longest being 144 years. This happened at the turn of the nineteenth and twentieth centuries, when healthcare levels worldwide were far too low. As the times advanced, the time required got shorter and shorter. It took Mauritius the shortest time, for only 12 years. But this is not the case for all latecomer countries, for example, India spent 41 years, so did the Philippines. Is

---

[6] Jean Dreze and Amartya Sen, *Huger and Public Action* (Oxford: Clarendon Press, 1989), p. 210.

**Table A.1** Number of years taken for mortality rate to drop from 20 to 10 per thousand in countries, regions, or races

| | Mortality rate 20‰ | Mortality rate 10‰ | Years taken | | Mortality rate 20‰ | Mortality rate 10‰ | Years taken |
|---|---|---|---|---|---|---|---|
| Mauritius | 1947 | 1959 | 12 | The Philippines | 1912 | 1953 | 41 |
| Singapore | 1939 | 1952 | 13 | India | 1946 | 1987 | 41 |
| Sri Lanka | 1940 | 1953 | 13 | Italy | 1906 | 1948 | 42 |
| Egypt | 1963 | 1978 | 15 | Cyprus | 1901 | 1944 | 43 |
| Mexico | 1944 | 1961 | 17 | Salvador | 1920 | 1963 | 43 |
| Malaysia | 1940 | 1959 | 19 | Uruguay | 1882 | 1926 | 44 |
| Russia | 1926 | 1946 | 20 | Germany | 1901 | 1948 | 47 |
| Taiwan (China) | 1932 | 1952 | 20 | Colombia | 1915 | 1962 | 47 |
| Barbados | 1936 | 1956 | 20 | Australia | 1854 | 1905 | 51 |
| Guyana | 1935 | 1958 | 23 | Venezuela | 1894 | 1952 | 58 |
| Chile | 1941 | 1964 | 23 | Japan | 1887 | 1950 | 63 |
| Rumania | 1930 | 1955 | 25 | France | 1901 | 1964 | 63 |
| Guatemala | 1953 | 1978 | 25 | Switzerland | 1883 | 1948 | 65 |
| Spain | 1922 | 1948 | 26 | Portugal | 1892 | 1962 | 70 |
| Jamaica | 1928 | 1955 | 27 | Bulgaria | 1881 | 1953 | 72 |
| Colored (South Africa) | 1950 | 1977 | 27 | Austria | 1912 | 1989 | 77 |
| Albania | 1929 | 1958 | 29 | Finland | 1870 | 1950 | 80 |
| Argentina | 1910 | 1940 | 30 | Greece | 1860 | 1946 | 86 |
| Poland | 1921 | 1953 | 32 | Belgium | 1887 | 1987 | 100 |
| Costa Rica | 1922 | 1954 | 32 | Ireland | 1864 | 1975 | 111 |
| Hungary | 1923 | 1955 | 32 | Norway | 1815 | 1930 | 115 |
| Czech | 1919 | 1952 | 33 | Sweden | 1824 | 1942 | 118 |
| Puerto Rico | 1913 | 1949 | 36 | England | 1876 | 1995 | 119 |
| Former Yugoslav | 1921 | 1957 | 36 | Denmark | 1816 | 1937 | 121 |
| Blacks (United States) | 1912 | 1953 | 41 | Scotland | 1855 | 1999 | 144 |

*Source* Palgrave Macmillan Ltd., *International Historical Statistics* (Basingstoke: Palgrave Macmillan; April 2013)

China "normal," or they are "normal"? Therefore, it is not very simple to say what is a "normal" average.

In fact, Judith Banister, one of the first American scholars to study the issue of the "Great Famine," noted this when she said that "China is a super-achiever in mortality reduction."[7] Wang Feng, a Chinese demographer working and living in the United States, also said in an article that "China has been an overachiever in the global process of demographic transition in the second half of the twentieth century."[8] If China had already been "super successful" in mortality reduction after 1949, what should we use as a "normal" average death rate?

As mentioned earlier, China's mortality rate in 1960 was 25 per thousand, which is the official figure. One might say that official data are not reliable, but a lot of unofficial data are even less reliable. Speaking of unofficial data, what we could look at should be those recognized more by the academic circles, such as the calculations by Judith Banister,[9] Ansley Coale,[10] Gerard Calot,[11] Basil Ashton,[12] and Jiang Zhenghua.[13] All these scholars agree that the peak mortality rate was in 1960, but as to how high the mortality rate was, their estimates vary, largely ranging from 30 to 45 per thousand (see Fig. A.7).

Suppose the worst mortality rate of the "Great Famine" ranged from 25 to 45 per thousand, what conclusions could be drawn from a comparison with the pre-New China years? There is a great deal of research on the mortality rate before the founding of New China, for which one can consult Table 2.3 of Chapter 2 of this book, which cites estimates

[7] Judith Banister and Samuel H. Preston, *Mortality in China*, Population and Development Review, Vol. 7, No. 1 (March 1981), p. 108.

[8] Wang Feng, *The Future of a Demographic Overachiever: Long-Term Implications of the Demographic Transition in China*, Population and Development Review, Vol. 37 (2011), p. 173.

[9] Judith Banister, *An Analysis of Recent Data on the Population of China*, Population and Development Review, Vol. 10, No. 2 (June 1984), pp. 241–271.

[10] Ansley Coale, *Rapid Population Change in China, 1952–1982* (Washington: National Academy Press, 1984).

[11] Gerard Calot, *Donnees Nouvelles Sur L'evolution Demographique Chinoise*, Population, No.4–5 (July–October 1984), pp. 807–834.

[12] Basil Ashton, Kenneth Hill, Alan Piazza and Robin Zeitz, *Famine in China, 1958–61*, Population and Development Review, Vol. 10, No. 4 (December 1984), pp. 613–645.

[13] Yuan Yongxi, *General Outline of China's Population* (Beijing: China Financial & Economic Publishing House, 1991), pp. 615–621.

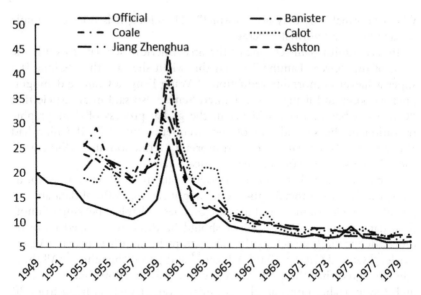

**Fig. A.7** Comparison of before and after Great Leap Forward: different estimates (unit: ‰)

more acceptable to the academic community. Table 2.3 indicates that the academic estimates of the "normal" mortality rate during the Republic of China years ranged from 25 to 45 per thousand. Some studies at the time also cited comparisons of mortality data from China, India, and other countries during the same period. We could see that the mortality rate during the Republic of China period was not only higher than that of India, but also higher than that of all the other countries with data available and was the highest in the world. It should be noted that the estimates cited here exclude the effects of wars (e.g., the War of Resistance against Japan and the Liberation War) and are estimates of the "normal" conditions of the Republic of China (especially the so-called "Golden Decade of 1928–1937"). In other words, the worst post-Great Leap Forward scenario was equivalent to the "normal" situation before the founding of New China. If not for the rapid progress after the founding of New China, the 1960 mortality rate might have been regarded as "normal." It should not be forgotten that 1960 was in fact only 11 years after the founding of New China!

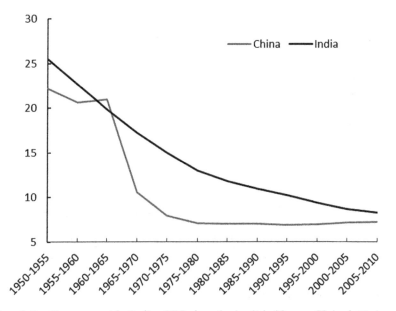

**Fig. A.8** Compare with India: UN data (unit: ‰) (*Source* United Nations Department of Economic and Social Affairs Population Division, *World Population Prospects: The 2012 Revision*, http://esa.un.org/unpd/wpp/index.htm)

To make a cross-country comparison with regard to what should be China's "normal" mortality rate, India is perhaps the most comparable case, since in 1960 both countries were poor, but India's GDP per capita (331 US dollars) was much higher than China's (191.8 US dollars).[14]

Two sets of data are shown below: Figure A.8 presents the United Nations' data, and Fig. A.9 presents the World Bank's data. As the United Nations' data indicate, in 1960, China's mortality rate was slightly higher than India's by 2 per thousand, while before that it was lower than India's by 4 per thousand, and after that the difference between the two was even greater.

The World Bank does not have mortality data for the period before 1960. China's mortality rate in 1960 was about 3 per thousand higher than India's; but in 1961 and through the early 1980s, China's mortality

---

[14] World Bank, GDP Per Capita (Constant 2010 US$): 1960–2017, https://data.worldbank.org/indicator/NY.GDP.PCAP.KD.

314  APPENDIX: A LOOK AT THE "GREAT FAMINE" ...

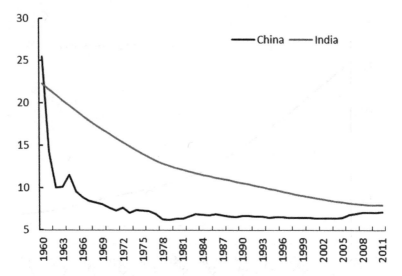

**Fig. A.9** Compare with India: World Bank data (unit: ‰) (*Source* World Bank, http://data.worldbank.org/indicator/SP.DYN.CDRT.IN)

rate was about 10 per thousand lower than India's. Comparing the mortality rates in China and India in the early 1960s, what exactly is a "normal" mortality rate?

As mentioned previously, people who study China's "Great Famine" are fond of quoting Amartya Sen, but they consciously or unconsciously ignore a few other quotes from him: "It is important to note that despite the gigantic size of excess mortality in the Chinese famine, the extra mortality in India from regular deprivation in normal times vastly overshadows the former. Comparing India's death rate of 12 per thousand with China's of 7 per thousand, and applying that difference to the Indian population of 781 million in 1986, we get an estimate of excess normal mortality in India of 3.9 million per year. This implies that every eight years or so more people die in India because of its higher regular death rate than died in China during the gigantic famine of 1958–1961. India seems to manage to fill its cupboard with more skeletons every eight years than China put there in its years of shame."[15] Here, Sen and his co-author

---

[15] Jean Dreze and Amartya Sen, *Huger and Public Action* (Oxford: Clarendon Press, 1989), pp. 214–215.

acknowledged that they used the highest estimate of the famine deaths in China (29.5 million), and if a lower estimate of deaths were to be used, it would have taken not eight years but much less time for India's excess deaths to surpass the excess mortality in China's 1958–1961 famine. Besides, Sen and his co-author assumed that the difference in mortality rate between China and India was 5 per thousand, but throughout the 1960s and 1970s, the actual gap between the two was 7–10 per thousand. Therefore, compared to China, with the exception of the 1958–1962 period, India's excess deaths every three or five years were much higher than the famine deaths in China as estimated by Sen and his partners.

In addition to India, we can also compare China in 1960 with other least developed countries, because China was one of them at that time. The horizontal axis in Figure A.10 represents the yearly GDP per capita, and the vertical axis is the crude mortality rate, with each plot representing a country, and China is represented by a small triangle. The official Chinese data of 25 per thousand are used in the chart, while mortality rates of the other least developed countries with their income levels similar to China's swing from 18 to 35 per thousand. If a same diagram is drawn with the 1962 data, China's triangle declines to about 10 per thousand, a level comparable with the developed countries at the time. That is to say, based on the official data of 25 per thousand, the worst year for China was equivalent to the average crude mortality rate in the least developed countries.

We can summarize the above observations as follows:

| Comparative Reference for 1958–1961 mortality rate | Observations |
| --- | --- |
| The Great Leap Forward and Its Aftermath | Steep rise of mortality rate, but a drastic decline recorded prior to the period |
| Years before the founding of New China | Equivalent to the "normal" situation before the founding of New China |
| Compared with India | China's worst time better than the "normal" situation in India |
| Compared with other least developed countries | About their "normal" situation |

Finally, by the way, let's discuss a question: Compared with the period before and after the "Great Leap Forward," what kind of people were most vulnerable to die prematurely in "hard times"?

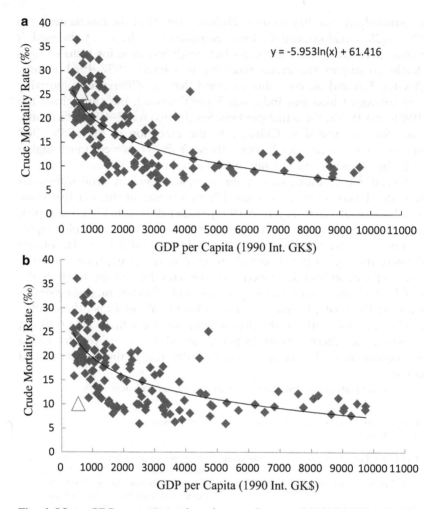

**Fig. A.10** a GDP per capita and crude mortality rate: 1960. b GDP per capita and crude mortality rate: 1962 (*Source* World Bank, http://data.worldbank.org/indicator/)

Many studies have found that malnutrition during infancy and early childhood may lead to high mortality rate later in life. For example, a study on Finland's 1866–1869 famine found that survival from birth to age 17 years was significantly lower in people born during the famine than in other people.[16] Another study focused on people in Italy who experienced hardships in infancy and childhood and found that these people were associated with higher mortality than others up to age 45.[17] Along this line of thinking, it is reasonable to assume that people born in the 1930s and 1940s before the Liberation were mostly malnourished, which might have contributed to their high mortality rate in China in 1959–1961. An indirect evidence of the nutritional deprivation among people born in this period is their average height (see Fig. A.11).

Numerous historical and comparative studies have found that within a country (assuming genetic homogeneity), the average height of different age groups (not individuals) is related to their health and nutrition during fetal and infant life. An Australian scholar studied the height of Chinese men and women born between 1935 and 1975. His statistics reveal that the average height of men born in 1935–1949 fluctuated from 1.67 to 1.68 meters. After 1949, the average height of men began to rise continuously, and by 1957 it was close to 1.7 meters. Women's average height was lower than men's, but the trend was similar. In other words, during the fetal and infant periods, the nutritional status of those born before 1949 was worse than their counterparts born after 1949. The average height of people born during the "hard period" after the Great Leap Forward went down about 0.3 cm, indicating that the nutritional status did affect their height. But even if it declined, this group was still 1.5 cm higher in the average height than those born in the late 1940s.

Nutritional deprivation was common among people born before 1949, who should be 10 years old or older by the late 1950s and the early 1960s. Table A.2 shows the age distribution of the population that died in rural Guizhou in 1958 and 1960. In general, infants and children should have been more vulnerable to die prematurely. But compared to 1958,

---

[16] Vaino Kannisto, Kaare Christernsen, and James W. Vaupel, *No Increased Mortality in Later Life or Cohorts Born during Famine*, American Journal of Epidemiology, Vol. 145, No. 11 (1997), pp. 987–994.

[17] Graziella Caselli & Riccardo Capocaccia, *Age, Period, Cohort and Early Mortality: An Analysis of Adult Mortality in Italy*, Population Studies, Vol. 43, No. 1 (1989), pp. 133–153.

**Fig. A.11** a Height and year born (Chinese men) (Year born). b Height and year born: 1935–1975 (Chinese women) (*Source* Stephen Lloyd Morgan, *Stature and Famine in China: The Welfare of the Survivors of the Great Leap Forward Famine, 1959-61* [February 2007], Available at SSRN: http://dx.doi.org/10.2139/ssrn.1083059)

**Table A.2** Age distribution of mortality in rural Guizhou, 1958 and 1960 (Unit: %)

| Age (years) | Rural Guizhou 1958 | 1960 | Range of change |
|---|---|---|---|
| 0 | 21.1 | 8.5 | −0.60 |
| 1 ~ 4 | 29.0 | 10.6 | −0.63 |
| 5 ~ 9 | 6.1 | 5.5 | −0.10 |
| 10 ~ 14 | 2.7 | 3.8 | 0.41 |
| 15 ~ 19 | 1.9 | 3.4 | 0.79 |
| 20 ~ 24 | 1.8 | 4.1 | 1.28 |
| 25 ~ 29 | 2.1 | 4.5 | 1.14 |
| 30 ~ 34 | 2.0 | 5.6 | 1.80 |
| 35 ~ 39 | 2.2 | 5.3 | 1.41 |
| 40 ~ 44 | 2.9 | 5.9 | 1.03 |
| 45 ~ 49 | 3.1 | 6.3 | 1.03 |
| 50 ~ 54 | 3.4 | 7.1 | 1.09 |
| 55 ~ 59 | 4.6 | 6.8 | 1.48 |
| 60 ~ 64 | 4.7 | 6.7 | 0.43 |
| 65 ~ 69 | 4.1 | 5.8 | 0.41 |
| 70 ~ 74 | 3.6 | 4.2 | 0.17 |
| 75 ~ 79 | 2.6 | 3.1 | 0.19 |
| 80 + | 2.1 | 2.7 | 0.29 |

*Source* Li Ruojian, *Preliminary Dissolution and Analysis of Mortality Rate in Difficult Times, Population Research*, Vol. 25, No. 5 (2001), p. 47

we found that in 1960, the proportion of mortality among age groups up to 10 years old (people born after the founding of New China) in the total deaths went down instead of up. Yet the mortality of groups over 10 years of age (people born before 1949) saw a rising proportion in the total deaths. This seems to suggest that people born before 1949 were more likely to die during the 1959–1960 "hard period" due to relatively worse fetal and infant nutritional deprivation. Compared with other provinces, Guizhou ranked second after Sichuan in crude mortality rate in the country from 1958 to 1962. Guizhou's data largely support the previous hypothesis that mortality rate in the famine was higher among people born before 1949 due to malnutrition at an early age.

Interestingly, someone has studied whether the mortality rate of people born during the "hard period" in the wake of China's Great Leap Forward was high, only to find that the famine-born cohort "does not show higher-mortality" than either the pre-famine or the post-famine cohort.[18] This may indicate that the "hard period" following the Great Leap Forward did not last long, so the nutrition of those born in that period soon recovered and their mortality rate did not go up. This contrasts with the persistent malnutrition among people born before the founding of New China.

No matter how to judge the "Great Famine," one thing must be made clear: originally, the famine history was as old as the history of China, as endless famines plagued China before the founding of the People's Republic. It is exactly the New China that ended the famine in China forever! This historical feat is worth volumes of writings.

---

[18] Shige Song, *Does Famine Have a Long-Term Effect on Cohort Mortality: Evidence from the 1959–1961 Great Leap Forward Famine in China*, Journal of Biosocial Science, Vol. 41, No. 4 (July 2009), pp. 469–491.